D1231379

The Story of the Tour de France

How a Newspaper Promotion Became the Greatest Sporting Event in the World

Volume 2: 1976–2018
Second Edition

Bill and Carol McGann

McGann Publishing

©Bill & Carol McGann 2019
Second Edition
All Rights Reserved

No part of this publication may be reproduced, stored in a retrieval system, or trans-
mitted, in any form or by any means, electronic, mechanical, photocopying, record-
ing, or otherwise, without the written permission of the author.

Photo credits: p.275 by Josh Hallett; p.304 ©Ludovic Péron; p.361 by Filip Bossuyt;
cover and all other photos are from the collection of and copyright Fotoreporter
Sirotti, and are reprinted with his permission.

Published by McGann Publishing
P.O. Box 864
McMinnville, OR 97128
USA
www.mcgannpublishing.com

**McGann
Publishing**

ISBN 978-0-9859636-9-9
Printed in the United States of America

Cover photo: Bernard Hinault winning stage eighteen of the 1981 Tour, alone, at
the top of Le Pleynet.

"What we need is something to nail his beak shut," groaned Henri Desgrange. If he didn't figure out a way to drive his arch-competitor out of business, he would be out of a job. But how? He needed a promotion, something incredible to capture the public's attention.

"Let's organize a race that lasts several days, longer than anything else. Like the six-days on the track, but on the road. The big towns will welcome the riders," offered one of his writers.

Desgrange chewed on the idea for a moment. "If I understand you right, *petit Géo*, you're proposing a Tour de France."

Map of France

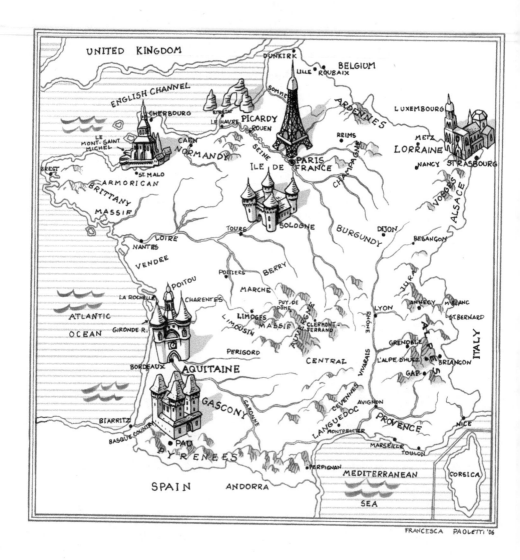

FRANCESCA PAOLETTI '06

Table of Contents

Acknowledgements

Our acknowledgments are this volume's first page of text because the unselfish assistance we received from so many kind people was crucial to the writing of this book. If this book has merit, it is because of their help.

Three men were particularly important to this enterprise. Two of them are familiar to any reader of cycling history: Les Woodland and the late Owen Mulholland. Both of these erudite men have put their profound knowledge of cycling, history and general culture at our disposal. They are generous men who made it clear that we were not to be shy about asking them for help. We took them at their word and as we noted in the first volume, we were rewarded with endless valuable insights and countless little-known facts, nearly all of which have been included in this work. Both allowed us to quote from their books and both gave us much needed advice. They have been good and kind friends.

Mr. Mulholland not only fielded countless questions, he reviewed the text and made many excellent suggestions.

The third man, James Witherell, has written a *magnum opus* on the history of the Tour, *When Heroes Were Giants*. Out of the blue, Mr. Witherell sent us a letter noting a couple of errors in the on-line version of this history. We entered into a correspondence that yielded his very gracious offer to review the text of this volume. He joyfully tackled the huge task of fact-checking our text as if it were his own book. We are extremely grateful to this bighearted man.

Scott Gibb and Mary Lou Roberts also scrutinized the text, making sure that people with varying levels of familiarity with the subject and jargon of cycling would understand the story. Sandra Lavigna and John Britt went over the text of both volumes, line-by-line, making many valuable suggestions. We ended up incorporating almost all of their suggestions.

Francesca Paoletti drew the map of France at the beginning of the book. We needed a map that was drawn specifically for a Tour de France history and Francesca has done a wonderful job.

Antonio and Mauro Mondonico and Valeria Paoletti also lent invaluable help. Our gratitude to them and the many others, listed in the bibliography, is profound.

Special thanks are due to Joël Godaert, Robert Janssens and Guido Cammaert, authors of the Tour Encyclopedie. In their words, they researched the results of each and every Tour like archeologists. I depended heavily upon their work, which is now largely posted on www.memoire-du-cyclisme.net. The *Memoire* site is a wonderful storehouse of information that was an essential tool in completing this story. The prodigious work the contributors to the site performed is a valuable service that has earned my deep gratitude.

Any errors are our own.

Preface

Doping has always been a part of cycle racing. In the early years riders used strychnine, ether, cocaine, brandy and a host of other drugs, anything to dull the pain and allow them to get through the ordeal of the impossibly long races of the early twentieth century. As time and technology progressed, the drugs and their efficacy improved. Out of this grew a riders' doping culture that became almost formalized with its own code of behavior. Almost no rider, even in retirement, spoke about doping to the press. A code of silence as effective as the *omertà* of the Mafia was imposed. As doping grew in sophistication and cost, the riders continued to behave as if they had a right to dope and intimidated anyone who spoke out. The management of teams by ex-riders has exacerbated the institutionalization of doping in cycle racing. Team management of doping programs described in the latter chapters of this volume was a natural outgrowth of this process.

Modern performance enhancing drugs are so effective that many riders have felt forced to either turn to them in order to remain competitive, or retire. The constant, ongoing drug scandals of the last two decades make this sad fact apparent. Clearly, drugs are an important part of our story.

For us, the problem is how to handle the accusations and suspicions of drug use. Several riders have noted that it is virtually impossible for a rider to prove the negative, that is, that he didn't use drugs. At the same time, recent cases have demonstrated that a rider can take drugs and evade even the most advanced and sophisticated tests. The defense that a rider is clean because he has been tested often is meaningless. Yet for an innocent rider, what other defense can he have?

Because of this problem, we assume for the purposes of this text that a rider is clean unless he has had a positive dope test, has had a court conviction for drug use or transport, or has confessed to using drugs. If events require that we note inconclusive evidence or accusations about doping in our narrative, we have done so. But again, barring our three tests of proof, the rider remains innocent.

Any writer delving into the history of the Tour finds himself in a morass of errors and self-serving propaganda. Since some of these fables are now part of the lore of the Tour, I have retold them anyway, pointing out where I believe they depart from fact.

A note on names. Many racers' names, especially Flemish ones, either have several possible spellings or their names were changed by French reporters. Often this French rendition is the way we know them. Jozef becomes Joseph. Ferdy Kübler becomes Ferdi Kübler. I have tried to use the names that the racers were either born with or at least as they were used by their countrymen. When following this rule would create more confusion, I have ignored it. For example, the Buysse brothers (Lucien was the winner of the 1926 Tour) were officially surnamed Buyze. Nowhere in the literature of the Tour have I found them so referenced, so Buysse they shall remain.

Please join us as we continue the wonderful story of the Tour de France, the greatest sporting event in the world.

Foreword by
Les Woodland

I think of myself, with conceited ease, as an *Eminence Grise* of cycle-racing. There are a great many of us, of course. Here in France we hold informal reunions in village bars, and over glasses of Pelforth we crystallise the advice we will entrust to the riders of the Tour de France.

It isn't easy to condense strategy into the few words that a cyclist can hear while negotiating a traffic chicane at 50 kilometers per hour. It isn't easy to drown out the radio ranting of some has-been team director who, for heaven's sake, can never have the clarity of vision that we in the bar can have.

That, I think, is why no Frenchman has won the Tour de France for more than 35 years. These guys almost deliberately don't listen.

But are we discouraged? No we are not. We shall be there again this summer, Dédé, Bernard, Jacques, Jean-Yves and me. We shall wait for the caravan as though it were some heavenly host and then we shall fight to retrieve the cheap key rings, leaking packets of coffee and silly cardboard hats that seem at that moment so important.

We will count and compare our booty and we will go home knowing our place in the pecking order of the cycling roost. And then our wives will ask what we've brought that rubbish home for and the whole lot will go in the bin.

Except for riders' bottles. There is no greater prize than a rider's bottle. Men who run international marketing conglomerates, men who plan naval manoeuvres, men who extract sick hearts... such people will fight in the gutter rather than let someone else go off with a bottle.

Does it matter that you could buy an exactly similar bottle—except that it's clean, not rimed with riders' flob and not scuffed from its collision with the ground—for two euros? No it doesn't. Naturally it doesn't.

Of course, not all Frenchmen like the Tour de France. I know a man called Delmas who views its fairground subtlety with the loftiness of a man who spent his working life professoring at the Sorbonne. He would be embarrassed if anyone assumed he knew the name of a single rider. To him, the Tour de France is Jerry Springer, but for a month. And you can't turn it off.

But do the rest of us care? Of course we don't. For four weeks we own France. We own the world. And we drink beer and shout our advice and then we go home and watch a Frenchman come thirty-second.

Introduction:
Our Story So Far

The first volume of our Tour de France history explains the Tour's origins in 1902 and tells the story of the Tour through 1975, after Frenchman Bernard Thévenet dramatically beat Eddy Merckx. In this volume we begin the story *in medias res*, jumping right in with the Tour's 1976 edition.

If the reader hasn't read the first volume, the following synopsis of the Tour's first 62 years will help make the narrative that follows understandable.

In the nineteenth century newspapers used a multitude of devices to increase their sales. Much of what both Charles Dickens and Alexandre Dumas wrote was serialized in newspapers. People breathlessly bought the next day's edition to learn how the Three Musketeers or Oliver Twist would get out of the fix the authors left them in at the end of the last installment. In the U.S., Darwin and Hattie McIlrath, sponsored by the *Chicago Inter Ocean* newspaper, went on a three-year trip around the world by bicycle while the paper printed weekly reports of their progress. Newspapers would often create their own news, for which they were the only suppliers in an era before radio and television.

Around 1862 Frenchman Pierre Lallement had the inspiration to connect pedals to a crank and the crank to a wheel and with that brilliant invention the bicycle was born. In 1867 Pierre Micheaux began manufacturing bicycles in Paris. Almost from that moment, the newspapers understood the magical appeal of men crossing great distances on these wonderful new machines and began promoting bicycle races. In 1869 *Le Vélocipède Illustré* sponsored the 130-kilometer Paris–Rouen race. Other papers jumped in and soon Europe was covered with races as people along the race routes eagerly bought papers that told the story of the race and listed the results. Both cycle racing and the papers thrived under this symbiosis.

In 1902 Henri Desgrange, the editor of the French sports newspaper, *L'Auto*, was desperately searching for some way to drive his competitor Pierre Giffard and his newspaper *Le Vélo*, out of business. Desgrange's paper was the creation of right-wing industrialists who were upset with both the liberal politics and high-priced advertising that characterized Giffard's paper.

At the suggestion of one of his writers, Desgrange took the audacious step of promoting a month-long bicycle race around France, a plan much grander than the one-day races that were the norm. His race would have the competitors ride six separate races, with rest days in between each race, in a grand tour of France. He then added up each rider's accumulated time for each race, or stage, with the winner being the rider with the lowest total elapsed time. This kind of multiple-race competition is called a stage race. This is the most glamorous and prestigious type of bicycle road racing and we can credit Desgrange and his staff with its invention and refinement.

The first running of this Tour de France in 1903 was a smashing success. *L'Auto's* sales soared, driving *Le Vélo* out of business. Despite a few missteps, Desgrange and his Tour (and believe me, it was his Tour) went on to become first a French and then an international institution. Of the twelve Tours run before the First World War, four were won by foreigners.

The Tour was almost killed by its success and the passions the race generated. Rampant cheating and spectator hooliganism marred the second Tour. To gain control of his race, Desgrange made several changes. The most important was that he altered the way the way the standings, called the General Classification (GC), were calculated. In 1903 and 1904 it had been based on elapsed time. He switched to adding up the riders' placings, or points. In a twenty-stage race, if a rider won all twenty stages he would have twenty points. This was much easier to measure and minimized cheating. But, it made for dull racing because if a rider came in second, 5 minutes or 2 hours behind first place, it was all the same. He also shortened the stages and increased their number. The 1905 edition took eleven stages to get around France.

In 1912 Eugène Christophe finished second in the Tour's General Classification, even though he had a lower elapsed time. In a move that characterized Desgrange's nimble and adaptable way of managing the Tour, he went back to using time to calculate the winner.

In 1905 the Tour also started to include mountains. At first the more modest of the Vosges and Alpine ascents were used. Because this was so well-liked, in 1910 Desgrange was talked into running the Tour over the high Pyrenees. Although he feared that this was asking more of the riders than they could do, they were up to the task and the drama of the mountains stages made the Tour even more popular.

Desgrange developed a very complicated rulebook. The most striking difference between the early Tours and today's was the requirement that a rider perform all of his own repairs. The most fabled story involving this rule was that of Eugène Christophe. In 1913 he broke his fork on a mountain descent and was forced to hike to the next town with his bike over his shoulder. Working at the blacksmith's forge for three hours, he fixed the fork and resumed the race. Because earlier that day the Tour's leader had abandoned, Christophe had been first in the General Classification when his fork broke. But with that catastrophe, his hopes of winning were dashed.

Over the next half-century the regulations regarding rider assistance were gradually relaxed. This amelioration reduced the effect a mechanical failure could have on the race's outcome. Several worthy riders lost probable Tour victories in the Tour's first 25 years because of the harshness of this rule. In spite of Desgrange's early rules that caused equipment failures to make the results seem to be the working of capricious chance, Belgian rider Philippe Thys won three Tours, 1913, 1914 and 1920. He would probably have won in 1922 except for a broken wheel. His feat would not be repeated until 1956.

Desgrange wanted his race to be inhumanly difficult. He wanted it to be a primitive test of a man's endurance, strength and character. He did all he could to make it an individual effort, but failed because in the end, bicycle racing is a sport contested by teams and won by individuals.

When Desgrange became convinced that Belgian teams colluded to help a sickly Maurice de Waele win the 1929 Tour, he had had enough. Desgrange hated teams and he hated sponsors. He couldn't do away with teams. The natural tendency of man, the social animal, to work together overcame all of Desgrange's efforts to isolate the competitors. But he could do something about the sponsors.

Until 1930, bicycle companies were the primary sponsors of the teams contesting the Tour. Boldly, Desgrange scrapped the trade team system and formed the teams along national lines. There was a team from France, one from Italy, etc. If he couldn't come up with enough national teams, he would add French regional teams. To help pay for the increased cost of supporting the riders during the Tour, since the sponsors couldn't be expected to, Desgrange charged a fee to firms that wanted to drive their logo'd cars and trucks along the Tour route. The publicity caravan is still with us and is an important part of the color and excitement of the Tour.

The public loved the national team system as much as the bicycle companies loathed it. For them, it was a three-week publicity blackout. The system gave France five straight victories in the early 1930s after a long period of Belgian domination.

Seeing that the cycling fans liked the Grand Prix des Nations individual time trial (an individual race against the clock) promoted by one of his newspaper competitors, Desgrange included the first individual time trial in the 1934 Tour. This gave big-gear men a chance to take back time from the smaller mountain climbing specialists. It gave the Tour a new balance and a new interest.

The conditions under which the first Tour riders competed were appalling by our standards. The bikes were single speed, the roads were mostly unpaved. In the mountains, the word "road" could be generous. Often the way over the high mountains was little more than a path. Even though bikes with gear changing systems were available before the First World War, Desgrange forbade the use of derailleurs. Desgrange's successor, Jacques Goddet, bowed to the force of change and finally allowed their use in the 1937 Tour.

The Tour was suspended during both World Wars. L'Auto, which had continued printing during the German occupation of the Second World War, was shuttered by the authorities after the war was over. Goddet formed a new newspaper, L'Équipe, and staged the first postwar Tour in 1947.

By 1951, the Tour had taken on the form we know today. Over the first three decades Desgrange had gradually increased the number of stages. By 1925 the Tour was run in eighteen stages, close to our current twenty or so. The racing slowly moved from an emphasis on the endurance required to complete the Tour's early stages that could approach 500 kilometers. By shortening the stages, the racing became more exciting as speed became an important element in the competition.

For the first half-century, the Tour's ever-changing routes had traced the hexagonal outline of France. In 1951 the Tour went inland into the hilly Massif Central for the first time. In 1951 the only major elements missing from a current Tour were the Prologue individual time trial and the resumption of trade teams.

In the post-war years France was rich with cycling talent. But because the French riders were unable to unite behind one designated leader, the Italians and the Swiss dominated the Tour. In 1953 Louison Bobet convinced the French National Team to race for him. With the help and protection of his teammates, Bobet won three straight Tours.

In 1957, Jacques Anquetil won the first of his five Tour victories. Anquetil had a unique style. He was a master time-trialist. He would stay with the climbers in the mountains, preventing their gaining any time on him. He would then destroy his competitors with a stunning time trial. His defensive riding style tended to alienate the public, but Anquetil cared only about winning and winning with the minimum effort. His duels with Raymond Poulidor, nicknamed "The Eternal Second", enlivened the Tours of the early 1960s. Poulidor was almost always second-best in competitions with Anquetil.

In the early 1960s the Parisian publisher Émilien Amaury became more financially involved with the Tour and promoted one of his writers, Félix Lévitan, to co-organizer of The Tour. Goddet remained the director of the Tour's sporting side and Lévitan became responsible for the race's finances. In 1962, bowing to pressure from bike manufacturers, the Tour reverted to using trade teams.

After Anquetil became the first racer to win five Tours, the Tour's next big shock was the arrival of Belgium's Eddy Merckx, whose 525 professional victories remains, by far, the record. On his way to matching Anquetil's five Tour wins, he shunned the tactical niceties that characterized Anquetil's racing. Merckx bludgeoned his competition with brute strength.

But Merckx was more than a powerful racing machine. He possessed courage and determination. In the 1975 Tour he was punched by a spectator near the top of a climb. That attack left him with an inflamed liver that forced him to take blood thinners. A few days later he crashed, breaking a cheekbone. Now he had to take painkillers as well. But pain, broken bones and drugs never stopped him from trying to win. Frenchman Bernard Thévenet won that year, but Merckx finished second, just 2 minutes and 47 seconds behind. Third-place Lucien Van Impe was another two minutes back.

Let's jump into the 1976 tour, the race's sixty-third edition.

one

1976–1982

Bernard Hinault is masterful in a Tour era deeply troubled by rampant doping and the Tour's declining financial position

1976 Eddy Merckx started 1976 by winning Milan–San Remo for a record seventh time, and he also won the Catalonian week. But that was it for Merckx in the win column for spring. He managed a second place in the Tirreno–Adriatico, but only sixth in Paris–Roubaix and Liège–Bastogne–Liège. In the Giro, he came in eighth. Not able to find his usual form and needing surgery for saddle-sores, he did not enter the 1976 Tour. There would be no rematch between Bernard Thévenet and Eddy Merckx that year.

There were plenty of other fine young cannibals, however. Bernard Thévenet arrived at the Tour fresh off a win in the Dauphiné Libéré, while Luis Ocaña, looking for another shot at glory, had come in second in the Vuelta and third in Paris–Nice.

But Joop Zoetemelk was the odds-on favorite. He won Flèche Wallonne and the Dauphiné Libéré, and had high placings in Amstel Gold and the Tour of the Mediterranean. He had been second in the Tour in 1970 and 1971 and had never finished worse than fifth.

Every Tour is different. Each year the cast of characters changes slightly as older racers retire and young men with fresh ambitions arrive. The route changes each year as well. With differing emphases on flat roads, time trials or mountains, different racers can find that some years suit their talents more than others. The 1976 Tour was clockwise, starting on France's west coast, circling north up to Belgium before heading south for the Alps. Here the 1976 Tour departed from tradition. Normally after one of the two mountain ranges, there are several transition stages before the hard climbing resumes. This year there were five days of climbing in the east, starting in the Vosges in stage seven and ending in stage eleven. Then there was just a rest day before four days in the Pyrenees. That was nine days in a row of mountains. If that wasn't enough, stage twenty finished at the top of Puy de Dôme. Importantly, five of the mountain stages ended with hilltop finishes. This is a huge advantage to smaller riders who rarely have the power to maintain a time advantage gained on a climb through a long descent and flat roll-in to a distant finish line. No wonder climber Lucien van Impe announced that he would be riding this Tour for the overall win rather than his usual King of the Mountains title.

Van Impe's changed circumstances involved more than just having a race itinerary that matched his talents. His previous manager, Jean Stablinski, was replaced with Cyrille Guimard, who had mounted a serious threat to Merckx in the 1972 Tour. Guimard was so recently retired, he was still the 1976 French Cyclocross Champion. In taking over the Gitane-Campagnolo team, he remade the squad to give van Impe better support.

There was a new comet in the heavens. Belgian Freddy Maertens turned professional in 1972. His fantastic sprinting, time trialing and overall strength let him win all but the steepest races. In 1976, his debut year in the Tour, he won 54 races including the World Pro Road Championships and the Belgian Road Championships. His erratic career peaked in 1976 and 1977 before it fell off to almost nothing. Then, in an astonishing act of will, he came back to win the 1981 World Championship.

Maertens did not disappoint Belgian fans unhappy with Merckx's absence. From the gun, he was on fire. He won the Prologue time trial, thumping a monstrous 55 x 12 gear, and then won the first stage. Next, he won the stage three time trial, beating such accomplished chrono men as Ferdi Bracke by 2 minutes, 23 seconds, Raymond Poulidor by almost 3 minutes, and Bernard Thévenet by 3 minutes, 32 seconds. When the Tour entered the Vosges, he won stage seven.

In stage eight, he managed only second to Peugeot's ace sprinter Jacques Esclassan. He explained, "I had already won four stages. For Peugeot, this was not good. They were at zero. We knew [Peugeot director Maurice] De Muer very well. Lomme [Driessens, Maertens' director] talked with De Muer and then talked to Pollentier, Demeyer and me. He said Peugeot needs to win a stage or they are finished. Also for my friends, Jacques Esclassan, Bernard Thévenet and the others. So I said to Lomme, 'Let's do it, okay?'"

Esclassan won the stage, but Peugeot rider Patrick Béon gave it all away by giving a victory salute while Esclassan was still twenty meters from the line. Writers said the victory "stinks a little of rubber," meaning they thought Maertens had put on the brakes.

With the riders poised to begin their days in the Alps in stage nine, the General Classification stood thus:

1. Freddy Maertens
2. Michel Pollentier @ 2 minutes 4 seconds
3. Hennie Kuiper @ 3 minutes 16 seconds
4. Jean-Pierre Danguillaume @ 3 minutes 23 seconds
5. Raymond Poulidor @ 3 minutes 31 seconds

Van Impe, Zoetemelk and Thévenet were all sitting about four minutes behind Maertens.

Stage nine was 258 kilometers that sent the pack up the Luitel before finishing at the summit of l'Alpe d'Huez, the first hilltop finish there since 1952. Even sprinter Freddy Maertens made it over the Luitel with the good climbers. But when Peugeot rider Raymond Delisle opened the hostilities on the Alpe, Maertens was quickly tossed. From then on Zoetemelk and van Impe attacked and counter-attacked each other all the way to the top, with Zoetemelk getting the win by 3 seconds. Poulidor, Thévenet, G.B. Baronchelli, Kuiper and the others were what military men call "collateral damage", incidental victims of a relentless shooting war between the two best climbers of the time. The result of the day's brawl was van Impe in Yellow with Zoetemelk trailing by 8 seconds. Maertens was third, down about a minute.

The next day was another *mano-a-mano* climbing fight between the two leaders. After ascending the Lautaret, the Izoard, and the Montgenèvre, Zoetemelk was able to beat van Impe and Thévenet by just one second and now trailed van Impe in the GC by 7 seconds. The pace was so hard that seven riders were eliminated for failing to finish within the time limit.

The third mountain stage was one of those races in which the peloton just doesn't feel like racing. They let José-Luis Viejo ride away without being chased. His gap of 22 minutes, 50 seconds was the Tour's largest postwar solo winning margin.

With the Alpine stages completed, here was the General Classification:

1. Lucien van Impe
2. Joop Zoetemelk @ 7 seconds
3. Raymond Poulidor @ 1 minute 36 seconds
4. Bernard Thévenet @ 1 minute 48 seconds

The first stage in the Pyrenees, the fourth mountain stage, was another odd day. Van Impe and Zoetemelk worried about each other, letting Raymond Delisle, an excellent though slightly aging racer, get away. Delisle, eighth when the stage started, was in Yellow when it ended, van Impe and Zoetemelk almost three minutes behind.

The next stage didn't affect the standings: the big guns held their fire. Stage winner Régis Ovion failed his drug test, his name stricken from the record and Willy Teirlinck was awarded the stage.

It was stage fourteen, the fifth of these mountain stages, that made history.

There were four big climbs that day. On the second, the Portillon, Ocaña attacked. While he was no longer the dominating rider he had been in the early 1970s, he was not to be ignored. Guimard told van Impe to go after him. Van Impe was reluctant; Guimard and van Impe did not completely agree on tactics, but feeling the moment was not to be lost, Guimard told van Impe that if he didn't go after Ocaña, he would run him off the road with his car.

That did it. Van Impe took off and caught Ocaña on the Peyresourde, the day's penultimate climb.

Zoetemelk didn't chase. He may have thought van Impe was hunting Climbers' points and not seeking the overall lead. And surely by now Ocaña was nothing more than a shell of his former self. Instead, Zoetemelk sat on the wheel of the man whose Yellow Jersey was threatened by the attack, Delisle. Normally this would be an astute strategy, forcing the leader to defend his position. It would have been astute if Delisle could have closed the gap. In fact, Delisle was exhausted and eventually lost over twelve minutes that day. Up the road, van Impe and Ocaña were flying.

Ocaña did the hard work on the flat road leading to the final climb. As he towed van Impe, Ocaña remembered how Zoetemelk had never helped him in his struggles with Merckx.

On the final climb to St.-Lary-Soulan, van Impe jumped away from Ocaña and won the stage and the Yellow Jersey. Realizing his tactical error, Zoetemelk came flying up the hill, going faster than van Impe. But he was 3 minutes, 12 seconds too late.

The Ocaña/van Impe/Zoetemelk attacks shattered the peloton. Forty-five of the remaining ninety-three riders finished outside the time limit. Peter Post, manager of the Raleigh team, asked on behalf of the riders that the Tour management waive the elimination rule for the stage, which they did.

The new General Classification with van Impe back in Yellow:

1. Lucien van Impe
2. Joop Zoetemelk @ 3 minutes 18 seconds
3. Raymond Delisle @ 9 minutes 27 seconds
4. Walter Riccomi @ 10 minutes 22 seconds
5. Raymond Poulidor @ 11 minutes 42 seconds

The final day in the Pyrenees, even with the Aspin, Tourmalet and the Aubisque, didn't change the top of the standings. The lions had to digest their kill.

The stage seventeen time trial showed that van Impe was a better-rounded rider than he was generally credited to be. Ferdi Bracke won the stage, but van Impe beat Zoetemelk by more than a minute. That put Zoetemelk four and a half minutes behind the Belgian climber with only one more chance to take the Tour leadership, the stage twenty climb to the top of Puy de Dôme. Zoetemelk won that stage, beating van Impe by an unimportant 12 seconds. Impressive, but to no real effect. That moment of careful, conservative calculation on the road to St.-Lary-Soulan had cost him the Tour. Zoetemelk may have been the better climber that year, but van Impe had the tactical genius of Guimard for the needed push.

Weakened by hepatitis, Thévenet had been losing time and finally abandoned in stage nineteen.

Lucien van Impe won the Tour, beating Zoetemelk by 4 minutes, 14 seconds. It was his only Tour victory and as of 2019 he remains the last Belgian to win the Tour. To this day, van Impe is troubled by Guimard's remarks that he would not have won the Tour without Guimard's encouragement and threats. Van Impe says Guimard talked to him as if he were a child; after the 1976 season, he changed teams.

Freddy Maertens won eight stages, equaling the record set by Charles Pélissier in 1930 and Merckx in 1970 and 1974.

Celestino Vercelli, riding with G.B. Baronchelli, Walter Riccomi and Wladimiro Panizza on the SCIC-Fiat team, talked to us about the 1976 Tour: "This was the year the Cannibal Eddy Merckx stayed home. This Tour was won by van Impe. Every stage of this Tour was very, very hard. Just to get an idea of the difficulties we faced, in Bordeaux, in incredibly hot weather, we raced three stages the same day. In the evening in the hotel (hotel is a big word for the place we stayed), we slept in big rooms together. I was running a high temperature, I was very tired and hot. I don't have words for that day on the bike.

"When we were riding the Pyrenean stages, the asphalt melted. You can imagine the huge difficulties we faced riding in the mountains in the soft asphalt. In the descent the situation was better with the tires holding the soft road very well. The big problem was the difficulty in removing the asphalt from our legs in the evening."

And Raymond Poulidor? He finished third, 12 minutes, 8 seconds behind van Impe. This was the fourteenth and final Tour de France for the now forty-year-old Poulidor. He abandoned the Tour only twice and finished with three second and five third places.

Poulidor's Tour Record:

> 14 participations
> 7 stage victories
> No overall victories and never a single day in Yellow, not one.

By the years:

> 1962: 3rd overall, 1 stage victory
> 1963: 8th overall
> 1964: 2nd overall, 1 stage victory
> 1965: 2nd overall, 2 stage victories
> 1966: 3rd overall, 1 stage victory

1967: 9th overall, 1 stage victory

1968: Did not finish

1969: 3rd overall

1970: 7th overall

1972: 3rd overall

1973: Did not finish

1974: 2nd overall, 1 stage victory

1975: 19th overall

1976: 3rd overall

Here's a selection of Poulidor's other victories: Milan–San Remo, Flèche Wallonne, Grand Prix des Nations (even though he wasn't a time trialist of Anquetil's caliber, he was still excellent against the clock), Vuelta a España, Critérium National, Dauphiné Libéré, Catalonian Week and Paris–Nice.

In 1974, at the Montreal World Road Championships, only 39-year-old Raymond Poulidor could stay with Eddy Merckx the last time up Mount Royal, finishing just 2 seconds behind. This was an extraordinary career by any measure.

Final 1976 Tour de France General Classification:

1. Lucien van Impe (Gitane-Campagnolo): 116 hours 22 minutes 23 seconds
2. Joop Zoetemelk (Gan-Mercier) @ 4 minutes 14 seconds
3. Raymond Poulidor (Gan-Mercier) @ 12 minutes 8 seconds
4. Raymond Delisle (Peugeot) @ 12 minutes 17 seconds
5. Walter Riccomi (SCIC) @ 12 minutes 39 seconds

Climbers' Competition:

1. Giancarlo Bellini: 170 points
2. Lucien van Impe: 169
3. Joop Zoetemelk: 119

Points Competition:

1. Freddy Maertens: 293 points
2. Pierino Gavazzi: 140
3. Jacques Esclassan: 128

1977

During the 1970s, Amaury's paper *Le Parisien Libéré* had been losing circulation, leading him to fire hundreds of workers. The dismissals were handled crudely, leading to years of sometimes violent labor troubles. After falling from a horse, Émilien Amaury died in January, 1977. Sympathetic to the workers' troubles, the left-wing paper *Libération* reported Amaury's death with the headline *Amaury falls from his horse: the horse is safe.*

Amaury's will left most of his estate to his daughter Francine. Since French law stipulates that all offspring receive equal shares, son Philippe sued for his legal portion. Settlement of the estate came six years later. Philippe got the papers and the Amaury Sport Organization (meaning the Tour and other important races), while Francine received magazines like *Marie-France*. Philippe reorganized his share of the empire, calling it Editions Philippe Amaury (EPA). In 2008 the Amaury family fortune was estimated to be about €450 million (about 600 million US dollars).

The 1977 Tour maintained its 4,000 kilometer length, 4,096 to be exact. There were five split stages and seven transfers to further sap the riders' strength. The organizers are always tinkering with their Tour, and in 1977 they decided to de-emphasize climbing after 1976's mountain extravaganza. From five, the number of hilltop finishes was reduced to just two. In addition, the individual time trial kilometers were increased from 89.8 to 105.2. An all-rounder with a powerful team to protect him on the flatter stages would find favor with this route. The rider who most perfectly fit that description was Bernard Thévenet with his black and white clad Peugeot team. Foreshadowing the 1977 Tour's disrepute, Thévenet was penalized in March for a positive dope test in Paris–Nice.

The Tour's favorites were easy to ascertain. Thévenet, of course, was at the top of the list. Van Impe planned to try for a second win even though the course was less suited to his talents. Merckx was back for what would be his last Tour. His 1977 spring had no major international victories.

Miko-Mercier supplied two contenders, Zoetemelk and Raymond Delisle, who had moved from Peugeot. The TI-Raleigh team had Hennie Kuiper, the 1975 World Road Champion and winner of the 1976 Tour of Switzerland.

Raleigh also had Dietrich "Didi" Thurau, who turned professional late in 1974. He was part of the magnificent West German pursuit machine that dominated the track discipline at the time, and was hailed as a god by German cycling fans looking for a new Rudi Altig. He looked the part, handsome with broad shoulders. During his first full year as a pro, he won five races including his National Championship and in 1976 he won eight. 1977 was his year: he won 25 races and had what would be a stunning start to the Tour de France.

The Prologue 5-kilometer time trial in Fleurance just north of the Pyrenees was the perfect distance for one of the world's finest pursuiters. Thurau won it, beating his teammate Gerrie Knetemann by 4 seconds and Merckx by 8. Thurau's first day in his first Tour put him in Yellow.

In the first road stage, 31 riders—a group that included Merckx, van Impe, Thévenet, Zoetemelk and Thurau—separated themselves from the rest of the pack, and by finishing with this front group, the young German preserved his small lead.

While the 1977 Tour may not have been set up as a climber's Tour, climbing was there and unusually, it started in stage two. The day's 253 kilometers included the Aspin, Tourmalet and the Aubisque. Thurau's ambitions were not unlike Rudi Altig's back in 1964 when he wanted to be the Yellow Jersey when the Tour passed into Germany. This year the Tour would head into Germany for stage thirteen, and Thurau deeply wanted to bring the Yellow Jersey to his home country. Stage two could ruin his chances.

On the Tourmalet, van Impe, Thévenet and Kuiper hammered out a two-minute lead over a chasing group that included Merckx, Ocaña, Thurau and Michel Laurent. Merckx asked Thurau for help in pursuing the leaders. Merckx, being the superior descender, led down the Tourmalet and working together, they regained contact with the trio on the Aubisque. After the Aubisque's descent, the stage finished on the motor-raceway in Pau. This allowed a regroupment that created a lead bunch of fourteen, with all the contenders except Ocaña: Thévenet, Thurau, Merckx, Zoetemelk, van Impe, Kuiper and Delisle. Thurau, a superb trackman, won the stage and dodged a bullet. He was still the leader, but Merckx was still only 8 seconds back. No one could feel confident with the Cannibal that close.

The next two mountain stages maintained the status quo. Instead of attacking in the Pyrenees, the climbers decided to wait for the Alps to contest the race.

At the Bordeaux 30-kilometer individual time trial Merckx was expected to deliver a devastating ride that would give him the lead. It did not turn out that way. Thurau took about a minute out of both Merckx and Thévenet, and now led Merckx by 58 seconds and Thévenet by 1 minute, 25 seconds.

As with many team time trials in the Tour's history, the four-kilometer stage seven-b race didn't count toward the individual riders' times; it was a race for team classification, with the riders of the top three teams getting small bonifications. Merckx's Fiat-sponsored squad won, with Thurau's Raleighs coming in third, costing Thurau 6 seconds.

At this point the overall standings were thus:

1. Dietrich Thurau
2. Eddy Merckx @ 51 seconds
3. Michel Laurent @ 1 minute 22 seconds
4. Bernard Thévenet @ same time
5. Hennie Kuiper @ 1 minute 40 seconds

Before stopping in Germany, the Tour detoured to Belgium. Patrick Sercu, whom Merckx called the most gifted rider he had ever known, won the stage into Charleroi after a 170-kilometer solo break, the peloton coming in six and a half minutes later. Not too bad for a sprinter! In case people might have thought the long break dulled the edge of Sercu's jump, he won the next stage (after a rest day) into Germany in a mass sprint that had all 95 riders still in the Tour finishing together.

Thurau did wear the Yellow Jersey into Germany, satisfying the delirious fans who surrounded his hotel, screaming their joy that one of their countrymen was in Yellow. He kept the lead for a little while longer, but the effort of holding off Merckx, Thévenet and the rest of the field was starting to show.

Before the stage fifteen-b individual time trial up the Avoriaz, the top six riders were close in time:

1. Dietrich Thurau
2. Eddy Merckx @ 51 seconds
3. Bernard Thévenet @ 1 minute 22 seconds
4. Hennie Kuiper @ 1 minute 40 seconds
5. Alain Meslet @ 2 minutes 9 seconds
6. Lucien van Impe @ 2 minutes 15 seconds

Zoetemelk had the fastest time up the 1,833-meter-high mountain, but it was later revealed he had failed the drug test. He was penalized 10 minutes and lost his placing, making van Impe the stage winner with Thévenet only 20 seconds behind him. Merckx came in at 1 minute, 16 seconds. Thurau, fatigued, was fifteenth at 1 minute, 53 seconds. Thévenet was now the leader with Thurau second at 11 seconds and Merckx third at 25 seconds.

During the stage sixteen climb up the Forclaz, Thurau was dropped. He fought his way back and made contact on the last climb of the day, the Montets. Once again, without a hill-top finish, Thurau was able to get control of the situation and win the sprint. Thévenet was in the same lead group and kept the overall lead.

It was in stage seventeen, a 184.5-kilometer trek over the Madeleine, Glandon and up l'Alpe d'Huez that the Tour sorted itself out. The Madeleine was a preliminary that had the effect of shelling Merckx, who was suffering from dysentery.

Easily escaping, van Impe romped up the Glandon and headed for l'Alpe d'Huez with Thévenet's Yellow Jersey in mind. He was only 33 seconds behind Thévenet in the GC, and his win last year had changed his ambitions. Even without Guimard to push and threaten him, he wanted a second Yellow Jersey and was willing to take chances to get it.

The wind was against van Impe as he rode in the valley leading to the Alpe. Determined, he persevered and arrived at the base of l'Alpe d'Huez alone.

Thévenet says that this ride was the hardest of his career. He chased the diminutive Belgian climber with Kuiper and Zoetemelk for company. Kuiper was sitting in fourth place at 49 seconds while Zoetemelk was fifth at 1 minute, 13 seconds. At this time, no one yet knew that Zoetemelk would be penalized for his stage fifteen positive dope test. The two of them sat on Thévenet's wheel and let the man with the Yellow Jersey perform the labor of defending his position. The strategy worked, the gap to van Impe growing smaller and smaller until they were so close that the follow vehicles behind van Impe had to pull out. As they did so, van Impe was hit by one of the television cars. Knowing the Tour was in play, van Impe immediately got back on his bike, only to have his rear wheel collapse.

Back with the chasing trio, Kuiper sensed victory and attacked, dropping Thévenet and Zoetemelk. While van Impe was getting a new wheel, first Kuiper and then Thévenet raced by him. With Kuiper almost a minute up the road, Thévenet's chase was a desperate fight to retain his lead.

Kuiper won the stage, slowing as he crossed the line, with Thévenet arriving 41 seconds later. Thévenet was still in Yellow, but by the skin of his teeth: 8 seconds. Van Impe's loss was heartbreaking. He finished 2 minutes, 6 seconds after Kuiper. Thurau came in seventeenth, at 12 minutes, 32 seconds.

Thévenet was furious with Zoetemelk and Kuiper who were willing to just sit on his wheel and let him do all the work. He called them *petits coureurs*, little riders. About that day, Thévenet said, "I believe that I never went as deep as in 1977, against Hennie Kuiper on l'Alpe d'Huez. That's the only time in my life I reached my limit."

The devastation wrought on the peloton by the hard stage was profound, thirty riders finished outside the time limit and were eliminated; Sercu and Bracke were among the dispatched.

Here was the General Classification situation after the Alpe d'Huez stage:

1. Bernard Thévenet
2. Hennie Kuiper @ 8 seconds
3. Lucien van Impe @ 1 minute 58 seconds
4. Francisco Galdos @ 4 minutes 14 seconds
5. Joop Zoetemelk @ 5 minutes 12 seconds
6. Dietrich Thurau @ 12 minutes 2 seconds

Doping problems continued. The first riders to cross the line at the end of stage eighteen, Joaquim Agostinho and Antonio Menéndez, were relegated after testing positive. Merckx, coming in third, was awarded the stage victory.

Thévenet won the stage twenty time trial, foiling Kuiper's only real chance to take the lead. Instead of gaining time on the Frenchman, Kuiper lost 28 seconds, putting the race out of the Dutchman's reach.

Thurau won the final day's time trial, showing the depth of his talent, but Thévenet was only 6 seconds slower. Kuiper lost another 12 seconds to the Frenchman, who in 1975 had begun a renaissance of French Tour riding that would last a decade.

This was Merckx's last Tour de France. In 1978 he rode only five races, winning none of them. He had worn himself out after entering about 1,800 races and winning over 500.

Final 1977 Tour de France General Classification:
1. Bernard Thévenet (Peugeot-Esso): 115 hours 38 minutes 30 seconds
2. Hennie Kuiper (TI-Raleigh) @ 48 seconds
3. Lucien van Impe (Lejeune) @ 3 minutes 32 seconds
4. Francisco Galdos (KAS) @ 7 minutes 45 seconds
5. Dietrich Thurau (TI-Raleigh) @ 12 minutes 24 seconds
6. Eddy Merckx (Fiat) @ 12 minutes 38 seconds

Climbers' Competition:
1. Lucien van Impe: 244 points
2. Hennie Kuiper: 174
3. Pedro Torres: 144

Points Competition:
1. Jacques Esclassan: 236 points
2. Giacinto Santambrogio: 140
3. Dietrich Thurau: 137

Doping was beginning to rear its ugly head. Or, more correctly, riders who doped were getting caught. Ocaña, Zoetemelk, Agostinho and Menéndez failed dope tests during the 1977 Tour. This was a strange time when it seemed the rules were not being enforced fairly. You will note that there were no Frenchmen in the above list of riders caught doping in the Tour. Rumors circulated about another three or four riders who had also failed their tests but had escaped penalties.

Thévenet would pay a high price for his drug taking. That winter he checked himself into a hospital because cortisone use had badly damaged his liver. He went public with his misdeeds, saying doping in the peloton was common. For this he was severely criticized by the press, by his fellow riders and by his sponsor Peugeot.

This would be a good time to stop and look at the bikes of the era. I had the good fortune to own a Team Raleigh bike built in the shop of Raleigh mechanic Jan Legrand that was typical of the era's bikes.

The frame was Reynolds 531 steel. The bike, being Dutch-built, was heavier than the normal 21-pound racing bike of the era. It was lugged, with a 25 millimeter diameter top tube and a 28 millimeter downtube. Tubing of that time for most uses was drawn to 0.6 millimeter thickness in the center of the tubes and 0.9 at the butts. This frame was fitted with short Campagnolo horizontal adjustable dropouts. It had no chrome. The groupset was Campagnolo Super Record. The hubs were 32-hole, laced to Martano rims. Tires were Clement Strada 66 cotton cold-treated tubulars.

Thévenet's 1975 bike was not of the same class. The Peugeot team rode stock Peugeot bikes with frames of 531 like the Raleighs, but with far inferior workmanship. Merckx, who rode for Peugeot early in his career, said the Peugeot bikes rode and handled like dogs. Like many champions (including Tom Simpson, Rik Van Looy and Freddy Maertens), Merckx had other builders supply him with frames that were then painted and decaled with the sponsor's name. Instead of crisp Campagnolo side-pulls, Peugeots used Mafac centerpull brakes that had been updated only slightly since the early 1950s.

The Simplex Super LJ derailleurs that Peugeot used were certainly up to the standards of the time, actually superior in their shifting to Campagnolo. The Maillard hubs had axles that were prone to breaking.

The Stronglight crankset was pretty and shiny. But, as anyone who rode one in competition could tell you, the spider was flexible so the chain rubbed against the front derailleur under even modest effort. The Maillard pedals were also inferior, having poor bearings and fragile axles.

And with that machine, one that any weekend duffer today would shun with horror, Thévenet won the Tour de France. It's the legs. By 1977, Peugeot had established a separate framebuilding shop to produce professional quality bikes and Thévenet won his second Tour on a world-class bike.

1978

At 3,908 kilometers, the 1978 Tour was a little shorter than previous Tours of the 1970s. It had only two split stages and two rest days, but it was again loaded with transfers: almost half the stages started in a different city than the previous day's finish. Anger over this had been brewing for years. The 1977 Paris–Nice stage race was marred by a rider's strike because of this kind of abusive scheduling. The Tour was courting the same trouble with its 1978 route.

The Merckx/Thévenet era was over; even though Thévenet would continue riding the Tour until 1981, Merckx had ridden his last race in March. 1978 marks the beginning of the Bernard Hinault regime. Hinault's nickname, *Le Blaireau* (The Badger) is apt. He said his solution for those times when he didn't feel good in a race was to attack. Hinault was a complete rider, able to climb, sprint and time trial. He raced classics, stage races, national and world championships, and won them all. He was one of the last of the breed.

He was only 23 years old, yet his accomplishments to date were substantial. The year before, Hinault had won Liège–Bastogne–Liège, Ghent–Wevelgem, the Grand Prix des Nations, and the Dauphiné Libéré. In 1978, he added the Vuelta and French Road Championship to his palmarès. This was a list of wins that most professionals would call a superb career, but Hinault was just getting started. In addition to being the most gifted rider of his age, on the Renault team he had Cyrille Guimard, the most tactically astute man in the business, for his director. Despite the cries of his countrymen for Hinault to ride the Tour, Guimard and Hinault waited until he had learned his craft and was ready to ride the Tour to win. Hinault, said Guimard, "…had the greatest athletic potential of any rider. By far."

Besides Hinault, the 1978 Tour was loaded with other potential winners. Zoetemelk, the true "Eternal Second" (he came in second in the Tour five times) was again riding in the pink, purple and white of Miko-Mercier. Kuiper, who had forced Thévenet to dig so deep on l'Alpe d'Huez the year before, had the strongest team behind him in the Peter Post-directed Raleigh squad. Van Impe had transferred to C&A, the company that had taken over sponsorship of Merckx's team. Peugeot, with a weakened Thévenet, had no real alternative. Michel Laurent had been hailed as the great new hope of French riding, but was unable to fulfill his nation's ambitions.

The 1978 Tour started in Leiden, Holland, with the Prologue held in torrential rain. Not surprisingly, the top four places of the time trial were taken by Dutch riders: Jan Raas, Zoetemelk, Kuiper and Gerrie Knetemann. All but Zoetemelk rode for TI-Raleigh.

Because of the appalling weather, the team directors held a meeting and agreed to petition the Tour management to have the results of the Prologue not count towards the General Classification. All of the directors, that is, except the expected holdout, TI-Raleigh's Peter Post. The Tour agreed to the directors' request; the results stood, but they would not be used in calculating the General Classification.

To make TI-Raleigh even unhappier, Jan Raas, winner of the Prologue, was denied the Yellow Jersey for the start of the first stage. Instead, it was planned to have last year's winner, Thévenet, don the *maillot jaune* for the first stage. He declined the privilege.

The Raleighs started the morning road stage angry, hammering through the day's terrible weather. Jan Raas was able to get clear of the field and elude a speeding Freddy Maertens to win the stage, and put on his Yellow Jersey with a 1-second lead. Raas said that if he never won another race, he was going to win that one.

The stage four team time trial was a cruel 153 kilometers long. Raleigh, bursting with talent, buried themselves to win it, putting Klaus-Peter Thaler in Yellow. Because Thévenet had crashed and his team had missed their feed, Peugeot finished thirteen minutes slower than Raleigh. Luckily for Peugeot, the era's usual practice was to not apply the team time trial times to the individual riders' General Classification. Small time bonuses were awarded to the winning teams, minimizing the stage's damage.

Stage eight was the first real test of the riders seeking overall victory, a 59.3-kilometer individual time trial. Hinault won the stage, beating Merckx's former right-hand man Joseph Bruyère by 34 seconds and Freddy Maertens by almost a minute. Bruyère of C&A was now in Yellow while Hinault had lifted himself to fourth.

During the time trial Merckx rode in the C&A team car following his good friend, screaming "Allez, Joseph! Allez!" while beating on the side of the car door.

Normally, in a time trial like this over rolling country with a pair of category four climbs, Bernard Thévenet would have been in the top five. His continuing health problems from doping were apparent with his twenty-second place at 4 minutes, 37 seconds.

At the end of stage nine, before the start of the climbing in the Pyrenees, the General Classification stood thus:

1. Joseph Bruyère
2. Jacques Bossis @ 2 minutes 7 seconds
3. Gerrie Knetemann @ 2 minutes 56 seconds

    4. Bernard Hinault @ 3 minutes 32 seconds

    5. Joop Zoetemelk @ 4 minutes 11 seconds

In the Pyrenees, Hinault gave confirmation that his climbing prowess was on the same level as his time-trialing. There was some skirmishing on the Marie-Blanque during stage ten, but the contenders finished together. Stage eleven ascended the Tourmalet and the Aspin to St.-Lary-Soulan. Zoetemelk attacked on the final climb but that day he fell short: Hinault and Mariano Martínez were able to catch and drop the Dutchman. Martínez won the stage but Hinault was closing in on Bruyère. Thévenet, who had lost over twelve minutes in the previous stage, was dropped on the Tourmalet, the day's first big pass, and abandoned.

The General Classification after stage eleven:

    1. Joseph Bruyère

    2. Bernard Hinault @ 1 minute 5 seconds

    3. Joop Zoetemelk @ 1 minute 58 seconds

    4. Michel Pollentier @ 2 minutes 47 seconds

Wednesday, July 12, had two stages scheduled, totaling 254 kilometers. The riders had to get up at 5:00 AM after an exhausting stage the day before, one that didn't see many riders in bed until 1:00 AM. Goddet was apprised of a planned rider's strike and tried to avert it with a compromise, offering the day's total prize money to the peloton if they would at least race the final hour. The racers, galvanized by Hinault's determined leadership, would have none of it. After riding so slowly they were an hour and a half behind the Tour's planned schedule, the riders stopped their bikes, dismounted and, still led by the 23-year-old Hinault, walked across the finish line in protest. The people of the little town of Valence d'Agen, where the stage finished, were furious that their six months of work preparing the city for the stage finish, as well as the fees paid to the Tour, organization were wasted. The police had to protect the riders from the angry fans.

The public, incorrectly thinking that the professional racers were wealthy athletes who should endure some hard work, generally failed to appreciate the striking riders' point.

The stage was annulled and the prize money was not awarded. Goddet showed no sympathy for the riders' complaints, noting that the race organization had consulted with the team managers several times before the route was unveiled. But it was the racers' point that while their employers had worked with the Tour, the riders themselves had not taken part in the route discussions.

Bastille Day featured a 52.5-kilometer individual time trial up Puy de Dôme. Perhaps 400,000 people were on the sides of the road to watch. With six kilometers to go, at the beginning of the climb proper, Zoetemelk changed to a lightweight climbing bike. Hinault's mechanic tried to do the same, but with the crowds pressing on all sides as he ran with the bike, the mechanic hit a spectator, ruining the front wheel of Hinault's lightweight bike. Zoetemelk won the stage with Pollentier just 46 seconds slower. Most surprising, Bruyère was only 55 seconds behind. On the day he had targeted to take the lead, after the bike switch fiasco, Hinault came in at 1 minute, 40 seconds.

This meant big Joseph Bruyère was still in Yellow. No one (Merckx excepted) expected him to do so well on the Puy de Dôme ascent.

Stage sixteen was another hard mountain stage. The racers would tackle the Col de la République, Luitel and finish at the top of l'Alpe d'Huez. Bruyère knew that it had been a miracle that he had been able to wear the Yellow Jersey this long and felt his hours in the lead were numbered. It was on the Luitel that he cracked.

But up the road, Michel Pollentier was scooting up the mountain, going over the Luitel with a 13-second lead on Zoetemelk, Kuiper, Hinault and Agostinho. The chasers were slow to get organized while Pollentier kept pressing his advantage in the Romanche Valley leading to l'Alpe d'Huez. He held his lead to the start of the hairpin turns of the Alpe where he had a gap of almost two minutes as Hinault, Kuiper and Zoetemelk closed in. Zoetemelk faltered in the final kilometers while Kuiper could see Pollentier up ahead as the tough little Belgian crossed the line. Pollentier was first, Kuiper second, then Hinault and Zoetemelk.

Two hours after winning the stage, Pollentier still hadn't visited the doping control as every stage winner must do immediately after the race is over. He was finally found and brought to the van with two other racers selected for random tests. One of the two, Antoine Gutierrez, seemed to have trouble producing a urine sample. The wary doctor, suspicious, pulled up his jersey and discovered a urine-filled bottle with a tube taped under his arm. Pollentier was found to have the same set-up. Pollentier's day in the sun was over and he was kicked out of the Tour.

Pollentier tried to explain that he had taken something for his breathing, but not knowing if it would trigger a positive test, he had tried to evade the controls. Later, it was found that he had taken amphetamines. Those certainly do trigger a positive dope test.

For years European reporters have cryptically referred to Pollentier having been bought and sold. When I asked his teammate Freddy Maertens about this, Maertens explained by accusing their team director, Fred De Bruyne, of warning the doctors about Pollentier's apparatus, saying De Bruyne was paid by another team to sell out his own rider.

The sordid episode was a sad end of the Tour for an immensely talented rider with the worst pedaling style in the pro peloton. Look at any picture of him and he's got his head cocked to one side, at least one elbow out and knees flailing. But he could make his bike go like hell. In 1977 he won the Giro d'Italia, the Tour of Switzerland and the Belgian Road Championships. Before the Tour started in 1978 he had already won the Dauphiné Libéré and again his National Championship. He entered the Tour three more times after this, but never finished. Like Freddy Maertens, he trusted other people with his money and they lost it for him. He ended up selling automobile tires out of his house.

Returning to the race.

Zoetemelk, who over the years had his own difficulties with dope testing, was sitting in second place when Pollentier was disgraced. Was this to be his breakout win?

There was one more Alpine stage, and with Kuiper having crashed descending the Granier and now out with a broken clavicle, there were now just two real protagonists, Zoetemelk and Hinault, who finished together. After stage seventeen and the climbing finished, Zoetemelk retained a fragile hold on the lead.

1. Joop Zoetemelk
2. Bernard Hinault @ 14 seconds
3. Joaquim Agostinho @ 6 minutes 13 seconds
4. Christian Seznec @ 8 minutes 25 seconds
5. Joseph Bruyère @ 10 minutes 25 seconds

He remained the leader until the inevitable meeting in the final time trial, stage twenty, 72 kilometers of what Hinault did best. Hinault—he said he knew he would triumph that day—beat Zoetemelk by 4 minutes, 10 seconds. With only one more stage, the Tour was his, the result of a careful, measured, controlled effort.

Final 1978 Tour de France General Classification:

1. Bernard Hinault (Renault-Gitane): 108 hours 18 minutes
2. Joop Zoetemelk (Miko-Mercier) @ 3 minutes 56 seconds
3. Joaquim Agostinho (Velda-Flandria) @ 6 minutes 54 seconds
4. Joseph Bruyère (C&A) @ 9 minutes 4 seconds
5. Christian Seznec (Miko-Mercier) @ 12 minutes 50 seconds

Climbers' competition:

1. Mariano Martínez: 187 points
2. Bernard Hinault: 176
3. Joop Zoetemelk: 155

Points Competition:

1. Freddy Maertens: 242 points
2. Jacques Esclassan: 189
3. Bernard Hinault: 123

1979

The 1979 edition of the Tour had five individual time trials totaling 165.3 kilometers, and two team time trials covering 176.8 kilometers. Previously, team time trials had counted only toward the team classification, with only small bonifications affecting the riders' General Classification. This year the team's real time in these stages counted toward the individual riders' elapsed times. This was a huge benefit for riders on powerful, well-drilled teams like TI-Raleigh and Renault-Gitane. If any Tour might be accused of being designed for a particular rider, this is the one. While Bernard Hinault could race well in any of the disciplines, he was the master of the chrono.

The route entailed many transfers. Drawn on a map, it looks like little random lines drawn from one point to another, bearing no relationship to each other. It was slightly shorter than the year before, at 3,765 kilometers with 25 stages. While there were many transfers, there were no split stages. The riders' strike of 1978 had finally gotten through to the organizers. Despite this, the Tour did continue to have occasional split stages until 1991. Since then the Tour has looked for other ways to find money rather than degrading the quality of the race.

There were really only two men entered who could be considered contenders for the Yellow Jersey in Paris, the same two who had made the race the year before: Hinault and Zoetemelk. This would be Zoetemelk's ninth Tour and there seemed to be no lessening of his powers, Zoetemelk having come in second in his first attempt in 1970 against Merckx, and second for a fourth time in 1978 when he finished four minutes behind Hinault.

The race started in a predictable way with Raleigh's Gerrie Knetemann winning the 5-kilometer Prologue in Fleurance, with Zoetemelk and Hinault tied at 4 seconds slower.

The 1979 Tour didn't offer any flat or transition stages to get the riders' legs used to the rhythm of mountain racing. There were no preparatory stages before the climbing. The first stage went directly from Fleurance, northeast of the Pyrenees, into the mountains, crossing the Col de Menté and the Portillon. With the stage's bad weather making the race dangerous, a teammate of Agostinho's, René Bittinger, was allowed the stage win. The Tour's elite watched each other, finishing together 47 seconds after Bittinger.

Stage two was a time trial up to Superbagnères, 23.9-kilometers of climbing to the 1,800 meter high ski station. Winning here put Hinault in Yellow with Zoetemelk and Agostinho at 53 seconds. Hinault ripped up the mountain so fast that five riders were eliminated for failing to make the time cutoff. Sean Kelly's Splendor team was particularly hard hit; two of the *hors délais* riders were his domestiques.

Stage three went over the Peyresourde, Aspin and the Soulor. Even with a puncture on the descent of the Aspin, Hinault won it from the thirteen men in the lead group.

By the end of the Pyrenees, the Tour had already sorted itself out:

1. Bernard Hinault
2. Joop Zoetemelk @ 53 seconds
3. Joaquim Agostinho @ same time
4. Hennie Kuiper @ 1 minute 49 seconds
5. Sven-Åke Nilsson @ 2 minutes 15 seconds
6. Giovanni Battaglin @ 2 minutes 19 seconds

Even with Hinault's squad taking a surprising fifth place in the team time trial the following day—won by the big, strong Dutch horses of Raleigh—Hinault remained in the lead, but the gap was narrowed to just 12 seconds over Zoetemelk. Kuiper, riding for Peugeot, says his director De Muer made a terrible mistake by selecting light, fragile tires for this stage. Suffering five punctures, Kuiper believes he lost a chance to wear the Yellow Jersey that day, since Peugeot finished 71 seconds behind Raleigh. Further, he wondered if that change to the dynamics of the race set him just far enough back to keep him from fighting Hinault on nearly equal terms.

Hinault improved his position slightly by taking Hot Spot intermediate sprints. The stage eight team time trial allowed Hinault, backed by his powerful Renault team, to add almost a minute to his lead, which was now 1 minute, 18 seconds.

Stage nine, a ride over the "Hell of the North"—the tough cobbles of Northern France—with a finish in the Roubaix velodrome, showed the world what Hinault was made of. At about the 100-kilometer point in the stage, Zoetemelk joined a dangerous group of escapees: Thurau, Pollentier, Ludo Delcroix, André Dierickx and Didier Vanoverschelde. Hinault missed the move and had to chase. He flatted. He chased again and was held up by strikers blocking the road. He got through and punctured again. Undeterred, he continued the chase while Zoetemelk pressed home his advantage. Hinault came into the Roubaix velodrome in a group with Kuiper, van Impe and Battaglin 3 minutes, 45 seconds after Zoetemelk's breakaway. Zoetemelk was in Yellow and Hinault was in tears.

Jacques Anquetil said that by showing such strength in adversity, fighting to regain the escapees and limiting his GC deficit to only 2 minutes, 8 seconds, Hinault had won the Tour. Or rather, that day Hinault did not lose the Tour.

The post-Roubaix General Classification:
1. Joop Zoetemelk
2. Bernard Hinault @ 2 minutes 8 seconds
3. Sven-Åke Nilsson @ 4 minutes 48 seconds
4. Ueli Sutter @ 4 minutes 49 seconds
5. André Dierickx @ 5 minutes 23 seconds
6. Hennie Kuiper @ 6 minutes 38 seconds

Stage eleven, in Brussels, was a 33.4-kilometer individual time trial. Hinault turned in an outstanding ride, beating Zoetemelk by 36 seconds. The gap between them was now 1 minute, 32 seconds, with Zoetemelk still the leader.

From Belgium the Tour headed south into the Vosges. Hinault and Zoetemelk didn't start shooting just yet. Italian hope Giovanni Battaglin was found positive for dope and received a 10-minute penalty, properly ruining his chances for a high placing.

The Tour then moved to the Alps where this Tour would be settled. Stage fifteen was a 54.2-kilometer hill-climb time trial going from Evian up to Morzine Avoriaz. Hinault won the stage, crushing Zoetemelk. This wasn't necessarily because Hinault was the stronger rider. Zoetemelk's hill-climb was a mechanical nightmare that required two bike changes. All in all, it was probably a fair thing, balancing the karmic books after Hinault's Roubaix stage problems. Hinault was now in Yellow with Zoetemelk at 1 minute, 48 seconds. Lest the reader think that Zoetemelk was a hopeless second-rater, GC third place Kuiper was 11 minutes, 47 seconds behind. Hinault and Zoetemelk were the class of the pack with Hinault the uniquely gifted racer of his generation.

The next day had three high passes, allowing Hinault to extend his lead by almost a minute. While Hinault was taking big pieces of time out of the Dutchman, he was also riding like the older Merckx, snagging little time bonifications in the intermediate sprints. For Zoetemelk, it was the Merckx nightmare all over again, chasing a relentless, aggressive competitor who would concede nothing.

Stage seventeen, with the Madeleine, Télégraphe, Galibier and hilltop finish at l'Alpe d'Huez compacted into 166.5 kilometers ended in a draw for the two leaders.

In stage eighteen, Zoetemelk finally beat Hinault, but only by 47 seconds. Originally the stage had been planned to be a trip over the Izoard, but road construction required a last-minute change. The stage started at the top of l'Alpe d'Huez, where the previous stage had ended, went over the Morte and then climbed back up the Alpe.

With the mountains finished, Hinault appeared to have earned his second Tour. He and Zoetemelk had opened up an astonishing gap on the rest of the field:

1. Berhard Hinault
2. Joop Zoetemelk @ 1 minute 58 seconds
3. Hennie Kuiper @ 21 minutes 23 seconds
4. Joaquim Agostinho @ 21 minutes 58 seconds
5. Jean-René Bernaudeau @ 23 minutes 40 seconds

Zoetemelk lost another minute in the final time trial. That was it. Or was it? In the final ride on the Champs Élysées, Zoetemelk slipped away from the peloton. Hinault himself went after him, bridging alone up to the fleeing Dutchman. Together they beat out a gap of 2 minutes, 18 seconds. Hinault won the final sprint and the Tour.

After the final stage Zoetemelk became the Tour's first rider to test positive for an anabolic steroid (Nandrolone, which he had had taken in 1978 without getting caught) and was penalized 10 minutes. Even so, Zoetemelk still finished second, so far ahead of the rest of the field were he and Hinault. Soigneur Willy Voet (more about Willy later) said that by the late 1970s, amphetamines (which could be easily picked up in tests) had been supplanted by anabolic agents: steroids and corticoids. Riders could now train harder and get stronger (and more muscular, as photos of the era show). A clean rider could still compete, but drugs could help a cheating rider more than ever.

Hinault was only 24 and had already won two Tours. At the other end, third-place Joaquim Agostinho was 37. Hinault won both the General Classification and the Points Classification. His domestique Jean-René Bernaudeau was the best young rider and Renault won the Team Classification.

Final 1979 Tour de France General Classification:
1. Bernard Hinault (Renault-Gitane): 103 hours 6 minutes 50 seconds
2. Joop Zoetemelk (Miko-Mercier) @ 13 minutes 7 seconds
3. Joaquim Agostinho (Flandria) @ 26 minutes 53 seconds
4. Hennie Kuiper (Peugeot-Esso) @ 28 minutes 2 seconds
5. Jean-René Bernaudeau (Renault-Gitane) @ 32 minutes 43 seconds

Climbers' Competition:
1. Giovanni Battaglin: 239 points
2. Bernard Hinault: 196
3. Mariano Martínez: 158

Points Competition:

    1. Bernard Hinault: 253 points

    2. Dietrich Thurau: 157

    3. Joop Zoetemelk: 109

Zoetemelk and Sven-Åke Nilsson of the Miko team sported the then-new seven-speed rear clusters when the norm was six cogs. This cost Zoetemelk in one wheel change when the mechanic had trouble finding a working replacement. The 1979 final podium was the same three men as the year before.

1980

There were some important realignments in the team rosters. Kuiper, second in the 1977 Tour and fourth in 1979, had changed teams a couple of times. He had been with the powerful TI-Raleigh team, but Kuiper and team boss Peter Post's relentless, driving management style weren't a good mix. He moved to the DAF Trucks team and then in 1979 switched to Peugeot, whose director Maurice De Muer had managed Thévenet to victory. Kuiper thought that if De Muer could win the Tour with Thévenet, he could turn Kuiper into a Tour winner as well.

Meanwhile, Zoetemelk left his old team of Miko and moved to TI-Raleigh. He now had the strongest team and Peter Post to help him win the Tour. This was 33-year-old Zoetemelk's tenth Tour attempt. He had placed second five times starting with his first entry in 1970 when he was runner up to Merckx. Even though the 1980 route wasn't as mountainous as other editions, Post was pleased. This is counter-intuitive given that Zoetemelk was an excellent climber, but Post figured his team of mostly big, strong Dutchmen could protect Zoetemelk for more of the race and he would spend less time isolated in the high mountains. Post took credit for motivating Zoetemelk, convincing him that his record of high Tour placings and other prestigious race wins meant he could actually win the Tour de France.

Hinault was planning on winning three Tours in a row, making him, at 25, Louison Bobet's equal. That spring he had already won the Giro by more than five minutes over Wladimiro Panizza. In addition to three sequential Tour wins he was hoping to add the rare Giro-Tour double to his palmares, joining Coppi, Anquetil and Merckx.

The weather during the first half of the Tour was terrible: cold, wet and rainy. This would have consequences for the peloton in a few short days.

The 1980 Tour started in Frankfurt, Germany. For the first time Hinault won the Prologue. He kept the lead until stage one-b, a 45.8-kilometer team time trial. The Raleighs almost always did well in this discipline and they delivered the goods this day, putting Gerrie Knetemann at the top of the standings. Knetemann didn't get a chance to get too comfortable in his Yellow Jersey because in stage two Rudy

Hinault riding to victory in the stage four time trial.

Pevenage led in the winning three-man break that included Yvon Bertin and Pierre Bazzo. The trio had extracted a ten-minute gap from the pack. This gave the lead to Bertin, one of Hinault's domestiques, second place to Pevenage and third to Bazzo. The next day Bertin finished in a small group of stragglers, fifteen minutes down. Pevenage was now the leader.

Hinault won stage four, the first individual time trial. It wasn't enough for Yellow, given the big advantage the stage two breakaways still had, but Hinault could surely see it on the horizon.

The General Classification after the time trial stood thus:

1. Rudi Pevenage
2. Pierre Bazzo @ 1 minute 4 seconds
3. Bernard Hinault @ 5 minutes 41 seconds
4. Gerrie Knetemann @ 6 minutes 58 seconds
5. Henk Lubberding @ 7 minutes 6 seconds
6. Joop Zoetemelk @ 7 minutes 11 seconds

The next day was ridden over the challenging pavé of Northern France in terrible weather, 250 kilometers of what Hinault called "those swinish cobbles". Hinault hated this kind of racing, even though his power and personal drive allowed him to excel in miserable conditions. He and Kuiper finished two minutes ahead of the field, putting him closer to the lead, three and a half minutes behind Pevenage.

As the peloton had been riding hard in the cold, wet weather, tendinitis had begun to appear. It was said that over 50 riders were racing in pain. Cynics thought the eruption of peloton-wide connective-tissue problems indicative of widespread steroid use. High steroid intake weakens tendons by suppressing the body's ability to repair damaged tissues. In the late 1990s Willy Voet wrote that his team doctor found he had to reduce the cortisone intake of riders transferring from other teams. Cortisone is a steroid the body produces in response to stress. "In spite of the sense of well-being which it brings, cortisone ends up destroying the muscles by increasing the demands which are made on them. This has the effect of making the tendons and joints far more fragile."

Hinault himself started to show the first symptoms of tendon problems in his knee (of course, this in no way specifically impugns Hinault, who never failed a drug test). Stage seven-a was a 65-kilometer team time trial. Raleigh won again. Ominously, Hinault could not take his pulls in the Renault pace line.

From here on, Hinault spent much time riding at the back of the peloton talking with the Tour doctor or with his director, Guimard. The press wrote reams about Hinault's knee, all done, in the words of Les Woodland, with the gravity normally reserved for dying kings.

Hinault took the Yellow Jersey from Pevenage in the stage eleven individual time trial, but Hinault was not riding at his best. It was Zoetemelk who had won the stage with Hinault coming in fifth, a rare show of weakness for the Badger. The day's top finishers:

1. Joop Zoetemelk
2. Hennie Kuiper @ 46 seconds
3. Joaquim Agostinho @ 1 minute 9 seconds
4. Bert Oosterbosch @ 1 minute 12 seconds
5. Bernard Hinault @ 1 minute 39 seconds

Yielding the following General Classification:

1. Bernard Hinault
2. Joop Zoetemelk @ 21 seconds
3. Rudy Pevenage @ 1 minute 29 seconds
4. Hennie Kuiper @ 1 minute 31 seconds
5. Pierre Bazzo @ 2 minutes 40 seconds

The next day, the Tour stood poised at the foot of the Pyrenees. Hinault had said he would never quit the Tour while in Yellow.

Yet, the pain was too much, even for Hinault. At 10:30 PM, the evening before stage thirteen, Guimard interrupted the Tour directors' dinner to inform them that Hinault had to withdraw (in fact he had already quietly left for Lourdes). The newspapermen had already sent in their stories and were livid, but Hinault wanted to duck out with a minimum of fuss. Hinault and Guimard knew that the next day's menu of the Aubisque, Tourmalet, Aspin and Peyresourde would far too much for a limping man struggling on the flat stages. It was ironic that this was Guimard's duty. Suffering from a painful knee, Guimard had to be lifted from his bicycle, in tears, in the 1972 Tour while in second place and holding the Green Jersey.

Zoetemelk says that at the time he was unaware of the dire state of Hinault's knee. He recalled, "My Tour started badly. I was never really well. But everything hinged on the second week, after Bordeaux, where I won the time trial. Bernard Hinault had an off-day. Normally he was much stronger than me, but he had knee problems. I didn't know he was going to abandon... I said to myself, if I won the time trial, why can I not win in the mountains? Now I had my chance!"

The lead was Zoetemelk's. The first and only big Pyrenean day showed he was not going to change his basic tactics. He continued to race not to win; instead he was riding not to lose. This negative, conservative approach had cost him dearly in years past, but now that he was in the lead and probably the strongest man on the strongest team, the Anquetil approach made sense. He let Miko rider Raymond Martin scamper away for a solo win (Martin was first over the three final climbs), but made sure dangerman Kuiper was kept on a short leash.

Zoetemelk came out of stage thirteen with a 1 minute, 10 second lead over Kuiper. Zoetemelk, like Merckx before when he had inherited the lead from Ocaña, refused to wear the Yellow Jersey the first day he was in the lead.

After stage thirteen, the General Classification:

1. Joop Zoetemelk
2. Hennie Kuiper @ 1 minute 10 seconds
3. Raymond Martin @ 4 minutes 37 seconds
4. Johan De Muynck @ 6 minutes 53 seconds
5. Pierre Bazzo @ 7 minutes 10 seconds

Three days later the Tour arrived in the Alps. There, Zoetemelk chose not to display his sparkling climbing skills, letting Belgian non-contender Jos Deschoenmaecker win stage sixteen to Pra Loup. Three kilometers from the top of the Pra Loup climb, one of Zoetemelk's domestiques, Johan Van der Velde, had his gears slip, causing him to swerve and crash Zoetemelk. Cut on both his thigh and arm, Zoetemelk quickly remounted and continued racing up the mountain. He did more than limit the damage, distancing himself from Kuiper by another 16 seconds, increasing his lead to 1 minute, 34 seconds.

The next day, with the Galibier, Madeleine and Joux-Plane, Zoetemelk showed the effects of the previous day's crash when he was dropped by the leaders early in the stage. He was protected and paced by his fellow Raleigh-riding Dutchmen who kept him in contention all day. Other riders who didn't have a chance for Yellow in Paris flew up the hills while Zoetemelk was content to finish thirteenth, but still a half-minute ahead of Kuiper. By riding carefully and conservatively, he was slowly building his lead.

During the third Alpine day he again let the non-contenders fly, but he showed he had plenty of strength, finishing with van Impe. Kuiper was weakening, coming in fourteenth, two and a half minutes behind Zoetemelk.

With the serious climbing finished, Zoetemelk was in control:

1. Joop Zoetemelk
2. Raymond Martin @ 5 minutes 22 seconds
3. Hennie Kuiper @ 5 minutes 39 seconds
4. Johan De Muynck @ 8 minutes 27 seconds

That left the individual time trial in stage twenty as the only serious obstacle to Zoetemelk's final victory. In St. Etienne, the center of what was then a thriving French cycle industry, Zoetemelk won his second time trial of the 1980 Tour, giving him a near bullet-proof lead with only two stages to go. Kuiper's fourth place that day was good enough to move him back into second place.

By the end of the Tour, Zoetemelk had hammered out a commanding lead, one for which there should be no apologies.

Final 1980 Tour de France General Classification:

1. Joop Zoetemelk (TI-Raleigh): 109 hours 19 minutes 14 seconds
2. Hennie Kuiper (Peugeot) @ 6 minutes 55 seconds
3. Raymond Martin (Miko-Mercier) @ 7 minutes 56 seconds
4. Johan De Muynck (Splendor) @ 12 minutes 24 seconds
5. Joaquim Agostinho (Puch) @ 15 minutes 37 seconds

Climbers' Competition:

1. Raymond Martin: 223 points
2. Ludo Loos: 162
3. Ludo Peeters: 147

Points Competition:

1. Rudy Pevenage: 194 points
2. Sean Kelly: 153
3. Ludo Peeters: 148

Much has been made of the fact the Zoetemelk was an excellent racer, but not a *patron*, a leader, an alpha male. He did not have the commanding authority of Merckx, Hinault, or even his own teammate, Jan Raas. Even after Zoetemelk took over the *maillot jaune*, teammates Knetemann and Raas were the team's leaders, giving the riders their directions.

Zoetemelk has suffered a lot of criticism over his victory, including claims that it was a gift because of Hinault's departure. Zoetemelk said it best, "Surely winning the Tour is a question of health and robustness? If Hinault does not have that health and robustness and I have, that makes me a valid winner."

Hinault agreed, "There is no need for him to say that he won because I abandoned. That would take away from his victory. My problems were of my own making. It is always the absent rider who is at fault. I was absent and he took my place." Ah, the supreme, generous confidence of a born winner.

The Zoetemelk of 1980, like the post-Blois-crash Merckx, was no longer at the peak of his powers. Jean-Paul Ollivier thinks Zoetemelk was at his best in 1974, before his Midi Libre crash and meningitis. His 1980 win at age 33 is a tribute to both his determination to return to the highest levels of competitive cycling and his persistence. He rode the Tour a total of sixteen times, finishing every time. He ended up winning the Dutch and World Championships, the Vuelta, Paris–Nice, the Tour de France (and was second six times), the Tour of Romandie, Amstel Gold and a host of other important races. Despite his numerous run-ins with the gas spectrometer, he was one of the finest racers to have ever turned a pedal.

Hinault recovered from his tendinitis soon enough to regain his form and win the World Road Championships that fall. But Guimard, worried about a successor to Hinault for his team, secretly signed Greg LeMond in Paris as Zoetemelk was riding up and down the Champs Élysées.

1981

The 1981 Tour still included two split stages, the second two-race day coming after a 246-kilometer stage to Roubaix, for a total of 25 stages, counting the Prologue. At 3,758 kilometers, it was slightly longer than current Tours.

Hinault had a superb spring. Wearing the Rainbow Jersey of the World Champion, he won Paris–Roubaix, Amstel Gold, the Critérium International and the Dauphiné Libéré. He didn't try the Giro this year, being content with an attempt to reassert his dominance of the Tour de France.

Who was there to challenge him? Zoetemelk was 34 years old. Van Impe and Agostinho, the other well-known Grand Tour men, were holdovers from the Merckx/Thévenet era and never displayed the ability to take on the Badger when he was on form.

The 1981 Tour started the same way the 1980 edition did. Hinault won the Prologue time trial and aggressively hammered the field in stage one. He might have gained several minutes if Guimard had not told him to let up and not take chances in the rain.

Raleigh won both the stage one-b and the stage four team time trials. That meant that Raleigh had won seven of these tests of team power and precision in a row. Also following the 1980 pattern, Gerrie Knetemann was the Raleigh man in Yellow. The 1981 team time trial rules were generous in the extreme to the teams that did well, giving the Raleigh team members a 2-minute bonus.

Stage five was the first day in the Pyrenees, 117.5 kilometers from St. Gaudens to St.-Lary-Soulan. Ever the commander, Hinault led over the Peyresourde. On the Pla d'Adet ascent, van Impe took charge, leading the remaining riders of the front group: Hinault, Alberto Fernández and a revelation, Australia's Phil Anderson. Van Impe won the stage by 27 seconds, but Anderson matched Hinault and Fernández stroke for stroke. Anderson, riding for Peugeot, became the first Australian to wear the Yellow Jersey.

Anderson's glory was short-lived. With a fragile 17-second lead over Hinault, he faced a 26.7-kilometer individual time trial the next day. As expected, Hinault won the stage and reclaimed the lead with Knetemann second, only 3 seconds behind. Anderson acquitted himself well, coming in third, 30 seconds slower than the Badger. Hinault, with the time bonus, now led Anderson by 13 seconds.

Over the next several days, the race made its way through northern France and Belgium. Anderson lost little pieces of time here and there as Hinault took the occasional bonus sprint and padded his lead. By the time the race reached Mulhouse for the stage fourteen individual time trial, the tenacious Australian was still in second place, but now 57 seconds behind. Hinault won the time trial, gaining another two minutes.

Before the Alps, the General Classification stood thus:

1. Bernard Hinault
2. Phil Anderson @ 2 minutes 58 seconds
3. Gilbert Duclos-Lassalle @ 6 minutes 37 seconds
4. Jean-François Rodríguez @ 8 minutes 35 seconds
5. Géry Verlinden @ 8 minutes 56 seconds
6. Lucien van Impe @ 9 minutes 38 seconds

Anderson's undoing started in stage sixteen with its four major climbs, including the Ramaz and the Joux-Plane. Both Anderson and Kuiper lost four and a half minutes on Hinault, who finished with climbers van Impe and Zoetemelk. Anderson was still second, but he was now 7 minutes, 39 seconds behind Hinault. Van Impe had moved up to third, two minutes behind Anderson.

Stage seventeen, with the Madeleine, Glandon and a finish at the top of l'Alpe d'Huez was where Anderson's dream ended completely. Blowing up on the Glandon, the Australian lost seventeen minutes, while Hinault and van Impe finished seconds behind stage winner Peter Winnen. Hinault had built a nine and a half minute lead over the new second place, van Impe.

Stage eighteen, the final day in the Alps, was a series of first- and second-category climbs, five in all. Hinault stamped his seal of authority on the Tour by riding away on the last ascent. As he led the lucky few remaining riders up the first category Pleynet, he made a strong backward look—perhaps glare would be a better word—at his followers, and with a couple of accelerations rode away. Bernaudeau tried to stay with him, but Hinault was not to be contained that day.

With the heavy climbing finished, the standings had taken this form:

1. Bernard Hinault
2. Lucien van Impe @ 12 minutes 12 seconds
3. Robert Alban @ 13 minutes 22 seconds
4. Joop Zoetemelk @ 15 minutes 9 seconds
5. Johan De Muynck @ 15 minutes 53 seconds

There remained one more time trial, 46.5 kilometers long and another opportunity for Hinault to further crush a field that could do nothing to stop the flying Frenchman. Hinault won and took another two minutes out of van Impe.

Freddy Maertens, who had been so good in the mid-1970s, winning as many as 54 races in a single year, won only two races in 1979 and one in 1980. In 1981 he came back. He earned his third Tour de France points title—the Green Jersey—winning six stages to do it, and later that year won the World Road Championship. In the remaining six years of his racing career he won only two more races.

Racing's finances were in transition. Greg LeMond is often given credit for the revolution in racer's pay. He deserves the credit, but his influence predates his famous 1985 contract with La Vie Claire. Phil Anderson is a natural entrepreneur and rather than accept 100 francs for holding up a Perrier bottle at the end of a Tour stage, Anderson contacted Coca-Cola which agreed to pay him to hold up a Coke instead, upsetting the Tour organizers. Back then, riders on the tight-fisted Peugeot team had to buy their own socks, gloves, and headbands. Anderson contacted Qantas Airlines and had them imprint some items with their logos. Peugeot soon figured they could do the same thing, costing Anderson his Qantas endorsement income.

After the 1980 season, Peugeot offered Anderson an increase of $690.00 a month, to the munificent total of $1,400 a month. Even accounting for decades of inflation, it wasn't much. Anderson was friends with the LeMond family, and Greg's father advised Anderson to hire a lawyer to negotiate for him. That created a stink (riders were supposed to know their place) but Anderson's lawyer had a point: Anderson was being offered less than the lawyer's secretary was being paid. With professional help Anderson was able to get a fair deal. Plus, he didn't have to buy his own racing socks any more.

Final 1981 Tour de France General Classification:

1. Bernard Hinault (Renault): 96 hours 19 minutes 38 seconds
2. Lucien van Impe (Boston) @ 14 minutes 34 seconds
3. Robert Alban (La Redoute) @ 17 minutes 4 seconds
4. Joop Zoetemelk (TI-Raleigh) @ 18 minutes 21 seconds
5. Peter Winnen (Capri-Sonne) @ 20 minutes 26 seconds

Climbers' Competition:

1. Lucien van Impe: 284 points
2. Bernard Hinault: 222
3. Jean-René Bernaudeau: 168

Points Competition:
1. Freddy Maertens: 428 points
2. William Tackaert: 222
3. Bernard Hinault: 184

One has to go back to 1973 and Ocaña's nearly sixteen-minute victory over Thévenet to find a larger winning margin. Hinault's 1981 Tour was a masterful, controlling ride—at a then-record pace of 37.844 kilometers per hour—performed by a rider who could do everything. That made three Tour victories for the Badger.

But, all was not well between Hinault and Guimard. Hinault claims that his using an agent to negotiate his contract with the team sponsors—rather than having Guimard act as an intermediary—started what Hinault called the "three year's war" between the racer and his mentor.

This was the first Tour with an American entered. Jonathan Boyer had been racing in Europe for the top Parisian amateur squad ACBB before turning pro in 1977. Guimard signed him to ride the 1981 Tour in support of Hinault where he finished a creditable thirty-second.

1982

Hinault didn't have his usual long list of spring wins this year. He had one major victory, the Giro d'Italia, with five stage wins (if you count the Prologue team time trial). Hinault still wanted to go where the air was thin and join Coppi, Anquetil and Merckx in the Giro-Tour Double Club. The last time he tried to become one of the immortals his knee couldn't take the effort of the two Grand Tours.

For the first time since 1968, the Tour started without Lucien van Impe. His Metauro Mobili team was not thought strong enough to ride both the Giro, which it had just finished, and the Tour. Van Impe tried to get a one-month contract with a team that would ride the Tour, but his efforts were fruitless.

The 1982 Tour started in Basel, Switzerland. Hinault won the Prologue and started the Tour in Yellow.

The ever-surprising Phil Anderson won stage two, from Basel to Nancy, France. He was part of a six-man break from which he escaped with about eight kilometers to go, coming across the line 4 seconds clear and taking the Yellow Jersey. As the Tour headed northwest back into France, Anderson kept his lead. Meanwhile, Hinault kept banging away, fighting with Sean Kelly for intermediate sprint time bonuses.

Stage five was scheduled to be a team time trial, but the leg had to be cancelled after several teams were already on the road. Striking steel workers, who had learned that 1,000 of their fellow employees were about to be fired, blocked the road. The French had generally decided to leave strikers alone, even when they broke the law by blocking roads. This allowed angry protesters to blow off steam and make their point, giving France a valuable safety valve.

Undeterred, the Tour organizers instead fit the time trial into the morning of stage nine. There, Raleigh showed it had lost none of its ability to dominate Tour team time trials, winning its eighth in a row. Hinault's Renault squad came in second and Anderson's Peugeots were fifth. Because the times were adjusted according to a system of bonuses rather than applying the real elapsed times, Anderson was still in Yellow with Hinault stalking him at 28 seconds.

Stage eight presented an interesting question, one that went unanswered. French Road Champion Régis Clère went away early and acquired a lead of almost thirteen minutes. The stage was to end with fifteen six-kilometer laps on a circuit at Châteaulin. It was Clère's audacious plan to arrive at the circuit, do a lap and then join the field when it arrived. Unfortunately for Clère, he got a flat tire just before arriving at the circuit. The wheel change was botched and his tire rubbed. It took two more stops before his bike was right. Too much time had been lost to put his plan into action and he was absorbed by the pack. Would drafting the lapped field have been legal? We'll never know. Frank Hoste, the Belgian champion, won the stage.

Hinault's appointment with destiny would not be postponed. Stage eleven was a 57.3-kilometer individual time trial. Gerrie Knetemann, who so often had come within seconds of matching Hinault in time trials, beat him by 18 seconds this time. Anderson came in twelfth, 3 minutes, 5 seconds behind Knetemann. The Badger was back in Yellow.

The General Classification stood thus:

1. Bernard Hinault
2. Gerrie Knetemann @ 14 seconds
3. Phil Anderson @ 2 minutes 3 seconds

Before the race ever hit the high mountains, Hinault was in control. The Pyrenees came first. Hinault didn't win or even make the podium

Stage fourteen time trial in Martiques. Zoetemelk loses 55 seconds to Hinault.

of the two Pyrenean stages, he simply rode as hard as necessary to keep the men who were threats in sight. Sean Kelly won the first day in the Pyrenees.

The final climb of the second of the two stages demonstrated the care Hinault could show in conserving his resources. There were eight riders left in the front group on the road to St.-Lary-Soulan. Swiss rider Beat Breu escaped, but since he was almost ten minutes down in the General Classification, Hinault ignored him. The other riders with Hinault, including Zoetemelk, Robert Alban and Bernard Vallet, refused to go to the front, forcing Hinault to lead. Two kilometers from the summit the attacks started. Hinault just rode at his speed, staying with Zoetemelk, knowing that Zoetemelk had decided he could not win and was riding for second place. And so Hinault played it, generating press speculation that he was weakening.

After the Pyrenees there was another time trial. This one Hinault won, and with that victory he fattened his already comfortable lead. Here was the Overall after stage fourteen with the Alps ahead:

1. Bernard Hinault
2. Phil Anderson @ 5 minutes 17 seconds
3. Joop Zoetemelk @ 5 minutes 26 seconds

In the Alps, Hinault again didn't bother doing anything more than marking his opposition. So far, he hadn't won any road stages.

Stage nineteen was the final time trial and again Hinault won it, with Knetemann 9 seconds slower. Hinault was going so fast at the end of his ride that he covered the last kilometer in exactly 1 minute: 60 kilometers per hour!

In the modern Tour de France, the final stage is a promenade into Paris with a furious finale as the race blasts up and down the Champs Élysées. Usually by this point the Tour's winner has been decided and the Yellow Jersey tries to stay out of trouble. But in 1979, Zoetemelk and Hinault had defied that tradition when Zoetemelk refused to lay down his arms in the final stage. He broke away and Hinault personally came after him and beat him in the sprint for the stage win.

In the final stage of the 1980 Tour, Zoetemelk had been terrified that with the bad weather, he might crash on the wet roads of the final stage and lose his best-ever chance to win the Tour. Similarly, in the 2004 Tour Lance Armstrong finished 19 seconds behind the leaders in the last stage, not wanting to get caught in a crash just before the end of the race.

Hinault was different. This year he joined the specialty sprinters in their elbow-banging, bike-thrashing final rush over the cobbles to the finish, beating them all. He finally had his road stage win, the most spectacular and prestigious of them all.

Tour writers have characterized Hinault's 1982 win as his most effortless. His form was so fine and his opposition so far below him that he seemed almost ordained the winner before the race even started. He had at last joined Coppi, Anquetil and Merckx in the elite group of riders who had won the Giro and the Tour the same year. That also made four Tour wins for Hinault. Only Anquetil and Merckx had more. Hinault intended to ride (and I assume win) the Tour four more times and retire upon turning 32 in 1986.

Sean Kelly claimed the first of his four Green Jerseys. Dutchmen ended in second through fourth place.

Final 1982 Tour de France General Classification:
1. Bernard Hinault (Renault): 92 hours 8 minutes 46 seconds
2. Joop Zoetemelk (Coop-Mercier) @ 6 minutes 21 seconds
3. Johan Van der Velde (TI-Raleigh) @ 8 minutes 59 seconds
4. Peter Winnen (Capri-Sonne) @ 9 minutes 24 seconds
5. Phil Anderson (Peugeot) @ 12 minutes 16 seconds

Climbers' Competition:
1. Bernard Vallet: 278 points
2. Jean-René Bernaudeau: 237
3. Beat Breu: 205

Points Competition:
1. Sean Kelly: 429 points
2. Bernard Hinault: 152
3. Phil Anderson: 149

two

1983–1990

A new generation of riders takes over, including the first Tour winner from the New World

1983 Who could beat Hinault? After his flawless victory in 1982 there seemed to be no one who could topple the mighty Breton. The question wasn't who would stop Hinault. It was "what". That spring he won the Vuelta and the Flèche Wallonne, but during the Vuelta his tendinitis flared up again, in the same right knee that had caused him to abandon the 1980 Tour. On the eve of the Tour's start Hinault, whose relationship with his director Cyrille Guimard was getting ever worse, announced that he would not ride. He had to quit racing immediately and let his body heal or risk irreparable damage. That left his Renault team without a captain. At first they thought they would go for stage wins and perhaps Marc Madiot or Laurent Fignon could win the Best Young Rider classification. After the Vuelta, Fignon was sure he had stage racing talent and thought he could win a stage, earn the White Jersey and finish in the top ten. As events will show, Renault really didn't know what they had on their team.

The Tour was again wide open with a new crop of young riders looking to contest the race. Colombia's national team was invited, bringing in several superb climbers, although only the most optimistic believed that any of them were real GC hopes. Merckx said Colombia's individualistic racing style with its solo breakaways in the mountains made them poor contenders for a high placing. The high-speed early stages over bad roads would sap their reserves and weaken them for the mountains.

Phil Anderson would again require watching, having come in tenth in the 1981 Tour, his first attempt. In 1982 he was fifth, wore Yellow for ten days and won the second stage. In the spring of 1983 he had already won Amstel Gold, Tour de l'Aude and the Tour of America as well as a second place in the Tour of Romandie. Anderson had two weaknesses. The first was his suspect climbing abilities. The second was the crucial problem of team support. Although he was Peugeot's number one protected rider, he couldn't count on his French team to support him, being a man from the English-speaking world. Those were different days.

Writer Pierre Martin gathered the prognostications of eight of the Tour's leading experts, including respected writers Philippe Brunel and Pierre Chany. The eventual winner was not on anyone's lists. The 1983 Tour was a cipher to all.

After the 1982 edition had tired the riders with too many transfers, the organizers promised no transfers in 1983. The promise was easy to make and difficult to keep. Instead, there were several, including a long one by high-speed train before the final stage in Paris.

Belgian Eric Vanderaerden won the Prologue, and kept the lead until the stage two team time trial, a 100-kilometer brute. Coop-Mercier won it, giving the Yellow Jersey to Jean-Louis Gauthier. When his teammate Kim Andersen got into a break the next day that beat the field by two minutes, the lead migrated to the Dane, the first man of his country ever to wear Yellow. Meanwhile, Zoetemelk's constant losing battle with the gas chromatograph continued. He turned up positive for dope again and was penalized his usual 10 minutes. Fignon got the hunger knock early in the stage and survived only because teammate Bernard Becaas gave Fignon all his food. Becaas paid dearly for his generosity by soon going weak from hunger himself.

This was to be a Tour in which misfortune played a large part, starting with Hinault's tendinitis. New super climber, Scotsman Robert Millar, crashed in stage three, losing almost seventeen minutes and ending his hopes for a high placing. A crash caused by Vanderaerden in the Roubaix velodrome took down Phil Anderson and French champion

Marc Gomez. Gomez had to retire. Because it happened in the last kilometer, even though he had to walk his bike across the finish line, Anderson lost no time. Fignon, having little experience riding the cobbles, rode the Roubaix stage with a death-grip on his bars, giving him big blisters on the palms of both hands, a source of misery in the stages to come.

As the racers made their way across Northern France, they had to endure stages long enough to remind one of the early days of the Tour. Stage four was 300 kilometers, stage five, 257. Through all of this, Kim Andersen kept the *maillot jaune*. Meanwhile, Sean Kelly had been chasing intermediate sprint bonuses and moving up the leader board while the already blistered Fignon came down with severe conjunctivitis.

In stage nine, Kelly took the lead, but only barely. Before the stage ten trip into the Pyrenees, here was the General Classification:

1. Sean Kelly
2. Kim Andersen @ 1 second
3. Phil Anderson @ 39 seconds
4. Joop Zoetemelk @ 1 minute 24 seconds

The first day in the mountains and the only Pyrenean stage was 201 kilometers going from Pau to Bagnères de Luchon. The riders would face the Aubisque, Tourmalet, Aspin and the Peyresourde. Van Impe led over the Aubisque, but it was Robert Millar who won the stage in front of Pedro Delgado. Pascal Simon was third at 1 minute, 13 seconds and became the leader. Seventh in the stage was Fignon, who had tried to go with Simon that day, but finished 4 minutes, 23 seconds behind Millar. Fignon later wrote that Simon was enjoying excellent form and didn't even bother to look at the young Renault rider when he went by.

And Phil Anderson? When he crashed on the Aubisque, his shoe came off. He had to undo the double knots (cycling shoes used laces back then) before he could get the shoe back on. Meantime, none of his teammates waited to pace him back up to the peloton. He did make contact with the leaders before the summit of the Tourmalet, the second climb, but the effort had cost him dearly. Since Kim Andersen had not been able to follow the leaders, Phil Anderson was now the virtual Yellow Jersey. And here's where the suspect support of the Peugeot team comes into play. Even though Anderson was the effective Tour leader, his teammate Pascal Simon attacked him. As writer John Wilcockson noted, Simon could do this simply because he was French and Anderson wasn't. After the crash and tiring chase efforts, Anderson finished twenty-fifth, 12 minutes, 41 seconds after the stage winner Millar.

Phil Anderson was demoted to being a domestique for Simon.

The standings:

1. Pascal Simon
2. Laurent Fignon @ 4 minutes 22 seconds
3. Jean-René Bernaudeau @ 5 minutes 34 seconds
4. Sean Kelly @ 6 minutes 13 seconds
5. Joop Zoetemelk @ 6 minutes 21 seconds (his penalty for doping wasn't announced until the end of stage eleven)

Earlier I noted that misfortune would be writ large on the 1983 Tour. Early in stage eleven, Joaquim Agostinho escaped with Simon's teammate Gilbert Duclos-Lassalle in hot pursuit. The Peugeot team, concerned that the formidable Agostinho was away, started working to pull him back. Agostinho's SEM teammate, Jonathan Boyer, went up front to be with the Peugeot chasers. Not wanting him there interfering with the chase, they tried to push him back, out of the way. There was a crash and two Peugeot riders went down, Bernard Bourreau and Simon. In his first day in the Yellow Jersey, Simon had fallen and broken his shoulder blade. He remounted and with help from his team, finished the stage in sixty-first place, in the same group as Kelly, van Impe and Fignon.

Fignon, though not knowing how badly Simon was suffering, felt he could win the Tour. Further, he believed Simon's Peugeot squad couldn't rule the peloton the way Renault under Hinault did. Guimard told Fignon to lay low, save energy, and be ready to act when the opportunity presented itself.

Patrick Clerc of the SEM team had been riding under a suspended sentence for refusing (along with Bernard Hinault) to give a urine sample after a criterium the previous year. It was announced that Clerc was the fourth rider of the 1983 Tour to fail a drug test. With this failure his suspended sentence should have been imposed automatically. To protest this potential penalty, the racers went on a go-slow ride in stage thirteen. It's said that Duclos-Lassalle rode up to Colombian rider Patrocinio Jiménez, who was off on a breakaway, and got him to cease his efforts and join the slowdown.

After trying and failing to talk the riders out of their plans to ruin the stage, and desperate to avoid a riders' strike, Lévitan capitulated and announced that the sentence had been abrogated and Clerc could continue to ride. The peloton was serious about defending its right to dope.

Stages eleven through sixteen were an agony for Simon. He did well as the Tour went through the Massif Central, losing only a little time to Fignon. He was aided by a perception in the peloton that it would be gauche to attack the wounded man in the leader's jersey. There was a feeling that he would eventually be forced to abandon.

It was in the stage fifteen time trial up Puy de Dôme where having only one working shoulder began to tell. Fignon had now closed to within 52 seconds of Simon. Simon's performance was remarkable because he was forced to climb the extremely steep final kilometer of the dead volcano sitting down. Phil Anderson, despite his domestique duties, had so far managed to stay in the top ten, but on this day Anderson fell to fourteenth place, probably ending his chances for a place on the podium in Paris.

The new General Classification:

1. Pascal Simon
2. Laurent Fignon @ 52 seconds
3. Sean Kelly @ 1 minute 29 seconds
4. Pedro Delgado @ 1 minute 45 seconds

The Pascal Simon drama had to end, and on stage seventeen it did. He had earned the love and respect of the fans, but his broken shoulder kept him from participating in each day's final ceremony where the Tour leader puts on his Yellow Jersey.

Facing six major climbs covering 223 kilometers and ending at the top of l'Alpe d'Huez, Simon's keeping the Yellow Jersey was out of the question. He abandoned after 95 kilometers and two climbs. Fignon, who took fifth in the stage, became the *maillot jaune*. Fignon said his first act upon being notified that he was leading the Tour de France was to commit a serious tactical error. He let Peter Winnen, a very dangerous rider, get away and gain two minutes.

The General Classification stood thus:

1. Laurent Fignon
2. Pedro Delgado @ 1 minute 8 seconds
3. Jean-René Bernaudeau @ 2 minutes 33 seconds
4. Peter Winnen @ 3 minutes 31 seconds
5. Sean Kelly @ 4 minutes 20 seconds

Because Fignon had already helped Hinault win the Vuelta, Renault boss Cyrille Guimard had not originally planned to bring his 22-year-old rider to the Tour. Troubled that Fignon already had one Grand Tour under his belt this year, Guimard didn't want to run the risk of over-racing his wonderful new young talent. With Hinault out of the Tour, Guimard decided that he needed Fignon's help and put him in the Renault roster, but planned to pull him the minute he looked tired.

There were two more Alpine stages, one a time trial. Fignon did not cover himself with glory. When a big break with Winnen, Angel Arroyo, Stephen Roche and others rode away on the Madeleine, Fignon couldn't answer the call. Guimard told him to remain calm and ride at his own pace. His third in the time trial stage was good enough to put Peter Winnen in second place.

By stage twenty-one, the penultimate day of the 1983 Tour, Fignon had a solid lead but had failed to win a stage. As the Tour had progressed, Guimard thought Fignon's grip on the lead was tentative and had him scrambling for intermediate sprint time bonuses. A win in the 50-kilometer individual time trial at Dijon let Fignon silence his critics and show that he was a deserving winner. Phil Anderson (the best-placed Peugeot rider) finished ninth.

At age 22, Fignon was one of the youngest winners of the Tour. He also joined another exclusive club, those who had won the Tour in their first attempt. The other freshman postwar winners were Coppi, Koblet, Anquetil, Merckx, Gimondi and Hinault.

At his team's celebration dinner Fignon said Hinault was kind and congratulatory to him without the slightest sense of jealousy. Yet when Guimard entered the room he instantly felt the strong dislike that had grown between Hinault and Guimard. He believed the icy coldness was the result of "arguments, differences, altercations". Fignon knew without being told that Hinault would change teams and was comforted by the fact that there would be no future intra-team rivalry between them.

Final 1983 Tour de France General Classification:
1. Laurent Fignon (Renault): 105 hours 7 minutes 52 seconds
2. Angel Arroyo (Reynolds) @ 4 minutes 4 seconds
3. Peter Winnen (TI-Raleigh) @ 4 minutes 9 seconds
4. Lucien van Impe (Metauro Mobili) @ 4 minutes 16 seconds
5. Robert Alban (La Redoute) @ 7minutes 53 seconds

Climbers' Competition:
1. Lucien van Impe: 272 points
2. Patrocinio Jiménez: 195
3. Robert Millar: 157

Points Competition:
1. Sean Kelly: 360 points
2. Frits Pirard: 144
3. Laurent Fignon: 126

1984

Sports are cruel. *L'Équipe* describes the 1984 Tour as an intergenerational conflict. Fignon at 23 represented the new guard and Hinault, at the ripe old age of 29, was of an older demographic cohort, close to being ready for the ash heap.

Fignon was nicknamed "The Professor" because of his scholarly appearance, oval wire-framed glasses and his time in college. And for a couple of years, could he ever ride a bike.

Coming to the Tour, Fignon was second in the Giro, losing the leader's Pink Jersey to Francesco Moser on the final day, a time trial. Fignon has made a good case for his belief that the Giro was stolen from him. The highest mountain stage was cancelled under weird circumstances, possibly saving Moser from a pummeling by Fignon, the superior climber. Then in the time trial, Fignon was the victim of another outrage (Moser strongly argues otherwise) when the television helicopter flew low and in front of Fignon, creating a headwind, while Moser had been followed by the same helicopter, creating a tailwind. The numerous pushes Moser received from the fans when he was climbing in the high mountains, ignored by the officials, were also questioned. But, Fignon was a man made for the Grand Tours and though he felt traumatized by the Giro's outcome, instead of tired, he came out of the Giro breathing fire. He was superbly fit and led what he thought was the best team in the world.

Moreover, Fignon said he had another advantage: he had Guimard at his side. "We both knew Hinault was an impulsive, angry rider who didn't have the best tactical awareness…when he needed to calculate, hold back and race with his head, he had dire need of Guimard."

As expected, Hinault had switched teams. He left Guimard and Renault, transferring to a new team, La Vie Claire, which sported distinctive Mondrian-inspired jerseys. After his knee operation, Hinault told Renault to choose between himself and Guimard. With Guimard's stunning record as a manager, they intelligently made the long-term decision to stick with Guimard. Hinault said a major reason for the change was his desire to have a greater say in team management. Further, either Hinault or Fignon had to change teams. It would be impossible for two of the finest racers in France (and perhaps in the world) to be on the same team, competing for the same victory. That never works. As Guimard said, "I found myself with two riders who had won the Tour. Then what? You can't keep them. One has to go… The problem was keeping two men, one of whom had won the four Tours, the other who was already a Tour winner at 22."

Hinault's spring racing seemed to say he had not returned with his old punch. The time out of competition while his knee was repaired was not without cost. Returning to the highest levels of sporting fitness takes time. He did win the Four Days of Dunkirk, but he took only second in the Dauphiné Libéré and third in Paris–Nice. His Classics placings weren't inspiring either.

Round 1: Hinault. Hinault won the Prologue for the fourth time, beating his former teammate Fignon by 3 seconds. Anquetil said that if he were Hinault, he would not have tipped his hand and let the others know that he was in such fine form by winning something as unimportant as a Prologue. For Hinault, I don't think there was ever an unimportant Tour win.

But wait, who's this at ninth with the same time as Zoetemelk and Stephen Roche? American racer Greg LeMond finished only 12 seconds behind the finest living time trialist, while beating one of the only men ever to best Hinault in a time trial when he was at the top,

Gerrie Knetemann. LeMond was riding his first Tour on Guimard's Renault team with Laurent Fignon. Showing signs of first-Tour jitters, LeMond had forgotten the mandatory sign-in and was still tightening his toe straps when the starter finished his countdown.

The year before, LeMond had won the Dauphiné Libéré in the spring, and in the fall he had become World Champion. His victory in the Worlds was a stunning solo win after more than seven hours of racing, showing both extraordinary strength, endurance and the ability to read a race. LeMond could display a superb understanding of the peloton's psychology, but he was also regularly caught strangely unaware and flat-footed.

Round 2: Renault and Fignon. Renault won the stage three 51-kilometer team time trial with Hinault's La Vie Claire a distant seventh at 55 seconds. The stage victory wasn't enough to give a Renault rider the Yellow Jersey, but it put Renault riders Fignon, Madiot and LeMond well up in the standings. The Colombian team, inexperienced in the highly technical and precise event, was last in the 51-kilometer stage. Their manager joked that the Colombian team fell apart only in the final 50 kilometers.

The General Classification after the team time trial stood thus:

1. Jacques Hanegraaf
2. Adri van der Poel @ 1 second
3. Marc Madiot @ 4 seconds
4. Ludo Peeters @ 9 seconds
5. Greg LeMond @ 10 seconds
6. Laurent Fignon @ 13 seconds

Stage five had one of those dopey early breaks that no one expects to succeed, unless success is defined as time on the world's televisions. Three riders took off in search of TV time: Paolo Ferreira, Maurice Le Guilloux and Vincent Barteau. Ferreira was a member of the unimportant (to this story, at least) Sporting Lisboa team. But Le Guilloux rode for La Vie Claire and Barteau was a Renault. The two most important teams in the Tour were neutralized because they would not chase down their own riders. Moreover, the politics of northern European racing had created an intense rivalry between the Raleigh-Panasonic team and the Kwantum squad. This paralyzed them as well and strangely prevented their chasing the break because neither had a rider up the road and they often, as in this case, only worried about each other. The break's lead grew until they were 17 minutes, 42 seconds ahead of the listless peloton. It was thought Barteau would easily win the sprint but Ferreira stunned everyone by crossing the line first.

This gave the crafty Guimard another card to play. His Vincent Barteau was now the Yellow Jersey while Le Guilloux was 1 minute, 33 seconds behind. Round three to Guimard.

Stage six was a sprinter's stage but it would have a lasting effect. Sean Kelly threw an elbow at Gilbert Glaus during the gallop to the line and was relegated to 140th place. The loss of the second-place points in the Green Jersey competition would cost him dearly. At the end of the Tour, Frank Hoste ended up beating Kelly by just 4 points. With a cleaner sprint in stage six, Kelly would likely have had the 1984 Green Jersey in his collection.

The first real contest to see who was ready to race was the 67-kilometer individual time trial of stage seven. Riding better than he had dared hope, Fignon beat Hinault where he lived, winning the stage and putting the Badger another 49 seconds back.

The General Classification was already starting to sort itself out.

1. Vincent Barteau
2. Maurice Le Guilloux @ 3 minutes 7 seconds
3. Paolo Ferreira @ 9 minutes 57 seconds
4. Laurent Fignon @ 12 minutes 54 seconds
6. Bernard Hinault @ 14 minutes 23 seconds
8. Greg LeMond @ 15 minutes 3 seconds

Hinault's third place in the time trial (Sean Kelly also finished ahead of him) brought about a change to Hinault's attitude and tactics. He saw this Tour would be difficult for him to win and started to fight for the intermediate sprint bonus seconds. In stage nine, Hinault and Kelly dueled for the third of the intermediate sprints. After Hinault won, they looked back and saw that they had created a sizable gap. They then put their heads down and pressed on with several other riders who had also detached themselves in the sprint. Caught napping because they expected the sprinters to slow and rejoin the peloton were LeMond, Fignon, Zoetemelk and Stephen Roche. A chase was organized and the two groups hammered down the road to Bordeaux at 60 kilometers per hour. Finally, facing a headwind and realizing that the gain would be too small for the effort, the Hinault/Kelly group sat up. But Hinault had once again shown that he was always willing to attack any time, any place. And Guimard, with his young team, had also proven that he could and would respond to the Badger's best efforts.

No one expected Barteau or his breakaway companions to come out of the mountains with their lead intact, but Barteau had some steel in his spine.

There was only one Pyrenean stage, 226.5 kilometers that went over the Portet d'Aspet, the Core, Latrape and a first category ascent to Guzet-Neige. Robert Millar was the angel with wings, winning stage eleven and leaving his closest follower, Colombian Luis Herrera, 41 seconds behind. LeMond, getting over a cold, had trouble and was dropped on the first climb, but being a superb descender, he regained contact and finished sixteenth, not far behind Hinault. Fignon, sensing Hinault's weakness, wanted to attack well before the finish. Guimard, wary, told Fignon to hold his fire until three kilometers from the summit, thus making it unlikely that Hinault would be able to regroup and respond. It worked perfectly, with Fignon taking almost a minute out of Hinault. Barteau surprised almost everyone by finishing only a little behind LeMond. He was still in Yellow.

Stage eleven results:

1. Robert Millar
7. Laurent Fignon @ 2 minutes 13 seconds
13. Bernard Hinault @ 3 minutes 5 seconds
16. Greg LeMond @ 3 minutes 42 seconds
19. Vincent Barteau @ 4 minutes 10 seconds

That left the General Classification thus:

1. Vincent Barteau
2. Maurice Le Guilloux @ 7 minutes 37 seconds
3. Laurent Fignon @ 10 minutes 33 seconds
5. Bernard Hinault @ 12 minutes 38 seconds
9. Greg LeMond @ 14 minutes 35 seconds

Round four to Renault.

Barteau was proving to be strongly attached to the Yellow Jersey. He survived the Pyrenees with a loss of only two minutes to the race's highest placed contender, Fignon. With their teammate in Yellow, Fignon and LeMond could sit on and if someone wanted to take the Yellow from Barteau, he would have to attack and get past Fignon, who was riding as he normally did, coolly, with no unneeded expenditure of energy.

Hinault now seemed unworried about such plebian concerns as conserving his strength for the best moment to take back needed time. He said his normal way was to attack if he felt weak or at a loss. It's a noble sentiment, but sometimes, nobility on those terms can be suicidal. As Tour father Henri Desgrange said, it's *la tête et les jambes* (head and legs). It didn't seem that Hinault had the legs and he certainly wasn't using his head.

Stage fourteen went through the rolling countryside of the Massif Central. Faded Belgian hope Fons de Wolf, in an extraordinary exploit, took off on a long solo break. At one point he had put 25 minutes between himself and the peloton and by the time the stage was over he still had 17 minutes, 40 seconds, lifting him to fourth place. The next day he paid for his effort, giving it all back and more, finishing 23 minutes behind the stage winner Frédéric Vichot.

While Hinault may have been riding with a touch of desperation, Fignon had also changed. He not only seemed to be getting stronger, but also more confident. On the day that de Wolf won, Hinault had attacked hard for second place in the stage. Fignon easily sped by the Badger, causing Raymond Poulidor to pronounce himself astonished at Fignon. The next day Fignon even won the field sprint.

The coming days held a 22-kilometer time trial and the Alpine stages. Even though he was riding in a state of grace, Fignon said that with only a two-minute lead over Hinault, he feared the slightest weakness would cost him dearly.

Stage sixteen was an individual time trial with an 800-meter climb in the final half. Seeming to fly up the mountain, Fignon beat Hinault, this time by 33 seconds.

Stage seventeen was a trip to the top of l'Alpe d'Huez, passing over three other highly rated climbs on the way. Here, Hinault had hoped he could wear down his young rival, but this seemed like an empty wish as Fignon was demonstrating a mastery that was Hinault's only a few years ago.

Hinault attacked five times on the penultimate climb, the Laffrey. Each time, Fignon closed up to him. After the fifth assault, Fignon was without teammates and the front group had been reduced to the climbing elite. Now it was Fignon's turn: he and Luis Herrera separated themselves from the others without attacking. They just rode faster than any other rider could. Over the top and on the descent Hinault chased like a madman. Riding through the valley leading up to the steep hairpins of l'Alpe d'Huez, Hinault caught the duo. Like a shark with the smell of blood in the water, the furious Hinault attacked and put some distance between himself and the Fignon/Herrera duo.

Looking back, Fignon said that the attack had in no way concerned him. He said he thought Hinault's effort laughable. Herrera, setting a blistering pace up the mountain with Fignon, Millar and Arroyo on his wheel, caught Hinault. As Herrera raced for the summit, Fignon was the last man dropped by the flying Colombian.

Stage seventeen results:

1. Luis Herrera
2. Laurent Fignon @ 49 seconds
3. Angel Arroyo @ 2 minutes 27 seconds
4. Robert Millar @ 3 minutes 5 seconds
5. Rafael Acevedo (another Colombian) @ 3 minutes 9 seconds
6. Greg LeMond @ 3 minutes 30 seconds
7. Bernard Hinault @ 3 minutes 44 seconds

Round five and the fight to Fignon. Herrera's stage win was the first by a Colombian, and the first by a non-European. The consequences of the stage were immense.

Barteau's dream was over. He gave up the Yellow Jersey to Laurent Fignon.

While the angry, raging Hinault had lost three minutes to Fignon, he was in no way subdued, looking for another opportunity to try to savage his competitors. Fignon, on the other hand, seemed to enjoy tormenting Hinault in press interviews. Samuel Abt astutely framed Fignon's attitude, "If you couldn't kick a man when he was down, when could you kick him?"

After Herrera's Alpe d'Huez stage victory the president of Colombia called him.

The General Classification after stage seventeen:

1. Laurent Fignon
2. Vincent Barteau @ 4 minutes 22 seconds
3. Bernard Hinault @ 5 minutes 41 seconds
4. Robert Millar @ 8 minutes 25 seconds
5. Greg LeMond @ 8 minutes 45 seconds

The next stage was challenging. It included the Galibier, Madeleine and a finish at La Plagne, all three rated *hors catégorie*. Hinault was soon dropped by the leaders but chased back on. By this point Hinault was so reduced in circumstances that he, the *patron* of the peloton, attacked in the feed zone. He was soon brought up short for that move by Fignon and LeMond's Renault team and was again dropped, on the Madeleine, and chased back on the descent.

Ever patient, Fignon assumed command on the final climb to La Plagne, dropping everyone, even the Colombians. This was the last element Fignon needed both to put the icing on the cake of this Tour and to silence those critics who carped that Fignon had yet to win a high mountain stage. He did this time, completely dominating his competitors. Hinault finished tenth, almost three minutes behind, but still moving him to second in the GC. Hinault now trailed the flying Fignon by 8 minutes, 39 seconds.

Two days later Fignon did it again, winning stage twenty, alone on the hilltop finish at Crans-Montana.

The Tour's penultimate leg was a 51-kilometer individual time trial. Fignon won again, although Sean Kelly, when the times were rounded to the nearest second, finished with the same time. Hinault lost another 36 seconds.

Guimard's Renault riders were the masters of the field. In Fignon's words, "As soon as we made up our minds, we could scatter the defeated bodies behind us, overwhelmed and wounded by our mastery." Yet, he said that even in 1984 he was not Hinault, who Fignon generously said was a better all-rounder, better against the clock and better at inflicting pain upon himself. "I did not have the class that was Hinault."

Guimard had now directed the winners of seven of the last nine Tours and though only 37, he would never guide another rider to Yellow in Paris.

Final 1984 Tour de France General Classification:

1. Laurent Fignon (Renault-ELF): 112 hours 3 minutes 40 seconds
2. Bernard Hinault (La Vie Claire) @ 10 minutes 32 seconds
3. Greg LeMond (Renault-ELF) @ 11 minutes 46 seconds
4. Robert Millar (Peugeot) @ 14 minutes 42 seconds
5. Sean Kelly (Skil) @ 16 minutes 35 seconds

Climbers' Competition:

1. Robert Millar: 284 points
2. Laurent Fignon: 212
3. Angel Arroyo: 140

Points Competition:

1. Frank Hoste: 322 points
2. Sean Kelly: 318
3. Eric Vanderaerden: 247

Bernard Hinault earned the admiration of cycling fans for his refusal to give up. Every day he went out looking for some chink in Fignon's armor, some way to break his young rival. It wasn't to be. In 1984 Laurent Fignon was vastly superior to any other rider and was never seriously challenged. With complete command of the race, he could and did ride patiently, opening up time on his rivals when it suited him. He wasn't content though. He always felt he had been robbed of one of cycling's most difficult accomplishments, the Giro-Tour double.

1985

Fignon could not return to defend his title. An inflamed Achilles tendon required surgery, forcing Fignon to sit this one out. So who was there to fill the vacuum? Hinault, of course. He could never be written off in any race he entered. Last year's Tour de France third-place Greg LeMond was also a possible winner.

The politics of this Tour were as complicated as any, and they would have repercussions for both Hinault and LeMond for more than just this Tour. Hinault's La Vie Claire team hired the talented LeMond away from Renault. Cynics say that this was to neutralize LeMond, the greatest single threat to Hinault's attempt for a fifth Tour win.

But why would LeMond go to La Vie Claire, centered around the single most driven racer in the world? What room would there be for LeMond? My understanding is that LeMond took a thoughtful approach to switching teams. He is said to have liked Paul Koechli, La Vie Claire's director, better than Renault's Guimard. His good friend Steve Bauer was on La Vie Claire, begging LeMond to come on over. Hinault seemed preferable to the often prickly Fignon. At the time, LeMond believed he was more talented than Fignon, an appraisal he has modified over the years, now saying Fignon had more ability than he gave him credit for.

In addition, Bernard Tapie, the owner of La Vie Claire, had scads of money and was using it to promote his various companies. LeMond made no secret of his belief that racers were underpaid for the value they brought to their sponsors and deserved a substantial pay increase. In no small way, over time, LeMond's financial demands elevated the pay of good racers on other teams as well. LeMond's contract with La Vie Claire was said to be for three years and worth a million dollars (actually it was $225,000 the first year, $260,000 the second year and $300,000 the third year). This was big money in those days.

Moreover, LeMond was unhappy with the way the Renault team and its sponsors had handled the use of his name and image. Manufacturers who had supplied the Renault team with its racing equipment had used LeMond's name and picture, claiming a personal endorsement of their products by LeMond. As was the usual practice of the time, they had done this without securing LeMond's explicit permission. LeMond sued several of the suppliers. I remember the stunned reaction European manufacturers had when they were served by LeMond's lawyers with lawsuits challenging what they had been doing for decades. LeMond had once again changed the game, refusing to accept the status quo.

Guimard believed he was in the driver's seat and told LeMond "You need me. I don't need you...if you don't stay with me you'll never win the Tour," refusing to give in to LeMond's demand to increase his then $125,000 salary. He wasn't asking Guimard to match Tapie's big bag of cash. He says he would have been happy with $150,000.

LeMond's situation on Renault had been far from ideal. It was a French team managed by a Frenchman, sponsored by a French company owned by the French government, with the hottest rider alive, Fignon, a Frenchman. Guimard remembered, "I realized very early on with Fignon and LeMond that I was going to have two bucks who would want to kill each other. You can't have two ten-point stags in the same herd of deer. You can't trust it. It can only end in one thing: mortal combat." As we shall see, it probably would have been better for both of them to have reached an accommodation. For starters, in this Tour without Fignon, Guimard didn't have a real General Classification contender.

I have long held that the single most talented bicycle racer to have ever turned a pedal in the post-Merckx era and probably since Fausto Coppi is Greg LeMond. While an amateur, he won everything and he did it with the natural ease of a born winner.

As a junior he went over to Belgium to race. Back in the 1970s and '80s many Americans traveled to Belgium to try to make it in the tough, high speed, ultra-competitive arena of the world's most bike-mad country. Almost all faltered or failed, going home broke, tired, sick and miserable. LeMond didn't falter, he thrived. During the week he was there, he won or placed second in every single race he entered. Then he won the Junior World Championships. It was one natural step after another. Winning the World Pro Road Championships in Switzerland at the ripe old age of 22 surprised no one. He was then signed by the finest team with the most respected director in the world, Renault and Cyrille Guimard. His freshman Tour in 1984 yielded a third place amid the blistering war fought by Hinault and Fignon.

I was in a race with LeMond only once (I can't say I raced him). It was a criterium in the little tourist town of Solvang, California, my last race as a category-one racer before I retired. From the gun the race was red hot. Lap after lap the peloton was strung out in one long line that extended halfway around the town. I was in the middle, saying my prayers, hoping I would not be the one who let the string break. Suddenly, the pace eased. I knew that whatever break had been off the front was either caught or was out of sight. A few laps later a slender rider went right by me, bumping me gently. It was LeMond. He had lapped a field with another rider, and was headed to the front for more. And he was still a mere junior!

Or, we can quantify his ability. VO_2 max is a measurement of the body's ability to transport oxygen in liters per minute. LeMond told me that at the time, his 92 was the second highest ever recorded (cross-country skiing legend Bjørn Dæhle had a freakish VO_2 max of 96). LeMond said Hinault's had been calculated at 88, the same as Miguel Indurain's. Lance Armstrong's was in the low 80s. LeMond was special.

To resume. It was announced that the La Vie Claire riders would protect Hinault or LeMond, whichever showed the best form. After LeMond had helped Hinault win the Giro in the spring, Hinault was going for his second Giro-Tour double.

Let's follow this Tour in detail because it is fascinating. Hinault used every tool at his disposal to keep LeMond, a man he knew to be at least his equal and possibly his superior, in a subordinate position.

Hinault showed his stuff by winning the Prologue with LeMond suffering a mechanical near the end and coming in fifth, 21 seconds back.

The first two stages were long eastward treks across northwestern France. By virtue of his excellent sprinting ability, Eric Vanderaerden was able to take the lead. He still had it after the La Vie Claire victory in stage three, a team time trial. When the time trial was over, Bernard Hinault's delirious fans ran out to greet their champion. He took terrible fright at the rushing, swarming crowd. He screamed at them to get away and started swinging his fists.

The relative position between Hinault and LeMond (still 21 seconds behind) had not changed much by the end of the three stages. The La Vie Claire team time trial win had put eight of their riders in the top ten.

In stage four, La Vie Claire rider Kim Andersen helped power a seven-man break that beat the pack to the finish by 46 seconds, earning him the *maillot jaune*. Stage six reminded the world that LeMond was a complete rider when, apparently on a lark, he sprinted with the kamikazes into Reims.

Vanderaerden won the sprint, which was far from clean. He was moving up through holes in the peloton that weren't really there and came even with Kelly. He started to force the Irishman into the barriers. Kelly pushed back. Vanderaerden responded by putting his arm out against Kelly. The sprint went to Vanderaerden but the two carried their argument all the way to the awards podium where Vanderaerden was given the Yellow Jersey. Then judges decided to relegate both of them. LeMond, who had crossed the line fourth was moved up to second in the stage and bagged the 20-second time bonus. He was now in third place, 2 seconds ahead of Hinault.

Seventy-five kilometers long, the stage eight individual time trial through the Vosges sorted things out. Hinault was by far the best man at the discipline that he had almost made his own. No one came within two minutes of him that day.

There had been some speculation as to why Hinault had not been chasing time bonuses this Tour as he had in recent years. Perhaps he had been saving his energy so that he could deliver a smashing time trial. Hinault caught his two-minute man Sean Kelly, and then, despite Kelly's efforts to remain close to the Frenchman, Hinault went on to take almost another minute out of him. German rider Didi Thurau was penalized for drafting Charly Mottet. When Thurau assaulted a racing official at the start of the next day's stage, the German was booted from the Tour.

The time trial's results:

1. Bernard Hinault
2. Stephen Roche @ 2 minutes 20 seconds
3. Charly Mottet @ 2 minutes 26 seconds
4. Greg LeMond @ 2 minutes 34 seconds

With only a couple of stages before the Alps, Hinault was back in his familiar Yellow Jersey. La Vie Claire was putting on an impressive display of force with Hinault, LeMond and Bauer in the top four.

The General Classification now stood thus:

1. Bernard Hinault
2. Greg LeMond @ 2 minutes 32 seconds
3. Sean Kelly @ 2 minutes 54 seconds
4. Steve Bauer @ 3 minutes 21 seconds
5. Phil Anderson @ 3 minutes 44 seconds

Stage eleven was the first day of hard climbing, 195 kilometers from Pontarlier, over the first-category Pas de Morgins, the second-category Le Corbier and finally up the first-category mountaintop finish at Morzine/Avoriaz. It was a classic Hinault performance.

He went away early with Luis Herrera, who was too far down to be a threat. Hinault made the usual deal, letting Herrera take the summits with their climbers' points and the stage win, while Hinault got the improvement to his overall time. Hinault wasn't interested in anything except gaining time, and doing it in such a way as to leave no doubt who was the leader of the team and the *patron* of the Tour. Herrera duly won the stage, with Hinault 7 seconds back. LeMond was blocked. He couldn't chase his teammate, but he eventually attached himself to Pedro Delgado and Fabio Parra, another of the Colombians, and finished fifth, losing 1 minute, 41 seconds. He was now 4 minutes behind Hinault while Stephen Roche was 5 minutes, 52 seconds adrift.

The Tour was telling on Hinault. The stage thirteen time trial was won by Eric Vanderaerden, with Hinault about one minute slower over the 31.8 kilometers. LeMond, hit yet again with mechanical trouble, lost another minute and a half to Hinault, being 2 minutes, 30 seconds slower than Vanderaerden.

The General Classification now stood thus:
   1. Bernard Hinault
   2. Greg LeMond @ 5 minutes 23 seconds
   3. Stephen Roche @ 6 minutes 8 seconds
   4. Sean Kelly @ 6 minutes 35 seconds
   5. Steve Bauer @ 8 minutes 23 seconds

Stage fourteen was a little detour through the Massif Central of France with a single first-category climb. Again Herrera took off early. LeMond joined Delgado, Millar and five others in pursuit. Back in the peloton, Hinault marked Roche and the others, hoping LeMond would stay away and solidify his hold on second place. The strategy worked when the Hinault group came to the finish two minutes behind winner Luis Herrera and one minute behind the LeMond group.

With less than a kilometer to go, the riders with Hinault had begun their sprint. Wheels touched and Hinault, Phil Anderson and four others crashed badly. Hinault lay on the ground for several minutes while being checked by the Tour's doctor. He climbed back on his bike and rode across the line, his face and particularly his nose, a bloody mangle of flesh. Hinault later accused Anderson of intentionally causing the crash.

When a rider crashes inside the final kilometer as Hinault did, Tour rules say he gets the same time as the group he was in. He had lost time on LeMond, but was still in Yellow. But, his nose was broken (he particularly regretted the loss of a pair of Ray-Ban sunglasses in the crash) and Hinault found it difficult to breathe. In addition, the fatigue that had appeared during that stage thirteen time trial seemed to be getting worse.

LeMond was now 3 minutes, 32 seconds behind Hinault (who was sporting two black eyes), with Roche at 6 minutes, 14 seconds. For once, LeMond had none of the various health problems that had dogged him; he was enjoying sparkling form.

They still talk about stage seventeen, a challenging Pyrenean 209-kilometer stage going from Toulouse, over the Aspin and the Tourmalet before finishing with a climb to Luz Ardiden.

On the Tourmalet, Guimard's Renault riders decided to test the wounded Yellow Jersey, sparking an angry response from The Badger, who chewed the Renault riders out for their aggression. Writer Richard Moore wondered if Hinault's anger was an unintentional signal to the others of the extent of his difficulty. This was a very different response from the Hinault who had traded leg-breaking attacks with Fignon the year before.

Hinault was in trouble and couldn't stay with the leaders. First LeMond, Roche and Delgado dropped him. Then, struggling with bronchitis in the moist air as well as having trouble breathing through his broken nose, Hinault also lost contact with his group containing Herrera, Millar, Kelly, Anderson and several others. On the descent Hinault rejoined Kelly's group.

Up ahead, Delgado was soaring away. Roche, with LeMond (who had been told to mark Roche), was chasing and feeling good. Roche wanted the stage win and possibly to move up to second, which would probably make LeMond the new leader. At the base of the road up to Luz Ardiden, a television crew told LeMond that the Hinault group was several minutes back. As Roche and LeMond continued to pull away from their chasers, both were aware LeMond was the stronger of the two.

When La Vie Claire assistant director Maurice Le Guilloux drove up next to LeMond, LeMond asked for permission to attack Roche and take the stage win. LeMond hadn't had a big win since taking the Rainbow Jersey in 1983. Le Guilloux responded with the orders from team director Koechli. Koechli was afraid LeMond would either take the lead and the Yellow Jersey or drag Roche up the mountain with him, providing the Irishman with a dangerous time gain. He told LeMond to wait for Hinault.

LeMond asked for the exact time gap. Le Guilloux, who had been Hinault's domestique, was evasive. LeMond pressed him harder and was told that Hinault was only 40 seconds behind. The momentum was coming out of the break as LeMond and Le Guilloux argued. Herrera caught and passed them. LeMond waited some more. Anderson and Kelly arrived next, but without Hinault.

Hinault was still several minutes back down the mountain. LeMond's decisive lead was melting away. The Tour could have been his right there. LeMond was getting stronger with every passing day as Hinault was weakening.

LeMond relates, "Koechli said to me, 'How dare you attack Hinault when he's in difficulty?'" Koechli denies saying this, but he did feel that LeMond was not yet strong enough to take on the responsibilities of Tour leadership.

Writer John Wilcockson talked to Koechli about this in 2005. Koechli denies making LeMond wait, saying that he authorized LeMond to make one attack and that he had to drop Roche. Roche was riding well and was too dangerous to play with. So, did Le Guilloux make up the orders? Someone gave the order for LeMond to wait; someone made the decision to lie to him about Hinault's whereabouts.

Koechli explained to Richard Moore, "If Greg had done what he wanted to do—ride [away] with Roche—then we go from having the top two riders, Hinault and LeMond, to first and third." Then discussing a following stage, "But let's imagine Greg punctures at that point. We lose the Tour. Roche wins. It doesn't need a big explanation. It's very easy."

Robert Millar noted that while Hinault was in trouble that day, he remained a calm professional and rode in his 25-tooth sprocket at his normal cadence rather than dropping to a bigger gear and ruining his legs for the next day in the mountains.

The stage results:

1. Pedro Delgado
2. Luis Herrera @ 25 seconds
3. Fabio Parra @ 1 minute 29 seconds
4. Sean Kelly @ 2 minutes 52 seconds
5. Greg LeMond @ same time
12. Stephen Roche @ 2 minutes 54 seconds
18. Bernard Hinault @ 4 minutes 5 seconds

The General Classification after stage seventeen:

1. Bernard Hinault
2. Greg LeMond @ 2 minutes 25 seconds
3. Stephen Roche @ 5 minutes 0 seconds

William Faulkner wrote that at least once in his life, every southern boy imagines that it's a hot day in July, referring to Gettysburg and particularly Pickett's Charge. How would he have reacted if he were ordered into that inferno? I think the same is true of every cyclist of the right age. We all imagine ourselves on the mountain, climbing to Luz Ardiden. In our imagination, awaiting us at the top of the mountain is a stage win in the Tour de France, the Yellow Jersey and cycling immortality. How would we react if we were told to slacken our pace for a wounded teammate? When we found that we had been lied to and Hinault was much farther down the hill, would we continue to wait? None of us could answer that question. I still can't over thirty years later. I do know that one of the greatest injustices in the history of sport was done to LeMond that day.

At the stage finish LeMond was in tears, frustrated with rage. Hinault, knowing that he had been handed his fifth Tour on a platter because LeMond had waited, promised to help him win the Tour next year. Greg said his goal had been a stage win and the Yellow Jersey for a few days. He felt that these were legitimate goals which he had the right to expect in this situation.

The next stage went over the Soulor and the Aubisque. Roche got his stage win and LeMond, understanding that La Vie Claire had decreed that Hinault was to win the Tour, took only 15 seconds out of Hinault. It should be noted that Roche was flying, and if he had taken a lot of time out of Hinault in stage seventeen he would have been extremely dangerous in stage eighteen. Koechli's concern about Roche was quite rational.

There was the formality of the final time trial. LeMond won it, his first Tour stage win, beating Hinault by only 5 seconds but confirming his ability as a natural stage racer, one who grew stronger during a three-week race.

Final 1985 Tour de France General Classification:
  1. Bernard Hinault (La Vie Claire): 113 hours 24 minutes 23 seconds
  2. Greg LeMond (La Vie Claire) @ 1 minute 42 seconds
  3. Stephen Roche (La Redoute) @ 4 minutes 29 seconds
  4. Sean Kelly (Skil) @ 6 minutes 26 seconds
  5. Phil Anderson (Panasonic) @ 7 minutes 44 seconds

Climbers' Competition:
  1. Luis Herrera: 440 points
  2. Pedro Delgado: 274
  3. Robert Millar: 270

Points Competition:
  1. Sean Kelly: 434 points
  2. Greg LeMond: 332
  3. Stephen Roche: 279

Hinault had claimed his fifth Tour, joining Anquetil and Merckx in the record books. He also earned his second Giro-Tour double.

Epilogue: In the 1987 Giro d'Italia Stephen Roche rode with Roberto Visentini on the Italian Carrera team. Roche had lost the lead to Visentini in a time trial. In the mountains Roche attacked. Roche's director told him to wait for Visentini. Roche refused and hammered up the mountain to take the lead for good.

Jacques Goddet, who had taken over management of the Tour when Desgrange took ill in 1936, retired from active direction of his share of the Tour, leaving Lévitan the sole manager of the enterprise. Goddet was responsible for restarting the Tour after World War Two and oversaw the Tour at a time when the nature of bike racing changed, from the use of one-speed bikes ridden on long stages that emphasized endurance, to the quicker sport we know today. Goddet worked to preserve Desgrange's original intent of making the Tour "inhuman" in its difficulty, causing him to be insensitive to the riders' demands that split stages be ended. Yet, he bent when he had to. His legacy to us is the Tour. All sports fans should be grateful for his determination to preserve the Tour's culture and to continue the race the world loves most.

Showing the increasing American influence in the Tour, Coca-Cola signed a twelve-year deal with the Tour to replace Perrier as the race's official drink.

1986

Hinault had said to LeMond, "In 1986 the Tour will be for you. I'll be there to help you." So easy to say in the heat of a moment after a teammate had made the sacrifice of a lifetime. In fact, LeMond was so furious after that infamous stage seventeen that he planned to abandon the Tour. Tapie and Hinault made peace with LeMond in his hotel room that evening with Hinault promising to work for the American. Hinault repeated the promise the evening after the final day of the 1985 Tour. Would Hinault have the character to fulfill his commitment when he could taste the immortality that would come with six Tour wins? And even if Hinault planned to be LeMond's domestique, how could he resist the French nation pleading for him to go for a sixth Tour? Even the president of France telephoned Hinault to ask him to ride for victory.

Fignon was back after ankle surgery and, having won Flèche Wallone; it was assumed that the real fight would be largely between the five-time and two-time Tour winners.

North Americans were coming in ever greater numbers. LeMond with his ace climbing friend Andy Hampsten and Canadian Steve Bauer were joined by the first American team to ride the Tour: 7-Eleven-Hoonved with Bob Roll, 1984 Olympic gold medalist Alexi Grewal, Chris Carmichael, Eric Heiden, Canadian Alex Stieda, Jeff Pierce, Mexican Raul Alcala, Davis Phinney, Doug Shapiro (who had ridden on Joop Zoetemelk's Kwantum-Decosol Tour team in 1985) and Ron Kiefel. After the Americans on La Vie Claire, they were the cream of the North American crop.

As troublesome as the politics and complicated jockeying amidst the tension of the La Vie Claire intra-team rivalry were in 1985, 1986 was even more difficult.

LeMond's spring had been good, but not spectacular: second in Milan–San Remo, third in Paris–Nice, fourth in the Giro d'Italia (a crash had cost him important time; it seemed that with LeMond, there was almost always something going wrong), and third in the Tour of Switzerland. Hardly the stuff of a rider who was to step into Hinault's shoes and lead the world's finest cycling team.

Andy Hampsten established his *bona fides* as a racer of the first rank when he won the Tour of Switzerland only a few short weeks before the Tour's start. Hinault used that win as fodder for his psychological war against LeMond, saying Hampsten's Swiss victory made Hampsten, not LeMond, his real heir.

Hinault's own spring was quiet with no top placings in important races.

Fignon wrote that he and Guimard had unintentionally revolutionized the structure of professional cycling teams. Teams were usually owned by the title sponsors, who set up a team's executive structure and controlled the cash. After Renault announced in July of 1985 that it would no longer fund its eponymous team, Fignon proposed to Guimard that they set up a corporation that would own the team and then sell space on their jerseys. Whatever was left over from the expenses of running the team would be theirs. This is how most teams are structured today. The French supermarket chain Système U liked the idea well enough to give the gents the 15 million francs a year they needed.

Thierry Marie won the first of his three Prologue victories at the kickoff of the 1986 Tour. Hinault was third at 2 seconds while Fignon and LeMond were seventh and eighth at 4 seconds.

7-Eleven's Alex Stieda took off at the 40-kilometer mark of stage one, an 85-kilometer race run in the outskirts of Paris. He was eventually joined by five other riders, but not until Stieda had collected the intermediate sprint time bonuses. The six stayed away from the charging field by only meters as they crossed the line. When the bonifications he collected were subtracted from his time, Stieda was the shock owner of the Yellow Jersey, the first North American to wear Yellow.

That same Saturday afternoon the teams lined up for a 56-kilometer team time trial. The 7-Eleven team was game to keep the Yellow Jersey but its efforts came apart when Eric Heiden crashed. Several other 7-Eleven riders scraped the curb to avoid following Heiden to the ground, weakening their tire casings and causing several flat tires. Stieda, exhausted from his morning effort, ran out of gas. Carmichael and Pierce had to drop back and nurse Stieda home, making sure they got him there in time to avoid having him eliminated by missing the time cutoff. Stieda made it to the finish in time, but his tenure in Yellow was over.

Fignon's Système U squad won the stage while La Vie Claire had a bad day, losing almost two minutes. Hinault said he slowed the team so that Guido Winterberg and Niki Rüttimann wouldn't get dropped. LeMond's memory is quite different, claiming Hinault was gasping and screaming at him because he couldn't keep up. Thierry Marie, a Système U rider, was back in Yellow with his teammates occupying the top seven places.

Stage three, ridden on the roads of Northern France, ended near the Belgian border where the freshman 7-Eleven team enjoyed another success. After having been in a break for much of the day, Davis Phinney won the sprint by inches, making him the first American to win a Tour road stage. As far as the Classification contenders were concerned, this was just another day to stay out of trouble.

Stage six brought bad news for LeMond. After getting second in an intermediate sprint, Hinault kept going, forming a serious escape with Roche and ten other riders. The attempt was neutralized, but Hinault's aggression remained unchecked.

Stage nine was a 61.5-kilometer individual time trial at Nantes. Now the Tour de France could begin in earnest.

The stage results:

1. Bernard Hinault
2. Greg LeMond @ 44 seconds
3. Stephen Roche @ 1 minute 1 second
32. Laurent Fignon @ 3 minutes 42 seconds

LeMond's performance was far better than his time showed. Saddled with his usual bad luck, a puncture had cost him almost a minute. LeMond believes that by winning the time trial, Hinault thought he had demonstrated his superiority and his right to lead the team, a condition LeMond says he never agreed to.

The General Classification:

1. Jørgen Pedersen
2. Stephen Roche @ 1 minute 5 seconds
3. Bernard Hinault @ 1 minute 10 seconds
8. Greg LeMond @ 1 minute 59 seconds

Stage ten into Futuroscope was hell for LeMond. He came down with a terrible case of diarrhea and was forced to ride part of the stage reeking with excrement dripping down his leg. Writer Paul Kimmage, who rode that Tour, said no one could call LeMond soft (as so many did) after he finished the stage under those conditions.

Stage twelve was the first day in the Pyrenees with four highly rated climbs, the last one being the category one Col de Marie-Blanque, followed by 45 kilometers of descent and flat before the finish at Pau.

Over the second climb, the Bargargui, Eduardo Chozas broke away on the descent, prompting Hinault, with teammates LeMond, Hampsten, Jean-François Bernard and a few other riders to give chase. After Chozas was caught, Hinault and Bernard escaped, with Delgado bridging up to them. They eventually spit out Chozas as the trio worked to put distance on the racers behind them. LeMond was stuck. He could not chase his two teammates, Hinault and Bernard, while neither Fignon nor Roche were in any kind of condition to assist with a serious chase and none of the others wanted to give LeMond any help. Hinault and Delgado tore up the road, gaining scads of time while LeMond sat fuming back in the chasing group. Finally LeMond was able to extricate himself, taking along only Herrera. Meanwhile, Hinault let Delgado have the stage, he had enough booty when LeMond came in 4 minutes, 37 seconds later. Hinault knew that if he were on the attack and in the lead, LeMond would be neutralized.

The General Classification at this point:

1. Bernard Hinault
2. Greg LeMond @ 5 minutes 25 seconds
3. Urs Zimmermann @ 6 minutes and 22 seconds
4. Pedro Delgado @ 6 minutes 57 seconds
15. Laurent Fignon @ 12 minutes 43 seconds

The stage had been so hard and the pace so hot, seventeen riders abandoned. The next morning two more quit, including Fignon, ill with a throat infection. At first LeMond was sure he had lost the Tour, as was the French press. Teammate Jean-François Bernard said, "….the game is done."

But that evening, furious at what had happened (Hinault was no less angry at LeMond for chasing with Herrera, though he didn't represent a GC threat), LeMond decided that the time had to be taken back, and he would do just that.

Stage thirteen was even harder than twelve, with the Tourmalet, Aspin, Peyresourde and the final climb to Superbagnères. Hinault escaped on the descent of the Tourmalet and by the time he reached the bottom, he had a lead of 1 minute, 43 seconds. Again, LeMond was stuck, unable to race and forced to let others do the chasing. By the bottom of the Aspin, the gap between Hinault and about 30 chasers was 2 minutes, 54 seconds.

On the Peyresourde, Hinault began to tire and might have been suffering from the hunger knock. A much-reduced chase group of Zimmermann, LeMond, Hampsten, Millar and Herrera cut the lead to 25 seconds and on the descent of the Peyresourde, Hinault was caught.

The climb to Superbagnères is sixteen kilometers of *hors catégorie* work. Hinault was riding with the group that had caught him until he attacked on this climb. Now it was just Hampsten, LeMond, Zimmermann, Millar and Herrera chasing, but with ten kilometers to go, again Hinault was caught.

Three kilometers later Hampsten jumped. No one countered. With that small gap in hand, Koechli drove up next to him and told Hampsten to take the stage and win the Tour de France. Hampsten was suffering the first stages of the hunger weakness himself and told Koechli he was using what energy he had solely to give LeMond a reason to attack. Finally LeMond bridged up to Hampsten, who continued to pound up the mountain.

Initially LeMond sat on Hampsten's wheel. Then, as Hampsten realized he could no longer keep up the infernal pace, he yelled at LeMond to take off and win the stage. At last, LeMond shed his hesitancy and raced up the mountain for the stage win as Hinault was being passed by rider after rider farther down the mountain. LeMond's gain on Hinault that day was 4 minutes, 39 seconds, almost the same amount of time he had lost the day before. Hinault was still in Yellow, but LeMond had shown that he could win the Tour and was now sitting only 40 seconds behind the fading leader.

Jean-François Bernard explained that La Vie Claire had two teams, "The team was divided in half, with the French supporting Hinault and the others supporting LeMond." Bernard is contemptuous of Koechli, arguing that the complicated job of managing the two strong personalities was beyond him and that it would have taken a managerial talent like Guimard to run the team. But Guimard was willing to toss redundant talent overboard in the interest of managing a cohesive team.

The stages after the Pyrenees across southern France heading towards the Alps changed nothing in the General Classification. But

Zimmermann with an attentive LeMond on his wheel in stage seventeen

during stage sixteen, Hinault again escaped, taking third-place Urs Zimmermann with him. LeMond was again unable to chase and asked Robert Millar to get his Panasonic team to close the gap, which they did. LeMond chewed out Hinault for giving the very dangerous

Zimmermann so much help. Hinault was unrepentant, "I'm the boss of this race, I know what I'm doing."

Stage seventeen, the first Alpine stage, was the scene of this story's denouement, with crossings of the Col de Vars, Col d'Izoard and a hilltop finish at the top of the Col du Granon.

Various groups attacked, leaving riders scattered all over the mountains. During the descent of the Izoard, Zimmermann, sitting in third, opened a gap. LeMond, acting as an attentive domestique, latched onto his wheel with Hinault trailing about 90 seconds behind. On the Granon, LeMond, ever dutiful, sat on Zimmermann as the Swiss rider poured on the gas. Hinault, now aware of the situation, attacked hard but Zimmermann with LeMond in tow was gaining time with every pedal stroke. Hinault simply couldn't close the gap. Eduardo Chozas, never in contention for the overall, had been off the front and won the stage, but that didn't matter to LeMond, who finished more than six minutes later. He was in Yellow.

The standings at this point:

1. Greg LeMond
2. Urs Zimmermann @ 2 minutes 24 seconds
3. Bernard Hinault @ 2 minutes 47 seconds
4. Robert Millar @ 6 minutes 19 seconds
5. Pedro Delgado @ 8 minutes 0 seconds

The next day was no easier with the Galibier and its little brother the Télégraphe, followed by the Croix de Fer and another hilltop finish, this time at l'Alpe d'Huez. LeMond had come close to a case of hunger knock in stage seventeen and was afraid he would neither recover sufficiently nor have the reserves to maintain his lead over such a difficult stage. Hinault had his own problems, including pain in a calf that made the Frenchman contemplate abandoning. Yet, come morning, Hinault was fine. He had told the team they must dispatch Zimmermann, who split LeMond and Hinault in the standings. LeMond knew that meant Hinault would be on the warpath and had to be constantly watched. LeMond and Hinault had spent much of the previous evening arguing about the race.

On the descent of the Galibier, Hinault attacked with Bauer on his wheel. LeMond, Zimmermann and Pello Ruiz-Cabestany caught them as they continued the descent. On the ascent up the Télégraphe, Hinault escaped for fifteen kilometers. LeMond, Bauer and Ruiz-Cabestany joined Hinault without bringing Zimmermann. The quartet put down their collective heads and started to work. The pace was too hot for Bauer and Ruiz-Cabestany, and on the Croix de Fer it was just Hinault and LeMond.

This was the day Zimmermann saw his chances for winning the Tour disappear. Seven kilometers from the top of the Croix de Fer, Zimmermann was in a group with Hampsten, Simon and Zoetemelk, 3 minutes, 10 seconds behind LeMond and Hinault. Zimmermann was desperate to get up to the duo. He closed the gap a little, but was still 2 minutes, 50 seconds behind at the top.

On the descent, Hinault and LeMond flew. Both were superb bike handlers. Years ago I spoke with former 7-Eleven rider Jeff Pierce about this stage and the one thing Pierce wanted to make sure I understood: LeMond could descend and do it extremely fast. Félix Lévitan was in the follow car and couldn't believe how fast the pair went down the mountain, "In all my years on the Tour de France I have never seen such a descent."

At the beginning of the climb to l'Alpe d'Huez, in Bourg d'Oisans, LeMond and Hinault were 4 minutes, 50 seconds ahead of Zimmermann. The pair continued to ride unbelievably fast up the mountain, LeMond following Hinault.

At the top LeMond generously joined hands with his tormentor and pushed Hinault ahead a bit so that he could take the stage victory. LeMond had survived another test from his difficult domestique, while Hinault had buried Zimmermann and risen to second place. And, by cannily convincing LeMond to ride behind Hinault up L'Alpe d'Huez so that French fans wouldn't attack him, he had remained in contention. Later Hinault claimed he could have "had LeMond's scalp" on L'Alpe d'Huez. In a post-stage interview Hinault said, "The race isn't over." You can imagine LeMond's dismay.

The General Classification after l'Alpe d'Huez:

1. Greg LeMond
2. Bernard Hinault @ 2 minutes 45 seconds
3. Urs Zimmermann @ 7 minutes 41 seconds
4. Andy Hampsten @ 16 minutes 46 seconds

Owen Mulholland wrote "As you note, Hinault attacked on the short two-kilometer climb out of Valloire that serves as the southern slope of the Col du Télégraphe. I'm not sure why Greg was caught napping so often by these surprise attacks. It's impossible to imagine, say, Merckx, missing such moves time after time. Anyway, once again Hinault was gone and Greg was stuck. However the descent of the Télégraphe is extremely sinuous and was made for Greg's fabulous descending skills. I remember his talking (laughing) to Hinault later about how he'd gotten rid of Zimmermann on that descent. It seems Zimmermann skidded across a corner trying to hang onto Greg's wheel and that's the last anyone up front ever saw of the poor Swiss that day! I believe (but am not absolutely certain) Bauer was already away, but in any event he was in the front, so when Greg and Bernard hooked up with him and a few others in the flat valley of the Maurienne, Steve lowered his head and motored to the foot of the Croix de Fer. Poor Zimmermann never stood a chance."

Stage twenty was a 58-kilometer individual time trial at St. Etienne. LeMond's hard luck continued when he crashed at kilometer 37. He remounted, and finding his brake rubbing, changed bikes, costing him still more time. Hinault rode his usual perfect time trial and won the stage, beating the trouble-prone LeMond by 25 seconds. Zimmermann was unable to present any challenge, finishing almost three minutes behind Hinault.

There was one more day in the mountains. Stage twenty-one went into the Massif Central, over several highly rated climbs, culminating in a hilltop finish at Puy de Dôme. The contenders had more or less accepted their positions while riders seeking individual glory in the closing days of the race sought their day in the sun. The only drama was during the final ascent when LeMond pulled away from Zimmermann, who had distanced himself slightly from Hinault. LeMond was now 3 minutes, 10 seconds ahead of Hinault and had only two more stages to survive.

LeMond's terrible luck stuck to him like a bad rumor. Shortly before entering Paris during the final stage, LeMond crashed badly enough to need a new bike. Hinault and his La Vie Claire teammates waited for him and paced him safely back into the field. Hinault, ever the competitor joined the final field sprint on the Champs Élysées, gaining fourth place to stage winner Guido Bontempi.

Paul Kimmage wrote about riding this final stage in his book *Rough Ride*. Many of the riders were on their last legs by the time the final day in Paris arrived. Of the 210 riders who started three weeks before, 132 finished. The veterans told Kimmage about the blistering speeds of the final kilometers on the Champs Élysées, and fearful of getting dropped while the whole world watched, more than a few took amphetamines. Kimmage asked the others if they weren't afraid of getting caught in the dope controls. No, he was told, only the winner and top finishers are tested after the final stage. They knew they were free to stick the needles in their arms.

The race was finally over and Greg LeMond had fulfilled the promise he made to himself when he was seventeen, of winning the Tour de France.

Final 1986 Tour de France General Classification:

1. Greg LeMond (La Vie Claire): 110 hours 35 minutes 19 seconds
2. Bernard Hinault (La Vie Claire) @ 3 minutes 10 seconds
3. Urs Zimmermann (Carrera) @ 10 minutes 54 seconds
4. Andy Hampsten (La Vie Claire) @ 18 minutes 44 seconds
5. Claude Criquielion (Hitachi) @ 24 minutes 36 seconds

Climbers' Competition:

1. Bernard Hinault: 351 points
2. Luis Herrera: 270
3. Greg LeMond: 265

Points Competition:

1. Eric Vanderaerden: 277 points
2. Josef Lieckens: 232
3. Bernard Hinault: 210

Hinault won the polka-dot Climber's Jersey, Hampsten earned the white Young Rider's Jersey and La Vie Claire won the Team Classification. This was a dominating performance in a Tour in which the only real question was which of the La Vie Claire riders would win.

Over the years the debate about this Tour has grown ever more heated.

Hinault has defended his actions repeatedly, saying that he was really helping LeMond by challenging him and forcing him to earn the Tour. Hinault's answer to his critics, "I'd given my word to Greg LeMond that I'd help him win and that's what I did. A promise is a promise. I tried to wear out rivals to help him but I never attacked him...It wasn't my fault that he didn't understand this. When I think of some of the things he has said since the race ended, I wonder whether I was right not to attack him...I've worked for colleagues all my life without having the problems I had with Greg LeMond."

Here's Owen Mulholland's view from his *Uphill Battle*, discussing Hinault's repeated attacks in the Pyrenees:

"[Hinault] once told me he liked to 'play' with cycling, and doing something this outrageous two days in a row may have been his idea of play. No one will ever know because when he explained himself, Hinault played with words. And when credibility disappears so does reliability. Was this a gamble to win in a super-dominant manner? Was he trying to tire out the opposition so LeMond could go easily into the lead? Was this a bold gesture for the hell of it, a 'playful' gesture? Who can tell because Hinault's actions could be interpreted in myriad ways, and his words, intentionally deceptive, meant nothing. On such a 'solid' basis LeMond had to make decisions."

1987

On March 17, Félix Lévitan found his office locked. The problem was said to be the finances involved with a proposed American race. Since Philippe Amaury was now the owner of *L'Équipe* and the Tour, Lévitan could no longer call upon the late Émilien Amaury's friendship to protect him. Lévitan was sacked, replaced by interim manager Jean-François Naquet-Radiguet, who lasted only a year.

In March, LeMond had broken his wrist and collarbone in the Tirreno-Adriatico and had gone back to the U.S. to recover. While he was turkey hunting in late April, he was accidentally shot by his brother-in-law. The forty shotgun pellets that tore into his body cost him three-quarters of his blood and a collapsed lung. Because of their location, thirty pellets could not be removed, including pellets in his heart lining, liver, small intestine and diaphragm. The short-term consequence of the accident was that LeMond could not return in 1987 to contest the Tour. The long-term effects on LeMond were even greater. The lead in his body left him damaged goods. Even though he returned in later years to earn wonderful victories, he was never the same.

Hinault, seeing that he could no longer ride at the top, retired. He rode his last race on his birthday in November of 1986.

So who was there? Laurent Fignon was still working on finding his old form. That spring he did rather well with third place in both Paris–Nice and the Vuelta a España, along with several other top-ten placings. But relations between Fignon and Guimard were not going well. Guimard, the team's administrator, was getting greedy. Though the team was well-funded, Guimard was now refusing to pay for top-flight racing talent and support personnel. Over the next couple of years Fignon said the team became amateurish.

Jean-François Bernard, now out from under the shadow of LeMond and Hinault, was expected to do well. His team, now called Toshiba-La Vie Claire was a superb formation with Steve Bauer, Kim Andersen and Niki Rüttimann to back him up.

Pedro Delgado had shown promise in previous Tours and his team, PDM, was one of the finest in the world. He would have such sterling riders as Gerrie Knetemann, Gert-Jan Theunisse and Steven Rooks helping him. Delgado's spring was an easy, low-key lead-in to the Tour with no notable wins.

Andy Hampsten, with a fourth in the 1986 Tour under his belt and now riding for 7-Eleven, should have been licking his chops at the mountainous 1987 Tour.

Stephen Roche, who played such a large part in LeMond's 1985 ride to Luz Ardiden, was having a wonderful year. Roche's racing had been up and down. A crash in the Paris Six-Day started a series of never-ending knee problems and attempts to correct them surgically. But in 1987 his knee was holding together. Coming to the 1987 Tour he had already won the Tour of Romandie and the Giro d'Italia. He had taken second in Liège–Bastogne–Liège (he says that if he had been more tactically astute, he would have won it: "I rode like an amateur that day.") and fourth in Paris–Nice.

The 1987 Tour was designed to be tough. It was, in Roche's words, "one of the most mountainous since the war," with 26 stages, counting the Prologue in West Berlin. Europe was still divided between East and West and would remain so until the autumn of 1989. Dutchman Jelle

Nijdam won the Prologue, but several of the Tour contenders, showing their form, were hot on his heels.

1. Jelle Nijdam: 7 minutes 6 seconds
3. Stephen Roche @ 7 seconds
7. Jean-François Bernard @ 9 seconds
8. Miguel Indurain @ 10 seconds
23. Pedro Delgado @ 19 seconds
26. Andy Hampsten @ 20 seconds

The Tour made its way across Germany and moved into France where stage five ended in Strasbourg. The Yellow Jersey had already changed hands a few times as the sprinters enjoyed their early, flat days in the Tour. The high speeds caused the large (207 starters) and nervous peloton to suffer repeated crashes. The Europeans blamed a lot of the falls on the Colombians, whom they considered poor bike handlers. After a Belgian hit a Colombian in the head with a water bottle during stage ten, a couple of other Colombians went after him and started a fight.

By the 87.5-kilometer stage ten individual time trial going from Saumur to Futuroscope, the only rider in the top fifteen with any real hope for a high final placing was Système U's Charly Mottet. The others had been riding quietly, trying to stay out of trouble while the big *rouleurs* and sprinters gained time bonuses that moved them up to the front of the leader's list. The time trial sorted things out. Roche won it with Mottet second at 42 seconds. That put Mottet in Yellow.

The General Classification at this point:

1. Charly Mottet
6. Stephen Roche @ 3 minutes 23 seconds
8. Jean-François Bernard @ 5 minutes 31 seconds
15. Pedro Delgado @ 6 minutes 41 seconds

Stage thirteen was the first day in the Pyrenees. On a day so hot the road tar melted, the contenders stayed together all the way to Pau even after four highly rated climbs. There was an attack on the descent of the second category Bargargui where the high speeds and hard braking melted the glue holding the tires to the rims. Some riders rolled the tires off their rims, others had their tires explode from the heat build-up, causing several crashes. This stage removed the non-climbers from the top of the rankings:

1. Charly Mottet
2. Jean-François Bernard @ 1 minute 52 seconds
3. Stephen Roche @ 3 minutes 23 seconds
6. Pedro Delgado @ 6 minutes 24 seconds
14. Andy Hampsten @ 11 minutes 24 seconds

The Tour headed towards the Massif Central. Stage eighteen's individual time trial up Mont Ventoux promised to shake things up and it did not disappoint. Jean-François Bernard executed the ride of his life, winning the stage and the Yellow Jersey. Never before had he risen to such heights. Look at some of the times of his competition to get an idea of how well the Frenchman rode those 36.9-kilometers:

1. Jean-François Bernard: 1 hour 19 minutes 44 seconds
2. Luis Herrera @ 1 minute 39 seconds
3. Pedro Delgado @ 1 minute 51 seconds
5. Stephen Roche @ 2 minutes 19 seconds
9. Charly Mottet @ 3 minutes 58 seconds
25. Andy Hampsten @ 6 minutes 12 seconds

The General Classification:

1. Jean-François Bernard
2. Stephen Roche @ 2 minutes 34 seconds
3. Charly Mottet @ 2 minutes 47 seconds
4. Pedro Delgado @ 3 minutes 56 seconds

Bernard was Hinault's chosen heir and the great hope of French cycling. He had a good lead and was climbing and time trialing well. The next day was a mountainous stage, and with the Tour soon turning into a Wild West shootout, he was not going to be allowed to keep the lead without mounting a serious defense.

Near the top of the first real climb, Bernard flatted and was unable to get his bike serviced before the other racers had disappeared up the mountains.

Bernard's luck didn't get any better. Mottet and his Système U teammates had hatched a plan to attack Bernard in that day's feed zone. They packed extra food to carry them through the long day, and for insurance, Mottet told Roche about the plan to make sure there would be enough horsepower to keep Bernard and his La Vie Claire team at bay.

Mottet knew the area and had seen that the feed zone was just after a narrow bridge, which would slow the peloton. Things happened exactly as Mottet predicted. Bernard, who had been chasing to get back on terms with the leaders after his flat tire, was forced to a halt when the peloton slowed upon reaching the bridge. Mottet, Delgado and Roche were already up the road and putting time between themselves and the soon-to-be furiously chasing Bernard.

Bernard was never able to rejoin the leaders and came in 4 minutes, 16 seconds after Delgado and Roche. Roche was in Yellow with Mottet only 41 seconds behind and Delgado close at 1 minute, 19 seconds. Ironically, Delgado and Roche had dropped Mottet, who had planned the day's skullduggery in the first place.

Stage twenty was another Alpine stage, with the first category Côte de Laffrey and a finish at l'Alpe d'Huez. The final climb up the Alpe had the riders coming in one at a time. Federico Echave won the stage and Fignon, finally starting to get his legs, rolled in sixth, 3 minutes, 25 seconds later, followed by Delgado. Roche was fifteenth that day at 5 minutes, 28 seconds. Delgado was the new *maillot jaune* with Roche 25 seconds behind. Spain was so transfixed by Delgado's struggle with Roche that the Spanish parliament suspended its deliberations so that the members could watch the stage.

The next day was finer still. The giant mountains kept coming at the riders. Stage twenty-one was 185.5 kilometers of pure effort. Along the way were the Galibier, the Madeleine and the final climb to La Plagne. Roche had insisted over and over that he wasn't a climber and knew the specialists like Delgado could give him trouble on their own turf.

Fignon launched a blistering attack and won the stage. But the real drama was Roche's story. In the November, 2003 *Cycle Sport* magazine he gave an interview about that fateful day:

> I had the Jersey at Villard-de-Lans [stage nineteen, won by Delgado]. But Delgado took it back from me the next day at the summit of l'Alpe d'Huez [stage twenty, related just above]. I was not a climber like him. Between the descent of the Galibier and the foot of the Madeleine [stage twenty-one, the stage we are discussing] I attacked because he was isolated. I passed him and rejoined the group ahead. Afterwards I climbed the Madeleine alone. Delgado and his teammates caught me again at the foot of La Plagne. I said to myself, "What am I going to do? If I stay

with him he'll kill me. I'll never get to the top." I let him go and conceded 1'10", 1'15".

But he didn't trust himself. And four kilometers from the line, I attacked at top speed. I gave it everything I had. And I got to within a few seconds of him. Psychologically, that was my most beautiful victory.

After his titanic effort to bring Delgado back, Roche collapsed at the finish and needed oxygen. He was taken to a hospital but was found to be perfectly fine.

The General Classification now, after Roche was penalized 10 seconds for taking an illegal feed:

1. Pedro Delgado
2. Stephen Roche @ 39 seconds
3. Charly Mottet @ 3 minutes 12 seconds

The next day, the last one in the Alps, Roche was able to take another 18 seconds out of Delgado. The Spaniard was tiring and they were only 21 seconds apart. Roche felt confident that his superior time-trialing abilities would give him the lead in the final race against the clock.

It came down to this penultimate stage, a 38-kilometer time trial at Dijon. Bernard's results let us know that this would have been an even more interesting race, if that were even possible, if he had not had that unfortunate flat.

The stage results:

1. Jean-François Bernard: 48 minutes 17 seconds
2. Stephen Roche @ 1 minute 44 seconds
7. Pedro Delgado @ 2 minutes 45 seconds

The Yellow Jersey was Roche's. And with only the final stage into Paris left, it was his to keep.

That last stage into Paris had a big surprise in store for the 7-Eleven team. Jeff Pierce won the stage in a solo victory with Steve Bauer only one second behind him.

In that same interview in *Cycle Sport*, Roche spoke kind words that reflected well on both Roche and Delgado.

"The memory of the Tour de France that will stay with me all my life is when I retook the jersey in Dijon. I went through the ceremony and then on the Jacques Chancel TV program Delgado was already in the middle of doing his interview. I arrived on the set and Delgado got up. He embraced me. Chancel said to him 'Less than an hour ago he took the Yellow Jersey from you and now you embrace him?' Delgado replied, 'I have had 4,500 kilometers in which to win the jersey, and I couldn't do it.' It was beautiful when he said that."

This was a fantastic Tour with eight different men wearing the Yellow Jersey, equaling the 1958 record.

Final 1987 Tour de France General Classification:
1. Stephen Roche (Carrera): 115 hours 27 minutes 42 seconds
2. Pedro Delgado (PDM) @ 40 seconds
3. Jean-François Bernard (Toshiba-La Vie Claire) @ 2 minutes 13 seconds
4. Charly Mottet (Système U) @ 6 minutes 40 seconds
5. Luis "Lucho" Herrera (Café de Colombia) @ 9 minutes 32 seconds

Climbers' Competition:
1. Luis Herrera: 452 points
2. Anselmo Fuerte: 314
3. Raul Alcala: 277

Points Competition:
1. Jean-Paul van Poppel: 263 points
2. Stephen Roche: 247
3. Pedro Delgado: 228

That year Roche won the Giro, the Tour and went on to win the World Championship. Only one other rider in the history of the sport, Eddy Merckx, has been able to win all three in a single year. *Erin Go Bragh*.

1988

Tour director Jean-François Naquet-Radiguet was replaced by his brother-in-law Xavier Louy. Naquet-Radiguet was thought to be a bit too independent and made too many important decisions on his own that seemed to reflect poor judgment, including a planned Montreal, Canada start for the 1992 Tour.

Roche had two knee operations between his World Championship win and the start of the new season and was unable to race the Tour.

LeMond had recovered from his hunting accident and signed with the PDM squad but injured his right knee in a Belgian *kermesse* in late

March and was troubled all spring with the injury. He attempted the Giro, but quit after five stages. He returned to the United States for surgery and recuperation.

Fignon's long climb back to competitiveness had started with a surprising win in Milan–San Remo. So surprising in fact that French TV had not even bothered to cover the race because the reporters felt no Frenchman could win. But by July Fignon, who started the Tour, had a tapeworm that soon rendered him unfit for racing.

That left Pedro Delgado, second the previous year, as the man to beat: he lost the 1987 Tour by only 40 seconds. At no time had Roche significantly outclassed him.

Andy Hampsten and the American 7-Eleven team entered, but Hampsten had just won the Giro, where the team had buried itself to keep him in the lead when he took the Pink Jersey after a remarkable ascent—and a frightening descent—over a freezing Gavia Pass. Would they recover enough to vie for the Tour?

Luis Herrera won the Dauphiné in early June by bounding up the Col de Porte in the final stage, taking the lead from Acácio Da Silva. Mottet had led in the early stages but had tired. Herrera showed superb form, but winning the Dauphiné is hard, draining work that often leaves its winner flat for the Tour.

At only 3,286 kilometers, the 1988 Tour was the shortest since Henri Desgrange recast the race in 1906. With twenty-two stages, the average stage length was only 149 kilometers, holding out the promise of a super-fast race.

The Tour was scheduled to open with a 6-kilometer Prologue. To comply with UCI rules, it was shortened to a "Prelude" that was run according to some rather odd rules. The teams rode a team time trial and let a single rider go with a flying start to ride the final kilometer, the only part that counted toward the General Classification. Guido Bontempi won with a time of 1 minute, 14 seconds. Bontempi's hold on the Yellow Jersey was almost as short as his Prelude. Steve Bauer beat the pack home in the first stage by 8 seconds, enough to put him in Yellow.

The next day it was Bauer's turn to give up the lead. Panasonic was the heir of the old TI-Raleigh squad and narrowly beat Bauer's Weinmann team in the 48-kilometer team time trial, earning the Yellow Jersey for Teun van Vliet.

In stage eight, the ever-attentive Bauer got into a sixteen-man break initiated by Herrera that beat the pack by 23 seconds, giving the lead back to Bauer. The Tour remained a simmering cauldron of hot competitors, and was turning out to be a fast one, setting a new record so far for average speed.

During stage eleven, going from Besançon to Morzine, the Tour got warmer. On the Pas de Morgins, Fignon and Bernard were dropped by the leaders after Urs Zimmermann opened the day's hostilities. Bauer was able to maintain contact with the front group, staying with them for the rest of the stage and preserving his lead. The real contenders finished together with the exception of Colombia's Fabio Parra, who soloed in 20 seconds ahead of the others.

Stage twelve was 227 kilometers that crossed the Pont d'Arbon, Madeleine, and Glandon before finishing at the top of l'Alpe d'Huez. Fignon abandoned that morning before even starting the stage.

Delgado shook things up when he attacked two kilometers from the summit of the Glandon, taking Steven Rooks along for company. In the final kilometers of the l'Alpe d'Huez's steep slopes they were caught by Fabio Parra and Gert-Jan Theunisse, but the chasing pack couldn't close the gap.

Things had exploded on the final run up the 21 hairpin turns of the Alpe. Fabio Parra repeatedly tried to get away, but he couldn't get through the crowds that blocked the leading motorcycles. Dutchman Steven Rooks managed (or was allowed) to escape, closely followed by Delgado and Rooks' good friend Theunisse. The rest of the field, including all of the erstwhile contenders, were scattered down the mountain. Pedro Delgado had established himself as the Tour's leader. Theunisse, in one of several run-ins with doping controls during his career, was found positive and had 10 minutes added to his time.

The General Classification now stood thus:
1. Pedro Delgado
2. Steve Bauer @ 25 seconds
3. Fabio Parra @ 1 minute 20 seconds
4. Steven Rooks @ 1 minute 38 seconds
5. Luis Herrera @ 2 minutes 25 seconds

The next day, Delgado tightened his grip on the race with his victory in the 38-kilometer uphill individual time trial with Bernard second at 44 seconds and Rooks third, 1 minute, 9 seconds off the pace. Bauer lost his second place to Rooks, who was now 2 minutes, 47 seconds behind the Spaniard.

Now came a rest day that transferred the race to the Pyrenees.

Delgado rode carefully yet masterfully in the Pyrenees. Stage fourteen, despite several challenging climbs, wasn't contested by the men seeking Yellow. It did show that even the Tour de France could have organizational snafus when a kilometer from the end, the follow cars were supposed to go straight while the riders were to bear left. In the confusion, the day's likely winner, Philippe Bouvatier, was mistakenly directed to go off-course with the cars. The stage winner, Massimo Ghirotto, recognizing Bouvatier's probable victory, offered Bouvatier the day's prize, a new Peugeot car. In those days, domestiques didn't make much money, making this a tremendous act of generosity on Ghirotto's part. The Tour organization came up with a second car so that Ghirotto could keep his.

Stage fifteen was the 1988 Tour's Queen Stage, with some of the great climbs of the Tour: Portet d'Aspet, Col de Menté, Peyresourde, Aspin, Tourmalet and Luz Ardiden. Delgado had let non-contenders Laudelino Cubino and Gilbert Duclos-Lassalle seek glory. In the final rush to the finish Delgado bolted, leaving such vaunted climbers as Parra, Theunisse and Rooks to do what they could to limit the damage. Generously, he eased before the line to let Gilbert Duclos-Lassalle take second place in the stage, Cubino having finished six minutes before. With the Pyrenees finished, Delgado had a 4 minute, 6 second lead on second-place Rooks. With a stage up to Puy de Dôme, where he should do well, and a 46-kilometer individual time trial looming as the only obstacles, Delgado should have been able to feel the Tour was his.

The standings after the Pyrenees:
1. Pedro Delgado
2. Steven Rooks @ 4 minutes 6 seconds
3. Fabio Parra @ 5 minutes 50 seconds
4. Steve Bauer @ 7 minutes 25 seconds
5. Gert-Jan Theunisse @ 7 minutes 54 seconds

In the evening after the finish of stage fifteen to Bordeaux, a rumor was reported on television: Delgado had tested positive for a banned drug. The journalists knew about the positive even before Delgado did. The next day Tour officials confirmed that Delgado had tested positive for Probenecid.

We'll stop here for just a second. Probenecid turns up every so often in dope tests. It is unusual that a healthy person would ever need the drug since it is rarely dispensed even to sick people. It acts as a diuretic and helps some people with gout. It can also increase the potency of antibiotics. Victims of drug-resistant gonorrhea are given Probenecid to increase the efficacy of their regimen of antibiotics. It is also called for in some AIDS cases. But Probenecid was found to have another effect: it drastically slows the urinary excretion of steroid metabolites. When an athlete pees into a bottle for a drug test, the testing scientist is often not looking for the drug itself, but for the by-products that the body produces as it metabolizes the drug.

Probenecid keeps these telltale chemicals from being present in urine, thus circumventing the drug test; the Probenecid itself can be fairly easily detected.

Here's where it gets interesting. Probenecid was then on the Olympic Committee's list of banned drugs. The UCI (cycling's governing body) was going to ban the drug after the Tour but it was not on the list of banned drugs as of July 1988.

After the drug positive, Tour boss Xavier Louy personally asked Delgado to withdraw from the Tour, but the Spaniard refused since he had broken no rules. Technically, Delgado had committed no offense. Two days after the positive test, the second sample (there is always an 'A' and 'B' sample tested independently for the racer's protection) was tested and the drug's presence confirmed. The Spanish government sent sports ministers and lawyers to France to argue Delgado's case. They were not going to surrender a third Spanish Tour winner (after Bahamontes and Ocaña) without a fight.

It was ruled Delgado could continue the Tour without penalty. The day of the announcement that Delgado was clear was also the day Theunisse received his ten-minute doping penalty. Ironically, it was steroids that showed up in Theunisse's test sample, the same class of chemicals that Delgado was thought to be hiding with Probenecid.

To this day, Delgado maintains his innocence and discusses his continuing the Tour under the drug cloud as if it were an act of heroism.

He said he took the Probenecid to help with problems with his legs. He later said that he was given a drink by a spectator on the route. Merckx thought the conflicting stories reflected poorly on the man, calling the defenses Delgado offered "rubbish".

Delgado is said to be a genuinely nice man, greatly liked by racers and fans. Because of this geniality, the riders staged a ten-minute strike the next day in sympathy for him.

During stage nineteen, with its ascent up Puy de Dôme, Johnny Weltz and Rolf Gölz had carved out a substantial lead, fifteen minutes with 50 kilometers to go. Then things stirred in the peloton. On the climb, Delgado demonstrated his complete mastery by easily dropping all the others and finishing third, five and a half minutes behind Weltz.

Delgado came close to winning the Dijon 46-kilometer individual time trial. He was ahead at every checkpoint but the finish line. The wind had come up during the day and finally it was too much for Delgado to overcome. His fourth place at 11 seconds to winner Juan Martínez-Oliver was still the best time of any of the top men. Rooks finished twentieth, 2 minutes, 26 seconds behind.

That settled the 1988 Tour. Delgado was by far the best rider that year and his more than seven-minute winning margin made that clear.

Hampsten and his team were indeed exhausted after the Giro. The Giro winner never displayed his normal brilliance in the high mountains. The 7-Eleven team was dogged by misfortune that began even before the race had started. Bob Roll crashed before the "Prelude" and had to be replaced at the last minute. During the second stage team time trial, Dag Otto Lauritzen crashed. Roy Knickman failed to make the time cutoff in the eighteenth stage to Limoges, and the next day Jeff Pierce, who had been struggling, was also eliminated.

Final 1988 Tour de France General Classification:
1. Pedro Delgado (Reynolds): 84 hours 27 minutes 53 seconds
2. Steven Rooks (PDM) @ 7 minutes 13 seconds
3. Fabio Parra (Kelme) @ 9 minutes 58 seconds
4. Steve Bauer (Weinmann-La Suisse) @ 12 minutes 15 seconds
5. Eric Boyer (Système U) @ 14 minutes 4 seconds
15. Andy Hampsten (7-Eleven) @ 26 minutes 0 seconds

Climbers' Competition:
1. Steven Rooks: 326 points
2. Gert-Jan Theunisse: 248
3. Pedro Delgado: 223

Points Competition:
1. Eddy Planckaert: 278 points
2. Davis Phinney: 193
3. Sean Kelly: 183

The 1988 Tour did live up to its expectation as a fast race. With an average speed of 38.909 kilometers per hour, it was the fastest Tour so far. And it was a strange Tour for Belgium. For the first time since 1910, not one rider from the bike-mad country won a stage.

In 2000 Steven Rooks admitted to having taken amphetamines and testosterone during his racing career. He just didn't get caught.

1989

Again the Tour organization changed directors. Jean-Marie Leblanc's appointment was one of the most important events in the history of the Tour de France. In its desperate search for income, the Tour had multiplied the various prizes and classifications, each having a sponsor. Most were unimportant to all but the most dedicated racing fans. Wanting to bring clarity and therefore credibility to the Tour, Leblanc slashed the list of competitions and then raised the cost of sponsoring the remaining, now more visible ones. Under Leblanc, the Tour underwent a renaissance, becoming wildly popular and financially sound. Leblanc's tenure coincided with the trend of the best stage racers making the Tour de France their only goal for the season. With ever-larger corporate money entering racing, the need for gigantic results to justify the big investments in teams drove more and more attention to the Tour. Leblanc's skillful management only served to magnify this tendency.

Leblanc, like all Tour directors before him except Naquet-Radiguet, was a former journalist. He had been *L'Équipe*'s chief cycling correspondent before becoming Tour boss. Moreover, Leblanc had also been a professional racer, having entered and finished both the 1968 and the 1970 Tours.

Both Greg LeMond and Laurent Fignon were back, and racing with dedication. They were in good form and finally achieving good results.

LeMond's recovery from his shooting accident and knee surgery was long and arduous. He had done reasonably well in the early season races. He was fourth in the Critérium International and sixth in Tirreno–Adriatico. LeMond had not won a race since his 1986 Tour de France victory.

In the Giro he suffered like a dog, finishing a lackluster thirty-ninth, almost an hour behind. It seemed he just could not find that old magic. Before the Giro ended, his wife, Kathy, flew to Italy to give him moral support. He stuck to it, refusing to give up. In the final stage, a 53.8-kilometer time trial, LeMond came in second, beating overall Giro winner Fignon by over a minute. The strength was returning. Both Fignon and Guimard were stunned by LeMond's superb Giro time trial. While Fignon was celebrating his Giro win, Guimard was the skunk at the picnic, warning Fignon, "LeMond will be up there at the Tour."

LeMond's team, however, was not a Grand Tour team. His ADR Belgians (including classics great Johan Museeuw) would be unable to give him the help he would need in the high mountains. He would have to race with his head.

Fignon, who hadn't been able to contend for a major stage race since he had surgery on his Achilles tendon in 1984, had found the way to win. In 1989 he had already won Milan–San Remo for a second time as well as the Giro d'Italia. Fignon also had an outstanding team in Super U that included future Tour winner Bjarne Riis. He said although he wasn't the rider he used to be, he could see a chance to achieve the Giro/Tour double. He thought that at nearly 29, this was the last year he could win the Tour, a final flowering of his physical ability. Fignon felt LeMond was the only name to be reckoned with in this Tour.

But, with Pedro Delgado also in good shape and seeking redemption after his tainted 1988 victory, this would indeed be an interesting Tour.

And that's just how it started out, interesting. At the Prologue, where every rider is assigned a specific start time, Delgado signed in twenty minutes early then went off to warm up. Somehow, he lost track of the time and showed up at the start house 2 minutes, 40 seconds late. The clock for a rider's time trial is quite indifferent: it starts with or without the rider. Delgado roared off, his time on the road being only 14 seconds slower than winner Erik Breukink. But because of his delayed start, he was now hamstrung with a deficit of almost three minutes at the Tour's opening. Fignon and LeMond both finished at the same time, 6 seconds off Breukink. The shootout between the two had started at the first possible opportunity.

The second stage, a team time trial, highlighted the teams' differences. Fignon's Super U squad won the stage, the team finishing intact, not losing any men on the road. Fignon said he felt ecstasy in his re-found strength and that for most of the stage, none of his teammates were able to share the pacemaking with him. LeMond's ADR team came in a respectable fifth, about a minute slower over the 46-kilometer course, despite losing three men along the way. Delgado's Reynolds-Banesto team finished dead last. Demoralized after his botched start to the Tour, Delgado couldn't keep up with his team. His teammates had to wait and nurse him to the finish. After two stages, Delgado was almost ten minutes down, a spectacular reversal of fortune from the year before.

The next test was stage five, the first individual time trial. At 73 kilometers, it would make a difference. Whatever morale problems Delgado may have been having in the first couple of stages, he was over them now. LeMond—whom Fignon called "unrivaled as a time trialist"—was using the new aerodynamic triathlon bars, which narrowed and thus streamlined the rider's frontal profile. They are standard equipment for any time trial bike today, but back then this was revolutionary stuff. Fignon thought these bars "strictly against the rules". He wrote, "Until then, the referees had only allowed three support points. For reasons that still elude me, Guimard and I didn't make a formal complaint…and the idle *commissaires* shut their eyes. The rules were being bent, and the consequences would be way beyond anything I could have imagined."

The stage results:

1. Greg LeMond: 1 hour 38 minutes 12 seconds
2. Pedro Delgado @ 24 seconds
3. Laurent Fignon @ 56 seconds
4. Thierry Marie @ 1 minute 51 seconds
5. Sean Yates @ 2 minutes 6 seconds

Which yielded these overall standings:

1. Greg LeMond
2. Laurent Fignon @ 5 seconds
3. Thierry Marie @ 20 seconds
4. Erik Breukink @ 1 minute 51 seconds
5. Sean Yates @ 2 minutes 18 seconds

LeMond wins the stage five time trial.

The first day in the Pyrenees went from Pau to Cauterets with the Marie-Blanque, Aubisque, Bordères and Cambasque in the way. Delgado's teammate, Miguel Indurain, was first over the final three climbs and won the stage. Delgado was back in action, completely revived and fighting, finishing about a minute and a half behind Indurain. LeMond chose not to defend his lead, Fignon and his team doing the work of policing the peloton. LeMond and Fignon trailed Delgado by 29 seconds, leaving no change to the General Classification except that Delgado continued to move up and LeMond had shown he would burn matches only upon necessity.

Stage ten with the Tourmalet, Aspin, Peyresourde and Superbagnères made little difference as both Fignon and LeMond were having off days. Fignon said he had to put on a big show to hide his physical distress.

On the final climb LeMond attacked. Fignon caught him and countered. LeMond tried to answer but couldn't, and Fignon put 12 seconds between himself and LeMond. Fignon now had the lead by 7 seconds and in Fignon's words, "the hand-to-hand battle had begun". That afternoon Fignon complained to the press about LeMond's negative riding, that it was unworthy of a Yellow Jersey.

Stephen Roche's knee flamed up again. He struggled in pain over the mountains, refusing to abandon during the stage. But that was it, Roche's Tour was over. Paul Kimmage says that during that evening while Roche was in misery in his hotel room, his team was already in talks with LeMond to see if he would come over to the Fagor squad the following year.

Fignon's 7-second lead remained until stage fifteen's 39-kilometer individual time trial with its two first-category climbs. Rooks won the stage, Delgado was fourth at 49 seconds and LeMond right behind him at 57 seconds. Fignon faltered and was tenth at 1 minute, 44 seconds. LeMond retook the Yellow Jersey with a 40-second lead over Fignon. Fignon said things were clear. LeMond was the superior time trialist and he was the better climber. If he didn't do something in the coming mountains, the results of that understanding would hold until Paris. To Fignon, a war of attrition had become an epic battle.

In the next day's stage with the Izoard, LeMond was able to gain another 13 seconds. Fignon wasn't able to stay with LeMond on the ascent and even after a kamikaze descent, he couldn't catch his prey. They say baseball is a game of inches. The 1989 Tour was a game of seconds, each a pearl beyond price as the two athletes battled with unabated intensity.

Stage seventeen, with the Galibier, the Croix de Fer and a finish up l'Alpe d'Huez, scrambled the eggs. After discussing things with Guimard, Fignon planned to attack as savagely as possible at the Alpe's first curve. As planned, Fignon attacked, but LeMond closed. Fignon went again, this time even harder, his legs burning with pain. LeMond came back. Then LeMond went, punching a giant gear, and this time Fignon had to dig deep to stay with his opponent. Fignon wasn't done. Somewhere he found the energy to go again, and again LeMond crawled back. They were seemingly perfectly matched. As they then slowed, others caught them.

Six kilometers from the summit Guimard drove next to Fignon and told him to attack, that LeMond was dying. Fignon said he couldn't, but after another kilometer he found the strength to jump, taking Delgado along. Guimard's superb racing sense was proved right again, LeMond couldn't answer. LeMond gave up 1 minute, 19 seconds and the lead to Fignon, who was now ahead by 26 seconds. Delgado had clawed his way to third place after being down almost ten minutes.

LeMond takes stage nineteen at Aix les Bains just in front of Fignon. Delgado and Theunisse also got the same time that day.

Guimard's reading of the two riders was masterful. Fignon regrets not taking Guimard's advice and attacking at the six-kilometers-to-go point, because he was taking twenty seconds per kilometer out of LeMond. Another twenty seconds would have changed things greatly.

Fignon was finding the Alpine air to his liking. He was having a super day during stage eighteen and escaped three kilometers from the top of the Côte de Saint-Nizier. He had a minute by the end of the descent, but ran into a headwind while LeMond chased with Delgado, Theunisse and Rooks, halving Fignon's lead. Still, he had won the stage and gained a precious 24 seconds, expanding his lead to 50 seconds. While publicly optimistic, LeMond is said to have privately conceded the race at this point. Fignon was sure he had won the Tour.

These men were so close, the degree of equipoise so perfect, this has to be one of the great races of history. Stage nineteen, with the Porte, Cucheron and Granier climbs proved it. LeMond won the stage with Fignon right with him, getting the same time. Neither was giving up a single second if it could be helped.

Here was the General Classification going into the final stage, a 24.5-kilometer time trial going from Versailles to Paris, the most famous and talked-about race against the clock in the history of the sport.

1. Laurent Fignon
2. Greg LeMond @ 50 seconds
3. Pedro Delgado @ 2 minutes 28 seconds
4. Gert-Jan Theunisse @ 5 minutes 36 seconds

LeMond had done wind-tunnel testing to perfect his riding position. For the time trial, he had an aerodynamic helmet and the aero bars which he had used to good effect in stage five. The run-in to Paris was slightly downhill. LeMond decided he didn't want to get time splits. He said he would just go as fast as he could and hope he didn't blow up before the end. The idea that he could take almost a minute out of an in-form Fignon in such a short distance was not preposterous, but it was unlikely. Being in second place, LeMond went before Fignon. LeMond thumped a monster 54 x 12 gear, driving it an astonishing 54.545 kilometers per hour. This was the fastest time trial ever ridden in the Tour de France and for years remained the record.

Fignon had other troubles besides LeMond. He had acquired a nasty saddle sore in stage nineteen. The pain had kept him from sleeping the night before, and by the day of the time trial, every pedal stroke was an agony, like the thrust of a knife. As he had done on every other occasion going back to his second place in the 1984 Giro, Fignon shunned the niceties of aerodynamics. He didn't use tri bars or an aero helmet. He even wore a wind-dragging ponytail. His saddle sore prevented his getting a proper warm-up.

As the race leader, Fignon had the privilege of going last. Despite riding the fastest time trial in his life, with each pedal stroke he lost time. Yet, when he came on to the Champs Élysées he still had the overall lead by two seconds. It was in those final meters that he lost those next, oh-so-precious 10 seconds. LeMond had to watch and wait in agony to see if his roll of the dice had succeeded.

The Tour was LeMond's. Fignon had lost the closest Tour in history. When Fignon learned that he had lost, he fell to ground with a moan, in tears, while LeMond yelped with joy.

Here's how the time trial went:

1. Greg LeMond: 26 minutes 57 seconds
2. Thierry Marie @ 33 seconds
3. Laurent Fignon @ 58 seconds

Final 1989 Tour de France General Classification:

1. Greg LeMond (ADR-Agrigel): 87 hours 38 minutes 35 seconds
2. Laurent Fignon (Super U) @ 8 seconds
3. Pedro Delgado (Reynolds) @ 3 minutes 34 seconds
4. Gert-Jan Theunisse (PDM) @ 7 minutes 30 seconds
5. Marino Lejarreta (Paternina) @ 9 minutes 39 seconds

Climbers' Competition:

1. Gert-Jan Theunisse: 441 points
2. Pedro Delgado: 311
3. Steven Rooks: 257

Points Competition:

1. Sean Kelly: 277 points
2. Etienne De Wilde: 194
3. Steven Rooks: 163

An aerodynamicist once calculated that if Fignon had just cut off his ponytail to reduce his drag, he would have gone fast enough to win the Tour. At the speeds LeMond and Fignon were traveling in the final time trial, the 8 seconds in the final Overall amounted to 82 meters, less than a football field after 3,257 kilometers. A manufacturer had offered Fignon and Guimard aero bars, but feeling they were against the rules, they chose not to take the risk. A couple of months later Fignon tried to use aero bars in the Grand Prix Eddy Merckx time trial, but was told that, indeed, they were against the rules, deepening the Frenchman's feeling that he had again been swindled.

That fall LeMond went on to cap his season with his second World Road Championship.

1990

At the start of the 1990 season, World Road Champion LeMond was noticeably overweight, a condition not improved by a bout of mononucleosis (Brits call it "glandular fever"). On the plus side, for the first time in his career, LeMond had a strong team that was dedicated solely to him. There were no split loyalties of the sort both he and Stephen Roche had been forced to deal with. And unlike his 1989 ADR team, his new team, sponsored by children's clothing company "Z", had riders who could assist him during the entire Tour, including climber Robert Millar, all-around strongmen Gilbert Duclos-Lassalle (a future two-time Paris–Roubaix winner) and Ronan Pensec. These were good men to have on one's side.

Meanwhile, Guimard and Fignon were engaged in a fight over management of their team, now sponsored by Castorama, which would result in a complete breakdown of their relationship in 1991.

While there may have been justifiable worries about LeMond's fitness to contest the Tour de France, these fears were put to rest with the Prologue time trial. Thierry Marie—who made a habit of winning these mini-time trials—won, with LeMond second at 4 seconds. Raul Alcala scored third with just about the same time, while Fignon was fifteenth at 19 seconds.

The first stage was another of those stages where a group of what was thought to be non-threatening riders was allowed to get away (Italians call such a break a *fuga di bidone*). The pack must have had a day of *non compos mentis* because this was actually a group of good racers.

Claudio Chiappucci, who never had any regard for conservative tactics, took off when the stage was only six kilometers old. Bauer, Pensec and Frans Maassen quickly joined him. After the first 30 kilometers the quartet had eked out a 30-second lead. Then, as is often the case, the peloton relented in its chase, perhaps slowed by a crash that took down Pedro Delgado. The lead quickly grew and by the end of the stage the pack was 10 minutes, 35 seconds behind the four speedy adventurers. All of these riders except Chiappucci were well-known quantities. Bauer was fourth in the 1988 Tour. Pensec had a sixth and a seventh in his past Tours. They were good riders who would surrender their time in the high mountains with great reluctance. But Chiappucci?

So far, Chiappucci had shown himself to be a competent but unspectacular racer. The previous year he was forty-sixth in the Giro and eighty-first in the Tour, but he did win the Giro del Piemonte and scored a second in the hilly Giro del Trentino. This year he had improved, with a seventh in Paris–Nice and a commendable twelfth in the Giro. This did not seem to be the stuff of a Tour contender. But wait, Chiappucci was King of the Mountains in this year's Giro. Hmmm…

Bauer was in Yellow yet again.

1. Steve Bauer
2. Frans Maassen @ 2 seconds
3. Claudio Chiappucci @ 9 seconds
4. Ronan Pensec @ 21 seconds
5. John Carlsen @ 9 minutes 3 seconds
6. Guido Winterberg @ 9 minutes 44 seconds
7. Thierry Marie @ 10 minutes 24 seconds
8. Greg LeMond @ 10 minutes 28 seconds

As the Tour went clockwise across northern France and then headed south for the Alps, the general situation remained unchanged, with the stage one breakaway quartet sitting on top of the leader board and Bauer in Yellow. A crash in stage four cost Robert Millar over nine minutes, eliminating the winner of the 1990 Dauphiné from contention.

Raul Alcala blistered the stage seven time trial, with Miguel Indurain second to him at a distant 1 minute, 24 seconds. LeMond picked up some time on the four breakaways, and was now 10 minutes, 9 seconds behind Bauer. Fignon, again suffering from poor form, abandoned. The four stage-one breakaways had ridden credible time trials; the closest rider to the four was Alcala and he was still over seven minutes behind Bauer.

Stage ten, with its finish at the Le Bettex ski station, took down the first of the Gang of Four. Bauer finished fiftieth, 4 minutes, 7 seconds behind stage winner Thierry Claveyrolat, who had escaped early in search of intermediate sprint points and then stayed away to the finish. Behind, on the final climb, Delgado blew up the chasing group but wasn't able to gain more than 19 seconds on the other contenders. More importantly, Bauer had come in behind Pensec and Chiappucci, the pair finishing in the LeMond group that included Rooks, Alcala, Indurain, Hampsten and Gianni Bugno. The Yellow Jersey was now the property of LeMond's teammate Ronan Pensec.

LeMond continued to chew away at the deficit in little bites. Stage eleven crossed the Glandon, Madeleine and finished atop l'Alpe d'Huez. Bugno and LeMond finished with the same time, Breukink just off their wheels. Pensec lost 48 seconds and Chiappucci lost 1 minute, 26 seconds. Pensec was still in Yellow with an increased lead over Chiappucci.

The standings after the Alpine climbing:

1. Ronan Pensec
2. Claudio Chiappucci @ 1 minute 28 seconds
3. Greg LeMond @ 9 minutes 4 seconds

Stage twelve was where it got interesting. The 33.5-kilometer individual time trial included a second-category climb and ended Pensec's hopes of taking the Yellow Jersey to Paris, while Breukink continued to display fine form by winning the stage. LeMond was fifth at 56 seconds. Chiappucci showed he was made of stern stuff with an eighth place, 1 minute, 5 seconds behind Breukink and only 9 seconds slower than LeMond.

The General Classification at this point:

1. Claudio Chiappucci
2. Ronan Pensec @ 1 minute 17 seconds
3. Erik Breukink @ 6 minutes 55 seconds
4. Greg LeMond @ 7 minutes 27 seconds
5. Pedro Delgado @ 9 minutes 2 seconds

Chiappucci had the Yellow Jersey and the Tour had a day of rest. During the next day's trip into the Massif Central, stage thirteen, Chiappucci missed the crucial break containing LeMond, Breukink, and Delgado, costing him almost five minutes. Doing a lot of the chasing himself, Chiappucci had at one point closed to within 33 seconds of his prey. But getting almost no help from the other teams, making contact with the talented riders ahead of him was an impossible task. He was the Yellow Jersey and it wasn't the other teams' job to defend it for him.

Breukink, who was having the Tour of his life, had pulled within 2 minutes, 2 seconds of Chiappucci, while LeMond was just a tad further back at 2 minutes, 34 seconds. If LeMond wanted the win, he had to get by both Chiappucci and a beautifully riding Erik Breukink.

In stage fourteen Breukink and LeMond took a small bite out of Chiappucci, 13 seconds. If they could keep up the pressure, the Italian would just bleed little dabs of time all over France. Would Chiappucci run out of Tour before he ran out of time?

Stage sixteen to Luz Ardiden, with the Aspin and the Tourmalet in the middle, decided the Tour and showed that both LeMond and Chiappucci were admirable athletes.

Chiappucci decided on a gigantic roll of the dice. He couldn't let LeMond and Breukink continue to ride their race, forcing him to give up time each stage. He lit the jets as soon as the race hit the first big climb, the Aspin, taking six others with him. Again Chiappucci was forced to do all the work. Leaving his companions, he was first over the summit, 34 seconds ahead of the first group. Chiappucci pressed on and by the time he was halfway up the Tourmalet he had extended his lead to 3 minutes, 20 seconds. LeMond grew alarmed. If Chiappucci held this much lead by the end of the day, he would probably be able to withstand any assault LeMond could mount with only one mountain stage and one time trial left.

LeMond dropped all but Delgado and Indurain as he raced to get back on terms with the small, courageous Italian. By distancing himself from Breukink, he had eliminated his only other threat as well.

LeMond performed a kamikaze descent that made up a whole minute and closed the gap to Chiappucci. LeMond and Chiappucci were now part of a small group in the lead that included Indurain, Fabio Parra and Marino Lejarreta. During the final ascent to Luz Ardiden, after riding at the front as long as he could, Chiappucci had to surrender when Fabio Parra attacked. LeMond and Indurain were among the small group who went with Parra; near the finish, Indurain attacked and LeMond had to let him go.

Indurain won the stage with LeMond 6 seconds back. Chiappucci came in fourteenth, 2 minutes, 25 seconds behind Indurain. That left Chiappucci with only a 5-second lead, a slim hold on the Yellow Jersey with a time trial coming up.

The last stage in the mountains, going over the Aubisque and Marie-Blanque, changed nothing; Breukink, LeMond and Chiappucci all finished with the same time. LeMond had a scare on the Marie-Blanque when Chiappucci and Delgado attacked. Seconds later LeMond flatted. He got a slow wheel change and then had to change his bike. With the two challengers up the road, LeMond chased with a surprising fury, again with a descent down the mountain that was frighteningly fast. The race marshal on the motor bike said that he had never seen a descent like LeMond's that day. Up ahead, Chiappucci had four Carrera teammates helping him while farther back the four "Z" riders who were with LeMond could just hang on while the World Champion blasted down the road.

Eventually contact was made, and LeMond made known his displeasure with the others who had attacked while he was getting a repair. LeMond said that at that moment he truly feared the race was lost.

After some brilliant riding, LeMond had things where he wanted them. He was to face a man with a 5-second lead who had never shown any special flair for riding against the clock.

The stage twenty 45.5-kilometer individual time trial played out exactly as LeMond had hoped and Chiappucci had dreaded.

1. Eric Breukink: 1 hour 2 minutes 40 seconds
2. Raul Alcala @ 28 seconds
3. Marino Lejarreta @ 38 seconds
4. Miguel Indurain @ 40 seconds
5. Greg LeMond @ 57 seconds
17. Claudio Chiappucci @ 3 minutes 18 seconds

LeMond had won his third Tour, this time without ever winning a stage.

Final 1990 Tour de France General Classification:
  1. Greg LeMond (Z): 90 hours 43 minutes 20 seconds
  2. Claudio Chiappucci (Carrera) @ 2 minutes 16 seconds
  3. Erik Breukink (PDM) @ 2 minutes 29 seconds
  4. Pedro Delgado (Banesto) @ 5 minutes 1 second
  5. Marino Lejarreta (ONCE) @ 5 minutes 5 seconds

Climbers' Competition:
  1. Thierry Claveyrolat: 321 points
  2. Claudio Chiappucci: 179
  3. Roberto Conti: 160

Points Competition:
  1. Olaf Ludwig: 256 points
  2. Johan Museeuw: 221
  3. Erik Breukink: 118

A team of Soviet riders sponsored by Alfa-Lum came to the Tour and did well with Dmitri Konyshev winning stage seventeen. Team members Piotr Ugrumov and Djamolidine Abdoujaparov would make a serious impression on the European pro circuit over time. East German Olaf Ludwig, riding for Panasonic, won the Green Jersey. Times were changing.

More than one writer has speculated that if Miguel Indurain had ridden for himself this year instead of for Delgado, he probably would have won the Tour. Who knows?

three

1991–1995

The Miguel Indurain Years

1991 Of course, after his 1989 and 1990 Tour victories, LeMond was the man to beat in 1991. His spring was less auspicious than ever. He abandoned the Giro and finished twenty-second in the Tour of Switzerland. But a less than sparkling spring was never a sign that LeMond should be counted out of the Tour de France.

Thierry Marie started the 1991 Tour the same way he had the year before, by winning the Prologue time trial.

Real racing started with the first stage when a break of serious Tour men got away, with LeMond, Breukink, Kelly and Rolf Sørensen among them. With the time bonuses and his good Prologue, LeMond was back in Yellow. This was a two-stage day. The afternoon was a team time trial: Sørensen's Ariostea squad won, putting him in the lead, which he kept until stage five when he hit a traffic island four kilometers from the finish, crashed and broke his clavicle.

Prologue specialist Thierry Marie showed he could do more than just a few kilometers at speed by winning the sixth stage with an astounding 234-kilometer solo break, the third-longest post-war escape by a single rider (Albert Bourlon's 253-kilometer ride in 1947 remains the postwar record). At the end of the stage he had 1 minute, 54 seconds to spare, enough to put him back in Yellow for a couple of days.

Stage eight's long 73-kilometer individual time trial brought out the real Tour riders.

The times of the day's top finishers:

1. Miguel Indurain: 1 hour 35 minutes 44 seconds
2. Greg LeMond @ 8 seconds
3. Jean-François Bernard @ 53 seconds
4. Erik Breukink @ 1 minute 14 seconds
5. Gianni Bugno @ 1 minute 31 seconds

This put LeMond back in the lead with Breukink at 1 minute, 13 seconds and Indurain 2 minutes, 17 seconds behind.

A couple of days later things got messy. Before the start of stage ten, two riders on the PDM team quit the Tour, and along the road to Quimper where the stage finished, two other PDMs retired. That evening it was revealed that several PDM riders including Breukink, Kelly and Alcala were ill. Only the riders and none of the support staff of the team were sick, which likely ruled out food poisoning. Team spokesman Jonathan Boyer said that it might have been a bad glucose drip (legal) that sickened the riders. The entire team withdrew from the Tour amid speculation that a doping program gone wrong was involved. Nothing was ever proven and the PDM team always denied using banned substances.

The real action of the Tour began with the first Pyrenean stage, going from Pau to Jaca, over two first-category climbs. A group got away on the first climb, the Soudet. When they arrived at the second-category Ichère, the break was well established and contained three high-class riders: Luc Leblanc, Pascal Richard and Charly Mottet. Meanwhile LeMond was unable to either get up to the break or enlist help from the other teams. With a winning margin of almost seven minutes over the LeMond group, Leblanc had gained the lead with LeMond down 2 minutes, 35 seconds.

It was stage thirteen—a 232-kilometer leg that went over the Pourtalet, Aubisque, Tourmalet and the Aspin before the final ascent to Val Louron—that changed the face of the 1991 Tour, and perhaps cycling itself.

LeMond broke away near the bottom of the Tourmalet. Indurain chased and caught LeMond, bringing with him Leblanc, Hampsten, Chiappucci, Bugno, Mottet and Gérard Rué. Near the top, just 500 meters from the crest, LeMond slowly slid off the back. He could do nothing as he watched the others ride away.

At the top, LeMond was only 17 seconds behind the leading group. Never one to give up, LeMond descended with that terrific ability that had saved him so many times before. He rejoined the leaders, but Indurain was gone. In a giant gear, LeMond bolted from the leading group, fully understanding the importance of what was happening. This was the Tour's pivotal moment. At the foot of the Aspin, he could see Indurain, but once the climbing began anew, LeMond lost ground, unable to keep pace with the soaring Spaniard.

Meanwhile, Claudio Chiappucci had also extracted himself from the leaders and was chasing Indurain. Getting word from his director that the Italian was on his way, Indurain slowed to allow Chiappucci to join him. The two relayed each other to the finish with Chiappucci taking the stage win and Indurain the overall lead. LeMond finished 7 minutes, 18 seconds later. The Yellow Jersey, Luc Leblanc, fared worse. As LeMond fought to get back on terms with Indurain and Chiappucci, Leblanc was jettisoned from the chasers and left to come in sixteenth, 12 minutes, 36 seconds after Chiappucci.

The General Classification after Indurain displayed his Tour abilities:
1. Miguel Indurain
2. Charly Mottet @ 3 minutes 0 seconds
3. Gianni Bugno @ 3 minutes 10 seconds
4. Claudio Chiappucci @ 4 minutes 6 seconds
5. Greg LeMond @ 5 minutes 8 seconds
6. Laurent Fignon @ 5 minutes 52 seconds
7. Andy Hampsten @ 7 minutes 25 seconds
8. Luc Leblanc @ 7 minutes 51 seconds

LeMond had absolutely no intention of giving up. Stage sixteen had no highly rated climbs, yet he fought to get into breaks and when caught, went again. His second place in the stage pulled back 26 seconds, a hard but successful day's work.

There was no avoiding the fate that awaited him the next day with its finish at the top of l'Alpe d'Huez after the Bayard and Ornon, both second category climbs. Bugno took the stage with Indurain and Leblanc right on his wheel. Chiappucci and Rooks were 43 seconds back; LeMond, Theunisse and Hampsten finished about two minutes behind.

The final Alpine stage was the cruelest of all, 255 kilometers that included the Aravis, Colombière and then the Joux-Plane. Thierry Claveyrolat won the stage with most of the contenders, including Indurain, about thirty seconds behind. LeMond was fifty-ninth at 7 minutes, 52 seconds, accompanied to the finish by his teammate Robert Millar.

LeMond broke away again on stage nineteen and snatched back a minute and a half. Because LeMond was no longer a threat, Indurain was content to finish in the middle of the pack.

The twenty-first and penultimate stage was a 57-kilometer time trial. Indurain won it, Bugno was second with LeMond third. The Tour was sealed.

On the final day, during the criterium that races up and down the Champs Élysées, Djamolidine Abdoujaparov, nicknamed the "Tashkent Terror", crashed spectacularly. With less than a kilometer to go, Abdoujaparov, the wearer of the Green Jersey, ran into a roadside barrier and went flying. It was a quarter of an hour before he would get up and cross the line.

Final 1991 Tour de France General Classification:
1. Miguel Indurain (Banesto): 101 hours 1 minute 20 seconds
2. Gianni Bugno (Gatorade-Chateau D'Ax) @ 3 minutes 36 seconds
3. Claudio Chiappucci (Carrera) @ 5 minutes 56 seconds
4. Charly Mottet (RMO) @ 7 minutes 37 seconds
5. Luc Leblanc (Castorama) @ 10 minutes 10 seconds
6. Laurent Fignon (Castorama) @ 11 minutes 27 seconds
7. Greg LeMond (Z) @ 13 minutes 13 seconds
8. Andy Hampsten (Motorola) @ 13 minutes 40 seconds

Climbers' Competition:
1. Claudio Chiappucci: 312 points
2. Thierry Claveyrolat: 277
3. Luc Leblanc: 164

Points Competition:
1. Djamolidine Abdoujaparov: 316 points
2. Laurent Jalabert: 263
3. Olaf Ludwig: 175

Miguel Indurain raced with the economical style of Jacques Anquetil, doing nothing more than necessary in the mountains. Only if an obvious or extraordinary opportunity presented itself did he attack, content to let his time trialing and watchful riding do the rest. A look at the final General Classification shows a generational shift. Delgado, LeMond and Fignon, who had been so dominant, were now well down in time while younger riders had surfaced.

Fignon said there were rumors going through the peloton in 1991 of a new drug, EPO (approved by the FDA in 1989), and by the next year, while he didn't think EPO use widespread, it was clearly being taken by some team leaders and few of the top domestiques. It may well be that from the moment it was available, athletes were taking the new drug and attaining astonishing performance improvements. Endurance athletes were also starting to die from mysterious heart ailments. During the early 1990s, at least a dozen riders died in their sleep. Writer Jean-François Quinet put the number of dead athletes much higher, estimating that as many as 80 riders (both amateurs and pros used the drug) perished as a consequence of EPO abuse.

In a 2004 interview in the French newspaper *Le Monde*, Greg LeMond said, "In 1990 I won the Tour and my team ["Z"] won the top-team classification. One year later, not one of us could follow the pace in the pack. There had been a radical change." He went on to note that when he was winning, his VO_2 max—maximum oxygen consumption, the basic measurement of an athlete's aerobic capacity—was tops among professional racers. In 2008, LeMond said, his energy output numbers would put him in the fifty-first percentile. In other words, the Greg LeMond of 1990 who won the Tour de France would be sent back for water bottles today.

Commenting on this interview, Andy Hampsten wrote "Like Greg, I, too, saw what I believe were the effects of EPO when it entered pro cycling in the early '90s. In the first years it grew from a few individuals reaping obscene wins from exploiting its 'benefits', to entire teams relying on it, essentially forcing all but the most gifted racers to either use EPO to keep their place in cycling, quit, or become just another obscure rider in the group."

1992

Indurain's spring racing results showed he had maintained his masterful 1991 form. He won the 1992

Giro d'Italia the same way he won the 1991 Tour de France—a la Anquetil. He contained his rivals in the mountains and won both time trials. He also won the Spanish Road Championships and the Tour of Catalonia. He was ready to join Coppi, Anquetil, Merckx, Hinault and Roche by going for the Giro-Tour double.

Gianni Bugno, who was second to Indurain in the 1991 Tour, was gunning for a Tour victory of his own. He came to this Tour as the reigning World Champion. His spring was quiet, but a third in the Dauphiné Libéré and a second in the Tour of Switzerland showed that his condition was coming on at just the right time. Chiappucci's second in the Giro (to Indurain) signaled that he too was ready to race.

The 1992 Tour flitted all around western Europe. To commemorate the signing of the Maastricht treaty, with its promise of an integrated European Union and a single market, the Tour schedule called for visits to Spain, Germany, Holland, Belgium, Italy and Luxembourg, in addition to France.

The action started with a Prologue in San Sebastian, Spain, and Indurain nailed it. In second place was a revelation, Swiss rider Alex Zülle. Riding for the Spanish ONCE team, he was just 2 seconds slower than Indurain. The next day, after winning an intermediate time bonus, Zülle was able to land the Yellow Jersey.

Zülle's ownership of the precious garment was short-lived. While the 1992 Tour mostly avoided the Pyrenees, it did make sure that the riders got a taste of the lash with a trip up the Marie-Blanque. That brought out another new face, Richard Virenque, a last-minute addition to his RMO team's lineup for the Tour. He was second in the stage and took the lead from Zülle, who finished twelve and a half minutes behind the flying Frenchman.

Virenque's possession of the lead would be just as short as Zülle's. In stage three, Pascal Lino, a teammate of Virenque's, was in the group of escapees who built a seven-minute gap over the peloton and he now took over the lead with two minutes over Virenque and six and a half minutes on third-place Indurain.

Virenque and Lino's RMO squad faced the 63.5-kilometer team time trial in stage four knowing that they would lose time. Some teams practice and become skilled at team time trials, riding close together, driving each other just hard enough so as not to tear the team apart.

They usually have riders who can put out the raw horsepower needed to propel the team at high speed on the flats. Other teams are terrible at the discipline and can lose tremendous amounts of time. Panasonic won while Chiappucci's Carreras were only 7 seconds behind, and Bugno's Gatorade team was third at 21 seconds. Motorola, with Hampsten, came in sixth, losing 48 seconds to Panasonic but coming in 2 seconds faster than Indurain's Banesto. Lino and Virenque's RMO squad was thirteenth at 1 minute, 45 seconds.

The General Classification after the stage four team time trial:

1. Pascal Lino
2. Richard Virenque @ 1 minute 54 seconds
3. Gianni Bugno @ 5 minutes 6 seconds
4. Claudio Chiappucci @ 5 minutes 20 seconds
5. Stephen Roche @ 5 minutes 28 seconds
6. Miguel Indurain @ 5 minutes 33 seconds
10. Laurent Fignon @ 5 minutes 49 seconds
12. Greg LeMond @ 5 minutes 55 seconds

For a race that was supposed to be dominated by the cool, unflappable, and dare I say it, dull Miguel Indurain, the surprises kept coming. Stage six was a rough, northern European classic-type stage with short, steep hills, bad weather and cobbles. The peloton broke into small pieces under the stress of a powerful breakaway that included some of the finest racers alive. Laurent Jalabert, Greg LeMond, Claudio Chiappucci and Brian Holm pounded away from the field, with Jalabert getting his first Tour stage win. Indurain was in the first chase group, 1 minute, 22 seconds back. Lino, with a healthy time cushion, had kept the lead. This put Chiappucci third (at 3 minutes, 34 seconds) and LeMond fifth (at 4 minutes, 29 seconds). This was good, aggressive tactical riding, not letting Indurain set all the terms of when and how the Tour would be contested.

As the Tour wound through the small countries of northern Europe, time bonuses slightly changed the relative positions of the riders.

In the stage nine 65-kilometer individual time trial in Luxembourg, Indurain delivered a lesson in the art of the chrono. Indurain caught Fignon, who had started 6 minutes earlier. In less than 80 minutes Miguel Indurain had completely changed the complexion of the Tour.

The stage times:

1. Miguel Indurain: 1 hour 19 minutes 31 seconds
2. Armand de las Cuevas @ 3 minutes 0 seconds
3. Gianni Bugno @ 3 minutes 41 seconds
4. Zenon Jaskula @ 3 minutes 47 seconds
5. Greg LeMond @ 4 minutes 4 seconds
6. Pascal Lino @ 4 minutes 6 seconds
7. Stephen Roche @ 4 minutes 10 seconds

The resulting General Classification:

1. Pascal Lino
2. Miguel Indurain @ 1 minute 27 seconds
3. Jesper Skibby @ 3 minutes 47 seconds
4. Stephen Roche @ 4 minutes 15 seconds
5. Greg LeMond @ 4 minutes 27 seconds
6. Gianni Bugno @ 4 minutes 39 seconds
7. Jens Heppner @ 4 minutes 52 seconds
8. Claudio Chiappucci @ 4 minutes 54 seconds

Through the French Jura, even though there were rated climbs and attacking riders who were not in contention for the Yellow Jersey, the real Tour men held their fire, keeping their powder dry for the first big Alpine day.

That day came in the thirteenth stage, 254.5 kilometers going from St. Gervais to Sestriere in Italy. The climbing was substantial. The riders faced the Saisies, Cormet de Roselend, Iseran, Mont-Cenis and the first-category climb to the finish at Sestriere.

Claudio Chiappucci was what Miguel Indurain wasn't. Where Indurain was cold, calculating, riding only to win and no more, knowing that whatever gaps he had allowed could be closed with a display of brute horsepower in the time trials, Chiappucci was the opposite. The Italian was willing to gamble, to take magnificent chances to gain time. He had to run these big risks because he was so vulnerable in time trials. Indurain said that he had to have eyes on the back of his head when he raced Chiappucci.

Americans often expressed contempt for Chiappucci with his wild excursions and attempts to break away, failing to understand that his flamboyant style served him well. His Grand Tour accomplishments are substantial. Tour de France: twice second, a third, and King of the

Mountains. For the Giro: twice second, plus a third, a fourth, and a fifth along with two King of the Mountains and one Points Jersey. This was consistent riding at the highest level.

As he had done in the 1990 Tour stage to Luz Ardiden, Chiappucci bet big on a roll of the dice. The first big climb of the day was the Saisies where Chiappucci escaped with some other riders, but without his main challengers, Bugno and Indurain. As far as they were concerned, this was far too early in such a monstrous stage to be romping around the Alps. By the time Chiappucci reached the top of the Iseran he was alone. Back in the leading group, the Banesto squad at last recognized the threat, assembled at the front and started working to bring the fleeing Italian back.

Bugno was riding the Tour to win and knew that this was the Tour's moment, yet he was trapped with Indurain while Chiappucci was riding away with the race. Bugno didn't want to go after Chiappucci knowing he would also be taking Indurain along for a free ride. He finally decided that it was better to take his chances with Indurain than to accept the sure loss by letting Chiappucci ride away to a mountain-top win. Bugno also knew Chiappucci would be finishing in Italy where the fanatical *tifosi* would lift him up the mountain with their excited cheers.

When Bugno attacked, as expected, he took along Indurain, as well as Hampsten and Franco Vona. The great chase was on. I still remember how exciting it was. I think everyone watching who wasn't Spanish was willing the lone, brave Chiappucci up the mountains, knowing the inexorable, machine-like Indurain would probably run him down before the end of the stage.

But Indurain couldn't catch this man. After riding alone for 125 kilometers, Chiappucci celebrated a brilliant victory. Vona came close, only 1 minute, 34 seconds down. Indurain, who ran out of gas in the final kilometers, was third, 11 seconds behind Vona.

Chiappucci's big gamble didn't yield him the Yellow Jersey as Indurain had ridden well enough to put himself solidly in the lead.

The General Classification after Sestriere:
1. Miguel Indurain
2. Claudio Chiappucci @ 1 minute 42 seconds
3. Gianni Bugno @ 4 minutes 20 seconds

4. Pascal Lino @ 7 minutes 21 seconds
5. Pedro Delgado @ 8 minutes 47 seconds

Another alpine stage followed with the Galibier, Croix de Fer and a finish on l'Alpe d'Huez, all three *hors catégorie*. Andy Hampsten was riding beautifully and this stage was the perfect showcase for

Hampsten wins big on l'Alpe d'Huez, stage fourteen.

his wonderful climbing abilities. He had been in the big break with Indurain the day before and acquitted himself well. Could he recover overnight from over 250 kilometers of mountainous racing and be able to take on the day's monsters?

On the Croix de Fer a couple of riders went clear of the now highly reduced, Banesto-led peloton. Alert to the opportunity, Hampsten and a couple of others joined them. In the group of five was dangerman Franco Vona, who had come in second the day before. Well clear of the pack, they went over the crest of the Croix de Fer as a group. In the valley leading to l'Alpe d'Huez the group worked well together, continuing to increase their advantage, starting up the Alpe with a lead of nearly four minutes.

Hampsten began the climb at a strong tempo and slowly wound it up, going from his 39-23 to the 21 and finally dropping to the 18! It's hard to explain to someone who has not ridden a climb of this severity how completely beyond the normal human experience it is to ascend a mountain this steep, this fast, after a day's racing. Only a few people in the world can do it.

With about seven kilometers to go, Hampsten was alone, riding to victory in the most prestigious of mountain stages. This was his seventh Tour and his first Tour stage victory. If you're going to win, you might as well win big.

Back down the hill, although Hampsten wasn't a General Classification threat, on the final climb Indurain and Chiappucci chased hard enough to pull back almost a half-minute, coming in together at 3 minutes, 15 seconds. Earlier in the stage, Gianni Bugno had cracked badly, coming in twenty-sixth, nine minutes after Hampsten. LeMond, tortured with saddle sores, could take no more and abandoned. Hampsten had catapulted himself onto the podium with his stage win.

The standings after l'Alpe d'Huez:

1. Miguel Indurain
2. Claudio Chiappucci @ 1 minute 42 seconds
3. Andy Hampsten @ 8 minutes 1 second
4. Pascal Lino @ 9 minutes 16 seconds
5. Gianni Bugno @ 10 minutes 9 seconds

The Tour then went over the Massif Central, but nothing changed. The only stage left that could affect the General Classification was the nineteenth, a 64-kilometer individual time trial. Again, Indurain distanced himself from his competitors. Bugno was only 40 seconds slower than the Spaniard, lifting himself back onto the podium after losing his place with his disastrous l'Alpe d'Huez stage. Andy Hampsten was the real loser that day, 5 minutes, 33 seconds slower than the Spaniard, costing him his place on the podium.

With only two stages left, the competition to win the Tour was over.

Final 1992 Tour de France General Classification:
1. Miguel Indurain (Banesto): 100 hours 49 minutes 30 seconds
2. Claudio Chiappucci (Carrera) @ 4 minutes 35 seconds
3. Gianni Bugno (Gatorade-Chateau D'Ax) @ 10 minutes 49 seconds
4. Andy Hampsten (Motorola) @ 13 minutes 40 seconds
5. Pascal Lino (RMO) @ 14 minutes 37 seconds

Climbers' Competition:
1. Claudio Chiappucci: 410 points
2. Richard Virenque: 245
3. Franco Chioccioli: 209

Points Competition:
1. Laurent Jalabert: 293 points
2. Johan Museeuw: 262
3. Claudio Chiappucci: 202

Indurain had his second Tour and his first Giro-Tour double. Chiappucci not only came in second, he was King of the Mountains and had ridden so consistently he was third in the competition for the points leadership. After an exhausting battle with Belgian classics specialist Johan Museeuw, Laurent Jalabert won the Green Points jersey.

The 1992 Tour was the fastest to date with an average speed of 39.504 kilometers an hour.

1993 The start of the 1993 Tour was much like the start of the 1992 edition. Again Indurain had won the Giro and had done it the same way as before, winning the two big time trials and never letting anyone dangerous get away from him in the mountains.

Chiappucci, hoping to challenge the mighty Spaniard's hegemony, was third to him in the Giro. Just as he had trailed Indurain by more than four minutes in the 1992 Tour de France, he finished over five minutes behind him in the 1993 Italian tour.

The 1993 Tour was run clockwise, starting near the western coast and working its way across the north of France. At 3,714 kilometers, it was about 250 kilometers shorter than the year before, but right in the range of current Tours.

The Tour's Prologue certainly had a familiar sound with Indurain winning and Zülle second, this time at 8 seconds while Bugno was third at 11 seconds.

Mario Cipollini was victorious in stage one, the first of what would eventually be twelve Tour stage victories. Despite his eight Tour starts, Cipollini would never finish a single Tour de France.

The second stage was won by Wilfried Nelissen, who started a six-stage speedster's fest as the jersey was shunted from sprinter to sprinter. There was a new face in that stage two sprint: 22-year-old Lance Armstrong, riding for Motorola, was seventh.

Stage four, an 81-kilometer team time trial, was won by Cipollini's GB-MG team, with the Spanish ONCE squad only 5 seconds behind. This was the start of ONCE's cultivation of the team time trial. The ONCE team strove to perfect their collective ability until their dominance was nearly as complete as the TI-Raleigh teams of the 1970s.

Tony Rominger's CLAS squad had a disappointing ride, finishing about two minutes behind GB-MG. Because the riders had given each other pushes along the way as well as a too-long tow from the team car while Rominger had a loose water bottle cage fixed, the entire team was penalized another minute. Rominger had lost more than three minutes and the Tour had barely begun.

Stage six was the fastest Tour road stage to date at 49.417 kilometers per hour. Winner Johan Bruyneel would go on to greater fame (or infamy) as the *directeur sportif* of the US Postal, Discovery and RadioShack teams of Lance Armstrong.

Other promising names of the future won the next two stages. Bjarne Riis won stage seven, while stage eight was Lance Armstrong's first Tour de France stage victory. He worked with Raul Alcala and Ronan Pensec to bridge up to three riders (including Stephen Roche) already off the front. Armstrong let the others lead it out and won the six-up sprint. Zülle crashed when a piece of trash got caught in his wheel, costing him more than two minutes. Bad luck seemed to hang on Zülle like a cheap suit his entire career.

Indurain was forced to wait until stage nine for the first individual time trial. Here he again he showed that, when it came to riding against the clock, he had no peer. The stage results for the 59-kilometer stage:

1. Miguel Indurain: 1 hour 12 minutes 50 seconds
2. Gianni Bugno @ 2 minutes 11 seconds
3. Erik Breukink @ 2 minutes 22 seconds
4. Tony Rominger @ 2 minutes 42 seconds
5. Alex Zülle @ 3 minutes 18 seconds

The resulting General Classification:

1. Miguel Indurain
2. Erik Breukink @ 1 minute 35 seconds
3. Johan Bruyneel @ 2 minutes 30 seconds
4. Gianni Bugno @ 2 minutes 32 seconds
5. Bjarne Riis @ 2 minutes 34 seconds

During the stages leading up to this time trial, Indurain had stayed out of trouble and avoided any serious time loss. But after just 59 kilometers of time trialing he was in command and could ride in his usual defensive and economical style.

After the time trial came a rest day and then the first day in the Alps, with the riders to go over the Glandon and Télégraphe, finishing on the Galibier. Rominger set out to push the pace and win the stage, but he could not dislodge Indurain. After five and a half hours of hard work, he and Indurain finished together with Motorola rider Alvaro Mejia. Hampsten was fourth at a little over a minute behind. Chiappucci suffered a bad day, finishing twenty-ninth, 8 minutes, 49 seconds behind, time that could never be made up on a rider of Indurain's class.

The next day was another Alpine stage with Louison Bobet's favorite mountain, the Izoard, followed by the Vars and two *hors catégorie* climbs, La Bonette and a finish at Isola 2000.

Rominger, again with Indurain for a shadow, won the stage. Indurain was perfectly content to let Rominger take the stage win, being interested only in the *maillot jaune*. Chiappucci, a bit resuscitated, was third at only 13 seconds back. Alvaro Mejia was again in the mix, finishing only 2 seconds behind Chiappucci.

Rominger (left) and Indurain finish together at the top of Isola 2000.

The Alpine stages seemed rather uneventful, with the colorless Indurain marking the aggressive Rominger. Yet the two days had left carnage in their wake. Before the two Alpine stages started there were 171 riders in the Tour, and after the mountains 151 remained. Indurain may have been riding conservatively, but the rest of the peloton was getting thrashed as Rominger repeatedly tried to drop the unflappable Spaniard.

Lance Armstrong quit the Tour after the first two stages in the Alps. His teammate Phil Anderson rode with him in the mountains and thought the young rider ill-suited for Grand Tours, "He was a one-day rider. I thought he could never, ever, win the Tour de France. Even he wouldn't have thought he could have won the Tour. He couldn't climb and he couldn't time-trial, two things you have to do to win the Tour."

The General Classification after the Alps:

1. Miguel Indurain
2. Alvaro Mejia @ 3 minutes 23 seconds
3. Zenon Jaskula @ 4 minutes 31 seconds
4. Tony Rominger @ 5 minutes 44 seconds
5. Bjarne Riis @ 10 minutes 26 seconds

The first Pyrenean stage was huge, a route over seven rated climbs. Colombian Oliviero Rincon set off for personal glory, getting away early with several other riders. He eventually dumped them all before soloing to victory. Back in the peloton, Rominger was still at it, refusing to lay down arms, battering away at Indurain again and again, but Indurain could take all the Swiss could dish out.

Stage sixteen was more of the same, with the Peyresourde and an ascent to Pla d'Adet. At the end of the day the standings remained unchanged. Zenon Jaskula won, with Rominger close by and Indurain 3 seconds behind them. There was one more stage in the Pyrenees, but it changed nothing. There was only one leg left that could affect the outcome, stage nineteen's 48-kilometer individual time trial.

Going into the time trial, the standings:

1. Miguel Indurain
2. Alvaro Mejia @ 4 minutes 28 seconds
3. Zenon Jaskula @ 4 minutes 42 seconds
4. Tony Rominger @ 5 minutes 41seconds

It looked as if Motorola had finally made the podium with Mejia sitting in second place.

The time trial results:

1. Tony Rominger: 57 minutes 2 seconds
2. Miguel Indurain @ 42 seconds
3. Zenon Jaskula @ 1 minute 48 seconds
4. Johan Bruyneel @ 2 minutes 16 seconds

5. Gianni Bugno @ 3 minutes 0 seconds

10. Alvaro Mejia @ 3 minutes 43 seconds

Rominger and Jaskula had blasted Mejia right off the podium. Once again Motorola had a pure climber close to a podium finish who couldn't mash the big gears in the time trials.

For Rominger, his victory in the time trial meant Indurain had tired and was vulnerable. Rominger felt that if he had worked on a General Classification victory from the first stage, avoiding the big time loss that hobbled him, he could have worn Indurain down enough to win the Tour. It's hard to know because Indurain, like Anquetil, never expended more energy than necessary. But Rominger might be right, Indurain was so exhausted from the 1993 Tour, that he skipped many of the lucrative post-Tour criteriums. Indurain had pulled off a Giro-Tour double in two consecutive years, the first racer to have ever done so. This made three Tours in a row for Indurain.

French stage racing was in a bad state. The highest placed Frenchman was Jean-Philippe Dojwa, fifteenth and more than a half-hour behind Indurain. Pascal Lino's stage fourteen win was the only French stage win in the 1993 Tour.

Fignon said he was shocked by the peloton's transformation over the past couple of years. Speeds were much higher, and indifferently talented riders now rode with commanding strength at the front.

Final 1993 Tour de France General Classification:

1. Miguel Indurain (Banesto): 95 hours 57 minutes 9 seconds
2. Tony Rominger (CLAS) @ 4 minutes 59 seconds
3. Zenon Jaskula (GB-MG) @ 5 minutes 48 seconds
4. Alvaro Mejia (Motorola) @ 7 minutes 29 seconds
5. Bjarne Riis (Ariostea) @ 16 minutes 26 seconds

Climbers' Competition:

1. Tony Rominger: 449 points
2. Claudio Chiappucci: 301
3. Oliviero Rincon: 286

Points Competition:

1. Djamolidine Abdoujaparov: 298 points
2. Johan Museeuw: 157
3. Maximilian Sciandri: 153

1994

The Italian Gewiss-Ballan team dominated the spring classics season. The squad demonstrated extraordinary strength in the Belgian Flèche Wallone semi-classic, run three days after Gewiss rider Evgeni Berzin had soloed to victory in Liège–Bastogne–Liège.

In this Flèche Wallonne, Berzin, Moreno Argentin and Giorgio Furlan seemed to effortlessly roll off the front about 80 kilometers from the finish. The trio took the day's podium; moreover, the first eight finishers in the Belgian race were all Italians.

Gewiss-Ballan had hired Dr. Michele Ferrari to be its team doctor. When the good doctor was asked about the EPO he was believed to have been using to "prepare" Gewiss riders, he replied that that which wasn't forbidden was allowed. Those in the peloton who hadn't tumbled on to what it took to win races in the early 1990s now began to understand what was happening and had no intention of letting a few Italian teams run away with all the prizes. The race to dope was on.

Cracks in the adamantine wall of Indurain's invulnerability started to show in the 1994 Giro d'Italia. Or at least they seemed to as Indurain failed to win any of the Giro's three time trials. In the stage one-b 7-kilometer individual time trial, eventual Giro winner Evgeni Berzin beat Indurain by three seconds. Stage eight was a fairer contest at 44 kilometers, but this time Berzin beat the Spaniard by 2 minutes, 34 seconds. In the final time trial, Berzin was 20 seconds faster over the 35 kilometers. Counting the final time trial in the 1993 Tour de France, this made four successive time trial losses for Indurain.

Moreover, climber Marco Pantani was able to get away on two consecutive days, gaining enough time to finish ahead of Indurain in the General Classification. This put a dagger in the heart of the Indurain strategy: contain the climbers in the hills, letting them gain only insignificant amounts of time and then kill them in the time trial. In the 1994 Giro, he could do neither.

The final podium for the 1994 Giro:
1. Evgeni Berzin
2. Marco Pantani @ 2 minutes 51 seconds
3. Miguel Indurain @ 3 minutes 23 seconds

Was this a portent for the Tour or just a careful training ride crafted so that Indurain would not be too tired to contest the final days of the Tour? Remember, late in the 1993 Tour he had run out of gas.

This Tour had a particularly large crop of good climbers. Given Indurain's past inability to ride in the mountains with the best mountain goats, riders such as Richard Virenque, Marco Pantani and Piotr Ugrumov were eager to take on the Spaniard.

The Tour's 7.2-kilometer Prologue in Lille was Chris Boardman's first day in his first Tour de France. What a spectacular result for him as he won the Prologue, beating Indurain by 15 seconds and Rominger by 19. He was now the Yellow Jersey, the first Englishman to own it since Tom Simpson wore it 32 years before. Simpson's last day in Yellow was four years before Boardman was born.

The next day, a 234-kilometer sprinter's stage from Lille to Armentieres, ended with one of the most spectacular crashes in Tour history. A policeman leaned into the road to take a picture of the final sprint. Wilfried Nelissen slammed into him, taking down Laurent Jalabert in the fall. Jalabert, who had won seven stages and the points competition in the Vuelta earlier that year, was looking forward to repeating the process in his home country. Instead, with terrible wounds to his face, he was taken to the hospital. Jalabert later said that the crash changed his way of riding. Under pressure from his wife, he no longer sought out the dangerous bunch gallops. Although Nelissen also returned to racing, he was never again the racer he was before that crash.

Boardman was able to keep his Yellow Jersey until the stage three team time trial, 66.5 kilometers contested at Calais. GB-MG won the stage with Motorola missing the win by just 6 seconds.

The GB-MG win gave Johan Museeuw the lead. Boardman, desperate to keep the Yellow Jersey for the next day's stage in England, had hammered his team. Being an inexperienced professional yet possessing extraordinary power (he had only turned pro in August 1993), he, as Armstrong would do in his early team time trials, took such hard pulls his teammates struggled to stay in his slipstream.

The Tour made another crossing of the English Channel, the first time since that less-than-successful journey of 1974. Back then, the crowds were sparse and the racing uninteresting. This time the crowds were huge and the racers rode the two English stages as if they were the

Tour de France. Boardman managed a fourth place in one of the stages, but he had lost too much time (1 minute, 17 seconds) in the team time trial to get back in Yellow. Ironically, Sean Yates, also a British rider, donned the *maillot jaune* on the Tour's first day back in France.

The Tour really started with the stage nine 64-kilometer individual time trial. Was Indurain faltering? Was his Giro performance a guide to his Tour? Look at the times:

1. Miguel Indurain: 1 hour 15 minutes 58 seconds
2. Tony Rominger @ 2 minutes 0 seconds
3. Armand de las Cuevas @ 4 minutes 22 seconds
4. Thierry Marie @ 4 minutes 45 seconds
5. Chris Boardman @ 5 minutes 27 seconds

With the possible exception of Rominger, Indurain had humiliated the field. Boardman was the reigning Olympic Pursuit Champion and would go on that year to become the World Time Trial Champion, but for all that ability, he was over five minutes slower than Indurain. Almost half the field finished more than twelve minutes behind the Spaniard.

The General Classification after the time trial:

1. Miguel Indurain
2. Tony Rominger @ 2 minutes 28 seconds
3. Armand de las Cuevas @ 4 minutes 40 seconds
4. Gianluca Bortolami @ 5 minutes 47 seconds
5. Thierry Marie @ 5 minutes 51 seconds

The time gaps were already beyond what anyone could ever recapture from an in-form Indurain unless misfortune took him down.

Stage eleven would reveal all with a new climb up the Hautacam to Lourdes, a 17.3-kilometer *hors catégorie* ascent. This is what the small, specialist climbers live for. Indurain may kill them in the time trials, but this was a chance to take the time back.

The first to take off up the mountain was Marco Pantani. Jean-François Bernard, who a few years earlier had been expected to inherit the mantle of Bernard Hinault, was now riding as a domestique for Indurain. Maybe he wasn't Hinault, but Bernard set a fiery pace up the Hautacam that shed most of the peloton. Halfway up, exhausted, he pulled off to let Indurain and the others take over. In past years, Indurain dared not let his climbing domestiques go all out in the high mountains because he couldn't match their pace. Now he could take what they could dish out and still be ready to hand out heaping helpings of suffering to those still on his wheel.

Indurain took over from Bernard and rode in his steady, smooth high-cadence style that was surprising for such a large man. Finally he was left with only two riders, both Frenchmen, Leblanc and Virenque. After another couple of kilometers, even Virenque couldn't take it. It was down to Leblanc and Indurain. The duo caught and passed Pantani. Leblanc tried to shed Indurain but could only gain a temporary gap that Indurain, with extreme effort, was able to close. At the summit, Leblanc sprinted ahead for the stage win.

This was a new Indurain. In the past, the mountains posed a threat, a manageable threat, but a danger to him nonetheless. Now Indurain could attack the field in the mountains and beat the best climbers at their own game. Look at the times for the stage:

1. Luc Leblanc
2. Miguel Indurain @ 2 seconds
3. Marco Pantani @ 18 seconds
4. Richard Virenque @ 56 seconds
5. Armand de las Cuevas @ 58 seconds
6. Pavel Tonkov @ 1 minute 26 seconds
7. Piotr Ugrumov @ same time
16. Tony Rominger @ 2 minutes 21 seconds

The General Classification:

1. Miguel Indurain
2. Tony Rominger @ 4 minutes 47 seconds
3. Armand de las Cuevas @ 5 minutes 36 seconds
4. Piotr Ugrumov @ 8 minutes 32 seconds
5. Luc Leblanc @ 8 minutes 35 seconds

The peloton was in tatters after the Tour's first serious climbing.

The next day was another Pyrenean stage with the Peyresourde, Aspin, Tourmalet and a final ascent to the Luz Ardiden ski station. With the field put in its place, Indurain let a group of non-contenders get away. Virenque led over the last three climbs, winning the stage by four and a half minutes over Pantani. Rominger, unwell, abandoned the next day.

The Tour headed towards the Alps. But before a second round of high mountains, there was stage fifteen, 231 kilometers going from Montpellier to Carpentras with Mont Ventoux in the way.

Big Eros Poli pedaled away from a completely indifferent peloton; by the time he reached the base of Mont Ventoux his lead was nearly half an hour. The climb up Mont Ventoux seemed to be almost beyond him. Exhausted, he could barely turn over the cranks. He cleared the summit, still with several minutes in hand, and sped down the other side, winning the stage 3 minutes, 39 seconds ahead of the first chasers. The contenders—Indurain, Pantani, Ugrumov, Virenque, and others— came in together 4 minutes later. While Poli's ride was indeed epic, nothing had changed in the General Classification.

The first day in the Alps with a climb up l'Alpe d'Huez didn't change much either. Riders with no GC hopes were allowed to escape, while Indurain kept Leblanc and Virenque on a short leash.

Stage seventeen, including ascents of the Glandon and Madeleine with a finish at Val Thorens, was the day Piotr Ugrumov finally went for a shot at glory. On a long break, he dragged Colombian Nelson Rodríguez to the finish, where the Colombian sprinted ahead of him for the stage win. Ugrumov was now sixth, a little over eleven minutes behind Indurain. The interesting stories of this Tour are these races for minor placings. No one believed that the 1994 Indurain could be shaken from his place at the top of the standings.

The next day with the Saisies, Croix Fry and the Colombière, all tough climbs, Ugrumov again escaped and this time achieved his solo victory. Indurain, unworried, rolled in second, 2 minutes, 39 seconds later. Ugrumov's solo adventure allowed him to leap past Pantani and others and onto the podium.

Stage nineteen was the clincher for the 1994 Tour, a 47.5-kilometer individual time trial that went over the second-category Les Gets and the first-category Avoriaz. Ugrumov turned in a stunning performance. Here are the stage results:

1. Piotr Ugrumov
2. Marco Pantani @ 1 minute 38 seconds
3. Miguel Indurain @ 3 minutes 16 seconds
4. Luc Leblanc @ 3 minutes 50 seconds
5. Charly Mottet @ 4 minutes 12 seconds

Virenque came in eighteenth at 6 minutes, 4 seconds. With that collapse, Ugrumov moved up to second while Marco Pantani regained third.

The final stage on the Champs Élysées was a fantastic, exciting race with Eddy Seigneur riding like a man possessed to take a solo win while American Frankie Andreu was second at only 3 seconds.

Final 1994 Tour de France General Classification:
1. Miguel Indurain (Banesto): 103 hours 38 minutes 38 seconds
2. Piotr Ugrumov (Gewiss-Ballan) @ 5 minutes 39 seconds
3. Marco Pantani (Carrera) @ 7 minutes 19 seconds
4. Luc Leblanc (Festina) @ 10 minutes 3 seconds
5. Richard Virenque (Festina) @ 10 minutes 10 seconds

Climbers' Competition:
1. Richard Virenque: 392 points
2. Marco Pantani: 243
3. Piotr Ugrumov: 219

Points Competition:
1. Djamolidine Abdoujaparov: 322 points
2. Silvio Martinello: 273
3. Jan Svorada: 230

That made four sequential Tour wins for Miguel Indurain. He was better than ever.

1995

Indurain skipped the 1995 Giro. Rominger, the only man to mount a serious challenge to the Spaniard's reign, did ride the Italian tour and won it by winning all three time trials, holding the leader's Pink Jersey from the second stage until the finish. In 1993, when Indurain had successfully ridden the Giro to victory, he was vulnerable to attack in the final week of the Tour. The Giro had grown too tough to be used as merely a steppingstone to the Tour.

Indurain had shown his fine form with wins in the important stage races leading up to the Tour, including the Dauphiné Libéré, the Midi-Libre and the Vuelta a Rioja. Miguel Indurain arrived at the Tour *départ* ready to roll.

The 1995 Tour was clockwise, starting in Brittany with a 7.3-kilometer Prologue time trial held in the early evening twilight. The first riders raced on dry roads but as the stage progressed, it started to rain and the last riders had wet, slippery streets. Last year's Prologue winner, Chris Boardman, crashed heavily on the slick road and was nearly hit by his own follow car. With both a broken ankle and a broken wrist, Boardman's Tour was over.

The Prologue winner was Jacky Durand, who had the good fortune to ride before the rain started. The favorites, seeded to ride later in the rain, were willing to give up a few seconds to remain upright. Indurain was thirty-fifth at 31 seconds, Rominger thirtieth at 26 seconds and Zülle twenty-sixth at 23 seconds. After all, you have to finish the race to win it.

During stage two, Jalabert won an intermediate sprint, acquiring enough bonus time to take the Yellow Jersey from Durand, keeping it until stage four when he lost almost a minute in a crash near the finish.

The Tour's first drama wasn't in the mountains and it wasn't in a time trial. Indurain chose to lay down the law during stage seven. Going from Charleroi to Liège over the lumpy Ardennes countryside, Indurain shot off the front. Only Johan Bruyneel, already up the road, was able to latch on to his wheel. As Lance Armstrong later explained, the rest of the peloton could only watch him ride away. Bruyneel sat on Indurain as he carved a 50-second lead for the two of them. Bruyneel sprinted away from Indurain for the stage win and the Yellow Jersey. But Indurain had shown how deep his stores of power were and given what was to come next, it was a powerful act of intimidation.

Bruyneel's ownership of the lead was short-lived. The next day was the first individual time trial, 54 kilometers long. This is what was extraordinary about Indurain's breakaway the day before. The core of Indurain's dominance was his time trialing, yet he felt so confident he was willing to spend precious energy attacking on a road stage whose final result could never be certain, instead of conserving his strength for the time trial. Indurain won the time trial and donned the Yellow Jersey.

The stage results for the stage eight time trial, from Huy to Seraing:

1. Miguel Indurain: 1 hour 4 minutes 16 seconds
2. Bjarne Riis @ 12 seconds
3. Tony Rominger @ 58 seconds
4. Evgeni Berzin @ 1 minute 38 seconds
5. Melchior Mauri @ 2 minutes 16 seconds

The General Classification after the time trial and just before the Tour's first day in the Alps:

1. Miguel Indurain
2. Bjarne Riis @ 23 seconds
3. Evgeni Berzin @ 2 minutes 20 seconds
4. Johan Bruyneel @ 2 minutes 30 seconds
5. Tony Rominger @ 2 minutes 32 seconds

The ninth stage took in four highly rated climbs ending with an ascent to La Plagne. Zülle exited the peloton with an escape that gave him the stage win and second place. Indurain, after calmly chasing Zülle during most of the latter part of the stage, decided to rocket up to La Plagne. None of his companions could stay with him, just as in the stage to Hautacam the year before. Indurain closed to within two minutes of Zülle while Tonkov, Pantani, Gotti, Virenque and the rest were scattered four minutes and more behind.

The new General Classification:

1. Miguel Indurain
2. Alex Zülle @ 2 minutes 27 seconds
3. Bjarne Riis @ 5 minutes 58 seconds
4. Tony Rominger @ 6 minutes 35 seconds
5. Ivan Gotti @ 6 minutes 54 seconds

The next day with the Madeleine, Croix de Fer and l'Alpe d'Huez, Pantani scooted away while Zülle and Indurain finished together.

Bastille Day, stage twelve, should have been an uneventful ride through the Massif Central as the peloton headed towards the Pyrenees. Should have been, but wasn't. Just 23 kilometers into the 222.5-kilometer stage, Jalabert and Dario Bottaro attacked. They were later joined by two members of Jalabert's ONCE team, Neil Stephens and Melchior Mauri, who was sitting in eighth place. Their lead grew to nearly eleven minutes, making Jalabert the virtual leader and Mauri virtual third place. With three ONCE riders in the break, it had both cohesion and power. Indurain's and Riis' teams finally woke up, smelled the coffee and started to bring them back. Too late. The chickens had flown the coop and all they could do was limit the damage. As the breakaway reached the base of the final climb, their lead was still over seven minutes.

After being led up the mountain by his teammate Mauri, Jalabert jumped away for a solo win. He had been away for 198 kilometers.

Back in the field, Pantani jetted up the mountain, eased to let Indurain and Riis join him, but then sprinted ahead to beat them at the end. After all this aggression, Indurain had again contained any menace and was still safely in Yellow.

The first day in the Pyrenees didn't change anything. Pantani escaped and Indurain controlled things, riding with second-place Zülle and third-place Riis to the finish. They were the elite of this year's Tour and were keeping a close eye on each other.

Stage fifteen was the Queen stage, taking in the Portet d'Aspet, Col de Menté, Peyresourde, Aspin and Tourmalet with a final ascent to Cauterets/Crêtes-du-Lys. Except for the second-category Aspet, these were all category one or *hors catégorie* climbs, a monumental day stuffed into 206 kilometers. Richard Virenque attacked and was first over every one of the passes and won the stage.

While Virenque was riding away from a demoralized peloton, several riders crashed on the descent of the Portet d'Aspet. Among them was Fabio Casartelli, the 1992 Barcelona Olympic Road Race Champion, riding for Motorola. The other riders were able to remount and continue, but Casartelli had hit his head at high speed (estimated by some at over 90 kilometers per hour) against a concrete barrier on the side of the road. He was airlifted from the scene, but shortly thereafter, he died in the hospital. Arguments continue to this day regarding his lack of a helmet, and whether wearing one would have saved his life.

It is amazing that Casartelli was only the third racer to die while riding in the Tour de France. If we eliminate Tom Simpson since his death was the result of a drug overdose (though Anquetil argued that he died because he didn't take enough dope!), the only crash deaths in a century of Tour de France racing have been Casartelli and Francesco Cepeda in 1935. The Tour is an astonishingly safe enterprise given the terrible chances the riders take day after day. Immediately following Casartelli's death there was the usual discussion and hand wringing as to whether the Tour should continue. Of course it did.

The next day's stage sixteen was ridden as a neutralized procession with the results annulled. At the end of the stage, the Motorola team was allowed to ride together across the line.

In stage eighteen, a small group escaped and Lance Armstrong, dropping his breakaway companions, came in alone to Limoges. Pointing the index fingers of both hands to the sky, he dedicated the win to his lost comrade. The team carried Casartelli's broken bike atop their team car for the rest of the Tour. Today it rests in the Madonna del Ghisallo chapel.

The only unfinished business left for the 1995 Tour was the final 46.5-kilometer time trial. Indurain made a clean win of it, beating second-place Riis by almost a minute.

Indurain had earned five sequential Tour wins, an unprecedented accomplishment. His 1995 Tour victory came without his winning a single road stage; the only stage wins were time trials. I am sure that it wasn't because he couldn't. It was because the stage wins were unimportant to him and represented needless wastes of energy. Only owning the Yellow Jersey in Paris mattered, and nothing could distract him from that goal.

By the start of the 1995 season, the entire professional peloton understood that without EPO a rider would be unable to win important races. In fact, because speeds were so high, even finishing a race without drugs became difficult. Several riders in the thought-to-be squeaky-clean Motorola team—desperate to get back on terms with the pack—finally gave up their fight to win races riding clean and began taking drugs. A rider later testified that Lance Armstrong's hematocrit had shot up from his normal low-to-mid forties to fifty percent. The team even had its own centrifuge to check its riders' hematocrits (percentage of blood that is red corpuscles). If blood is not being manipulated, there is no need for a racer to use a centrifuge.

Final 1995 Tour de France General Classification:
1. Miguel Indurain (Banesto): 92 hours 44 minutes 59 seconds
2. Alex Zülle (ONCE) @ 4 minutes 35 seconds
3. Bjarne Riis (Gewiss-Ballan) @ 6 minutes 47 seconds
4. Laurent Jalabert (ONCE) @ 8 minutes 24 seconds
5. Ivan Gotti (Gewiss-Ballan) @ 11 minutes 33 seconds

Climbers' Competition:

1. Richard Virenque: 438 points
2. Claudio Chiappucci: 214
3. Alex Zülle: 205

Points Competition:

1. Laurent Jalabert: 333 points
2. Djamolidine Abdoujaparov: 271
3. Miguel Indurain: 180

four

1996–1998

A new generation of powerful drugs, lax enforcement and the riders' belief in their entitlement to dope explodes into the Tour's greatest crisis

1996 Why shouldn't Miguel Indurain have been considered a shoo-in for a record-breaking sixth Tour win? He was the reigning World Time Trial Champion. In June he won the Dauphiné Libéré against most of the riders he would face in July, winning two of the eight stages along the way. Rominger was second to the Spaniard in that race and Virenque third. Indurain's other major threat, Telekom's Bjarne Riis, didn't even finish the Dauphiné. 1994 Giro winner Evgeni Berzin could not be ignored, but having come in tenth in the 1996 Giro, over fourteen minutes behind winner Pavel Tonkov, he seemed an unlikely man to topple Indurain.

Zülle didn't ride the Dauphiné. Riding for the Spanish ONCE outfit, his efforts centered on Iberian races, two of which he won.

Riis, like Indurain, had been slow to mature. He rode his first Tour de France in 1989, coming in an undistinguished ninety-fifth. He didn't finish the next year, while in 1991, he was 107th. 1993 was his breakout year, with a stage win and fifth overall. The next year he slid to fourteenth but still captured a stage win. 1995 was even better with a spot on the podium and a day in Yellow. In the winter, tired of friction with Evgeni Berzin, he moved from Gewiss to the well-financed and organized German Telekom team, managed since 1992 by Belgian tough-guy Walter Godefroot. Godefroot was a champion with 150 pro victories to his name. He expected his riders to be filled with the same discipline that drove him to win Paris–Roubaix, the Tour of Flanders, Liège–Bastogne–Liège and ten Tour stages. He was not the right manager for men of a gentler mentality; and as the years progress, we'll see him squander some of the finest talent in the world. But for now, Riis, also a man of drive and self-confidence, was the rider Godefroot was looking for. His team lacked a first-class Grand Tour man, someone who might unseat Indurain. Riis' leaving the Gewiss team was the answer to Godefroot's prayers.

Most teams racing in modern Tours qualify automatically, with a few vacancies called "wild cards" filled at the organizer's discretion. Usually the Tour selects a couple of lower-ranking French teams to help French cycling. The value of TV rights can figure into team selection as well. To get more American television viewers for the Tour, the US Postal team was given the nod.

The 1996 Tour started with a Prologue in 's Hertogenbosch in Holland, went south to the Alps, then into the Massif Central, and on to the Pyrenees. After the mountains, the Tour headed north through Aquitaine on the southwest coast of France. From there, the riders would endure a transfer for the final stage into Paris. This was one of those rare Tours that went through neither Normandy nor Brittany. While there were 103.4 kilometers of individual time trialing, there were no team time trials.

Zülle was one of the finest riders in the world when racing against the clock (he became World Time Trial Champion that fall) and he proved it when he won the Prologue on wet, slippery roads, beating specialist Chris Boardman by two seconds. Riis and Indurain were almost tied, being 11 and 12 seconds slower, respectively. Indurain said that he rode carefully, wanting to avoid an accident.

The first five stages, with the exception of stage four, were the playground of the sprinters. Frédéric Moncassin, Mario Cipollini and Erik Zabel, the fastest men in the world, each won stages. Only in stage four were they unable to control events, when a five-man break with a four and a half minute lead stayed away. GAN rider Stéphane Heulot was the highest placed of the escapees and took the lead.

During stage six, in miserably wet and cold weather, Lance Armstrong climbed off his bike. He felt poorly and thought he had bronchitis. He said would concentrate on preparing for the Olympics in Atlanta. His Olympic rides that fall were well below what was expected of a man soaring to the top of cycling. Still, top professional team Cofidis signed him to a $2.5-million, two-year contract. That fall that he was diagnosed with testicular cancer that had metastasized all over his body. We'll pick up his story in 1999.

Before the climbing started, the General Classification after stage six looked like this:

1. Stéphane Heulot
2. Mariano Piccoli @ 20 seconds
3. Alex Zülle @ 4 minutes 5 seconds
4. Laurent Jalabert @ 4 minutes 6 seconds
5. Evgeni Berzin @ 4 minutes 8 seconds
6. Abraham Olano @ 4 minutes 12 seconds
7. Bjarne Riis @ 4 minutes 16 seconds
8. Miguel Indurain @ 4 minutes 17 seconds

The contenders were all clustered at or near four minutes. Heulot and Piccoli would surely be dispatched in stage seven—200 kilometers with the Madeleine, Cormet de Roselend ascents and a final climb to Les Arcs. The stage started collecting its toll almost from the start when Jalabert was dropped about eight kilometers from the summit of the Madeleine, which was enveloped in a thick, wet mist. The elite riders went over the top together with Riis willing to descend a bit faster than the others on the damp, slippery roads. With no company and lots of climbing still to come, he slowed and waited for the others. Heulot stayed with the leaders on the Madeleine but on the Roselend he abandoned, suffering horribly from tendinitis pain in his right knee.

Descending the Roselend, Zülle crashed twice but refused to give up, rejoining the leaders. On the climb to Les Arcs, Leblanc, who was well back in the GC because of a stage six crash, attacked but did not draw a response from the group with Virenque, Riis, Indurain, Olano and Rominger. Indurain himself looked good as he rode the first two climbs, meaning the others were probably again competing for second place.

Then, just near the end of the Les Arcs ascent, about three kilometers from the finish, the unbelievable happened. Indurain was in trouble! The Riis group dropped him, and probably for the first time in anyone's memory, he looked to be suffering. He signaled for a feed by wiggling a phantom bottle. Indurain had ran out of food and was suffering from the "bonk". Other riders took pity on him and gave him food, but it was a shock to all that an otherwise faultless rider would commit such an error. Indurain struggled in over four minutes behind stage winner Leblanc. Zülle, paying the price of his earlier crashes, managed to finish 50 seconds ahead of Indurain. Both Zülle and Indurain had given up so much time in the first hard day in the mountains that the other challengers felt, for the first time in years, the Tour was in play. Berzin became the first Russian in Tour history to wear the Yellow Jersey.

The General Classification after stage seven:

1. Evgeni Berzin
2. Abraham Olano @ same time
3. Tony Rominger @ 7 seconds
4. Bjarne Riis @ 8 seconds
5. Jan Ullrich @ 30 seconds
6. Richard Virenque @ 31 seconds
11. Alex Zülle @ 2 minutes 30 seconds
14. Miguel Indurain @ 3 minutes 32 seconds

That was Saturday. Sunday, July 7, was a 30.5-kilometer uphill individual time trial to Val d'Isère that showed Berzin's ownership of the Yellow Jersey was no fluke. Indurain lost still more ground to Riis and Berzin.

Results of the Val d'Isère time trial:

1. Evgeni Berzin: 51 minutes 53 seconds
2. Bjarne Riis @ 35 seconds
3. Abraham Olano @ 45 seconds
4. Tony Rominger @ 1 minute 1 second
5. Miguel Indurain @ same time
6. Jan Ullrich @ 1 minute 7 seconds

Indurain was now eleventh, 4 minutes, 53 seconds behind the Russian.

Monday was a big day, with the Iseran, Galibier, Montgenèvre and a finishing climb to Sestriere on the menu. The weather wouldn't cooperate; winds clocked at over 100 kilometers per hour blew snow around the summits of the Iseran and the Galibier. This prompted the organizers to shorten the stage to just 46 kilometers, leaving the riders to contest just the Montgenèvre and the final ascent to Sestriere.

Almost from the start, Riis started shooting. Three times he attacked and was brought back. The fourth attack Riis unleashed was too much for the others, and up the Montgenèvre he flew. He crested 20 seconds ahead of the fifteen riders left in the front chase group. On the final climb, Riis extended his lead, while Berzin couldn't take the pace set by Leblanc, Indurain and the others. When the smoke had cleared, Riis was the new leader. He had ridden over the two mountains at an incredible average speed of 39.02 kilometers per hour.

The results of the stage:

1. Bjarne Riis
2. Luc Leblanc @ 24 seconds
3. Richard Virenque @ 26 seconds
4. Tony Rominger @ 28 seconds
5. Miguel Indurain @ same time
14. Evgeni Berzin @ 1 minute 23 seconds

The stage yielded a new General Classification, with Riis' young teammate Jan Ullrich the big surprise. Indurain was in a deep hole that looked hard to climb out of:

1. Bjarne Riis
2. Evgeni Berzin @ 40 seconds
3. Tony Rominger @ 53 seconds
4. Abraham Olano @ 56 seconds
5. Jan Ullrich @ 1 minute 38 seconds
6. Peter Luttenberger @ 2 minutes 38 seconds
7. Richard Virenque @ 3 minutes 39 seconds
8. Miguel Indurain @ 4 minutes 38 seconds

The hardest Alpine climbing was completed; now the riders had to face the Massif Central. The French had hoped Laurent Jalabert, the current world number-one rider, would be the man to wear Yellow in Paris, but he had to abandon during stage ten with gastroenteritis. While stage ten had the Montgenèvre (again), it came too early in the stage for the climbers to stay away. Telekom's Erik Zabel won, giving Telekom firm grips on both the Green and the Yellow Jerseys.

During the next couple of stages, Telekom controlled the race, letting breaks of non-contenders get away but carefully policing any real threats. That left things to be settled in the Pyrenees, which started with stage sixteen and its single climb, an ascent to Lourdes/Hautacam. It was one of the most astonishing stages in racing history. I saw it on television and its defining moment is still clear in my mind. It was a 200-kilometer stage that had the best riders together at the start of the final climb. Laurent Roux—who had been away for 160 kilometers—was still slightly off the front. As soon as the climb began in earnest, Zülle took off like a rocket and steamed right past Roux. Virenque dragged the elite climbers up to him, losing Rominger in the process.

With nine kilometers to go, Riis tested the others with a probing attack and Indurain was able to stay with him. Riis turned the power down a bit. He went again and this time only four riders could stay with him. Then he did what I've never seen before or since. He eased a bit at first as if he were in trouble and rode next to the others, looking carefully at each of them. Convinced that they were all riding at their limits, he went again and shot up the hill, leaving the others to their only option, limiting their losses to the super-strong Dane. He finished alone, almost a minute ahead of Virenque, 2 minutes, 28 seconds ahead of Indurain and almost three minutes ahead of Berzin.

Riis gave what can only be called an unusual performance, giving up position and momentum on a steep mountain surrounded by the finest climbers in the world. Only the most profound confidence could have allowed him to do what he did. And Indurain, who was hoping to celebrate his thirty-second birthday with something more than another time loss to the Dane, was clearly not the man he had been the year before.

A side note about this stage: Part of this dominating Hautacam performance's effect on the others was that Riis seemed to doing a lot of the difficult climbing in the big chainring. Years later, someone with the Danish federation told my friend Larry Theobald that Riis was among the first to use a compact chainset with smaller chainrings. This might have been bit of psy-ops on Riis' part, specifically done to demoralize his opponents.

If there was to be any chance of breaking Riis' grip on the lead, it would have to come in stage seventeen with its seven climbs, of which five were second-category or better: the Soulor, Aubisque, Marie-Blanque, Soudet and the steepest, the Port de Larrau. On the Soudet, Riis kept the pace high and there the first real selection occurred with eleven riders surviving. Festina's Virenque and Laurent Dufaux hammered the remaining riders, putting Indurain out the back door. In the final run-in to Pamplona, Dufaux and Riis escaped, with Dufaux outsprinting the almost invulnerable Dane. With the finish in Pamplona, Spain, Indurain's fans were out in force, hoping for a miracle. The day's route even took the riders past Indurain's childhood home. Despite the results, both the public and Riis paid tribute to the man who had hoped for better that year.

In interviews that afternoon, Riis said that in addition to being directed by Godefroot, he was getting tactical advice from Laurent Fignon. It was Fignon who had spotted young Riis' talents and talked him into changing teams and riding for Guimard's Système U team. With his 1989 narrow loss to LeMond still burning, Fignon told Riis to beware of playing with fate by being content with a one-minute lead. Knowing how such a small margin can evaporate, Fignon advised Riis to continue being aggressive and increase his margin over his competitors. But, after stage seventeen, look who was sitting in second place: his young domestique, a product of the East German sports machine.

1. Bjarne Riis
2. Jan Ullrich @ 3 minutes 59 seconds
3. Richard Virenque @ 4 minutes 25 seconds
4. Laurent Dufaux @ 5 minutes 52 seconds
11. Miguel Indurain @ 15 minutes 36 seconds

Telekom now had the first two places on the podium, the Green Jersey, and in Jan Ullrich, the Best Young Rider.

The only way Riis could miss winning the Tour now was to stumble during the penultimate stage, a 63.5-kilometer individual time trial. Riis didn't stumble but he did falter. Looking tired after three weeks, he turned in a time that was good enough to keep his lead. But young Ullrich stormed the course at 50.452 kilometers per hour, beating second place Indurain by 56 seconds, and his team leader by 2 minutes, 18 seconds. Ullrich's win meant he was one of those rare, titanically talented men, like Greg LeMond, who grow stronger during even the hardest Tour. Indurain praised him with words that, as we'll see in the Armstrong years, had a touch of prophecy, "He is as strong as an ox and his performances in the mountains and in the time-trials makes him a definite winner, as long as he stays fit."

It took Riis eleven years as a pro to attain this level. Since that Tour victory, Riis was dogged by accusations of drug use, accusations that Riis steadfastly denied until 2007. Riis' confession was an important part of the dramatic events that rocked the 2007 Tour. We'll save the details of that episode for later. Ullrich became the first German since Kurt Stoepel in 1932 to make the Tour's podium.

Final 1996 Tour de France General Classification:
1. Bjarne Riis (Telekom): 95 hours 57 minutes 16 seconds
2. Jan Ullrich (Telekom) @ 1 minute 41 seconds
3. Richard Virenque (Festina) @ 4 minutes 37 seconds
4. Laurent Dufaux (Festina) @ 5 minutes 53 seconds
5. Peter Luttenberger (Carrera) @ 7 minutes 7 seconds

Climbers' Competition:
1. Richard Virenque: 383 points
2. Bjarne Riis: 274
3. Laurent Dufaux: 176

Points Competition:
1. Erik Zabel: 335 points
2. Frédéric Moncassin: 284
3. Fabio Baldato: 255

1997 Bjarne Riis set about winning a second successive Tour. He would be over 33 years old, but so were Scieur, Lambot, Zoetemelk, Buysse, Bartali and Pélissier when they won. Only Zoetemelk, of that group, had won in the last 40 years. Although he had abandoned in the Tour of Switzerland, Riis had good results in the spring, including winning the Amstel Gold Race. Moreover, he had a superb team, brimming with good, dedicated talent, such as the previous Tour's second place, Jan Ullrich.

There was one problem. Ullrich, while riding as a domestique for Riis, had finished a close second to the Dane. As the 1996 Tour was drawing to a close and Riis was struggling with exhaustion, Ullrich was stronger than ever, winning the final time trial. I remember the dueling TV interviews early in the summer of 1997 with Riis asserting that Ullrich would ride for him, since Riis was the team captain. Ullrich seemed to demur on that point. Anyone watching could see that the chains of servitude were not as strongly forged as Riis wanted to think they were. After the 1996 Tour and his second place, Ullrich declared that the Tour would be the centerpiece of his career.

Ullrich had turned pro for Telekom late in the 1994 season. He was a shoo-in to ride for Germany in the 1996 Atlanta Olympic Games but chose instead to ride the Tour to help Riis.

There was no rematch with Miguel Indurain. He retired at the end of the 1996 season after becoming the Olympic Time Trial Champion in August and starting but abandoning the Vuelta a España in September. The mantle of leadership of the Banesto team fell to Abraham Olano, who had finished a creditable ninth in the 1996 Tour, 3 minutes, 14 seconds ahead of Indurain.

Other men who could wear Yellow in Paris included Virenque, Zülle, Berzin and a rising Italian star, Marco Pantani, a cycling type whose equal had not been seen since Charly Gaul. He was what the Italians call a *scattista-scalatore*, a man who can explode on a steep climb when the others are already at their limit. This type of climber is the bane of men like Indurain, Ullrich and Hinault, who settle into a rhythm on an ascent and can climb at a high rate, but don't react well to sudden changes of speed. Pantani in 1994, his second year as a pro, scored a second in the Giro and a third place in the Tour. In 1995 it looked as if his career was over after he suffered a terrible crash that shattered his left tibia and fibula. He doggedly set out to prove the doctors were wrong to doubt he would ever walk again, let alone race a bicycle. By early 1997 he was fully competitive. He abandoned the Giro after a crash, but earlier had come in fourth in the Critérium International. Like Gaul, Pantani was a bomb who could go off any time the road went up.

The 1997 Tour was counter-clockwise (Pyrenees first) and designed to give the riders a relentless pounding in the mountains. The hard climbing started in stage nine and continued non-stop through the Massif Central and the Alps. After finishing the Alps in stage sixteen, the riders faced a dose of the Vosges in stage eighteen. Not since the

1976 Tour stacked up all the climbing in nine sequential stages had the mountains been all run up against each other like this. 1976 had produced Lucien van Impe, the finest climber of his age, as the winner. Might the 1997 Tour be as kind to Richard Virenque or Marco Pantani?

Chris Boardman did the job he was paid to do: win the Tour's 7.3-kilometer Prologue time trial, but Jan Ullrich was just two seconds slower and Zülle was only 5 seconds off the winner's pace. So strong were these men who would contend for Yellow, they were almost able to beat the speedy Prologue specialist at his own game.

Sprinters dominated the first four stages, run through Brittany and Normandy, with Italian Mario Cipollini winning the first two. Then Zabel won stage three and Nicola Minali bagged stage four. From the end of the first stage, Cipollini had been wearing the Yellow Jersey.

It was rumored that tension between Riis and Ullrich started with the first stage, where Riis was caught in a massive crash and Ullrich didn't wait to help him get back up to the field. These fast-moving early stages claimed two victims: Zülle fell several times and finally gave up after the fourth stage, and Tony Rominger had to withdraw with a broken collarbone.

Cédric Vasseur went on a 147-kilometer break and won the fifth stage by two and a half minutes, 27 years after his father Alain had won a Tour stage. But unlike the father's win, Cédric's earned the Yellow Jersey.

As the Tour headed for the Pyrenees, the sprinters continued to own the race, with Zabel winning three stages so far. His job was made easier because the ranks of the speedsters were considerably thinned. Belgian Tom Steels was thrown out of the Tour for throwing a water bottle at Frédéric Moncassin while Djamolidine Abdoujaparov was tossed from the Tour for a positive dope test and Mario Cipollini quit with an injured knee.

After stage eight and before the climbing began, the General Classification stood thus:

1. Cédric Vasseur
2. Erik Zabel @ 1 minute 21 seconds
3. Chris Boardman @ 2 minutes 54 seconds
4. Jan Ullrich @ 2 minutes 56 seconds
5. Stuart O'Grady @ 2 minutes 59 seconds

Stage nine, held on Bastille Day, July 14, took the race over the Soulor, Tourmalet, Aspin and up the Col de Val Louron-Azet before descending to Loudenvielle. Virenque was aggressive the entire day while Ullrich stayed with Riis, who was having a difficult start in the mountains. When Virenque attacked on the final climb, Ullrich left Riis behind and had no trouble staying with the Frenchman. Pantani and Laurent Brochard led over the top. Brochard sped off on the descent, but Ullrich was uninterested in Brochard and kept his eye on Virenque. While Ullrich had no trouble marking Virenque, he initiated no attacks of his own, perhaps because Godefroot had not yet decided to give his young rider complete freedom to seek the big win. Vasseur kept the lead for another day. The new General Classification showed that even though the Tour was still young, things had already begun to sort themselves out.

1. Cédric Vasseur
2. Jan Ullrich @ 13 seconds
3. Abraham Olano @ 1 minute 14 seconds
4. Bjarne Riis @ 1 minute 43 seconds
5. Richard Virenque @ same time

Riis continued to tell the press that he was still the team leader. In fact, he was doing well with a good position in the standings, but Ullrich was the stronger rider.

The next day was even harder, 252.5 kilometers that went over the Portet d'Aspet, Port, Port d'Envalira and the Ordino with a final 32-kilometer ascent to Arcalis. Now Godefroot moved to backing Ullrich as his man. On the big last climb, with ten kilometers to go, the now unleashed Ullrich accelerated twice; and with the second acceleration, even the finest pure climbers in the world, Pantani and Virenque, were helpless before his demonstration of power. Ullrich smoothly rolled up the mountain and into the Yellow Jersey.

The stage's results:

1. Jan Ullrich
2. Marco Pantani @ 1 minute 8 seconds
3. Richard Virenque @ same time
4. Francesco Casagrande @ 2 minutes 1 second
5. Bjarne Riis @ 3 minutes 23 seconds

Which yielded a new General Classification:

1. Jan Ullrich
2. Richard Virenque @ 2 minutes 58 seconds
3. Abraham Olano @ 4 minutes 46 seconds
4. Bjarne Riis @ 4 minutes 53 seconds
5. Marco Pantani @ 5 minutes 29 seconds
10. Cédric Vasseur @ 7 minutes 31 seconds

The post-stage comments indicated a new appreciation of Ullrich's extraordinary physical talents. Bernard Hinault thought Ullrich would be able to dominate the Tour for another seven or eight years while Virenque hoped Ullrich wouldn't go on a five-Tour winning streak.

After a rest day, a hilly 55.5-kilometer individual time trial was scheduled. Virenque's ambition was to lose only a couple of minutes in what all thought to be Ullrich's specialty. His director didn't think a loss of four or more minutes would be a surprise.

Virenque was the penultimate starter with Ullrich his three-minute man. Near the finish Ullrich caught and passed Virenque, increasing his lead to 5 minutes, 42 seconds. Virenque had no intention of giving up, saying that with the Alps coming, he would be racing on roads that would play to his advantage.

Stage thirteen presented an opportunity to take a chunk of time out of Ullrich, if that were indeed possible. It was an easterly run from St. Etienne over flattish country with an ascent to the top of l'Alpe d'Huez. The steep slopes of the Alpe might give the climbers a chance to shake Ullrich. Ullrich was in fact dropped, but only by Pantani, and not until the riders were well onto the climb. Making his way through many thousands of fans who formed a narrow defile, Pantani beat Ullrich to the top by 47 seconds. Jean-Paul Ollivier says Ullrich intentionally eased to let Pantani win the stage, being careful not to let the diminutive climber gain too much time. Virenque's hope to challenge Ullrich on the fabled Alpe turned out to be an empty one as he lost another 40 seconds to the German, while Pantani had moved up to third place. At this point Ullrich thought Virenque had lost too much time to be considered a threat to his Tour leadership.

Two climbing stages remained. Stage fourteen started at Bourg d'Oisans, near the bottom of l'Alpe d'Huez, and went over the Glandon and Madeleine before the first-category ascent to Courchevel. The previous evening, after the Alpe d'Huez stage, Virenque had been told that Ullrich was suffering from food poisoning. Virenque's Festina team decided that this would be the perfect time to deploy a set-piece

The major protagonists of the 1997 Tour in the mountains. Pantani leads Virenque and Ullrich.

assault on the ailing German. Once on the Glandon, Festina, which had some good climbers, went all-out. By the time the front group crested the Glandon there were about twenty riders in the main lead group, and Ullrich was isolated without teammates.

In addition to being a fine climber Virenque was a first rate descender and raced down the Glandon aggressively with Ullrich close on his tail. Ullrich was riding a poor-handling, super-light climbing bike that brought him close to grief more than once on the treacherous descent. At the bottom, Ullrich slowed for some help from teammates, while Virenque pressed on alone. Riis now put himself at Ullrich's service, towing him back to Virenque in time for the final climb. There, Ullrich stayed with Virenque no matter how hard the Frenchman tried to get away. Virenque got the stage win, but now he was left with just one climbing stage to take back 6 minutes, 22 seconds.

The day had been a hard one. Frank Vandenbroucke led in a group of 93 riders who finished 36 minutes, 56 seconds after Virenque. This was beyond the time elimination cutoff, and the officials made special dispensation to keep the peloton from being reduced to 62 riders at one stroke.

If there might be a stage where Virenque could recover some time, it was the fifteenth with the Forclaz, Croix Fry, Colombière and the Joux-Plane. It turned out to be a stage without drama. Pantani had been complaining of a sore throat and breathing trouble since the Alpe d'Huez stage and had threatened to abandon. Instead, he broke away on the final climb, and also being a gifted descender, rode off for the stage win while Ullrich kept an eye on Virenque.

With the Alpine stages finished, the General Classification stood thus:

1. Jan Ullrich
2. Richard Virenque @ 6 minutes 22 seconds
3. Marco Pantani @ 10 minutes 13 seconds
4. Bjarne Riis @ 11 minutes 55 seconds
5. Fernando Escartin @ 16 minutes 5 seconds

A chink in the German's armor showed in stage eighteen, the Vosges stage. During the penultimate climb, Ullrich was unable to stay with Virenque. Showing grit, Ullrich regained contact and finished with Virenque in the main group. Now there was only the last time trial the day before the final stage into Paris. Ullrich didn't win it, but after defending his lead since the tenth stage, he could be allowed a second place to Olano, one of the world's finest time trialists. Virenque, tiring from his constant efforts to unseat Ullrich, lost almost another three minutes to Ullrich over those 63 kilometers.

Also tired, having been unwell in the Alps, was Riis. His final time trial was terrible. After first damaging his bike in a fall, he suffered a series of mishaps as his mechanics couldn't get his wheel in correctly. He finally threw his bike to the ground in fury.

While Ullrich worried that something might go wrong in the final stage, nothing did and he won what everyone assumed would be the first in a long series of Tour victories.

To this writer it seemed that Ullrich was well-nigh invulnerable during the 1997 Tour. But Festina soigneur Willy Voet says that the effort of taking the lead during the climb to Arcalis had left him tired and vulnerable. Had Virenque and the rest of the Festina squad systematically and intelligently attacked him in the Vosges when

Ullrich's team was exhausted, Voet thinks the race might have had a different outcome.

Final 1997 Tour de France General Classification:

1. Jan Ullrich (Telekom): 100 hours 30 minutes 35 seconds
2. Richard Virenque (Festina) @ 9 minutes 9 seconds
3. Marco Pantani (Mercatone Uno) @ 14 minutes 3 seconds
4. Abraham Olano (Banesto) @ 15 minutes 55 seconds
5. Fernando Escartin (Kelme) @ 20 minutes 32 seconds

Climbers' Competition:

1. Richard Virenque: 579 points
2. Jan Ullrich: 328
3. Francesco Casagrande: 309

Points Competition:

1. Erik Zabel: 350 points
2. Frédéric Moncassin: 223
3. Mario Traversoni: 198

1998

Always looking for ways to make the Tour interesting as well as profitable for its owners, the organizers had the 1998 edition start in Dublin, Ireland. The Prologue and the first two stages were to be held on the Emerald Isle. Then, without a rest day, the riders were to be transferred to Roscoff on the northern coast of Brittany, followed by a trip inland for a couple of stages before turning directly south for the Pyrenees, then the Alps and finally Paris. This wasn't a race loaded with hilltop finishes, but it did have 115.6 kilometers of individual time trialing. This should have been a piece of cake for Ullrich. In 1997 he had not only won the Tour, he also won the HEW Cyclassics and the German National Championship, both prestigious and important races.

Ullrich was a well-rounded rider who could do anything and deserved his number-two world ranking. But the demands of fame were more than he could handle. His autobiography *Ganz oder Ganz Nicht* (All or Nothing at All) is disarmingly frank and honest about his troubles. After the 1997 Tour he signed endorsement contracts so lucrative he would never have to worry about a paycheck again. Over the winter his weight ballooned. In his words, he had begun 1998 with a new personal best: he weighed more than he had ever weighed in his entire life. He said that after winning the Tour, training was the furthest thing from his mind. He fell into a vicious cycle. He couldn't find good condition and good health. He would lie in bed frustrated, and shovel down chocolate. He would then go out and train too hard for his lapsed form and get sick all over again.

"I can't just train all year long. My life consists of more than cycling," he told himself. Meanwhile, his trainer Peter Becker ground his teeth in frustration seeing his prodigiously talented client riding fewer than 50 kilometers a day.

The results of his winter excess and lack of training were obvious. He attained no notable successes in the spring, but in the new era of Tour specialization, this wasn't necessarily a sign that things were going wrong. Yet in Ullrich's case, there were few signs that things were going right. In March he pulled out of the Tirreno–Adriatico only 30 kilometers into the first stage.

Ullrich had a new foe in the 1998 Tour. Marco Pantani had been a Charly Gaul-type racer who would detonate on a climb and bring himself to a high placing in a single stage. In May, he proved that he could do more than just climb when he won the Giro d'Italia. A sign that Pantani was riding on a new level came in the penultimate stage, a 34-kilometer time trial. He lost only 30 seconds to one of the masters of the discipline, Sergey Gonchar.

During the early 1990s, both Greg LeMond and Andy Hampsten had warned that EPO was changing racing. It was doing just that, and not for the better. Hematocrit is the measurement of the percentage of blood volume that is occupied by red blood cells, the tools the body uses to feed oxygen to the muscles. Normal men of European descent have a hematocrit percentage in the low to mid 40s. It declines slightly as a response to the effects of training and stage racing.

When the body needs more red blood cells, it produces the hormone erythropoietin, which signals the bone marrow to increase red blood cell production. Endurance athletes were now injecting a synthetic erythropoietin (EPO) to increase their hematocrit and realizing astonishing performance improvements.

This is not without danger because as the hematocrit rises, so does the blood's viscosity. By the early 1990s (and perhaps even the late

1980s) those athletes we mentioned earlier who were dying in their sleep were expiring because their lower sleeping heart rates couldn't shove the thick, red sludge through their blood vessels. Until 2004 there was no way to detect synthetic EPO, so the only limit to how much EPO an athlete would use was his willingness to tempt death. A friend traveled with a famous Spanish professional racing team in the 1990s and was horrified to see the riders sleeping while wearing heart monitors hooked up to alarms. If the athlete's sleeping heart rate should fall below a certain number, he was awakened, given a saline injection, and put on a trainer.

In January, 1997, the UCI implemented the 50 percent rule. If a rider were found to have a hematocrit exceeding 50 percent he would be suspended for two weeks. Since there was no test at the time to determine if a rider had synthetic EPO in his system, the two-week suspension wasn't considered a positive for dope, it was to give the rider a rest so he could "regain his health". There were ways for cagey riders to get around the 50 percent limit, but that is a story for 1999.

EPO vastly improved a rider's work capacity (the blood could carry up to 20 percent more oxygen), making it nearly impossible for an undoped rider to win. We've seen EPO use spread: first it was used by Italian racers and then by the rest of the professional peloton.

More evidence of how EPO was queering results: Lance Armstrong was the reigning World Road Champion during the 1994 season. He possessed an incredible engine that was custom-made for difficult, single-day races. Armstrong (who was probably doping with "just" cortisone and testosterone at the time) won no European races in 1994, because it was over the 1993–1994 winter that EPO became widely used in the European peloton.

In 1995, after Eddy Merckx introduced Armstrong to Dr. Michele Ferrari, the American racer traveled to Ferrara, Italy to meet with the Italian doctor with the sulfurous reputation. He would hide the relationship as best he could (there is no mention of Ferrari in his autobiography *It's Not About the Bike*) but Armstrong would use Ferrari as a consultant, trainer and advisor for the rest of his career.

The writing on the wall was easy to read, if anyone wanted to read it. Festina's director Bruno Roussel asked UCI boss Hein Verbruggen to do something about the Italians, who were doping up a storm and winning everything, saying his team would have to either use EPO as well or go out of business. Racing teams are in the business of winning, and if they don't, they lose financial support from their commercial sponsors.

Verbruggen pretended there was no problem, praising the successful dopers for their work ethic while blaming the clean riders for being lazy, failing to train as hard as the Italians. In the mid-1990s, riders on teams not using the drug were tired of getting whipped, tired of watching sprinters climb hills with ease while they were dropped. They demanded EPO from their directors and doctors. As one-time US Postal rider Tyler Hamilton wrote about hematocrit, "It was not just another number; it was *the* number, capable of making the difference between having a chance at winning and not."

Hamilton explained, "The answer is simple: the longer the race, the more doping helps—especially EPO. The rule of thumb: If you don't take any therapy in a three-week race, your hematocrit will drop about two points a week, or a total of six points. It's called sports anemia. Every one percent drop in hematocrit creates a one percent drop in power—how much force you can put into the pedals."

Doping was and is part of the sport. As we proceed through the sordid story of 1998, the actions of the riders to protect themselves and their doping speaks volumes.

And just because a rider has never tested positive for dope doesn't mean that he has been riding clean. Many riders who never failed a drug test were later found by other means to have been cheaters.

The Prologue for the 1998 Tour was on July 11, but the story of the Tour starts in March when a car belonging to the Dutch team TVM was found to have a large cache of drugs. Fast forward to July 8. Team Festina *soigneur* Willy Voet's team car was searched at a customs stop as he was on his way from Belgium to Calais and then on to the Tour's start in Dublin. What the customs people found in his car set the cycling world on fire. Among the items Voet was transporting were 234 doses of EPO, testosterone, amphetamines and other drugs that could have only one purpose, to improve the performance of the riders on the Festina team. For now, we'll leave Voet in the hands of the police, who took him to Lille for further searching and questioning.

In Dublin, Chris Boardman won the 5.6-kilometer Prologue at the scorching speed of 54.2 kilometers per hour. Ullrich momentarily silenced his critics when he came in sixth, only 5 seconds slower. Tour Boss Jean-Marie Leblanc said that the Voet problem didn't concern him or the Tour, the authorities would sort things out. Bruno Roussel, the director of the Festina team, expressed surprise over Voet's arrest.

The first stage was run under wet and windy conditions, with Tom Steels winning the sprint. But the cold rain didn't cool down the Festina scandal. Police had raided the team warehouse and found more drugs, including bottles labeled with specific rider's names. Roussel expressed mystification at these events and said he would hire a lawyer to deal with all of the defamatory things being written about the team. The next day Erik Zabel took over the Yellow Jersey by accruing intermediate sprint bonifications.

When the Tour returned to France on July 14, Casino rider Bo Hamburger became the Tour leader. Meanwhile, Voet had started to talk to the police and explained he was acting on instructions from Festina team management. Roussel said he was "shocked". The next day things got worse for Festina. Roussel and team doctor Eric Rijckaert were taken by the police for questioning. Leblanc continued to insist that the Tour was not involved with the messy Festina events and that if no offenses occurred during the Tour, there would be no action taken to expel Festina.

While the race continued on its way to the Pyrenees with Stuart O'Grady in the lead—the first Australian in Yellow since Phil Anderson and the second ever—the Festina affair continued to draw all of the attention. The UCI suspended Roussel, but both the Andorra-based Festina watch company and Leblanc continued to voice support for the team's continued presence in the race.

July 15 turned the entire cycling world upside-down. Roussel admitted that the Festina team had systematized its doping. His excuse was that since the riders were doping themselves anyway, often with terribly dangerous substances like perfluorocarbon (synthetic hemoglobin), it was safer to have the doping performed under the supervision of the team's staff. Leblanc expelled Festina from the Tour. Several Festina riders, including Virenque and Laurent Dufaux, called a news conference, asserted their innocence and vowed to continue riding in the Tour.

There was still a race going on amid all of the Festina doings, and the first sorting came with the 58-kilometer time trial of stage seven. Ullrich again showed that against the clock he was an astounding rider. American Tyler Hamilton was second but he could come only came within 1 minute, 10 seconds of the speedy German. Another American rider, Bobby Julich of the Cofidis team, turned in a surprising third-place ride, only 8 seconds slower than Hamilton.

The General Classification with two stages to go before the mountains:

1. Jan Ullrich
2. Bo Hamburger @ 1 minute 18 seconds
3. Bobby Julich @ same time
4. Laurent Jalabert @ 1 minute 24 seconds
5. Tyler Hamilton @ 1 minute 30 seconds

Virenque announced the Festina riders would not try to ride the Tour after their expulsion. That took Zülle, World Champion Laurent Brochard, Laurent Dufaux and Christophe Moreau, among others, out of the action.

The Tour then subjected 55 riders to blood tests and found no one with banned substances in his system. The Tour declared this meant the drug use was confined to just a few bad apples. What it really meant was that over decades, riders and their doctors had learned how to dope so the drugs didn't show up in the tests. And, in 1998 there was still no test for EPO. The team doctors protested that the Festina affair was bringing disrepute upon the other teams and their profession. The fans hated to see their beloved riders singled out and thought that Festina was getting unfair treatment. But given the carload of very expensive drugs Voet was ferrying to the Tour, it was apparent the UCI had completely failed in its job to run a clean sport and to protect the health of the young and ambitious athletes it was responsible for.

US Postal soigneur Emma O'Reilly said she had been told by another Postal staff member that her team was worried about being caught that evening by the police who seemed to be everywhere and that they had flushed $25,000 worth of medical products down the toilet of the team's camper van. The whole sport was rotten.

Reflecting upon both the easy ride TVM had received in March when their drug-laden car was found and the new scandal, officials reopened that case.

Stage ten, the long-anticipated showdown between Ullrich and Pantani, had finally arrived. It was a Pyrenean stage, going from Pau to Luchon over the Aubisque, Tourmalet, Aspin and the Peyresourde. With no new developments in the drug scandals, attention could finally be focused back on the sport of bicycle racing. It was cold and wet in the mountains, conditions that can sap a rider's energy as much as or more than a hot day. It was on the Peyresourde that the action finally started. Casino rider Rodolfo Massi was already off the front when Ullrich got itchy feet and attacked the dozen or so riders still with him. Pantani then responded with his own acceleration and in a flash, was gone. At the finish he had closed to within 36 seconds of Massi while Ullrich and nine others, including Julich, came in a half-minute after Pantani. After having lost the lead in stage eight when a break of non-contenders was allowed to go, Ullrich was back in Yellow with Pantani eleventh, 4 minutes, 41 seconds back.

Stage eleven, on July 22, had five climbs rated second category or better with a hilltop finish at Plateau de Beille, an *hors catégorie* climb new to the Tour. As usual, the best riders held their fire until the final ascent. Ullrich punctured just before the road began to bite, but he was able to rejoin the leaders before things broke up. And break up they did when Pantani took off. No one could hold his wheel, leaving Ullrich to chase with little help. Pantani was first to the top with the Ullrich group a minute and a half back. While Pantani had said he was too tired from the Giro to consider winning the Tour, he was slowly closing the gap.

After the Pyrenees and with a rest day next, the General Classification stood thus:

1. Jan Ullrich
2. Bobby Julich @ 1 minute 11 seconds
3. Laurent Jalabert @ 3 minutes 1 second
4. Marco Pantani @ same time

Festina director Roussel, still in custody, issued a public statement accepting responsibility for the systematic doping within the team.

On July 24, the day of stage twelve, the heat in the doping scandal was raised a bit more, if that were possible. Three more Festina team officials, including the two assistant directors, were arrested. A Belgian judge performing a parallel investigation found computer records of the Festina doping program on team doctor Erik Rijckaert's computer.

Rijckaert said all the Festina riders contributed to a fund to purchase drugs for the team. Six Festina team members were rounded up and questioned by the Lyon police: Zülle, Dufaux, Brochard, Virenque, Pascal Hervé and Didier Rous. The scandal grew larger still when TVM manager Cees Priem, the TVM team doctor, and a TVM mechanic were arrested. A French TV reporter said that he had found dope paraphernalia in the hotel room of the Asics team.

How did the riders handle this growing stink? Much as they did when they were caught up in the Wiel's affair in 1962. They became indignant. They were furious that the Festina riders had been forced to strip in the French jail. They were fuming that so much attention was focused on the ever-widening doping scandal instead of the race. In 1962 Jean Bobet had talked the riders out of making themselves ridiculous by striking over being caught red-handed. As Willy Voet wrote, "Suddenly I'd stopped being a masseur and had become a drug dealer. I was being taken for something I wasn't. What had I done that they should treat me like that?"

There was no Jean Bobet to be voice of sanity in 1998. The riders initiated a slow-down, refusing to race for the first 16 kilometers.

On July 25 several Festina riders confessed to using EPO, including Armin Meier, Laurent Brochard and Christophe Moreau. The French newspaper *Le Monde* thought the 1998 Tour should be cancelled. The riders should have been outraged when confronted with the undeniable fact that they were racing against cheaters. Instead, the peloton defended the fraudsters.

As the Tour lurched towards the Alps, the top echelons of the General Classification remained unchanged. Zülle issued a statement of regret admitting his use of EPO, saying what any rational observer should have assumed, that Festina was not the only team doping.

On Monday, July 27, the Tour reached the hard alpine stages. Stage fifteen started in Grenoble and went over the Croix de Fer, Télégraphe and Galibier, with a hilltop finish at Les Deux Alpes. It was generally assumed that if Ullrich could stay with Pantani until the final climb he would be safe, since the climb to Les Deux Alpes averages only 6.2 percent despite an early section of a little over 10percent gradient. Ullrich's big-gear momentum style of climbing would be well suited to this ascent.

Pantani didn't wait for the last climb. On the Galibier, in terrible conditions, he exploded into action, quickly disappearing up the mountain. At the top, with two and a half minutes on Ullrich, he then used his superb descending skills on the treacherous descent to increase his lead on the now isolated German. By the start of the final climb, Pantani had a lead of more than four minutes. On the road to Les Deux Alpes Ullrich's lack of deep, hard conditioning showed. He was in trouble and needed teammates Riis and Udo Bölts to pace him up the mountain.

At the top, the catastrophe (as far as Telekom was concerned) had become complete. Pantani was in Yellow, having taken almost nine minutes out of the German who wobbled in twenty-fifth that day. The new General Classification shows how dire Ullrich's position was:

1. Marco Pantani
2. Bobby Julich @ 3 minutes 53 seconds
3. Fernando Escartin @ 4 minutes 14 seconds
4. Jan Ullrich @ 5 minutes 56 seconds

Stage sixteen was the last day of serious climbing with the Porte, Cucheron, Granier, Grand Cucheron and the Madeleine. Ullrich did better than the day before; he attacked and had only Pantani for company. Since Pantani was the leader with the luxury of riding defensively, he let Ullrich do all the work. If Ullrich couldn't drop Pantani, he could at least put some distance between himself and Julich and Escartin, which he did. Pantani and Ullrich came in together, with Ullrich taking the stage victory in Albertville. Julich and Escartin followed the duo by 1 minute, 49 seconds. Ullrich was back on the Podium:

1. Marco Pantani
2. Bobby Julich @ 5 minutes 42 seconds
3. Jan Ullrich @ 5 minutes 56 seconds
4. Fernando Escartin @ 6 minutes 3 seconds

Ullrich said he knew how good Pantani was, but given how difficult the Giro's final week had been, the German had expected Pantani to be too tired to compete for Yellow in July.

Wednesday, July 29, stage seventeen: the remaining riders staged a strike. They started by riding slowly and at the site of the first intermediate sprint they sat down. After talking with race officials, some took off their numbers and then they all rode slowly to the finish in Aix-les-Bains with several TVM riders lined up in the front holding hands to show the solidarity of the peloton. Along the way, the Banesto, ONCE and Risso Scotti teams abandoned. The Tour organization voided the stage results, allowing those riders who were members of teams that had not officially abandoned to start on Thursday.

Why all this anger now? First of all, the day before, drugs were said to have been found in a truck belonging to the Big Mat-Auber 93 team, though the next day this turned out to be untrue. Then the entire TVM squad was taken into custody and the team's cars and trucks were seized. They, like the Festina team, were handled roughly by the police, sparking outrage from those riders not yet in jail.

Thursday, July 30, stage eighteen: Kelme and Vitalicio Seguros now quit the Tour. That meant all four Spanish teams were out. Rodolfo Massi, winner of stage ten and wearer of the King of the Mountains jersey, was taken into custody, though a French court would clear him of all charges two years later. At the start of the stage, there were only 101 riders, down from 189 starters.

Friday, July 31, stage nineteen: TVM abandoned the Tour. ONCE's team doctor Nicolás Terrados was also put under arrest after a police search found drugs on the team bus that later turned out to be legal. The situation was as Willy Voet had described it, "…drug taking is to top-level sport what batons are to a majorette troupe: you rarely find one without the other."

Some riders argued that if they had taken drugs, it was without their knowledge, that they had submitted to injections from team doctors and soigneurs, trusting that the substances were legal. Voet says this is untrue. He wrote, "They have always known exactly what they are taking. Probably better than I used to: because they know their own bodies, how they react, what moment to put something in, what drug to take, and what dose. Riding as a professional means being professional on every level."

Ullrich's last chance to take the Tour was the 52-kilometer stage twenty time trial. But Pantani was too good; he gave up only 2 minutes, 35 seconds to Ullrich. That sealed the Tour for Pantani. Ullrich acknowledged that he had not taken his preparation for the Tour seriously and had paid a high price for his lack of discipline. He promised to work harder in the future and not repeat his mistakes.

Of the 189 starters, 96 finished.

None of the Festina riders had triggered a positive drug test. Writer David Walsh summed up the 1998 Tour disgrace when he wrote, "It may be forgotten what bike Marco Pantani rode when winning the '98 Tour de France, but it is widely known that Voet drove a Fiat." Pantani was on a Bianchi.

Final 1998 Tour de France General Classification:

1. Marco Pantani (Mercatone Uno): 92 hours 49 minutes 46 seconds
2. Jan Ullrich (Telekom) @ 3 minutes 21 seconds
3. Bobby Julich (Cofidis) @ 4 minutes 8 seconds
4. Christophe Rinero (Cofidis) @ 9 minutes 16 seconds
5. Michael Boogerd (Rabobank) @ 11 minutes 26 seconds

Climbers' Competition:

1. Christophe Rinero: 200 points
2. Marco Pantani: 175
3. Alberto Elli: 165

Points Competition:

1. Erik Zabel: 327 points
2. Stuart O'Grady: 230
3. Tom Steels: 221

Pantani became the first Italian to win the Tour since Felice Gimondi in 1965 and became the seventh man to do the Giro-Tour double, joining Coppi, Anquetil, Merckx, Hinault, Roche and Indurain.

The drug busts of 1998 did little to alter rider and team behavior. There would be more drug raids and more outraged screams from the riders, but the police knew what they were dealing with. The riders had formed a conspiracy to cheat and break the law. Their code of silence was nothing more than a culture of intimidation that enabled the riders to do what they had done for more than 100 years, take drugs to relieve their pain, allow them to sleep and improve their performance. Their anger at the treatment they received from the police arose from a sense of entitlement, that using drugs was something that they could and sometimes had to do.

French law allows the police to detain a person for 24 hours and question him extensively without letting him see a lawyer. ONCE rider

Neil Stephens was interrogated from 2 PM to 1 AM. The riders were jailed under detestable conditions designed to break a prisoner's will. But their complaint that they should be treated in a dignified manner and that perhaps the police should wait until after the Tour before continuing their investigation was silly. Crime was being committed and it is the duty of the police to stop it.

The French Cycling Federation decided to do what it could to clean up the doping mess by setting up longitudinal testing of French riders. Instead of looking for specific instances of doping, shifts in a rider's blood values would trigger a suspension. It must have been effective because big wins by French riders immediately became far less common. The French had unilaterally disarmed.

five

1999–2005

The Armstrong years: Lance Armstrong focuses on winning the Tour and dominates it as no other rider in its history.

1999 Over the winter, more allegations of drug use surfaced. The only conclusion possible was that the situation was probably even worse than the 1998 Tour had led one to believe. After stage five in the 1999 Giro, the Italian National Sports Council/Olympic Committee (CONI) subjected sixteen riders from three different teams to a new comprehensive blood and urine test. Two of the riders tested positive for dope but no penalties were levied. The riders, as they have been since the start of testing, were incensed. Marco Pantani, Oscar Camenzind, Laurent Jalabert and Mario Cipollini held a press conference, declaring that if the national sports organization intruded any further upon the testing regimen, which had heretofore been the responsibility of the toothless and compliant UCI, they would stop racing. Of that group of four, Pantani was not the only rider who would have drug problems. In 2004 Camenzind retired after receiving a two-year suspension for EPO, while in 2013 Cipollini was the object of accusations of drug use during his cycling career. Also in 2013, Jalabert, when confronted with positive tests for EPO from 1998, made a statement saying he couldn't say for sure whether or not he was doped, but never took banned substances knowingly.

Before the start of the penultimate stage of the 1999 Giro, Pantani was awakened for a blood test. His hematocrit of 52 percent resulted in his being ejected from the Giro after he had won four stages and was leading the General Classification. The cycling world was stunned. Pantani's *squalificato* seemed to affect many racing fans far more deeply than the Festina scandal, probably because of Pantani's powerfully heroic image. He had triumphed over a horrible accident and saved the Tour during its great crisis. Pantani partisans made accusations of a conspiracy.

In fact, the riders have long known how to foil a hematocrit test. When they knew they would be subjected to a test (and they often got advance warning) they would take saline injections, aspirin, guzzle liters of water, and in no time their hematocrits were within the legal limit. Some teams even provided the riders with small centrifuges so that they could "manage" their own red blood cell concentration. For reasons that have never been fully explained, Pantani did not take measures before the test to bring his hematocrit down or somehow believed he was below the limit. The Italian was too devastated by the disqualification to consider riding the Tour.

In mid-June the Tour announced that the TVM team along with several individuals (including ONCE manager Manolo Saiz and rider Richard Virenque) would not be allowed to participate in the Tour. But missing from the list of banned riders were the Festina and Mercatone Uno teams and Marco Pantani. Later, the UCI overruled the Tour organization and insisted that Virenque and Saiz be allowed to participate.

And the doping in pro racing continued, with four riders tossed from the Tour of Switzerland for high hematocrits.

In June, Ullrich announced he had injured his knee in the Tour of Germany and would not be able to compete in the Tour. With Pantani and Ullrich out, the press cast about for a favorite. At the top of many lists were Pavel Tonkov (1996 Giro winner), Alex Zülle, Fernando Escartin, and Ivan Gotti (1997 and 1999 Giro winner).

And there was another rider to consider. He had withdrawn from the 1996 Tour and could not ride the 1997 and 1998 editions as he endured surgery and chemotherapy to cure what should have been a life-ending case of testicular cancer. In the fall of 1997 he announced the resumption of his professional cycling career. That return was bumpy with intermittent successes and withdrawals.

But by mid-1998 he had returned to the top ranks of professional cycling with a win in the Tour of Luxembourg, fourth in the Vuelta and fourth in the World Time Trial Championships. Late in 1998 this rider, Lance Armstrong, told Greg LeMond of his plans to win four Tours. LeMond was encouraging, but later, knowing the kind of rider Armstrong had been, he told his wife Kathy, "I feel sorry for him. He's delusional."

But in 1999 Armstrong won the Prologue of the Dauphiné Libéré and narrowly lost a two-up sprint to Michael Boogerd in an important classic, the Amstel Gold Race. Lance Armstrong had returned.

When Armstrong was diagnosed with cancer he had just inked a $2.5-million, two-year contract with the French team Cofidis. Kevin Livingston, Bobby Julich and Frankie Andreu had also moved from Motorola to Cofidis. Cofidis promised to support Armstrong even if Armstrong couldn't fulfill his contract. Later, saying that he did not hear much from Armstrong (who was busy trying to stay alive), Cofidis boss François Migraine sent Alain Bondue to the U.S. to find out exactly what was happening and to renegotiate the contract.

Cofidis offered Armstrong a new contract for 1998 at a reduced salary of $180,000 plus performance incentives. Migraine thought that he had a deal with Armstrong at this point. Saying he had only an offer from Cofidis, Armstrong searched for a new team that would offer better terms. He signed with the American US Postal squad for $200,000 plus performance incentives and it was in their blue kit that he was riding the 1999 Tour.

While Armstrong was not on many possible Tour winner lists, Miguel Indurain had said that he thought Armstrong had a serious chance of winning the Tour.

With Pantani, Ullrich and Riis not starting, 1999 was one of those rare years in which there were no former Tour winners.

Fearing that after the 1998 debacle, doping would get more intense scrutiny this Tour, several French teams asked their riders to stop doping in advance of the Tour. Feeling lots of other teams would continue using EPO during the Tour, US Postal didn't slacken its use of performance-enhancing drugs.

Armstrong and Bruyneel felt US Postal's doctor, Pedro Celaya, wasn't aggressive enough with the dope, and winning in that era was impossible without chemical help. Celaya was released and replaced with Luis Garcia del Moral, a skilled and enthusiastic dispenser of performance-improving drugs, legal or not.

The Tour started in the Loire Valley town of Le-Puy-du-Fou and went clockwise up to northeastern France followed by a big transfer to begin the Alps on stage nine. After the Alps came the Massif Central, the Pyrenees and then the final time trial on the penultimate stage.

A bad start. Before the Tour begins, all the riders undergo a public medical examination. Armstrong was worried about bruises on his upper arm from injections and had them covered with makeup. Why worry about something so banal since riders get many perfectly legal injections? Different medicines are injected in different parts of the body and vaccinations, insulin, EPO and growth hormone are put into the upper arm. One could presume Armstrong was not concerned about being questioned about getting a series of vaccinations. Bruyneel was so worried that several of his riders had hematocrits close to 50 that they had to take salt tablets and drink as much water as they could to get their numbers down.

Armstrong showed that he had now mastered the first component of a successful Tour rider, time trialing. Though he had never shown any particular talent for riding against the clock before his return from cancer, he won the 6.8-kilometer Prologue, beating Zülle by 7 seconds.

The Tour was upended in the second stage. Starting at Challans, southeast of Nantes, the riders were sent to the island of Noirmoutier before returning to the mainland and a finish in St. Nazaire. They had to negotiate the Passage du Gois, a narrow four-kilometer road that is normally submerged, except at low tide. Even when exposed, it is slippery and dangerous. Worse, there was a hard crosswind. Making the situation even more dire, the entire peloton reached the constricted road intact. Armstrong, Olano, Escartin, Tonkov, Virenque and Julich were in the front of the pack when it made the treacherous crossing and emerged unscathed. But behind them was chaos. A crash took down Zülle, Gotti and Boogerd, who were badly delayed in the mess. The teams that had managed to get clear without damage now drove the lead group hard. The Zülle group came in 6 minutes, 3 seconds after Tom Steels led in the lucky 70 front riders. At one terrible, early blow, Zülle, a wonderfully talented but accident-prone rider, was out of contention. By earning time bonuses, Estonian sprinter Jaan Kirsipuu was the leader, with Armstrong only 14 seconds back in second place.

Tailwinds during stage four allowed the riders to set a new record for the fastest road stage, 50.356 kilometers per hour, beating Johan Bruyneel's 1993 record.

As they raced over the flatter roads of Northern France, the fast finishers enjoyed the time in the Tour when they could strut their stuff. While there were several fine sprinters in the 1999 Tour, the finest, far and away, was Tuscan Mario Cipollini. By the end of stage seven he had done what no postwar rider had done, win four stages in a row. One must go back to 1930, when Charles Pélissier was the reigning speed demon, to find the last four-consecutive-stage winner.

The next day, in Metz, the riders faced a 56.5-kilometer individual time trial. Then the mountains had to be conquered. The Tourmen would come out of hiding after the early stages when their primary job was to avoid trouble.

During the time trial, misfortune struck two important contenders. Bobby Julich crashed and had to abandon and Abraham Olano also fell, losing so much time that the man who started after him, Armstrong, caught and passed him. Armstrong's victory in the stage was substantial. Zülle, who came in second, could come within only 58 seconds of him.

The General Classification before a rest day to be followed by the first Alpine stage:

1. Lance Armstrong
2. Christophe Moreau @ 2 minutes 20 seconds
3. Abraham Olano @ 2 minutes 33 seconds
4. Stuart O'Grady @ 3 minutes 25 seconds

After his time trial performance, the remaining big question was whether Armstrong could climb with men like Zülle, Escartin and Virenque. Before he came down with cancer, he couldn't. The ninth stage would certainly settle the question with the Tamié, Télégraphe, Galibier, Montgenèvre and a hilltop finish at Sestriere. It was a cold, wet day with hail on the descent of the Montgenèvre. Virenque escaped on the Galibier and was the first over the Montgenèvre, but he couldn't hold his lead. On the descent, Escartin and Gotti took wild chances, building a gap of about thirty seconds. During the final climb, a group of five of the best, including Armstrong and Zülle, were together. With less than seven kilometers to go, Armstrong jumped away, catching and passing Escartin before going right on by a dumbfounded Gotti. With the encouragement of Bruyneel coming over his earphone, Armstrong rode ever harder and farther away from his chasers. The only credible threat coming up the road was from Zülle, but he couldn't close the gap. Armstrong crossed the line alone, 31 seconds ahead of Zülle and two and a half minutes ahead of Virenque. Armstrong, never before a formidable climber, had made it look easy. TV commentator Paul Sherwen said Armstrong had bridged to the leaders, "…like they were standing still."

The new standings:

1. Lance Armstrong
2. Abraham Olano @ 6 minutes 3 seconds
3. Christophe Moreau @ 7 minutes 44 seconds
4. Alex Zülle @ 7 minutes 47 seconds

Armstrong was in an ideal position. He had a healthy lead, one so large that he could ride economically and keep his dangermen in sight. He didn't have to waste energy on offensive exploits. In fact, he had been in control since the crash in stage two, but insecurity about Olano's climbing abilities had prevented US Postal from relaxing. Armstrong adopted exactly that conservative strategy for the next day's stage to the top of l'Alpe d'Huez. With over six minutes in hand, he planned to avoid disaster and let the others try to take the race from him. At the base of the Alpe, the fast pace caused Olano to drop off. Part way up the climb, Italian Giuseppe Guerini took flight with Tonkov hot on his tail. Tonkov couldn't catch Guerini but he was just dangerous enough that Armstrong went after him. Near the top, a photographer got in Guerini's way and the two went down. Guerini jumped back on his bike and was able to regain his momentum and won the stage, beating Tonkov by 21 seconds. The Armstrong/Zülle group came home within four seconds of Tonkov. The day's net result with Olano's two-minute time loss was that Armstrong now had a lead of 7 minutes, 42 seconds over the still second-placed Spaniard. Zülle was third, 5 seconds behind Olano.

Armstrong had taken on a new responsibility, enforcing the riders' code of silence regarding drugs. Earlier in the season, rider Jean-Cyril Robin had quite reasonably complained that there were now two

178

racing speeds, the French with their longitudinal testing and the rest of the world, which raced faster. Armstrong told Robin that it would be best if he didn't say things like that.

During the Tour, Christophe Bassons, an enormously talented rider who was trying to race without dope, was writing a column about the difficulties of riding clean. David Walsh recounted the on-the-road conversation between Bassons and Armstrong:

"You know, what you're saying to the journalists, it's not good for cycling."

"I am simply saying what I think. I have said there is still doping."

"If that's what you're here for, it would be better if you returned home and found some other kind of work."

"I'm not going to leave when I haven't changed anything. If I have things to say, I will say them"

"Ah, fuck you."

The angry peloton, with Armstrong as its *patron*, soon drove Bassons out of the Tour and out of the sport.

After the Massif Central there remained three stages that could affect the Tour's outcome: the two days in the Pyrenees and a 57-kilometer time trial. If the pure climbers wanted to take back time from Armstrong, time was running out.

Stage fifteen had six big mountains: the Ares, Menté, Portillon, Peyresourde, Val Louron, and a hilltop finish at Piau Engaly. The attacks started with the first mountain pass. Virenque, Brochard and others shattered the peloton. In the now-reduced pack, US Postal kept up a warm pace, since most of the breakaways presented no threat to Armstrong's lead. But when Escartin escaped on the Portillon, Armstrong himself went after him. Escartin went again on the Peyresourde and began to work with riders who were already off the front. Escartin dropped them and soloed in for the win. Virenque and Zülle, who had been able to withstand Armstrong's attacks, beat the Yellow Jersey to the finish by 9 seconds.

For Armstrong and his team, the final kilometers of that stage represented a rare episode of support failure. Running out of food, Armstrong got the hunger knock, explaining his inability to stay with Virenque and Zülle. Again Olano had been the main casualty, this day coming in seven minutes after Escartin, losing his second place.

That afternoon rumors of a possible Armstrong dope positive became more solid when the French paper *Le Monde* announced that a drug test had shown Armstrong to be using a corticosteroid. It is possible twenty or thirty other riders might also have been positive for the same drug, and the results may have been suppressed because the Tour did not want a repeat of 1998. Banned since 1978 except when prescribed by a doctor, corticosteroids, like EPO, had previously been undetectable.

Before the Prologue it had been announced that a test for corticosteroids (widely used) had been developed, and it would be implemented the next day. This sent a shock through the peloton. But it seemed the riders weren't going to get hammered by the testers. It looked like everyone was going to be allowed to skate, thereby avoiding a second consecutive Tour drug scandal.

The source of Armstrong's drug positive was explained to be the skin cream containing minute traces of cortisone that he had been using to fight saddle sores, which the Armstrong camp claimed had been cleared by the Tour authorities for use.

Or, maybe there was something else afoot. On the form that all professionals must submit, listing all the prescription drugs they are taking, Armstrong wrote that he was taking nothing and he reiterated that position in a news conference before the positive was known. When *Le Monde*'s reporters questioned US Postal about the positive, Armstrong's soigneur Emma O'Reilly said there was panic in the team before the team had its doctor write a back-dated prescription.

This wasn't the first time a back-dated prescription had been used to save a racer with a doping positive. After winning the 1997 World Championships, Laurent Brochard was positive for Lidocaine, inadvertently a part of the mix of drugs he was taking. A prescription was ginned up and given to the UCI (which Willy Voet says turned a blind eye to the messy affair) and Brochard kept his rainbow jersey. How many other times this has happened, we'll never know.

The cycling press could not believe that Armstrong could emerge from cancer and an earlier career of stage-racing mediocrity to become this extraordinary Tour racer. When a *Le Monde* reporter at a press conference asked Armstrong why the drug was not on his exemption form, Armstrong replied, "Mr. *Le Monde*, are you calling me a liar or a doper?" That was the end of the corticoid questioning, but a pattern for future inquiries about Armstrong's possible drug use was set: outrage, name calling, bullying and coercion became the usual tools to protect the Armstrong franchise, while the press, afraid of losing access to riders, failed to ask hard questions.

Stage sixteen would be tough, with the Aspin, Tourmalet, Soulor and the Aubisque. With a descent into Pau after the final climb, this stage would not give the pure climbers a chance to gain time should Armstrong falter. While there was action off the front, Armstrong stayed focused on his rivals. On the Tourmalet, a hard acceleration by Postal rider Kevin Livingston caused Virenque to lose contact. The main worries were Escartin and Zülle, who both seemed indefatigable and strong. At the top of the Tourmalet, Escartin attacked and took Zülle and Armstrong with him. Escartin tried again on the Soulor and again Armstrong stayed with him. In the final drive to Pau, Armstrong let the others go, not needing to fight for a stage win or further tire himself.

After the Pyrenees the General Classification stood thus:

1. Lance Armstrong
2. Fernando Escartin @ 6 minutes 15 seconds
3. Alex Zülle @ 7 minutes 28 seconds
4. Laurent Dufaux @ 10 minutes 30 seconds
5. Richard Virenque @ 11 minutes 40 seconds

Armstrong chose to ride the stage nineteen time trial to win, rather than playing it safe and riding carefully. He beat Zülle by 9 seconds. The main loser of the day was Escartin, who, not unexpectedly, lost gobs of time and his second place. David Walsh noted that before his cancer, Armstrong had been a very consistent time trialist, losing about six minutes during each of the long time trials of the 1993, '94 and '95 Tours. Now he was the master of riding against the clock, and the Tour was now Armstrong's.

Like the 1971 Tour (when Ocaña crashed out while in Yellow), this is a Tour that invites speculation. What if Zülle had not crashed in the Passage du Gois and lost six minutes? If Zülle had not lost that time, then perhaps Armstrong would not have had the luxury of a defensive ride. It would surely have been a closer Tour that might have gone another way.

The imposition of longitudinal testing of French riders clearly put that country's cycling at a low ebb. The highest-placed Frenchman was Virenque, eighth at 17 minutes, 28 seconds. For the first time since 1926 (the era of Belgian Tour hegemony), no Frenchman had won a single stage. The highest-placed French rider in 1926 was eighth as well.

In an era crazy with drug use, I noted that the French had unilaterally disarmed. Writers lashed the French for being lazy, for no longer being hungry for victory. Feeling smug and superior, Americans laughed at them. The French riders complained about cycling's two speeds, the slower speed raced by the more rigorously tested French versus the winning speeds ridden by the rest of the professional peloton. No good deed goes unpunished.

Final 1999 Tour de France General Classification:
1. Lance Armstrong (US Postal): 91 hours 32 minutes 16 seconds
2. Alex Zülle (Banesto) @ 7 minutes 37 seconds
3. Fernando Escartin (Kelme) @ 10 minutes 26 seconds
4. Laurent Dufaux (Saeco) @ 14 minutes 43 seconds
5. Ángel Casero (Vitalicio Seguros) @ 15 minutes 11 seconds
6. Abraham Olano (ONCE) @ 16 minutes 47 seconds

Climbers' Competition:
1. Richard Virenque: 279 points
2. Alberto Elli: 226
3. Mariano Piccoli: 205

Points Competition:
1. Erik Zabel: 323 points
2. Stuart O'Grady: 275
3. Christophe Capelle: 196

2000 The lead-in to the expected rematch between the three active Tour winners began to look like a soap opera. While Armstrong studiously trained and reconnoitered the important roads of the 2000 Tour (Armstrong was far from unique in this, Anquetil and other successful Tour riders had also familiarized themselves with Tour roads in advance), Ullrich and Pantani suffered trouble-filled pre-seasons. In January, Pantani announced that both the Giro and the Tour would be the centerpieces of his 2000 season. He spent part of the winter training in the Canary Islands while Ullrich escaped the cold of his native Germany by training in Mallorca. As the early season races drew nigh Pantani postponed his racing start, feeling that things were not "tranquil". He was dealing with the stress of returning to racing after a long absence. After his 1999 Giro expulsion, Pantani had simply hung up his bike. Moreover, Pantani was harassed by a judicial investigation into his 1999 Giro disqualification. In Italy there is a crime called "sporting fraud" and Pantani was potentially culpable. Later an inquiry would also be opened into the circumstances of his 1995 Turin crash and the disturbingly high hematocrit the hospital technicians found him to have.

In March, Armstrong pulled out of Paris–Nice, but this was due to a case of bronchitis. Ullrich rode the Tour of Murcia and finished ninety-third, almost an hour behind winner David Cañada. The message from the T-Mobile team regarding Ullrich was *alles ist in ordnung* (everything is in order). Late in February, Pantani entered and retired from the Tour of Valencia. Ominously, his doctor started talking openly about stress and indications that Pantani's mental condition wasn't ideal.

When March came, Ullrich entered Tirreno–Adriatico. He was so fat his team managers tried to keep photographers away from him. The team said he had to lose about three kilos while other racers said Ullrich had to shed at least ten kilograms to be competitive. By late March, Pantani was still postponing the restart of his racing season. Meanwhile Armstrong was testing his legs in spring races and getting top placings.

On May 12, after a long series of yes-and-no signals about his riding the Giro, Pantani announced he would indeed ride the Italian national tour. Ullrich attempted to ride the Midi Libre, but abandoned after a poor time trial and a shelling in the mountains. Pantani finished the Giro an hour down and in twenty-eighth place. He had helped his friend and teammate Stefano Garzelli win, showing improving form in the Giro's latter stages with a second place in the mountainous stage nineteen.

At the end of June it looked like Ullrich might have pulled a rabbit out of his hat when he was fifth in the Tour of Switzerland, finishing only two minutes behind the winner, Oscar Camenzind, and beating Virenque by 15 seconds.

In the drug war, a test for synthetic EPO had been developed, but because there were too many questions about its reliability, it was decided not to implement it for the Tour, though it was used in the 2000 Sydney Olympics. Once the test was finally put into use, the riders were ready. Instead of a couple of large injections of the drug during the Tour, a closer-spaced series of micro-doses kept the level of EPO below the detectable threshold. As the testing became more sensitive, riders went from injecting EPO in the skin to get a slow release of the drug, to putting it directly in the vein to reduce "glow time", the period when the drug was at a detectable level. And when that became insecure, the riders went back to good, old-fashioned blood doping. Some were crazy enough to do homologous blood doping (blood from another person, as performed by the US Olympic cycling team at the 1984 Los Angeles Olympics), but the riders getting the best medical help performed autologous doping (reinjecting an athlete's own saved blood). Blood would be extracted just after the Dauphiné and then reinfused a couple of times during the Tour, usually during rest days. It gave a potent boost to performance and at that time, was still undetectable.

At the Tour's start Armstrong looked to be rock-solid, while his two main challengers were really unknown quantities. It was hard to know exactly what kind of fitness they would bring to the race.

The other important character in this, the Millennium Tour, was the route. The Prologue (now called stage one) was lengthened to 16.5 kilometers, perhaps putting it out of reach of the short-distance men who specialized in doing well in the usual pure-power start-up to the race. For the first time since 1995, the Tour included a team time trial. Armstrong said he relished the addition, as well he should, given the strength of his team. The team time trial also favored ONCE with Olano and Jalabert, and Ullrich's Telekom squad. There was only one extended individual time trial, 58.5 kilometers coming on the third-to-last stage. To honor the Tour's history, stage fourteen would go over the historic route that took in the Allos, Vars and Izoard—last used in 1949 and won by Gino Bartali. After the Pyrenean stages, there was only a short respite before three days of climbing in the Alps, a schedule that would favor the climbers.

The Tour started at the Futuroscope amusement park where David Millar squeaked past Armstrong by 2 seconds to take the first Yellow Jersey. Signaling fair-enough form, Ullrich was fourth, 14 seconds slower than Millar. Marco Pantani, however, showed his Tour build-up was far from ideal, finishing a lowly 136th, giving away two minutes to his rivals.

Millar kept the lead until the stage four team time trial. Spanish racing had certainly changed from the early days when Spaniards were only interested in and good at climbing. By the 1990s Spaniards were among the most accomplished time trialists in the world. Jalabert's and Olano's well-oiled ONCE machine won the stage, even after a 20-second penalty for using a team car to tow a dropped rider back to the team. Jalabert was in Yellow, a fact that did not displease the other contenders since it was assumed Jalabert could be depended upon to dutifully give up the lead in the mountains, and yet his powerful team would be responsible in the short term for controlling the race.

During the team time trial Armstrong showed that he had more to learn about being a team leader. As Postal crossed a giant bridge over the Loire River, Armstrong took a hard pull. With the steep ramp up the big bridge combined with the day's strong crosswinds, Armstrong's efforts blew the team apart. They struggled to get back together, but it showed that even a team that has done the most careful practice and preparation can make serious mistakes in the heat of competition. Even with that error, US Postal came in second, 26 seconds behind ONCE.

Pantani's Mercatone Uno team did better than expected, losing only 3 minutes, 14 seconds while finishing ninth on the day. For Zülle, it was almost like 1999 again. His Banesto team lost four minutes, time that would be almost impossible for him to take back from Armstrong. Again, his Tour was almost over before it started. Escartin was in even worse shape: his Kelme squad came in fourteenth, almost five minutes slower than ONCE. A Tour win for him was out of reach.

The General Classification after the stage four team time trial:
1. Laurent Jalabert
2. David Cañada @ 12 seconds
3. Lance Armstrong @ 24 seconds
4. Abraham Olano @ 35 seconds
5. Viacheslav Ekimov @ 43 seconds

Jalabert kept the lead for only two days. Early in stage six, while he was taking a "natural break", a group of twelve riders rolled off the front and quickly formed a smooth working group. ONCE, Pantani's Mercatone-Uno team and US Postal chased, but the twelve men would not be denied, preserving a lead of over seven minutes to the finish. ONCE showed they had higher ambitions than Jalabert's temporary stint in Yellow by shutting down their own pursuit efforts after only a few kilometers. The man with the good fortune to have snagged the Yellow Jersey after the day's successful break was one of the oldest men in the peloton, 36-year old Alberto Elli of Telekom. Now, how much energy would Telekom expend defending Elli's lead? Telekom's manager predicted that Elli would keep the Yellow Jersey until the climbing started in stage ten.

The next day Telekom did work, but not too hard, to defend Elli's lead when French rider Christophe Agnolutto went on a successful solo break (the first one for a French rider in the Tour since 1997). Near the end of the stage when Elli joined an escape, US Postal jumped to the front of the pack and shut it right down. They didn't want things to get out of hand. The next day, when Dutch rider Erik Dekker slipped away, it was again US Postal with help from Mercatone Uno who did the work of keeping the gap manageable.

At the end of stage nine, with the Pyrenean climbing coming the next day, here was the General Classification. Most of the higher-ranking riders were members of that stage six break:

1. Alberto Elli
2. Fabrice Gougot @ 12 seconds
3. Marc Wauters @ 1 minute 15 seconds
4. Pascal Chanteur @ 2 minutes 56 seconds
14. Laurent Jalabert @ 5 minutes 40 seconds
16. Lance Armstrong @ 5 minutes 54 seconds

Stage ten, with its hilltop finish at Lourdes/Hautacam, went 205 kilometers with the Col de Marie-Blanque, the Aubisque and then its little brother the Soulor before the final ascent. The day started with cold, rainy weather, which Armstrong preferred and Ullrich loathed. It had now rained during nine out of the first ten stages. Kelme rider Javier Otxoa went over the Aubisque first, followed by eight riders in a group containing Escartin and Virenque. About three minutes further back were the main contenders, Armstrong, Zülle, Ullrich and Pantani among them.

Very soon into the final ascent, Pantani attacked, taking Armstrong and Zülle for company. Then, in a move that astonished all who were watching, Armstrong jumped and dropped first Zülle and then… Pantani.

He then went after the others up the road catching all but Otxoa, who was too far ahead. Armstrong came charging in just 42 seconds after Otxoa had won the stage, followed by the tossed, gored and now former contenders. Ullrich's poor preparation had cost him dearly; he finished thirteenth, four minutes behind Otxoa. Pantani was twenty-first, almost six minutes back. In a single day, on a single climb, Armstrong had checkmated his rivals. Christophe Moreau, grasping for any silver lining, thought Armstrong might be vulnerable because his team wasn't as strong as in 1999.

The new General Classification:

1. Lance Armstrong
2. Jan Ullrich @ 4 minutes 14 seconds
3. Christophe Moreau @ 5 minutes 10 seconds
4. Marc Wauters @ 5 minutes 18 seconds
5. Peter Luttenberger @ 5 minutes 21 seconds

Stage twelve, which finished at the top of the dreaded Mont Ventoux, was held on the thirty-third anniversary of Tom Simpson's death in 1967. US Postal was well-prepared. During the rest day, Tyler Hamilton says he, Armstrong, and Livingston were each given a pint of their saved blood.

At Mont Ventoux's base, Hamilton and Livingston set such a hot pace Zülle, Escartin and Moreau were soon dropped. So much for Moreau's being able to take advantage of the weaker 2000 Postal team. Soon only seven riders remained: Armstrong, Ullrich, Pantani, Virenque, Roberto Heras, Santiago Botero and Joseba Beloki. Pantani was yo-yoing on and off the back as Ullrich drove the group hard.

After the riders climbed above the tree line, with about five kilometers to go, Pantani surprised everyone by moving to the front and delivering a series of hammer blows, the last of which was more than the others could withstand. The man called "the Pirate" was gone. But it wasn't over. Armstrong took off after Pantani and caught him.

Pantani wins the Mont Ventoux stage.

Armstrong wrote that as they fought the hard winds together near the top, he tried to encourage Pantani by yelling, "*Vince*", for victory. Pantani misunderstood and thought Armstrong said "*Vitesse*" [go faster], trying to antagonize him. At the top, Armstrong said he eased to let Pantani have the win (and that's exactly how it looked), the usual practice when the Yellow Jersey has worked with another rider to gain time on his rivals.

Baxter

Pickup By:
6/11/2021

dclibrary.org

Baxter

Pickup By:
6/11/2021

.

.

.

.

.

In a post-stage press conference Armstrong said he had indeed let Pantani win the stage, enraging and humiliating the Italian, who possessed a terrible inferiority complex. Pantani lashed back, saying that he was the better rider and had fairly won the sprint. The dispute hit its nadir when Armstrong crudely called Pantani "*Elefantino*", a nickname Pantani detested because it made fun of his prominent ears.

Despite the sordid little episode, Armstrong had delivered another punch to the peloton's solar plexus. The new General Classification:

1. Lance Armstrong
2. Jan Ullrich @ 4 minutes 55 seconds
3. Joseba Beloki @ 5 minutes 52 seconds
4. Christophe Moreau @ 6 minutes 53 seconds
5. Manuel Beltran @ 7 minutes 25 seconds

After a transition stage came stage fourteen, the one designed to commemorate the 1949 Tour. Here Kelme unleashed a storm of aggression and was rewarded with a solo stage win by Santiago Botero, but the upper echelons of the General Classification remained unchanged.

When reviewing the final two Alpine stages, one can't help but think of that famous advice from Machiavelli's *The Prince*: "And let it be here noted that men are either to be kindly treated or utterly crushed, since they can revenge lighter injuries, but not graver." This is often paraphrased as "Never do an enemy a small harm." Pantani had been stewing over Armstrong's post-Ventoux tail-twisting and was bent on revenge. Remember, *vendetta* is an Italian word.

Stage fifteen was a climber's dream, going from Briançon over the Galibier and the Madeleine, with a hilltop finish at Courchevel. From the early kilometers on the Galibier, there had been another Kelme-inspired break. The chasing peloton stayed together until the ride up to Courchevel. Pantani blasted off early in the final ascent and only Armstrong could go with him. Then Pantani attacked again and Armstrong couldn't resist. Pantani rocketed up the road, seeking the early breakaways, catching them all and soloing in for a victory that could not be considered a gift of any sort. Armstrong came in 50 seconds after Pantani, but had benefited from the Pirate's move as he distanced himself still farther from Ullrich and Beloki.

Stage sixteen had four big mountains: the Saisies, Aravis, Colombière and the Joux-Plane. Armstrong expected another war to erupt between Pantani and himself. War he may have expected, but he probably didn't count on the mutually assured self-destruction that ensued. On the Saisies, with over 120 kilometers of hard alpine racing remaining, Pantani was gone, searching for earlier breakaway riders, leaving Armstrong's Postal team no choice but to chase. Pantani made common cause with Escartin and a teammate of Virenque's, Pascal Hervé. The trio still had a lead when they went over the Colombière, but by the descent's end, the Postal-led peloton had caught them. On the Joux-Plane Pantani faded and lost contact with the Armstrong group. It looked like Pantani's second day of trying to punish Armstrong had failed.

But the hours of relentless chasing had taken their toll on the others. The front of the peloton was down to four riders, Ullrich, Armstrong, Virenque and Heras. Armstrong had felt so good during the chase, he rolled right through the feed zone and didn't pick up any food, a failing he later called, "a feeble mistake, an unthinkable one for a professional."

On the climb, with twenty kilometers to go, Armstrong couldn't keep up with the others, and ten kilometers from the summit he got the hunger knock. For the second year in a row, Armstrong had failed to eat enough and found himself in trouble. Seeing the opportunity, Ullrich started to pound up the hill for all he was worth. Armstrong, through an enormous effort of will, got himself up the final kilometers of the Joux-Plane and then hurtled down the other side of the mountain into Morzine. Because Ullrich did not have anywhere near the form that won the Tour in 1997, he couldn't capitalize on Armstrong's failure. Virenque won the stage but Armstrong lost only a minute and a half to Ullrich. Armstrong was blessed in the quality of his competition.

Pantani's team said he spent the evening suffering from gastric problems (more likely he was out of gas after those difficult stages), and The Pirate retired from the Tour the next day. Armstrong was deeply resentful of Pantani's kamikaze attack and said that those agonizing minutes on the Joux-Plane were the worst in his cycling career. Despite his own loss, Pantani had fulfilled beyond his wildest dreams his desire to "blow the stage up".

Armstrong still had a solid lead and had only the final time trial to worry about. Starting in Freiburg im Breisgau, Germany, and finishing in Mulhouse, France, Ullrich had the home-court advantage in the 2000 Tour's only long individual time trial. Armstrong, with a 5 minute, 37 second lead, didn't have to worry about losing the Tour to Ullrich unless misfortune struck, always a possibility in a time trial where the rider is going all-out. Over the first ten kilometers, Ullrich was able to stay even with Armstrong, who started last, 3 minutes after the German. Then, after getting approval from Bruyneel, Armstrong upped the tempo and slowly forged a lead as he passed the crowds lining the road, estimated at one million strong. At the end, Armstrong had gained his only stage win of the 2000 Tour, beating Ullrich by 25 seconds. It was the second fastest time trial in Tour history at 53.986 kilometers an hour, just off the 1989 mark of 54.545 set by LeMond.

The Postal team was the only squad to finish the Tour complete.

There was another race going on, the race for the Points Leader's Green Jersey. Telekom's Erik Zabel took his fifth *Maillot Vert*.

Final 2000 Tour de France General Classification:
1. Lance Armstrong (US Postal): 92 hours 33 minutes 8 seconds
2. Jan Ullrich (Telekom) @ 6 minutes 2 seconds
3. Joseba Beloki (Festina) @ 10 minutes 4 seconds
4. Christophe Moreau (Festina) @ 10 minutes 34 seconds
5. Roberto Heras (Kelme) @ 11 minutes 50 seconds

Climbers' Competition:
1. Santiago Botero: 347 points
2. Javier Otxoa: 283
3. Richard Virenque: 267

Points Competition:
1. Erik Zabel: 321 points
2. Robbie McEwen: 203
3. Romāns Vainšteins: 184

2001

The year started with what by now had become the usual press releases from Telekom, explaining that Ullrich's preparation was on track. He did train harder than the year before, but in March he was still responding to questions about his weight. By riding the Giro for training in May and June he came to the Tour with his best form since 1997.

Armstrong was tired of the constant sniping from the French press who, not unreasonably, questioned how an indifferent climber and time trialist had come to dominate a drug-fueled peloton. He lashed out in January, "It's unfortunate that the biggest bike race in the world is in France. We're living in an era of French innuendo and insinuation." This was churlish. It is the French culture and the French people who made possible the great race that Armstrong devoted himself to winning.

A French investigation into allegations of US Postal doping resulted in testing of archived urine and blood samples from the 2000 Tour. Limited by the state of drug detection at the time, they were found to be clean.

Tyler Hamilton wrote that Armstrong told him he had tested positive in the Tour of Switzerland, "You won't fucking believe this, I got popped for EPO. No worries, dude. We're gonna have a meeting with them. It's all taken care of." Armstrong and Bruyneel did have a meeting with the drug lab director. Incredibly, the lab created a terrible conflict of interest by later accepting $125,000 from Armstrong, said to help buy more testing equipment. The UCI denied any *quid pro quo* and says that while Armstrong's samples were suspicious, they did not trigger a doping positive.

Pantani, buffeted by three judicial investigations into doping allegations, competed in Spain in February but was unable to finish a race. With Pantani's physical and mental form highly questionable and with one of his teammates having been caught earlier in the season with a high hematocrit, the Tour decided against inviting his Mercatone Uno team. Sprint specialist Mario Cipollini's Saeco team also did not get an invitation, partly because one of its riders was also under the cloud of doping problems. After 1998 and 1999, the Tour wanted nothing to do with any potential scandal. The result was a Tour heavily weighted toward French teams.

For all the talk of cleaning up the sport, doping in the pro peloton continued unabated. Italian police raided the riders' hotel rooms during the San Remo stage in the Giro. The huge cache of drugs seized and the substantial number of renowned riders involved generated a complete crisis within Italian cycling. There could be no doubt. The peloton was both highly drugged and skilled at evading doping controls.

The 2001 Tour went clockwise, the first climbing coming with the stage six entry into the Vosges. After two days in the Alps, the riders faced three Pyrenean stages, all of which had hilltop finishes. At 3,453 kilometers and twenty stages, the 2001 Tour was a little shorter than the 2000 edition.

Christophe Moreau, 2000's fourth place, won the 8.2-kilometer Prologue in Dunkirk with Armstrong third, only 4 seconds slower, and Ullrich fourth at 7 seconds.

During the early stages as the Tour veered into Belgium, the racing was aggressive. After stage three, Credit Agricole rider Stuart O'Grady was in Yellow. A capable rider, O'Grady could be expected to hold the lead at least until the mountains. The question was, should the team defend the lead and burn themselves out or leave O'Grady to the wolves in order to work for Bobby Julich who was third in 1998? When a break went clear in stage four, Credit Agricole was fortunate enough to have Julich in it. That put the onus on US Postal and ONCE to bring back the break, which they did. With a team time trial the next day, neither of the chasing squads wanted to expend the energy, but Julich was too dangerous to be allowed any freedom.

The team time trial was a surprise. Credit Agricole won it, thereby giving O'Grady more time in Yellow. US Postal had a disaster when Christian Vande Velde slipped on the wet road, taking down Roberto Heras. The team waited for them, losing about a minute and a half.

After the stage five team time trial, with the Vosges showing up the next day, here was the General Classification:

1. Stuart O'Grady
2. Jens Voigt @ 26 seconds
3. Bobby Julich @ 27 seconds
4. Igor Gonzalez de Galdeano @ 57 seconds
5. Joseba Beloki @ 1 minute 7 seconds
15. Lance Armstrong @ 1 minute 53 seconds
19. Jan Ullrich @ 2 minutes 20 seconds

When the race hit the hilly, twisty roads of stage seven, Credit Agricole director Roger Legeay did the unexpected. Instead of defending O'Grady's lead, he sent another of his riders, Jens Voigt out on a break, a move which succeeded brilliantly. Voigt was now the *maillot jaune.*

The next day, stage eight, set the Tour on its ear. Bike racing strategy is almost always a gamble. In a three-week stage race, the director wants to minimize the work his team does. When a break goes, he has to calculate whether or not to put his men at the front and start chasing. If the break is filled with riders who could not possibly be threats to the overall win, they may be allowed to get away through the inaction of the top teams. Or, the sprinters' teams may decide the break must be retrieved in order to bring the race together for a mass romp at the end. Early in stage eight a group of fourteen riders escaped, eventually amassing a lead of thirty-five minutes. In that break were O'Grady and journeyman riders Andrei Kivilev and François Simon. O'Grady was back in Yellow and some good but unspectacular riders had made the coming two weeks of the race interesting.

The new General Classification:

1. Stuart O'Grady
2. François Simon @ 4 minutes 32 seconds
3. Bram de Groot @ 21 minutes 16 seconds
4. Andrei Kivilev @ 22 minutes 7 seconds
24. Lance Armstrong @ 35 minutes 19 seconds

The stage was set for the first day in the alps, and what a day it was, with three *hors catégorie* climbs: the Madeleine, the Glandon and a hilltop finish at l'Alpe d'Huez. Telekom attempted to win the stage by keeping the speed high. Over the Madeleine, Armstrong moved back from the front of the peloton, looking uncomfortable and out of sorts. Catching Armstrong on a bad day, Telekom kept the pace fast. On the Glandon, Armstrong continued to look distressed. At the base of the Alpe with the Telekom riders burning watts at a prodigious rate, Postal rider José Luis Rubiera suddenly went full gas with Armstrong, Ullrich and Kivilev on his wheel. After Rubiera did his work and pulled off, Armstrong did a probing acceleration, slowed a moment and looked back, staring at the others, particularly Ullrich. Comfortable that they couldn't go with him, he then rocketed away for a solo win. Momentarily stunned, Ullrich re-found his momentum and finished second, almost two minutes later.

The entire stage with Armstrong's supposed trouble during the first two climbs had been a US Postal tactical set-piece. They knew the team directors all had televisions in their cars. If Armstrong were in difficulty, the other teams would know and act upon that information. Telekom was suspicious, but the opportunity to take back time from Armstrong doesn't occur every day. The chance had to be seized.

Things had changed dramatically, though Armstrong voiced regret that Kivilev, an excellent rider, had been allowed to gain so much time.

1. François Simon
2. Andrei Kivilev @ 11 minutes 54 seconds
3. Stuart O'Grady @ 18 minutes 10 seconds
4. Lance Armstrong @ 20 minutes 7 seconds
5. Joseba Beloki @ 21 minutes 42 seconds
6. Christophe Moreau @ 22 minutes 21 seconds
7. Jan Ullrich @ 22 minutes 41 seconds

The next day was a time trial up to Chamrousse. Armstrong won the stage and took another minute out of Ullrich and six from Kivilev. While Simon was still in Yellow, Kivilev now had only two minutes on Armstrong.

Stage twelve came after a rest day and transfer to Perpignan for the Pyrenees stages. With a first-category hilltop finish, the twelfth leg was exactly the kind of stage that Armstrong had used over and over to gain time on his rivals. During the final climb to Plateau de Bonascre, the best of this Tour—Armstrong, Ullrich and Kivilev—were off the front. Ullrich attacked, dropping Kivilev. Near the top Armstrong jumped and took another 23 seconds out of Ullrich, bringing him to within 28 seconds of Kivilev. Simon remained in Yellow with a nine-minute lead on Armstrong.

The 2001 Tour's Queen Stage was the 194-kilometer stage thirteen, featuring six highly rated climbs and ending with the *hors catégorie* ascent to Pla d'Adet/St.-Lary-Soulan. Jalabert had decided to forego chasing the General Classification, trying instead for the polka-dot jersey. At kilometer 25 he escaped with a small group of non-contenders. Over each of the peaks, starting with the Col de Menté, Jalabert was first. By the time he reached the final climb he was exhausted and cramping, but the French crowds were delirious with joy over his exploit.

Back in the peloton on the Peyresourde, Telekom upped the tempo. The increase in speed was too much for Simon who had dreamed of hanging on to his Yellow Jersey for another day. Along with most of the peloton, he was shelled. With the lead group down to just 23 riders, Ullrich accelerated, taking along only Armstrong. Together they crested the Peyresourde, but on the descent Ullrich misjudged a corner and went tumbling off the road. Armstrong waited for Ullrich, who was unharmed by the fall.

The delay allowed for a small regroupment, with Postal riders Heras and Rubiera, along with Beloki and Kivilev, rejoining them. Rubiera set a fiery pace up the final climb and after he pulled off it was again down to Armstrong and Ullrich. They traded hard pulls but Ullrich couldn't quite match Armstrong's speed. Sensing the moment was at hand, Bruyneel radioed Armstrong to deliver the *coup de grace*. Armstrong put Ullrich to the sword, leaving him an even minute behind. Armstrong had taken the Yellow Jersey.

The new General Classification:

1. Lance Armstrong
2. Andrei Kivilev @ 3 minutes 54 seconds
3. François Simon @ 4 minutes 31 seconds
4. Jan Ullrich @ 5 minutes 13 seconds
5. Joseba Beloki @ 6 minutes 2 seconds

The final day in the mountains took in the Aspin, Tourmalet and final ascent to Luz Ardiden. At the base of this last climb, remnants of an early break were caught by the fast-moving Postal-led peloton. With about ten kilometers to go, Basque rider Roberto Laiseka exploded out of the Armstrong/Ullrich group and raced for the summit. Meanwhile, Postal riders Heras' and Rubiera's prodigious efforts chewed up what was left of the front chasing group until only Ullrich and Armstrong remained. Together they raced for the top. As they crossed the line, Ullrich reached out for Armstrong's hand and they crossed together. The Tour was effectively over and Ullrich was acknowledging as much. Armstrong said that he was in the best condition of his life. It showed.

There was now only the 61-kilometer individual time trial in stage eighteen to affect the results. Ullrich was tiring and lost 1 minute, 39 seconds to Armstrong, the stage winner.

There was still one battle left to fight, the ownership of the sprinters' Green Jersey. Zabel had won the penultimate stage, leaving Stuart O'Grady with 212 points and Zabel with 210. This would be settled on the Champs Élysées. Czech rider Jan Svorada won the final sprint, but Zabel was second and O'Grady third, giving Zabel a record sixth Green Jersey. Armstrong had joined the elite group of Louison Bobet, Jacques Anquetil, Eddy Merckx and Miguel Indurain as a winner of three consecutive Tours.

Final 2001 Tour de France General Classification:

1. Lance Armstrong (US Postal): 86 hours 17 minutes 28 seconds
2. Jan Ullrich (Telekom) @ 6 minutes 44 seconds
3. Joseba Beloki (ONCE) @ 9 minutes 5 seconds
4. Andrei Kivilev (Cofidis) @ 9 minutes 53 seconds
5. Igor Gonzalez de Galdeano (ONCE) @ 13 minutes 28 seconds

Climbers' Competition:

1. Laurent Jalabert: 258 points
2. Jan Ullrich: 211
3. Laurent Roux: 200

Points Competition:

1. Erik Zabel: 252 points
2. Stuart O'Grady: 244
3. Damien Nazon: 169

Armstrong had not only won the Tour de France three times, he was becoming rich and powerful. When Greg LeMond learned that Armstrong was working with Michele Ferrari, he voiced doubts about Armstrong's achievement, "If it is true, it is the greatest comeback in the history of sport. If it is not, it is the greatest fraud."

Armstrong reacted with fury, telling Frankie Andreu, "I'm going to take him down."

LeMond got a series of calls from cycling industry heavyweights as well as threats from Armstrong's attorneys, all intended to scare LeMond into issuing a retraction. US Postal backer Tom Weisel told LeMond, "You know, what you're saying about Lance isn't good for you. You better be careful."

Overwhelmed and frightened about the financial security of his family, LeMond did issue a retraction. Others who spoke out would also feel the strong arm behind Armstrong's brass knuckles.

The tentacles of Armstrong's organization seemed to be everywhere. UCI boss Hein Verbruggen allowed both the UCI and himself to be compromised by letting Jim Ochowicz, founder of the 7-Eleven (later morphing into Motorola) team, start a brokerage account for him. Investment banker Tom Weisel, the main backer of Armstrong's team, began managing some of Verbruggen's assets in 2001. This was a clear conflict of interest that made many wonder if Armstrong, who almost always seemed to know in advance when a surprise dope test was coming, got special treatment in return.

2002

In January Ullrich traveled to the Tour of Qatar where his *directeur sportif* Rudy Pevenage said, "Jan is in excellent shape." But on February 12 the bad news started. Ullrich began to feel pain in his knee and was told to reduce his training. In March, Ullrich's knee was still inflamed and it was announced that Ullrich would be out of action for three weeks. The injury stubbornly refused to heal and plagued him all spring. In early May he announced that with his knee problem keeping him from racing, he could not ride the Tour. At one stroke, the road to Armstrong's fourth win was made smoother.

Later in May Ullrich had knee surgery. In June, after an out-of-competition drug test that all professional riders are subject to, Ullrich was found to have amphetamines in his system. It wasn't a matter of doping for performance enhancement, Ullrich wasn't racing. He had been at a clinic undergoing rehabilitation of his knee and was growing depressed over his inability to race. At a disco he had taken Ecstasy, which is a chemical relative of amphetamine.

Even after the operation, Ullrich's knee still wasn't getting better and he feared he might never race again. Following the drug positive, the German cycling federation suspended Ullrich for six months.

He then underwent a second knee operation, and this time he was able to resume training. Because of the suspension he could not begin racing until March 23, 2003. With no rider on the team capable of competing for the General Classification, Telekom was forced to build its team around Erik Zabel and his quest for a seventh Green Jersey.

While Ullrich was imploding, Armstrong's preparations were monitored by Michele Ferrari. Armstrong's US Postal team was thought to be stronger than even the year before.

At 3,276 kilometers, the 2002 Tour was the shortest since 1905. With twenty stages and the usual two rest days, the average stage length was down to 163 kilometers. It was run counter-clockwise, starting in Luxembourg, heading west across Normandy and Brittany, the transferring to Bordeaux to ride south to the Pyrenees before hitting the Alps. To keep up the suspense, several of the key mountain stages were saved for the end.

That Armstrong's preparation had been on target showed when he won the 7-kilometer Prologue. The highly technical course pushed the pure-power specialists like David Millar off the podium.

The first stage gave an excellent example of what happens when a strong rider takes an intelligent chance. After Rubens Bertogliati took a flier, the sprinters looked at each other to see who would chase him down. The answer was no one, and Bertogliati became the new Yellow Jersey. Zabel allowed Bertogliati only two days in the lead. With the time bonuses accrued in the intermediate sprints and a second place in stage three, Zabel was in Yellow for the first time since 1998.

Stage four was the team time trial, which ONCE had made their specialty for years. Riding a nearly flawless race, they beat US Postal by 16 seconds, making Igor Gonzalez de Galdeano the leader. ONCE director Manolo Saiz finally had a true General Classification contender in Joseba Beloki, who was third in 2001. Does he defend the Yellow Jersey for as long as possible and tire his team or does he save his team's energy to help Beloki?

The General Classification after stage four:

1. Igor Gonzalez de Galdeano
2. Joseba Beloki @ 4 seconds
3. Lance Armstrong @ 7 seconds
4. Jörg Jaksche @ 12 seconds
5. Abraham Olano @ 22 seconds

Saiz was a banal, unadventurous tactician. He answered the question early the next day when a group of moderately dangerous men broke away. ONCE quickly went to the front and shut it down. Saiz seemed to be conceding the race to US Postal, preferring to keep the Yellow

Jersey he had for as long as possible rather than work for the Yellow Jersey he might keep in Paris.

As the Tour raced at near-record speed across northern France, ONCE worked with the sprinters' teams to keep the race together, sparing US Postal the trouble of policing the peloton. With the exception of a minor crash in stage seven that cost Armstrong 27 seconds, coming into the first individual time trial US Postal had made no mistakes and had suffered no serious misfortune.

Colombian rider Santiago Botero surprised everyone when he beat Armstrong by 11 seconds in the 52-kilometer time trial while Gonzalez de Galdeano rode well enough to preserve his lead, riding just 8 seconds slower than Armstrong. Writers looking for something to hang a story on started speculating that perhaps Armstrong might not be invulnerable. The answer would come over the next few days.

The General Classification stood thus:

1. Igor Gonzalez de Galdeano
2. Lance Armstrong @ 26 seconds
3. Joseba Beloki @ 1 minute 23 seconds
4. Sergey Gonchar @ 1 minute 35 seconds
5. Santiago Botero @ 1 minute 55 seconds

Stage eleven, 158 kilometers long, went over the Aubisque before ascending part way up the Tourmalet to the La Mongie ski station. Jalabert was trying to repeat his capture of the polka-dot jersey, and on the Aubisque he joined and then dropped a small escaping group. Back in the peloton, Postal set the pace. On the Aubisque the speed was tolerable and by the time the bunch reached the base of the Tourmalet it was still about 70 men strong. It was here that Postal lit the fuses of their two rockets, Rubiera and Heras. First Rubiera pulled, setting a pace so fast, superb riders like Gonzalez de Galdeano, Moreau and Julich were dropped. With about five kilometers to go, Heras took over. Only Armstrong and Beloki could hold the small Spanish climber's wheel as they zoomed past the tiring Jalabert. Near the end of the ascent, Armstrong jumped to take the sprint with Beloki seven seconds back. Armstrong said that it took all he had to hold Heras' wheel.

After La Mongie the General Classification stood thus:

1. Lance Armstrong
2. Joseba Beloki @ 1 minute 12 seconds

3. Igor Gonzalez de Galdeano @ 1 minute 48 seconds
4. Raimondas Rumšas @ 3 minutes 32 seconds
5. Santiago Botero @ 4 minutes 13 seconds

The next day, stage twelve, with its climbs over the Menté, Portet d'Aspet, Core, Port with a final ascent to Plateau de Beille, was almost a carbon copy of the day before. Jalabert went off looking for King of the Mountains points while US Postal kept the peloton working hard all day. On the final climb, again Rubiera started things going, then Heras took over and rocketed up the mountain. This time Armstrong escaped farther from the finish and took a full minute out of Beloki, the only other rider who could stick with Heras.

Two days later, the stage fourteen climb to the top of Mont Ventoux showed that even the Postal team was vulnerable. Rubiera performed his usual set-up in the earlier part of the ascent. Heras, having a bad day, couldn't help, leaving Armstrong isolated. ONCE tried to take advantage of the situation and sent Beloki on the attack. Armstrong not only closed up to him but countered, leaving the rest of the peloton behind. Farther up the road, Virenque had been in a break for almost 200 kilometers, eventually shedding all of his fellow escapees. He was now, alone, laboriously turning the pedals, struggling to stay ahead of the hard-charging Armstrong. Virenque hung on to win the stage, but Armstrong closed to within two and a half minutes.

Beloki had a terrible day on the baking hot slopes, losing almost two minutes. Even worse, Botero, who had been thought a likely contender for the podium, lost about thirteen minutes. The tactics so far employed by the Spanish, who had at the beginning of the Tour had proclaimed that it would be "wide open" race, full of Iberian aggression, had been amateurish. Rather than trying to put US Postal on edge, sending riders up the road, attacking at unexpected times, trying to isolate Armstrong, they had been content to sit on the Postal team, trying to hang on for dear life on the final climb. Of course it was there, at each hilltop finish, that Postal would set the stage ablaze, destroy the peloton and release Armstrong for another win.

After a rest day the Tour faced three Alpine stages. The first one, with its final climb to Les Deux Alpes didn't change the top rankings. Botero, who had failed so dramatically on Mont Ventoux, rode to a solid solo victory.

In many ways, stage sixteen with the Galibier, Madeleine and La Plagne climbs was just like the Pyrenean stages. Dutchman Michael Boogerd went off on a solo adventure at around the hundredth kilometer of the 180-kilometer stage. Early in the final climb Rubiera again lit the jets, leaving most of the remaining peloton in the dust. Five kilometers from the finish, Armstrong took off. He didn't catch Boogerd, but he put another half-minute between himself and Beloki.

The General Classification with the climbing completed:
1. Lance Armstrong
2. Joseba Beloki @ 5 minutes 6 seconds
3. Raimondas Rumšas @ 7 minutes 24 seconds
4. Santiago Botero @ 10 minutes 59 seconds
5. Jose Azevedo @ 12 minutes 8 seconds

Armstrong won the 50-kilometer time trial, avenging his stage nine loss. He was fortunate in the misfortune of the man who came in second. Raimondas Rumšas was ahead of Armstrong at the first time check, but his aero bars came loose, surely costing more than the 53 seconds he finished behind Armstrong. That put the icing on the cake, giving Armstrong four consecutive Tour wins, joining Anquetil (1961–1964), Merckx (1969–1972) and Indurain (1991–1995).

Again, the ownership of the Green Jersey came down to the final day in Paris where Australia's Robbie McEwen denied Erik Zabel his seventh sprinter's crown.

Final 2002 Tour de France General Classification:
1. Lance Armstrong (US Postal): 82 hours 5 minutes 12 seconds
2. Joseba Beloki (ONCE) @ 7 minutes 17 seconds
3. Raimondas Rumšas (Lampre) @ 8 minutes 17 seconds
4. Santiago Botero (Kelme) @ 13 minutes 10 seconds
5. Igor Gonzalez de Galdeano (ONCE) @ 13 minutes 54 seconds

Climbers' Competition:
1. Laurent Jalabert: 262 points
2. Mario Aerts: 178
3. Santiago Botero: 162

Points Competition:

1. Robbie McEwen: 280 points
2. Erik Zabel: 261
3. Stuart O'Grady: 208

Edita Rumšas, wife of third-place finisher Raimondas, had been following her husband throughout the Tour. She was arrested near Chamonix in the French Alps on the final day of the Tour, her car filled with various pharmaceuticals that one could only assume were doping products. She was taken to jail where she insisted the drugs were simply medications for her mother. While Mr. Rumšas was accepting the award for third place in the Tour in Paris, he knew that his wife was in custody. Edita spent several months incarcerated while her husband avoided going back to France where he could be arrested. In 2006 the courts gave both husband and wife suspended sentences for importing illegal substances. Though tested several times, Rumšas never failed a drug test during the 2002 Tour. Tyler Hamilton's conclusion from the episode, given the substantial cache of drugs Edita was ferrying, was that "…it was possible to microdose a boatload of drugs during the Tour and not get caught."

The following year, in the sixth stage of the 2003 Giro, Rumšas was positive for EPO. Because Rumšas passed all drug tests given to him during the Tour, his 2002 third place remains on the books. In fact, all of the dope tests in the 2002 Tour were negative leading to the declaration that the riders were clean and free of drugs. As noted by Willy Voet—whose misfortune precipitated the 1998 Festina scandal—the Tour's 141 drug tests merely showed that the riders remained far ahead of the testers.

2003 In September of 2002, still under a racing suspension for his Ecstasy drug use, Ullrich announced that when his contract with Telekom expired at the end of 2002 he would not re-sign, preferring to find another team and a new beginning. Autumn is usually a difficult time to begin looking for a new team as most of the squads have their budgets for the following racing season settled as well as their rider contracts. This late in the year, few teams have the spare funds to take on a new and extremely expensive rider. But a man who can compete for a Grand Tour victory is a rare commodity, so the bidding was spirited, with Bjarne Riis' CSC team trying to bring him on board. Also Kelme, Phonak and the financially troubled Coast squad of Germany bid for his services. He came close to an agreement with a new team to be sponsored by the German Postal Service, but the deal was nixed when a new business plan for the German Post Office called for firing 40,000 postal employees. The politics of giving Ullrich a rich contract to ride bikes while tens of thousands of people were put out on the street had Ullrich looking elsewhere.

The sagest advice anyone gave during this troubled time in Ullrich's life came from Armstrong, who advised Ullrich to ride for Riis for free. Armstrong understood that the difficult-to-coach rider needed direction, not more money. Riis said that if Ullrich came to ride for him, his free and easy ways were over, he would ride and train under Riis' strict instructions. Ullrich said that since Riis wasn't exactly forthcoming about how much money he could pay, he chose Coast amid complaints from many of Coast's riders that they had not been paid their salaries for the second half of the 2002 season. Some surmised Ullrich chose Coast over Riis because Ullrich wanted no part of the structured life and training that Riis had promised.

The UCI had put Coast under a set of strict requirements regarding rider payments. On March 6, unhappy with Coast's foot dragging and endless excuses, the UCI suspended the team. Later in March, the suspension was lifted but Zülle, fed up with the turmoil and loss of racing time in March, bolted for the Swiss Phonak team.

In early May, Coast was suspended again. Team bike supplier Bianchi, who had assisted the Coast team with increased funding so that they could afford Ullrich, took over the team and its UCI license, thereby assuring Ullrich (and Bianchi bikes) a place in the Tour.

Meanwhile super-sprinter Mario Cipollini's Domina Vacanze squad had not been invited to the Tour. Noting that Cipollini always left the Tour before the high mountains and that he had never finished a Tour, Leblanc justified his decision by noting that the 2003 Tour's mountains started after only a week of racing. Cipollini would surely ride only a few stages before abandoning.

It again looked to be a rematch between the troubled Ullrich and the perfectly prepared Armstrong. Armstrong rode a lighter pre-Tour race schedule but showed good form when he won the Dauphiné.

While that win was by 72 seconds over Iban Mayo, it was a pyrrhic victory because he had to go deep into his reserves to win. At the start of the Tour he was still tired. One of Armstrong's coaches said that they should have let Mayo win the Dauphiné.

Ullrich seemed to being doing better than had been predicted. Though overweight, he was fifth in the Tour of Germany.

Telekom's new Tour GC man was Alexandre Vinokourov, who had just won the Tour of Switzerland. Gilberto Simoni, victor in the recently completed Giro, boasted that with his superior climbing prowess, he would be able to take the Tour.

This was the Centenary Tour. One hundred years before, Georges Lefèvre and Henri Desgrange had cooked up the idea of a stage race on the roads of France to help promote the ailing circulation of their paper, *L'Auto*. To commemorate the Tour's centennial at the October presentation of the 2003 route, 22 of the 23 living Tour winners were gathered together: Ferdy Kübler (1950), Roger Walkowiak (1956), Charly Gaul (1958), Federico Bahamontes (1959), Felice Gimondi (1965), Lucien Aimar (1966), Jan Janssen (1968), Eddy Merckx (1969, '70, '71, '72, '74), Bernard Thévenet (1975, '77), Lucien van Impe (1976), Bernard Hinault (1978, '79, '81, '82, '85), Joop Zoetemelk (1980), Laurent Fignon (1983, '84), Greg LeMond (1986, '89, '90) Stephen Roche (1987), Pedro Delgado (1988), Miguel Indurain (1991, '92, '93, '94, '95), Bjarne Riis (1996), Jan Ullrich (1997), Marco Pantani (1998) and Lance Armstrong (1999, 2000, '01, '02 and eventually '03, '04 and '05). Only 1967's winner Roger Pingeon missed the gathering.

To further solidify the historic nature of the 2003 Tour, the route visited the six original stage cities: Paris, Lyon, Marseille, Toulouse, Bordeaux, and Nantes with a complex series of prizes and competitions involving those who did well in those stages. As it had been the custom in earlier Tours, Henri Desgrange's initials were returned to the Yellow Jersey.

The Prologue in Paris yielded a few surprises. Australian Bradley McGee won, but probably because David Millar's mechanic chose to lighten Millar's single-chainring bike by removing the front derailleur. Near the finish, after hitting a bump, Millar dropped his chain since it was not kept on the ring by front derailleur. He was forced to settle for a seething, furious second place.

Ullrich showed that his spring preparation might have been good enough with a fourth at 2 seconds, while Armstrong was seventh, 7 seconds slower. In addition to being simply tired from the Dauphiné, Armstrong had crashed in that race and had taken antibiotics that didn't agree with him. Making things even worse, in the week leading up to the Tour Armstrong was suffering from gastroenteritis causing diarrhea that lasted right up until the Tour's start. Given all these handicaps, Armstrong's Prologue was impressive.

Armstrong's problems weren't over. He had changed shoes on the Thursday before the race start, resulting in a slightly different pedal-cleat interface that irritated his hip. He tried to mask the pain during the first week, but it contributed to his sub-par performance. Every rider has small and large problems along the way, but this was an unusual series of difficulties for a rider who usually came to the Tour perfectly prepared.

As part of the Centennial, the Tour stopped for a moment outside the restaurant *Le Réveil Matin* (The Alarm Clock) in Montgeron, where the Tour started its first stage in 1903.

Just before Alessandro Petacchi's stage one sprint victory, a nasty left turn caused a pile-up that brought down several important riders including Armstrong. While Armstrong was unhurt, others including Rabobank's Levi Leipheimer, had to abandon. Tyler Hamilton broke his clavicle, but decided to endure the pain and continue riding.

Stage four's 68-kilometer team time trial created the year's first sorting. US Postal beat Beloki's ONCE by 30 seconds and Ullrich's Bianchi squad by 43 seconds. This put Postal domestique Victor Hugo Peña in Yellow and Armstrong in second place, 1 second behind, with the climbing commencing in three days. Peña kept the Yellow Jersey for those three days, but US Postal caught heat for sending Peña back to the Postal car to get water bottles. Many thought the Yellow Jersey deserved more respect. What it showed was the absolutely unwavering manner in which the entire Postal team viewed their task of helping Armstrong win the Tour.

Stage seven started with several category two and three climbs to soften the riders' legs before the Col de Ramaz, a category one summit twenty kilometers before the finish. Ridden in terrible heat, the stage had a profound effect upon the Tour. Simoni said he was exhausted from both his Giro win and especially from the Tour's stage-four team time trial. He could not stay with the leaders and lost ten minutes. 2000 Giro winner Stefano Garzelli struggled, also attributing his difficulty to the team time trial.

About forty kilometers into the stage, Virenque bolted, bridging up to several others who were already off the front, including teammate Paolo Bettini. Bettini got the hunger knock, leaving Virenque on his own. Virenque maintained his lead to the top of the Ramaz, then held on to the finish in Morzine, beating the pack by almost four minutes and putting him in Yellow with Armstrong still in second, now back 2 minutes, 37 seconds.

Stage eight had a few category two and three climbs before the Galibier and a hilltop finish at l'Alpe d'Huez. While Armstrong may not have been quite at the top of his game, Ullrich was suffering with intestinal troubles, as were others in the peloton. The stronger riders reached the base of the Alpe together. Then, in a shock to not only the peloton but also to the Postal team, new Postal recruit Manuel Beltran hit the bottom of the mountain with all jets blazing. His speed shattered the pack and put both Ullrich and Virenque out the back door. The other climbers, sensing that Armstrong and the Postal team had been riding easily over the Galibier for a reason, started attacking. Beloki tried a couple of times to get away. Then Iban Mayo jumped and made it stick. Vinokourov made good his escape as well. Even Tyler Hamilton had a go, but was brought back. Mayo won the stage, followed a couple of minutes later by Vinokourov. A half-minute later Armstrong led in six survivors. Armstrong was in Yellow but it seemed as if the Tour, for the first time in years, was in play. Armstrong regretted not riding the stage harder because he felt he could have taken more time out of Ullrich.

The new General Classification:
1. Lance Armstrong
2. Joseba Beloki @ 40 seconds
3. Iban Mayo @ 1 minute 10 seconds
4. Alexandre Vinokourov @ 1 minute 17 seconds
5. Francisco Mancebo @ 1 minute 37 seconds
6. Tyler Hamilton @ 1 minute 52 seconds

Stage nine had the Lautaret and the Izoard, but both came before the 100-kilometer mark of this 184.5 kilometer stage. Late in the stage came the second-category St. Apollinaire and the third-level Côte de La Rochette before a descent into Gap. They shouldn't have had too much effect upon the race, but affect the race they did. Armstrong had been unable to deliver a *coup de grace* on l'Alpe d'Huez. The others had hit Armstrong with all they had, yet he was still the man in Yellow. But the sense that he could be challenged gave new life to the race. Most of the good riders were together for the final climb when Vinokourov blasted off the front, drawing no reaction.

Further up the Rochette Armstrong hit the pack hard, taking a few riders with him, including Beloki, Mayo and Ullrich. They crested 15 seconds behind Vinokourov, but it was on the descent that the race changed completely. On the serpentine road with its soft asphalt melted by the heat, Beloki went down hard. In a tight corner his rear wheel locked up, the tire rolled off the rim and exploded. Armstrong, who had been right on his wheel, reacted quickly by going off the road to his left, cyclocrossing through a farmer's field, then back onto the road to rejoin the race.

Beloki, in agony with a broken finger, elbow and femur, still wanted to get back on his bike. Just before the crash, his manager Manolo Saiz had told Beloki to let Armstrong take the lead. Now Saiz cradled the shattered racer in his arms, knowing that his Tour (and his career as a top racer) was over. With Beloki out, Vinokourov's stage win and its time bonus put him in second place, 21 seconds behind Armstrong.

In intense heat, the Tour rode stage ten to Marseille; a day of rest followed. Postal's 43-second margin of victory over Bianchi in the stage-four team time trial was looking crucial. Without that superb effort, Vinokourov would have been in Yellow at this point.

Stage twelve continued the drama. The day was a roasting 35° centigrade (95° Fahrenheit) and Armstrong suffered terribly from dehydration during the 47-kilometer individual time trial. Ullrich won the stage while Armstrong, who had been going as fast as Ullrich for the first half of the stage, was second at 1 minute, 36 seconds.

The General Classification stood thus:
1. Lance Armstrong
2. Jan Ullrich @ 34 seconds

3. Alexandre Vinokourov @ 51 seconds
4. Tyler Hamilton @ 2 minutes 59 seconds
5. Haimar Zubeldia @ 4 minutes 29 seconds
6. Iban Mayo @ same time

The Tour was now set for three days in the Pyrenees. Stage thirteen had two big climbs, Port de Pailhères and a hilltop finish at the Ax-3 Domaines ski station. Bruyneel sent José Luis Rubiera up the road, and by the crest of the Pailhères he was in a break a couple of minutes ahead of the Armstrong/Ullrich group and ready to assist Armstrong should he need help.

On the final climb, Rubiera was caught by the Armstrong group, but Carlos Sastre, who had been part of the break, stayed away, persevering on to win the stage alone. Farther back, Postal had Roberto Heras attack the Ullrich/Armstrong group, leaving just shattered remnants, several of whom took turns attacking: Zubeldia, Vinokourov and then finally Ullrich. Sitting in the saddle Ullrich was able to ride the others off his wheel and come in second behind Sastre. Armstrong closed to within 7 seconds of Ullrich, which left the General Classification still close:

1. Lance Armstrong
2. Jan Ullrich @ 15 seconds
3. Alexandre Vinokourov @ 1 minute 1 second

The second Pyrenean day included six big passes: Col de Latrape, Col de la Core, Portet d'Aspet, Col de Menté, Portillon and the Col de Peyresourde, whose summit came eleven kilometers before the finish. On the Portillon, Virenque, Dufaux and Simoni emerged from an earlier break and were able to stay away to the end. Simoni, recovering from his earlier efforts in the Giro and the Tour, won the stage. On the Peyresourde, Vinokourov joined a break that again generated no reaction from Ullrich or Armstrong. The Kazakh stayed away, narrowing his time gap a bit more. Armstrong later said that at this point, he believed that his chances of winning the Tour were at best 50 percent.

The General Classification podium now stood thus:
1. Lance Armstrong
2. Jan Ullrich @ 15 seconds
3. Alexandre Vinokourov @ 18 seconds

Stage fifteen, 159.5 kilometers going from Bagnères-de-Bigorre to Luz Ardiden, was the final Pyrenean stage. On the Tourmalet Ullrich got away, but Armstrong closed back up to him. During the descent, Armstrong gapped Ullrich a few times on the tricky corners, but the best riders were together for the final ascent.

Climbing with nine kilometers to go, Mayo put in a hard acceleration which Armstrong answered. Then, as the riders were going around a tight corner Armstrong took the shortest line (he liked to ride close to the edge of the road and deny others his slipstream) and caught his bars in the straps of a spectator's musette. Down he went, taking Mayo with him as Ullrich swerved to avoid them. Armstrong and Mayo remounted while up ahead Ullrich slowed. Finding that the others weren't so interested in waiting for the Yellow Jersey, Hamilton went to the front and put his arm out to slow them. Armstrong, after having trouble with his cleats, finally rejoined. Mayo took off again, and then Armstrong jumped after him so hard no one could follow. Ullrich, who is a momentum climber like Indurain, never did well when the speed changed on a climb. He had a hard time getting going again as Armstrong went by Mayo and took the stage, beating Mayo, Ullrich and Zubeldia by 40 seconds. Ullrich did get his big body up to speed, pulling back 10 seconds out of Armstrong's gap in the upper slopes of the climb, but he ran out of mountain too soon.

The resulting General Classification:

1. Lance Armstrong
2. Jan Ullrich @ 1 minute 7 seconds
3. Alexandre Vinokourov @ 2 minutes 45 seconds
4. Haimar Zubeldia @ 5 minutes 16 seconds
5. Iban Mayo @ 5 minutes 25 seconds

After the awards ceremony where Armstrong donned the Yellow Jersey, Bernard Hinault greeted him with the simple words, "Welcome to the club." Barring misfortune Armstrong would become a member of the five-time Tour winners club.

The stage nineteen time trial didn't disappoint for drama. It was raining hard that morning. Ullrich loathed the cold and wet while Armstrong thrived in it. Unlike Armstrong, Ullrich didn't go out on the course in the morning to familiarize himself with the roads, preferring to stay in bed and watch a videotape of the route. The race itself turned out to be fraught with danger. Several of the riders who rode before Ullrich and Armstrong had crashed, one breaking several ribs. Understanding the Tour would be decided during the coming hour, Ullrich shook with anxiety in the start house. He took off cleanly and for much of the distance he was leading, with a record individual time trial speed of 55.21 kilometers an hour. Perhaps in any other era Ullrich's effort would have won him the Tour. But at only a couple of seconds slower, Armstrong was nearly matching Ullrich's effort.

Then disaster struck. In a roundabout, as the weather was getting wetter and windier, a gust of wind caught Ullrich's rear disc wheel and sent him to the ground. The Tour was over. Armstrong slowed to avoid crashing, letting David Millar win the stage and Hamilton take second. It's important to note that since Ullrich was ahead of Armstrong by only 6 seconds in the time trial when he fell, but was down by 1 minute, 5 seconds in the Overall, the race was in fact already over and the crash didn't change the final outcome.

Again, the Green Jersey's owner wasn't settled until the final stage in Paris, Robbie McEwen and Baden Cooke being separated by only 2 points. Cooke took second in the final sprint to Frenchman J.P. Nazon, while McEwen was third, giving Cooke the Points classification.

Armstrong joined Anquetil, Merckx, Hinault and Indurain in the elite club of five-time Tour winners, but only he and Indurain had achieved their wins consecutively. Virenque joined Bahamontes and van Impe as six-time winners of the climbing competition.

Waiting for Armstrong in stage fifteen was a grand sporting gesture which probably cost Jan Ullrich the Tour. Comparisons have been made to the 2001 Tour when Armstrong waited for Ullrich after he crashed on the descent of the Peyresourde, but the situations are not comparable. Going into that stage Armstrong led Ullrich by four minutes. Even though François Simon was in Yellow, that race was over. The 2001 Tour was not in play for Ullrich. In 2003 it was.

The 2003 Tour was raced at the record speed of 40.94 kilometers/hour.

Final 2003 Tour de France General Classification:
1. Lance Armstrong (US Postal): 83 hours 41 minutes 12 seconds
2. Jan Ullrich (Bianchi) @ 1 minute 1 second

3. Alexandre Vinokourov (Telekom) @ 4 minutes 14 seconds
4. Tyler Hamilton (CSC) @ 6 minutes 17 seconds
5. Haimar Zubeldia (Euskaltel) @ 6 minutes 51 seconds
6. Iban Mayo (Euskaltel) @ 7 minutes 6 seconds

Climbers' Competition:

1. Richard Virenque: 324 points
2. Laurent Dufaux: 187
3. Lance Armstrong: 168

Points Competition:

1. Baden Cooke: 216 points
2. Robbie McEwen: 214
3. Erik Zabel: 188

Among other endeavors, Italian sports physiologist Dr. Francesco Conconi had been advising athletes since the early 1980s. In addition to "preparing" Francesco Moser for his successful 1984 World Hour Record attempt with blood doping (unethical, but not against the rules in 1984), Conconi has been accused of introducing EPO to the sport of cycling. On November 23, 2003, Judge Franca Oliva acquitted Conconi of doping charges that had been pending against him, because the charge of "sporting fraud" had not been a crime when the acts in question had been committed. Moreover, there was no specific evidence proving Conconi had been personally involved with helping riders break any drug laws.

In March of 2004, Judge Oliva issued a 44-page report on the lengthy Conconi investigation and prosecution. While Conconi and his assistants weren't legally guilty of a crime, Oliva stated unequivocally that they were morally guilty of helping others dope. The report was damning in its list of Conconi clients who had exhibited highly volatile hematocrit values. Hematologists hired by the Italian government said these highly variable blood values could be assumed to show EPO use. Among the riders the report said had used EPO were Giro/Tour/World Champion Stephen Roche, Marco Pantani, Claudio Chiappucci and Giro winners Evgeni Berzin, Marco Pantani, Ivan Gotti and Gianni Bugno. It was Conconi that Michele Ferrari had worked with in the early 1980s as they studied their own brand of sports physiology.

2004

Two riders seemed ready to challenge Armstrong for supremacy. Tyler Hamilton's new team, Phonak, was generously funded with a $9.6-million budget and Hamilton had a purpose-built team to work for him just for the Tour. Hamilton's form looked nearly perfect with a win in the Tour of Romandie and second in the Dauphiné, beating Armstrong in the time trial up Mont Ventoux. His high placing in 2003's Tour, accomplished with a broken collarbone, spoke well for his abilities.

Ullrich was back with Godefroot, the same team but with a new name. Telekom became T-Mobile. Godefroot had been bitter about the 2002–2003 breakup. Even though Ullrich was welcomed back into the fold, Ullrich's personal trainer and good friend Rudy Pevenage was still *persona non grata* and was not allowed to travel with the team. He was forced to take care of Ullrich by traveling on his own at Ullrich's expense. Ullrich's winning the Tour of Switzerland seemed to signal that his condition would be good. But, would his usual too-rapid weight loss in the weeks before the Tour again sap his strength?

Tragically, there was one missing rider. In February, Marco Pantani was found dead in a hotel room from an overdose of cocaine.

The 2004 Tour was run counter-clockwise, Pyrenees first. The route had some difficult stages planned with an interesting twist. The first individual time trial was up l'Alpe d'Huez allowing the climbing specialists to worry about time losses only in the Prologue and Besançon time trial, the penultimate stage.

A "stop-loss" rule was instituted for the team time trial. The most a rider could lose was three minutes, outraging Armstrong partisans who saw a nefarious French plan to keep the US Postal freight train from gaining the time it deserved. But many previous Tours have awarded the winner of the team time trial only a small time bonification, and some editions had allowed the team time trial to affect only the team standings, leaving the individual times unchanged.

The accusations of doping continued. Several members of the Cofidis team, most notably David Millar, the World Time Trial Champion, were found to have been habitual users of performance enhancing chemicals. Millar wasn't found out through drug testing. Like almost all of the pro peloton, he had been able to finesse the testing regimen. The French police raided his home, and upon finding doping products, extracted a confession from the man who had for so long denied that he cheated.

Another doped rider who was finally caught put it this way, "I was tested 200 times during my career, and 100 times I had drugs in my body. I was caught, but 99 other times, I wasn't. Riders think they can get away with doping because most of the time they do."

Armstrong had been at the center of doping accusations from almost the first moment he showed that he could successfully contest the Tour. A French judicial inquiry into accusations of Armstrong and Postal team doping had been proceeding at a glacial pace. The inquiry took 21 months to complete. Finally, in September, 2002, the investigation was closed for lack of evidence.

In June 2004, a book titled *LA Confidential: the Secrets of Lance Armstrong* came out, accusing Armstrong of systematically doping. It put together a compelling series of accusations and disturbing evidence. Armstrong swore he would bring the writers to account in court, but didn't. For Armstrong fans, convincing proof was still missing, but Armstrong did not pursue his accusers in French courts except for an attempt to compel the publisher to include a denial by Armstrong of the book's accusations in every copy. Armstrong's request was denied.

He did sue the London *Times* when one of the authors, David Walsh, suggested Armstrong was doping. The *Times* settled, paying Armstrong £300,000. To advance the story, in August of 2005 the French newspaper *L'Équipe* discovered the results of retrospective testing of frozen 1999 Tour urine samples. The newspaper said that six of Armstrong's samples were positive for EPO. Armstrong flatly denied that he had doped, suggesting the samples had been spiked. The UCI was more concerned about the disclosure of confidential data than it was about the near certainty that cycling's franchise rider was cheating. UCI boss Verbruggen had a friend investigate the accusation and the resulting report was a whitewash, again more troubled about the leak and Armstrong's supposed rights than the doping that was making the sport as believable as professional wrestling.

At the time, Armstrong was involved in several lawsuits against writers, publishers and individuals who had accused him of doping. Yet, though *L'Équipe* had unabashedly called Armstrong a liar and invited him to sue, Armstrong did not take legal action against the paper.

Armstrong was contemptuous of the few riders who either admitted to doping or spoke out against its use in the peloton. He used all of his power to terrorize anyone who hinted that his accomplishments were attained with the help of banned drugs. He continued to vigorously enforce the professional riders' *omertà*, the code of silence regarding dope.

Back to the race:

The Prologue time trial was held in Liège, Belgium on wet, slippery streets. Ullrich's teammate, Sergei Ivanov crashed earlier in the day prompting Ullrich to ride carefully, as did Hamilton.

Armstrong rode full gas, coming in second and putting 15 to 20 seconds between himself and his challengers before the first stage. Ullrich's time was slower than it should have been, even accounting for his caution. He was coming down with a cold.

The third stage had two sections of pavé, the first being almost three kilometers long. All the riders were desperate to be at the front as they approached the cobbles. As the peloton accelerated to a near flat-out pace, and just before the first pavé sector, Iban Mayo and US Postal rider Benjamin Noval locked handlebars and went down along with Thor Hushovd, who was the *maillot jaune*. Postal hammered the front. Postal, like nearly all riders in Tour history, had no trouble forgetting the traditional race courtesy of waiting for a fallen Tour leader when it didn't suit them.

All of Mayo's team, including their number two Classification man Haimar Zubeldia, dropped back to pace him back to the field. But US Postal stayed at the front, riding the cobbled section blisteringly fast. First George Hincapie and then more powerfully, Viacheslav Ekimov put in hard, long pulls, splitting the field into several groups. The front group, with most of the top riders, steamrolled away from a second chase group that contained not only Mayo, but top French hope Christophe Moreau as well. This group lost almost four minutes, ending Mayo's and Moreau's hope for a top overall finish on only the second stage.

The stage four team time trial was held on 64.5-kilometers of smooth but wet road. US Postal executed their ride perfectly and won the stage, putting Armstrong in Yellow. Armstrong was impressive, taking kilometer-long pulls.

Because Phonak chose narrow, lightweight, thin tires that were too fragile for the wet roads, Hamilton's team suffered five punctures as well as several mechanical problems, finishing with just five riders. Yet, their ride was impressive. Phonak came in second after waiting twice for riders with problems and running a short team. Thanks to the new team time trial rules, Hamilton's loss was only 20 seconds.

Gilberto Simoni, Saeco team leader and twice winner of the Giro, seemed to forget that he had to finish with his team to get the protection of the new rule. Coming into town and fearing a crash on the cobbles, he let himself get separated from his team, costing him 2 minutes, 42 seconds.

Armstrong said he would not defend his lead this early in the Tour. In stage five, a small group escaped and finished with a gap of twelve and a half minutes. In the wind and bad weather and with a crash in the peloton, it had become difficult to keep the break from running away, resulting in the young French Road Champion, Thomas Voeckler, putting on the Yellow Jersey, with Armstrong more than nine minutes behind. This was not the result Postal wanted; they remembered the trouble caused in 2001 when they let a break get such a big lead.

During this stage, US Postal domestique Floyd Landis rode up to Tyler Hamilton to tell him that Armstrong had called UCI boss Hein Verbruggen to accuse Hamilton of doping. Armstrong was burning after Hamilton had beat him in the Dauphiné's Mt. Ventoux time trial. And sure enough, the UCI sent a letter to Hamilton, asking him to come to UCI headquarters to have a talk with Mario Zorzoli, the UCI's chief medical officer. In fact, Hamilton had shown signs that he had undergone a homologous blood transfusion.

The stages leading up to the first rest day after stage eight were all run under wet and windy conditions across the north of France, with frequent crashes putting the riders on edge. It was said that more than 100 of the remaining 176 riders had been involved in at least one crash. At the one-kilometer-to-go sign in stage six, a terrible pile-up stopped most of the field and sent Hamilton flying. He landed on his back, breaking his helmet in the process.

Here were the standings before the Tour headed to the Massif Central for stage nine:

1. Thomas Voeckler
2. Stuart O'Grady @ 3 minutes 1 second
3. Sandy Casar @ 4 minutes 6 seconds
4. Magnus Backstedt @ 6 minutes 27 seconds
6. Lance Armstrong @ 9 minutes 35 seconds
7. George Hincapie @ 9 minutes 45 seconds
11. Tyler Hamilton @ 10 minutes 11 seconds
20. Jan Ullrich @ 10 minutes 30 seconds

Tour management had put in three transition stages, intended to be challenging with "heavy" roads that would be tough on the peloton. Jean-Marie Leblanc said he included these stages in the hope that some of the Tour contenders would try to shake things up with tactical, aggressive riding rather than just sitting in Postal's wake, riding tempo and waiting for the mountains and Armstrong's inevitable assault.

It was not to be. Each day, opportunistic, non-threatening breaks were allowed to go, then controlled. These stages across the Massif Central of France had no real effect on the standings and thanks to his hard working team, Voeckler hung on to his Yellow Jersey.

Stage twelve started with a long, slow rise out of Castelsarrasin in the Pyrenees followed by two climbs: a ride up the Aspin and then a trip partway up the Tourmalet to La Mongie. It would be an astonishing day. Ullrich, Mayo, Zubeldia and Hamilton all cracked early on the Tourmalet. The day had turned cold and nasty, bad news for Ullrich, who was now sick enough to require antibiotics. When asked over his radio if his team's number two man, Andreas Klöden should wait and escort him to the finish, Ullrich, knowing that he was going to lose a lot time that day, gave Klöden his freedom. Only CSC's Ivan Basso could stay with Armstrong, surprising many by beating the five-time Tour winner to the line.

Ullrich, Hamilton and Mayo all shared the same doping doctor, Eufemiano Fuentes. Hamilton said he had been transfused with bad blood. Perhaps Fuentes had botched the other riders' transfusions as well.

Stage thirteen was more of the same, a 205.5-kilometer ride over the Portet d'Aspet, Core, Latrape, Agnes and then up to Plateau de Beille.

Early on, Hamilton abandoned. Injuries to his back from the crash in stage six had kept him from being able to ride out of the saddle, and he was unable to apply any real power to his pedals.

Later on, Mayo played out a repeat of Federico Bahamontes' attempts to quit the Tour fifty years before. Suffering badly in his second day in the mountains, Mayo fell off the pace and at one point got off his bike. His manager convinced him to get back on and continue. After riding just a few meters he started to take his shoes out of the pedals. His teammates kept pushing him along, not letting him quit. Even Fabian Cancellara of the Fassa Bortolo team came up beside him and started pushing him. He finished the stage 38 minutes behind the winners.

US Postal completely controlled the race, keeping the tempo high. By the penultimate climb, the Col d'Agnes, there were only twenty-two riders left in the Armstrong group, seven of them Postal riders. This team domination probably has no equal in modern Tour history and alarmed observers who knew this could not be the result of riding *paniagua* ("bread and water", a racer's term for riding without drugs). Within the first couple of kilometers of the final climb, the Armstrong group was reduced to about a dozen riders. As Postal's José Azevedo increased the intensity, it was soon down to just three: Azevedo, Armstrong and the young Italian rider from the day before, Basso. After Azevedo had done his work for Armstrong and swung off, it was Basso and Armstrong trading pace to the line. This time, Armstrong was the better while Basso showed the strain of the two days in the mountains.

Plucky Thomas Voeckler looked like he was finally going to lose his Yellow Jersey as he struggled up the final kilometers to Plateau de Beille. He had dropped behind the lead group on each of the climbs and chased back on the descents, fearlessly blazing down the mountainsides. As he passed under the two-kilometers-to-go banner, his manager drove up next to him and told him that if he pushed it, he could keep the Yellow Jersey. Exhausted, Voeckler dug even deeper and kept his lead by a whisker-thin 22 seconds over Armstrong; Ivan Basso was third at 1 minute, 39 seconds.

The utter collapse of nearly all the fancied challengers after just two days in the mountains was a stunner.

Cyrille Guimard, coach of van Impe, Hinault, Fignon and LeMond, called the day a massacre. He thought only Ivan Basso had a chance at final victory after stage thirteen, and that was doubtful because he was only as strong as Armstrong, not stronger. Armstrong was the better time trialist, making it unlikely that Basso could take enough time out of Armstrong in the remaining days unless Armstrong were to have a bad day.

After the Pyrenees and stage thirteen, before a rest day and the Alps, here were the standings:

1. Thomas Voeckler
2. Lance Armstrong @ 22 seconds
3. Ivan Basso @ 1 minute 39 seconds
4. Andreas Klöden @ 3 minutes 18 seconds
5. Francisco Mancebo @ 3 minutes 28 seconds
8. Jan Ullrich @ 7 minutes 1 second

The first Alpine stage's climax was expected to be the second category Côte de Chalimont, whose summit was followed by quick descent before a mild climb to the finish.

Ullrich knew he had to do something, and soon. He would run out of opportunities quickly with all the climbing and time trialing packed into this last week. Riding with the Armstrong group on the Col de l'Echarasson, he heaved his big body up the road in a furious attack. In the Pyrenees he had pedaled with a ponderous, slow, ineffective cadence, but here he was spinning his long cranks, looking fresh and as powerful as the old Ullrich. He went over the mountain about a minute ahead of the Armstrong group, picking up some remainders of a fraying breakaway, Garcia-Acosta and Santos Gonzalez.

CSC hit the panic button. Not being confident that Ivan Basso could challenge Armstrong for first place, Ullrich's attack was seen more as a threat to the podium place Basso currently held (assuming Voeckler would be dispatched). Playing it safe, Riis told Jens Voigt, who was up the road in an earlier break, to ease for the small Yellow Jersey group behind him that also had Carlos Sastre, Basso and two Postal riders. Together, CSC and US Postal brought Ullrich back to the peloton.

When this group came into the finish area, Armstrong was sitting in the back, in the big ring, cross-chained, ready to dump the gear for a sprint. He jumped and emphatically won the stage. Armstrong was now in Yellow.

Stage sixteen was the wildly anticipated individual time trial up l'Alpe d'Huez. Before the collapse of almost of all of Armstrong's competitors, it had the potential to be an electrifying day that would showcase Armstrong, Ullrich, Hamilton and Mayo in a terrific, dramatic race.

Riding through a tightly packed defile of race fans, Armstrong executed a convincing victory, beating Ullrich by 61 seconds and catching Ivan Basso with about four kilometers to go. Germans were furious with countryman Jens Voigt, who had been instrumental in chasing Ullrich down the day before. They heckled him and held up signs calling him "Judas". After the stage Ullrich explained that this was Voigt's job, to work for his team.

Stage seventeen, the Queen Stage, was 204.5 kilometers that went over the Glandon, Madeleine, Tamié, Forclaz and the Croix Fry. T-Mobile figured this was an important opportunity to put Ullrich and Klöden in second and third places and announced that they would attack Basso.

As the racers rode kilometer after kilometer, US Postal set a fast pace causing all but the last few of the contenders to go out the back door without so much as a single attack. The confidence seemed to have gone out of the legs of Ullrich and Klöden as T-Mobile just sat behind Postal the entire way.

Floyd Landis led up the Croix Fry, reducing the front group to just himself, Armstrong, Ullrich, Klöden, and Basso. In the final descent into Le Grand-Bornand, first Landis ("Run like you stole something", Armstrong told him) attacked, but was brought back by Ullrich. Then Klöden counter-attacked. Armstrong, upset at Ullrich for pulling back Landis, chased him like a fiend and caught him at the line. No change to the top placings.

During the eighteenth stage, an Italian rider with a troubled doping history, Filippo Simeoni, bridged up to a break. Armstrong soon came roaring up to the escaping group as well, a strange act for the Yellow Jersey. The other escapees knew their break would soon be caught because the peloton would not tolerate the Yellow Jersey riding off the front. They begged Armstrong to drop back to the bunch, but Armstrong wouldn't budge unless Simeoni also returned to the peloton, which they both eventually did.

Armstrong was punishing Simeoni for testifying that Michele Ferrari had been Simeoni's training advisor and had given him prescriptions for EPO and Human Growth Hormone. Since it was slowly becoming known that Armstrong also employed Ferrari (since 1995), Armstrong needed to squash any idea that Ferrari was a doping doctor and now called Simeoni a liar. By joining the break, Armstrong was ruining Simeoni's chances of winning a stage, thereby enforcing the doping code of silence.

When Simeoni rejoined the pack, other riders, including Filippo Pozzato, Giuseppe Guerini and Daniele Nardello, gave Simeoni grief. Without shame, Armstrong moved his hand across his mouth with a "zip the lips" gesture. During the Tour's final stage, Simeoni would again attack, and this time the other riders spat on him.

The penultimate stage, nineteen, was a 55-kilometer individual time trial, an oblong loop over the rolling countryside starting and ending in Besançon. At the first time check, 18 kilometers into the stage, Ullrich had already lost 43 seconds. Ullrich had hoped to do well enough to make it to the podium but fell far short of that goal, while Klöden beat Basso by a large enough margin to move into second place.

And that's how it ended. Armstrong made history by winning a sixth consecutive Tour de France. Richard Virenque won a record seventh King of the Mountains title, passing Federico Bahamontes and Lucien van Impe, who had six each.

Final 2004 Tour de France General Classification
1. Lance Armstrong (US Postal): 83 hours 36 minutes 2 seconds
2. Andreas Klöden (T-Mobile) @ 6 minutes 19 seconds
3. Ivan Basso (CSC) @ 6 minutes 40 seconds
4. Jan Ullrich (T-Mobile) @ 8 minutes 50 seconds
5. Jose Azevedo (US Postal) @ 14 minutes 30 seconds

Climbers' Competition:
1. Richard Virenque: 226 points
2. Lance Armstrong: 172
3. Michael Rasmussen: 119

Points Competition:
1. Robbie McEwen: 272 points
2. Thor Hushovd: 247
3. Erik Zabel: 245

After coming close to being found positive for homologous blood doping at the Athens Olympics, Tyler Hamilton was popped for the same offense at the Vuelta a España in the fall. Bobby Julich's reaction to Hamilton's trouble at the Olympics: "…But the rest of us at the Olympics passed the test. Why didn't he? I'm sick of people who cheat, sick of cleaning up their mess and trying to explain it…" In October of 2012 Julich would confess to having used EPO from 1996 through July of 1998, the month he was third in the Tour de France.

2005

Professional racing underwent a profound re-organization with the institution of the Pro Tour when the president of the UCI, Hein Verbruggen, rammed through his personal vision of how the sport should be run. The twenty best teams were given a "Pro Tour" license good for four years. The most important races, which included the Grand Tours and the classics, were given Pro Tour status. The Pro Tour teams would be required to send riders to all of the races on the Pro Tour calendar. The idea was to give stability to the teams and a high quality peloton to all of the important races.

Not happy with what they saw as a bald UCI power grab, the Grand Tour owners pushed back, complaining that many of the Pro Tour rules encroached on their ability to run their races as they saw fit. While negotiations between the UCI and the organizers dragged on, both sides agreed to disagree for the moment and run the season under a flag of truce. The Tour de France sent invitations to all twenty Pro Tour teams, leaving them only one wild card. Facing a 200-rider limit to the peloton, there was some speculation that the Tour would have eight-man squads, allowing more, smaller teams to compete. It didn't come to pass and only one discretionary invitation was issued, to the French Ag2r team.

Instead of a short prologue, the 2005 edition started with a 19-kilometer individual time trial, a change with the potential to drastically alter the complexion of the first week's racing. Normally, sprinters do reasonably well in the short, power-intensive prologues; at worst they start the first road stage a few seconds out of the lead. Their hope is to accrue time bonuses along the way to gain the Yellow Jersey before they hit the mountains. With a longer time trial, the gaps between the better time trialists and the sprinters would most likely put the lead out of time-bonus reach. Some thought this would reduce the desperation and aggression in the early stages and make the racing safer. Given the intensity of Tour competition, this was unlikely.

The 2005 Tour went clockwise (Alps first), then headed to the Pyrenees and finished the climbing in the Massif Central before heading to Paris.

There had been some doubt as to whether Armstrong would ride the 2005 Tour and attempt to extend his winning streak to seven consecutive Tours. In February he announced that he would, indeed, be on the line in July. His contract with his team's new sponsor, the Discovery television channel, required him to ride one more Tour, but he could choose to ride in either 2005 or 2006.

Ullrich had already put in 2,500 training kilometers by New Year's Day, announcing that unseating Armstrong remained his primary goal.

In the pre-Tour tune-up races, the Dauphiné Libéré and Tour of Switzerland, both Ullrich and Armstrong did well enough. Ullrich led the Swiss Tour for a while before coming in third, a minute and a half behind winner Aitor Gonzalez. Armstrong was fourth in the Dauphiné while T-Mobile's other Tour hopeful, Alexandre Vinokourov, was fifth, three seconds behind Armstrong.

Armstrong's teams had been put together for a single purpose, to deliver Armstrong to Paris in Yellow, while Ullrich's teams usually had split ambitions. Besides working for the General Classification, stage victories were important to the German teams and in the pre-Armstrong years this had worked well for them. In 1997 they won both the Yellow and the Green Jerseys, courtesy of their successful dual-pronged Ullrich and Zabel attack. For the 2005 Tour, T-Mobile announced a team selected with the sole purpose of winning the Yellow Jersey. The team was strong, with 2004 second-place Andreas Klöden and 2003 third-place Alexandre Vinokourov. To make room on the team for another domestique who could help in the mountains, six-time Green Jersey winner Erik Zabel was left off the roster. Still, the real question was, given the rough parity Armstrong and Ullrich had in time-trialing, did Ullrich bring enough horsepower to the Tour to withstand Armstrong's explosive bursts of power in stages with hilltop finishes? That was where the big time was lost, stage after stage, year after year. With the exception of 2003, Armstrong had about clinched each of his Tours with a rocket-like explosion of irresistible speed on the year's first hilltop finish.

T-Mobile seemed intent upon confirming its image as the team that couldn't quite get things right. The day before the first stage, team director Mario Kummer was motorpacing Ullrich (driving a car or motorcycle with a rider following in the vehicle's slipstream), when he hit the brakes without warning, sending Ullrich through the rear window and into the car. Amazingly, Ullrich seemed fine despite the mishap.

At 54.676 kilometers per hour, CSC rider David Zabriskie's stage one ride was the fastest individual time trial in Tour history, beating LeMond's fabled 1989 record of 54.454. Armstrong, who started a minute after Ullrich, caught and blew by the slower-moving German.

1. David Zabriskie: 20 minutes 51 seconds.
2. Lance Armstrong @ 2 seconds
3. Alexandre Vinokourov @ 53 seconds
12. Jan Ullrich @ 1 minute 8 seconds

Michele Ferrari said that after a crash, the body's diversion of precious energy and resources measurably impairs a racer. At the first stage Ullrich had given up a minute he shouldn't have.

Zabriskie kept the lead until the fourth stage, a 67.5-kilometer team time trial going from Tours to Blois. CSC, having the Yellow Jersey, was the last team to ride. At each checkpoint throughout the ride it was ahead of Discovery by a few seconds. As CSC blazed the day's final two kilometers, Zabriskie probably suffered a lapse of concentration. One moment the team was in perfect formation and the next Zabriskie was flying through the air in a terrible crash. The team continued while Zabriskie limped in a minute and a half later. Discovery had won the stage by 2 seconds and Armstrong was now the Tour leader. Discovery's 57.325 kilometers per hour was the fastest Tour team time trial on record.

The next day's start was delayed because Armstrong, following an old tradition of not wanting to wear the Yellow Jersey the day after inheriting it from a rider who has lost it from misfortune, was told he would be ejected from the Tour if he did not put on the Yellow Jersey. That settled it, Armstrong was in Yellow.

Alexandre Vinokourov would need watching. Just before the finish of stage six, as the pack was closing in on fading escapee Christophe

Mengin, Vinokourov and Lorenzo Bernucci took off, catching Mengin. Mengin crashed in the dangerous final corner, forcing Vinokourov to slow, allowing Bernucci to take the stage. But with the 12-second time bonus for second place and the 7-second gap to the field, Vinokourov had elevated himself to third.

Gently lumpy stage seven took the Tour into Germany. Seeing that riders were getting shelled on easier climbs in these early stages, Armstrong said that the high speed of this Tour was taking its toll. The riders were already getting tired.

Stage eight went into Germany's Vosges mountains before taking the riders back into France. On the day's final climb, the second category Col de la Schlucht, Armstrong found himself isolated. The day's hot pace had caused his already tired team to be dropped. Vinokourov tried several savage attacks; all were neutralized. Then T-Mobile launched Klöden, who caught escapee Pieter Weening. Their break stuck and Klöden moved to 1 minute, 50 seconds behind Armstrong, who remained in Yellow. Armstrong, knowing he could not win the Tour without a working team to defend him, was angry at being left alone and promised hard talk at the team's dinner table.

The reason for Discovery's poor performance came out later. Blood that had been extracted from team members after the Dauphiné wasn't reinjected until the rest day that came after stage nine. Knowing it was being watched, the team had grown wary and would only re-infuse the blood when it felt safe from prying eyes. One time the team bus driver feigned a mechanical problem and pulled off the road. While mechanics pretended to repair the bus, riders laid down on the bus floor to receive transfusions.

The next stage, number nine, went over the French Vosges. Looking to conserve energy and give the Discovery domestiques a rest from protecting the Yellow Jersey, Discovery allowed a three-man break containing CSC's Jens Voigt to go. This was exactly what Discovery wanted, to hand over the responsibility of the Yellow Jersey to a man who would not be a long-term threat. Voigt was just such a man and he now had the lead with a rest day before the real climbing began. Again Ullrich crashed, this time at high speed early in the stage. He was able to rejoin the field with little trouble.

This Tour was shaping up to be a fast, hard-fought race with an average speed of 46.2 kilometers per hour over the 1,493.5 kilometers covered so far.

The General Classification after stage nine:

1. Jens Voigt
2. Christophe Moreau @ 1 minute 50 seconds
3. Lance Armstrong @ 2 minutes 18 seconds
4. Michael Rasmussen @ 2 minutes 43 seconds
5. Alexandre Vinokourov @ 3 minutes 20 seconds
6. Bobby Julich @ 3 minutes 25 seconds
7. Ivan Basso @ 3 minutes 44 seconds
8. Jan Ullrich @ 3 minutes 54 seconds

Into the Alps. Stage ten was a simple enough stage, with the Cormet de Roselend rearing up midway through the 181-kilometer stage and a hilltop finish at Courchevel. Now topped off with fresh blood, this time there were no problems with Armstrong's team. They were able to escort him until the final kilometers of the stage, setting a fiendishly fast pace, especially from the end of the descent of the Roselend until the start of the final climb. In the first eight kilometers of that climb Heras, Vinokourov and Beloki were dropped. Then Ullrich came off while Landis (now riding for Phonak) was also shelled. T-Mobile sacrificed Klöden to escort Ullrich up the mountain.

Meanwhile Armstrong did the lion's share of the work as men who had spent almost a year preparing for the Tour were tossed and gored. With a kilometer to go, Armstrong revved it up some more and took only Alejandro Valverde for company. Valverde, being the better sprinter, won the stage and with that, the 2005 Tour was turned upside down.

The new General Classification after several important riders had inexplicably failed their first test:

1. Lance Armstrong
2. Michael Rasmussen @ 38 seconds
3. Ivan Basso @ 2 minutes 40 seconds
4. Christophe Moreau @ 2 minutes 42 seconds
5. Alejandro Valverde @ 3 minutes 16 seconds
8. Jan Ullrich @ 4 minutes 2 seconds
16. Alexandre Vinokourov @ 6 minutes 32 seconds

Stage eleven was another day in the high Alps with the Madeleine, Télégraphe and Galibier before a long descent to Briançon. On the Madeleine, Vinokourov joined a break of about ten riders. As they rode

Armstrong and Basso finish stage fourteen.

over the three mountains, almost all of the Kazakh's fellow breakaways were eliminated until he was left with only Santiago Botero. Back in the reduced field, Discovery rode at tempo, not too worried about a rider with a six-minute deficit. Vinokourov outsprinted Botero for the stage win, and with the 1 minute, 15 second time gap to the field plus the 20-second stage-win time bonus, Vinokourov moved up to twelfth, 4 minutes, 47 seconds behind Armstrong.

With the Alps done, the tired riders sweated their way across Southern France in heat so oppressive that at one point the officials had a melted section of the road hosed down to cool it off.

Still in baking heat, stage fourteen started with a series of third- and fourth-category Pyrenean climbs that ended with the Port-de-Pailhères and a hilltop finish at Ax-3 Domaines. Again, an early break without riders who could be considered GC threats was allowed to ride unchallenged to the finish. Back in the peloton, T-Mobile rolled the dice and set a fast pace up the Pailhères, but their tactics seemed to be in disarray. Vinokourov rocketed away from the now-reduced group and Ullrich chased him down, creating a gap to Armstrong, who was without teammates. After waiting a few minutes, Armstrong then calmly closed up to the leaders. It was an impressive display of power and sangfroid.

At the base of the climb to Ax-3 Domaines, Vinokourov, who had been dropped after his earlier attack, rejoined and again attacked. This time Klöden brought him back and then dropped him. Now it was Basso, Ullrich, Armstrong, Landis and Levi Leipheimer. In the climb's final kilometers, just Ullrich, Basso and Armstrong remained. Shortly before the end, Ullrich was dropped and Armstrong jumped hard enough to slightly distance Basso, solidifying his lead.

Stage fifteen was the year's hardest mountain stage. At 205.5 kilometers, it included the Aspet, Menté, Portillon, Peyresourde, and Val Louron-Azet, with a hilltop finish at St.-Lary-Soulan/Pla d'Adet. On the Col de Menté, a break of fourteen went clear. Wanting to be up ahead to help Armstrong in the latter part of the stage, George Hincapie was in the break. As they rode up and over the Pyrenees, one by one the others dropped off. By the time they were on the final climb, it was just Óscar Pereiro and Hincapie. Pereiro, understanding that Hincapie was an Armstrong domestique and would not be allowed to help, did all of the work, dragging Hincapie in his wake. After sitting on Pereiro for nearly the entire climb, Hincapie jumped around the Spaniard for his first Tour stage win. Though he understood the game, Pereiro was nonetheless bitter about doing all the work, only to lose the stage.

The real race was back down the road. By the time the peloton went over the Peyresourde, the Yellow Jersey group was reduced to eighteen riders and the Hincapie/Pereiro break was long gone. On the Val Louron-Azet, Basso hit the front hard and gapped Ullrich, who clawed his way back, but Armstrong and Basso knew the German was vulnerable. On the descent there was a small, temporary regroupment. Early on the final climb Basso accelerated, taking Armstrong along but shelling Ullrich. Armstrong did not contest the sprint when Basso led him over the line.

The General Classification stood thus:

1. Lance Armstrong
2. Ivan Basso @ 2 minutes 46 seconds
3. Michael Rasmussen @ 3 minutes 9 seconds
4. Jan Ullrich @ 5 minutes 58 seconds

Even though the final day in the mountains included both the Marie-Blanque and the Aubisque, the finish line was over 70 kilometers from the crest of the Aubisque, preventing any major change to the standings. Pereiro, still burning from his loss to Hincapie, got into the winning break, where this time Australian Cadel Evans did the lion's share of the work while Pereiro sat on and zipped around for the stage win.

The year's longest stage was the 239.5-kilometer run from Pau to Revel, with a sawtooth profile of third- and fourth-category climbs. T-Mobile was not surrendering. During the final climb Vinokourov gave the front group a hard hammer blow followed by an equally savage pull by Ullrich. Moreau, Landis and Evans were caught unawares by the move and were shelled. To make life still more miserable for the dropped trio, Armstrong and the rest of the remaining Discovery riders went to the front and drove the separated group hard. Armstrong collected his seventy-ninth Yellow Jersey, tying Bernard Hinault, but well behind Merckx's closetful of 96.

Stage eighteen brought the Tour into the center of the Massif Central. Just before the finish, there was a three-kilometer climb with a ten-percent gradient. While the usual break of non-contenders was ten minutes up the road, the peloton was being whittled down by the pack's high speed as it rode over the region's relentless climbs. Just into the final ascent, Basso lit the jets and then there were four: Evans,

Ullrich, Basso and Armstrong. The losers of the day were Michael Rasmussen, whose third place was now in jeopardy since Ullrich was only 2 minutes, 12 seconds behind him with the final time trial coming, and Vinokourov, who could not match the Basso move.

The stage twenty time trial was important because there were so many positions in play.

Going into the time trial the standings were thus:

1. Lance Armstrong
2. Ivan Basso @ 2 minutes 46 seconds
3. Michael Rasmussen @ 3 minutes 46 seconds
4. Jan Ullrich @ 5 minutes 58 seconds
5. Francisco Mancebo @ 7 minutes 8 seconds
6. Levi Leipheimer @ 8 minutes 12 seconds
7. Cadel Evans @ 9 minutes 49 seconds
8. Alexandre Vinokourov @ 10 minutes 11 seconds

The 55.5-kilometer time-trial course had a third-category climb followed by a descent that required care. Ullrich ripped the course, showing again that his preparation was, as usual, too late. His move to third place was aided by Rasmussen's catastrophe: first, Rasmussen crashed, then flatted and got an incompetent wheel change requiring several bike changes before he could continue. To add to his misery he fell on the descent. Rasmussen finished seventy-seventh that day, 7 minutes, 47 seconds behind the day's winner, Lance Armstrong, who chalked up his twenty-fourth career Tour stage win.

The results of the time trial:

1. Lance Armstrong: 1 hour 11 minutes 46 seconds
2. Jan Ullrich @ 23 seconds
3. Alexandre Vinokourov @ 1 minute 16 seconds
4. Bobby Julich @ 1 minute 33 seconds
5. Ivan Basso @ 1 minute 54 seconds

This yielded a slightly changed General Classification. Note that now only two seconds separate Leipheimer and Vinokourov:

1. Lance Armstrong
2. Ivan Basso @ 4 minutes 40 seconds
3. Jan Ullrich @ 6 minutes 21 seconds
4. Francisco Mancebo @ 9 minutes 59 seconds

5. Levi Leipheimer @ 11 minutes 25 seconds

6. Alexandre Vinokourov @ 11 minutes 27 seconds

7. Michael Rasmussen @ 11 minutes 33 seconds

The final stage was confusing because light rain made the streets slippery. Not wanting to have a mass crash changing the final outcome, officials announced that the winner's final time for the General Classification would be fixed when the Tour crossed the finish line on the Champs Élysées for the first time. But the time bonuses for the second intermediate sprint and final sprint were still in play. Leipheimer had to keep worrying about Vinokourov. Vinokourov took a couple of bonus seconds in one of the intermediate sprints despite Leipheimer's team's best efforts to control the situation. Now Vinokourov was behind Leipheimer by only a fraction of a second. Then a ruling seemed to come down saying that the stage's remaining time bonuses had been cancelled.

In the final kilometer Vinokourov jetted away, winning the stage and the 20 bonus seconds which, to the surprise of Leipheimer, turned out to be up for grabs after all.

Final 2005 Tour de France General Classification:

1. Lance Armstrong (Discovery): 86 hours 15 minutes 2 seconds

2. Ivan Basso (CSC) @ 4 minutes 40 seconds

3. Jan Ullrich (T-Mobile) @ 6 minutes 21 seconds

4. Francisco Mancebo (Illes Balears) @ 9 minutes 59 seconds

5. Alexandre Vinokourov (T-Mobile) @ 11 minutes 1 second

6. Levi Leipheimer (Gerolsteiner) @ 11 minutes 21 seconds

Climbers' Competition:

1. Michael Rasmussen: 185 points

2. Óscar Pereiro: 155

3. Lance Armstrong: 99

Points Competition:

1. Thor Hushovd: 194 points

2. Stuart O'Grady: 182

3. Robbie McEwen: 178

The 2005 Tour was raced at an average speed of 41.654 kilometers per hour, an increase of about four kilometers per hour over Greg

LeMond's 1989 Tour. This ten percent increase in speed required an extraordinary jump in rider energy output. Straight-line increases in bicycle speed cause the cyclist's aerodynamic drag to go up by the square of the speed. While not all of a rider's efforts go into fighting the wind, there are other losses such as chain drag and tire rolling resistance, the overall effect is to require perhaps a quarter again as much energy to ride the Tour at this higher speed. There were 143 urine and 21 blood tests performed during the 2005 Tour without a single positive.

During the final awards ceremonies, Armstrong, now the winner of a record-breaking seventh consecutive Tour, was allowed to address the crowd. Bristling from doping accusations, he said, "I'm sorry you don't believe in miracles. But this is a hell of a race. You should believe in these athletes, and you should believe in these people. I'll be a fan of the Tour de France for as long as I live. And there are no secrets—this is a hard sporting event and hard work wins it."

It turned out miracles are hard to find.

six

2006–2011

Cycling begins to fight doping while the Grand Tours continue a turf war with the UCI.

2006

Philippe Amaury died on May 23, 2006. His widow Marie-Odile became the majority stockholder of Editions Philippe Amaury, the owner of *L'Équipe* and the Tour. As of 2014 the Amaury family owned 100 percent of the media group with its more than 3,000 employees and turnover of nearly €700 million (about a billion US dollars).

With Armstrong retired, the Tour organization was hoping a new era had arrived. Tour boss Jean-Marie Leblanc had taken the doping accusations against Armstrong to heart. When the 2006 route was unveiled, he and his successor, Christian Prudhomme, said, "On the 24th of July we turned a page on a long, very long chapter in the history of the Tour de France. And one month later, current events made it clear to us that it was just as well that this was so." Leblanc was even more blunt in a later interview with the Associated Press, saying that "[Armstrong] was not irreproachable in '99. EPO is a doping product. So this tempers and dilutes his performances and his credibility as a champion." Armstrong replied with his usual bluntness, "Jean-Marie Leblanc says the Tour deserves a better fate, I believe it deserves a better leader."

Leblanc himself had been planning to retire for some time, originally hoping to turn over the reins of Tour leadership after the 2003 Tour to Daniel Baal, deputy director of the Tour. But, as Leblanc hung on year after year, Baal gave up and resigned. Christian Prudhomme, a television journalist, was brought in as the new deputy to Leblanc, with Leblanc finally retiring after the 2006 Tour.

There were several men poised to make the 2006 Tour perhaps the hardest-fought race at least since 2003.

Jan Ullrich seemed to have banished his eating and training demons. He kept his weight under control over the winter and applied himself to his training with rigor. In spring, a knee inflammation kept him off his bike for a while, but he recovered enough to ride the Giro for training. During the Italian Tour he never pushed himself except in the stage eleven time trial which he won, beating an on-form Basso by 28 seconds over a flat, 50-kilometer course. Perhaps for only the second time since he had won the Tour in 1997, Jan Ullrich was in shape and ready to contest the Tour. He was the only former Tour winner entered.

Ivan Basso had been maturing as a stage racer and in 2005, could stay with the best on the climbs. His 2006 Giro win had been a study in effortless domination. Backed up by the strongest team in the race, he was able to pick his moments and deliver blow after lethal blow to his competitors. But, could Basso hold his magnificent form over such an extended period?

Floyd Landis had also enjoyed a superb spring, winning the Tour of California, Paris–Nice and the Tour de Georgia. His trainers insisted that Landis had such an abundance of strength that he didn't have to dig too deeply for his spring victories. He did have an incredible natural athletic talent, including an extraordinary VO_2 max of 90, close to LeMond's and well above Armstrong's, which was in the low 80s. Plus, Landis was a fearless and skilled bike handler, one who could descend mountains with astonishing speed.

Landis had been part of the Armstrong machine for three years, but after the 2004 Tour, he left the Postal team for Phonak. As had happened with other riders who had gone from being domestiques to competitors, Armstrong reacted to Landis' team change with anger and bitterness.

While considered a serious challenger in the 2005 Tour, by stage eleven Landis was already four minutes behind Armstrong. Some attributed Landis' final 12 minute, 44 second deficit to the psychological war Armstrong waged against him, an argument Landis says is wrong. But Landis seemed to have lost much of his fighting spirit once it became clear that a place on the 2005 Tour podium wasn't to be his.

And what about the Discovery team? Though now without Armstrong, it was still brimming with talent, talent that could help a great rider win the Tour. But Discovery didn't have a Grand Tour man except Paolo Savoldelli who was probably still cooked from the Giro.

The 2006 Tour was a counter-clockwise race, starting with a 7.1-kilometer Prologue individual time trial in Strasbourg. With 116.1 total kilometers of individual effort, this Tour placed a strong emphasis on time trialing. With just three hill-top finishes, there were fewer opportunities than in some previous editions for the pure climbers to put the *rouleurs* to the sword.

Once again, the pall of a doping scandal hung over professional cycling. On May 23, after a months-long investigation involving hidden cameras, the Spanish Civil Guard arrested five men, accusing them of an assortment of doping crimes. Among them were Liberty Seguros director Manolo Saiz, and José Ignacio Labarta, the assistant sports director of the Comunidad Valenciana squad. Immediately, the Liberty Insurance Company withdrew its sponsorship. Since Liberty Seguros was Kazakh rider Alexandre Vinokourov's team, a group of businessmen from Kazakhstan quickly replaced the missing funds and the team became Astana-Würth. Not being a Pro Tour team, Comunidad Valenciana was going to ride the Tour with a wild-card invitation, which was withdrawn in the face of the growing scandal.

The weekend before the start of the Tour is the traditional time for most National Championships, allowing the newly minted champions to ride the Tour wearing their national flag jerseys. On the Sunday morning of the championships, a Spanish newspaper leaked major details of the ongoing investigation, called *Operación Puerto*, showing that many riders and their teams had a deep involvement in systematized doping. The Spanish riders—as usual feeling that doping was their business and outraged at the publicity the story showered upon their illicit practices—staged a strike and refused to ride the Spanish Road Race Championship. As usual, the riders weren't outraged that there were cheaters amongst them. Their anger was at the publicity. Nothing but the drugs used to cheat had changed.

On the Thursday evening before the Saturday, July 1, Tour start, the Tour organization gave dossiers to the team managers documenting the growing case against the riders involved in the Spanish doping scandal. The team managers and Tour organization met and decided that since the Pro Tour code of ethics said, "No team will allow a rider to compete while under investigation in any doping affair", the riders, from several different teams, who were part of the inquiry would have to be excluded. Ullrich was in the team bus on the way to a Friday pre-Tour presentation when he was informed of his suspension. CSC director Bjarne Riis had to tell Basso he would not be able to ride the Tour. Also removed from the start list were Francisco Mancebo, Óscar Sevilla, Joseba Beloki, Isidro Nozal, Sérgio Paulinho, Allan Davis and Alberto Contador. For the first time since 1999 there would be no former Tour winners on the start line.

Vinokourov was collateral damage. Even though he wasn't suspended, his team lost too many riders because replacements weren't allowed when a rider is excluded for doping problems. Tour rules require six riders on a team and Vinokourov's Astana-Würth squad was now down to five. In a stunning admission of a failure to perform even the most elementary due diligence, Vinokourov said that he only learned after he had signed for the team that team owner and boss Manolo Saiz was engaged in an ongoing war with the Tour. Back in 1998, at the height of the Tour's crises, Saiz had pulled his ONCE team out of the Tour in order to...no, what he said he was doing to the Tour is unprintable. But Saiz had surely set both himself and his team up for a fall by striking at the Tour at its moment of greatest difficulty.

The start list was now whittled down to 176 starters, the smallest field since 1984's 170 riders. Last years' first through fifth place would not be competing, the highest-placed 2005 Tour finisher entered was Levi Leipheimer, who had finished sixth.

The effect of the exclusion raised the hopes of many riders who's dreams were previously limited to just a place on the podium. Leipheimer, winner of the Dauphiné, thought he could win. Others such as Cadel Evans, Andreas Klöden and Bobby Julich were now considered potential winners. Damiano Cunego, who said he was riding the Tour just to learn, voiced the hope that he now had a chance to win.

Big, strong Thor Hushovd (2005 Green Jersey) won the Prologue, keeping George Hincapie out of Yellow by only three-quarters of a second. Mechanics discovered cuts in Landis' rear tire just before he started. Not wanting to take a chance, they replaced it, forcing Landis to roll up the ramp late and take off immediately, probably costing him eight seconds.

Early in the first stage, Hincapie bagged 2 bonus seconds in an intermediate sprint, giving him his first Yellow Jersey in ten Tour attempts. Maybe Discovery was starting its first post-Armstrong Tour well.

The next day, Discovery director Bruyneel indicated he was looking for more than just an early capture of the Yellow Jersey. Not wanting to tire his team, he chose not to defend Hincapie's lead.

Stage three, another Northern European stage, left several riders with race-ending injuries, most notably Valverde, who crashed and broke his collarbone in the final kilometers of the stage. The intense heat (35°C) and high speeds made for a fatigued peloton with riders susceptible to moments of inattention.

Laurent Fignon, who had replaced Bernard Thévenet as the race commentator for the France 2 television channel, explained why the carnage in a professional race crash can be so great. When the peloton is racing hard (and the pros do ride closer together than amateurs), all the rider sees is the back of the rider in front of him and a peripheral view of the riders to his side. He doesn't see much of what is going on up ahead as he fights to maintain his position while riding all-out. When the helicopters following the race come down low and close to the bunch during a crash, riders can't hear the squeal of brakes and the riders' shouts and the sounds of folding bikes. The din of the helicopter's engine and rotors drowns that all out. The riders continue down the road and race into the waiting mess, blind and deaf to the carnage that awaits them.

The Spanish doping scandal continued to roil the waters. Würth (of Astana-Würth) and the Comunidad Valenciana pulled their sponsorships. French sports minister Jean-François Lamour accused the UCI of failing to attack doping seriously. UCI president Pat McQuaid bristled in response, basically admitting the current state of the drug detecting art could not catch a modern, sophisticated doper.

This is true, and is why the riders caught up in *Operación Puerto* had never tested positive for dope. As Lamour said, only the naïve get caught in drug tests.

As the Tour moved across Normandy and into Brittany, the race remained the plaything of the sprinters. World Champion Tom Boonen wasn't able to win a stage, but through his consistent high placings, with their attendant time bonuses, he was able to secure the Yellow Jersey after stage four and to hold it until the seventh stage's 52-kilometer time trial. Boonen was the first man since Greg LeMond in 1990 to trade a Rainbow Jersey for one of Yellow.

The time trial in the Brittany town of Rennes was filled with surprises and heartbreak. The general expectation was that American riders or those in the American Discovery and the Danish CSC teams would dominate. Midway through the stage this hope received its first blow. CSC, which had already sent Basso packing, lost another of its best riders when Bobby Julich crashed out of the Tour as he had in 1999. This time, going through an "S" curve at nearly full speed, he hit some gravel and went flying. David Zabriskie, usually one of the fastest men in the world against the clock, lost almost two minutes, blaming it on his failure to pre-ride the course. Leipheimer, who had won the Dauphiné only a couple of weeks before, dropped six minutes. Discovery riders Hincapie and Savoldelli also did poorly.

The emergent winners after the time trial? T-Mobile had four men in the top six of the General Classification (Gonchar, Rogers, Sinkewitz, Klöden) with Ukrainian Sergey Gonchar—pounding a monstrous 55 x 11 gear—winning the day and the Yellow Jersey. Landis again had a late start. This time officials forced him to modify the placement of his aero bars. After he started, they soon came loose, forcing a bike change. Still, he came in second, losing only a minute to Gonchar.

The General Classification after the stage seven time trial:

1. Sergey Gonchar
2. Floyd Landis @ 1 minute 0 seconds
3. Michael Rogers @ 1 minute 8 seconds
4. Patrik Sinkewitz @ 1 minute 45 seconds
5. Marcus Fothen @ 1 minute 50 seconds
6. Andreas Klöden @ same time

After seeing the results, Johan Bruyneel said, "It's lucky Jan Ullrich is not here, otherwise the Tour would be over."

Behind the scenes of the Tour, the UCI and the Grand Tour organizers had been holding talks to see if their disagreements over the Pro Tour could be bridged. Patrice Clerc, spokesman for the Tour, announced that at this point the negotiations were dead, meaning the Grand Tours would not participate in the Pro Tour.

During the first rest day, Landis announced that after the Tour he would undergo hip replacement surgery. Landis had broken his hip in 2003 and it had never healed correctly.

Stage ten, from Cambo-les-Bains to Pau featured the Col d'Osquich, Soudet and the first-category Marie-Blanque. It was rightly predicted that with the finish line 40 kilometers after the summit of the Marie-Blanque, the day would be one of careful watching and perhaps one of attrition, as the accumulated kilometers took their toll on the riders' legs. T-Mobile did some work defending Gonchar's Yellow Jersey, giving Landis and the other contenders a free ride.

Juan Miguel Mercado and Cyril Dessel got completely clear on the Marie-Blanque and drove their break all the way to the finish. They had been granted so much freedom that Dessel, who had been adventuring for climber's points, gained enough time to take the lead. In the final kilometers, Mercado tried to make a deal with Dessel, telling him that since Dessel would gain both the Yellow and Polka-Dot Jerseys, he should let Mercado take the stage win, a not unusual sharing of the spoils. Dessel was so sure of his strength and so desperately wanted the stage win that he refused the offer. Mercado immediately stopped working, forcing Dessel to pull the pair over the final five kilometers. Mercado easily won the sprint and Dessel took the lead. Dessel's choice would have interesting consequences.

If the contenders had been keeping their powder dry, it was for stage eleven. With the Tourmalet, Aspin, Peyresourde, Portillon and a hilltop finish at Pla-de-Beret, there would now be the clarity that had been lacking because of the best riders' conservative riding. On the penultimate climb, the Portillon, T-Mobile massed at the front and increased the tempo. The effect was to shell many riders who had been struggling all day. Over the top, Klöden, Landis, Evans, Denis Menchov, Cunego, Simoni, Boogerd and Rasmussen were among the survivors.

For Discovery, the news was bleak. Only Azevedo had been able to stay with the leaders; Hincapie, Savoldelli and Yaroslav Popovych had been dropped. Dessel, the Yellow Jersey, also came off.

At the base of the final ascent, Rabobank had an embarrassment of riches with Rasmussen, Boogerd and Menchov having made the cut. Menchov told his teammates that he was feeling good. In response, Boogerd and Rasmussen set a pace only Menchov, Evans, Landis, Leipheimer, Sastre and Klöden could withstand. After Rasmussen sat up, depleted from his efforts, Boogerd continued to drive hard, dropping Klöden. T-Mobile's General Classification hope had crumbled under the pressure of the withering heat and high speeds. With eight kilometers to go, the lead group was down to Landis, Menchov, Leipheimer, Sastre and Evans. Leipheimer mounted two attacks, reducing the group to Menchov, Landis and himself. Menchov won the stage and Landis took the lead. But it didn't have to end that way. Race leader Dessel punished himself, racing for the finish line with all he had, ending the day 4 minutes, 45 seconds behind Landis, the exact difference in their General Classification times. Landis' 8-second time bonus for third place gave him the edge in time and levered him into the Yellow Jersey. If Dessel had cooperated with Mercado the day before, he would surely have arrived at that finish more than eight seconds sooner and would have still been in Yellow at least until the Alpe d'Huez stage the following Tuesday.

After stage eleven, the General Classification stood thus:
1. Floyd Landis
2. Cyril Dessel @ 8 seconds
3. Denis Menchov @ 1 minute 1 second
4. Cadel Evans @ 1 minute 17 seconds
5. Carlos Sastre @ 1 minute 52 seconds
6. Andreas Klöden @ 2 minutes 29 seconds

That was it for the Pyrenees. The next day, Discovery's Popovych got into the winning break and soloed home to salve the open wound of the team's general collapse. That savvy move lifted Popovych to tenth, 4 minutes, 15 seconds behind Landis, making him the best-placed Discovery rider.

The Spanish doping investigation rolled on. A German newspaper alleged the records of Eufemiano Fuentes, the doctor at the heart of the scandal, showed that Jan Ullrich took insulin, cortisone, and various hormones including testosterone, as well as a unit of his own blood, in preparation for the 2005 Tour.

July's relentless heat continued to bake the riders. Saturday's stage thirteen was the year's longest at 230 kilometers, and was held on possibly the hottest day of the 2006 Tour. A break of four strong riders, all low in the standings, was allowed to gain a half hour, probably because Phonak wanted another team to take and defend the lead. Óscar Pereiro of the Illes Balears team, the best-placed rider in the break, was perfect for the task. He had lost a lot of time in the Pyrenees (he was forty-sixth at the start of the stage) and could be expected to suffer badly in the Alps and surrender his lead, at this point only 1 minute, 29 seconds. Surely the Yellow Jersey was an unexpected development for the Spanish team and they would work like dogs to keep the lead for the next stage so that they could bask in it during the rest day. Phonak could relax and be ready for the real fight in the Alps.

Indeed, Pereiro's team did work hard to defend his lead during stage fourteen, a transitional stage, giving the Phonak their desired rest.

Stage fifteen, with the Izoard, Lautaret and hilltop finish on l'Alpe d'Huez, was the first of three days in the Alps. As usual, a break of non-contenders went clear early, while the Classification men stayed together until the base of l'Alpe d'Huez. T-Mobile started things rolling by sending their men to the front to whip up the pace. Then a Phonak rider went even harder and almost instantly it was down to Landis, Menchov, Evans and Klöden. Landis accelerated and dropped all but Klöden. Then others, including earlier dropees Leipheimer and Sastre, regained contact, but they couldn't withstand another surge, this time by Klöden. Up ahead, Luxembourger Frank Schleck, who had been away most of the day, hung on to an 11-second lead for the stage win. Landis emerged from the battle in the Yellow Jersey.

The General Classification after stage fifteen:
1. Floyd Landis
2. Óscar Pereiro @ 10 seconds
3. Cyril Dessel @ 2 minutes 2 seconds
4. Denis Menchov @ 2 minutes 12 seconds
5. Carlos Sastre @ 2 minutes 17 seconds

After Landis' masterful performance in stage fifteen, the even more difficult sixteenth leg should have been a platform from which he could solidify his lead. The day included the Galibier, Croix de Fer, Mollard and a first-category hilltop finish at La Toussuire. Rasmussen jetted away from a break on the Galibier with Tadej Valjavec and Sandy Casar in tow. The peloton, knowing that worse than the Galibier was in store for them that day, continued to ride tempo with Landis looking quite comfortable. On the Croix de Fer, Rasmussen was now alone and riding powerfully with a seven-minute lead on the peloton.

When the Croix de Fer started to bite, T-Mobile lifted the pace, costing Landis most of his team. For the first time, Landis was sitting farther back in the peloton instead of his usual place near the front. On the second-category Col du Mollard, Landis looked a bit distressed while riding at the very back of his group. When the peloton arrived at the base of the final climb there had been some regrouping, but Landis had just one teammate, Eddy Merckx's son Axel.

Carlos Sastre then took off on a solo flight followed by a blast of speed from T-Mobile and with that, Landis' legs exploded. After displaying weeks of mastery, he was suddenly unable to stay with the leaders. He was soundly dropped and in the final kilometers to the summit, lost about a minute per kilometer.

Up ahead, Rasmussen crossed the line first after being away for 173 kilometers. Sastre had been closing fast, but came up 1 minute, 41 seconds short. The big surprise was Óscar Pereiro, who came in third and retook the Yellow Jersey. Landis limped in twenty-third, ten minutes after Rasmussen.

At this point, it was assumed that Landis' quest for the overall win was over. As to why he suffered a *défaillance* on this most crucial of days, Landis was less than candid, saying, "I had a very bad day on the wrong day." Bernard Hinault speculated that he had suffered a terrible hunger knock.

That evening, instead of giving up, Landis and his team planned how to get back in the race. Eddy Merckx told Landis that the race wasn't over. Word got out to the other pros that he was going to do something spectacular early in the stage. Some of them asked him not to be so foolhardy. He told them he was going on the first hill.

If possible, stage seventeen was the hardest stage yet, with few kilometers of flat road. It was almost all rising or falling terrain. For their final day in the Alps, the exhausted riders had to climb first the Saisies, then the Aravis, followed by the Colombière, the Châtillon and finally the *hors catégorie* Joux-Plane. A break went clear in the first kilometers. On the Saisies, Phonak massed at the front and drove hard. Klöden and Landis attacked and few could go with them. Landis attacked again and was alone. Up the Saisies he flew, riding as if he had never suffered any trouble at all the day before, lending credence to Hinault's explanation as to why Landis had collapsed the previous day.

Landis' recovery was so complete, he ascended the 6.4 percent Saisies in the big ring. At the summit he was over three minutes ahead of the peloton and within three minutes of the leaders. He descended the Saisies hell-bent to make up his previous day's losses. He caught most of the leading break on the lower slopes of the Aravis, but didn't wait or rest. He went right through them, taking along just Daniele Righi and Patrik Sinkewitz. Over the top of the Aravis, Landis had built his lead to 4 minutes, 31 seconds. Back in the peloton, Pereiro was down to one teammate. By the base of the Colombière, Landis' lead had grown to 5 minutes, 30 seconds.

When he topped the Colombière, Landis had an astounding 8 minutes, 30 seconds. So far, T-Mobile, CSC, Davitamon-Lotto and Ag2r, all teams with riders in the hunt for the Yellow Jersey, had been playing a dangerous game of poker, depending on Pereiro's remaining two teammates to perform the chase. It wasn't working, but still they did nothing while Landis continued to ride away with the Tour de France.

On the descent of the Colombière, Landis pushed his lead to nine minutes. Finally the other teams woke up. CSC started to work to protect Sastre, and eventually T-Mobile helped. That effort cut the gap, but by the time Landis reached the base of the steepest climb of the day, the Joux-Plane, he still had 7 minutes, 25 seconds. Sinkewitz, who had been sitting on Landis' wheel, was finally dropped. Landis was now alone. Behind, Sastre escaped the peloton and climbed strongly in pursuit.

At the top of the difficult Joux-Plane, Landis led Sastre by five minutes and Pereiro's group by seven. The descent of the Joux-Plane to Morzine is technical and dangerous, perfect for a man with Landis' descending skills. He dropped down the mountain as if his hair were on fire, extending his lead by another 30 seconds. He crossed the line 5 minutes, 42 seconds ahead of Sastre and 7 minutes, 8 seconds in front of Pereiro. In addition, by virtue of his stage win, second intermediate sprint win and climber's bonuses for being the first over the mountains, Landis accumulated about 30 seconds in bonifications. He was back in the race.

The new General Classification:

1. Óscar Pereiro
2. Carlos Sastre @ 12 seconds
3. Floyd Landis @ 30 seconds
4. Andreas Klöden @ 2 minutes 29 seconds
5. Cadel Evans @ 3 minutes 8 seconds

The next day, anticipating the crucial 57-kilometer individual time trial, the contenders pulled back their claws. This would be settled on the penultimate stage.

T-Mobile announced that they had fired both Jan Ullrich and Oscar Sevilla. Both men had been given 30 days by the team to establish their innocence. Ullrich equivocated, refusing to take a DNA test that could exonerate him. He argued that a man doesn't have to prove his innocence, others must prove his guilt. True in court, false in cycling. T-Mobile said that even if Ullrich were eventually cleared, he would have to find employment with another team.

The Tour was settled during that final time trial, or so it seemed. While time-trial specialist Sergey Gonchar set the fastest time, over the first fourteen kilometers, Landis was only a second slower. But, not wanting to blow up or worry about matching the speed of a man who was two hours down on the General Classification, Landis continued at his own pace. Pereiro was tenacious, losing only 10 seconds to Landis at the first time check. By the second time check, at 34 kilometers, Pereiro had relented, giving up a full minute and the lead. There were two surprises: Sastre's less-than-stellar performance, costing him his podium placing, and Klöden's brilliant second-place ride, moving him up to third. Landis had now regained the lead with only the promenade to Paris left to go.

There were no surprises as the remaining 139 riders blistered the Champs Élysées. Thor Hushovd took advantage of the peloton's disorganization following a series of hard attacks by Discovery.

Without the lead-out trains keeping things together, it was every man for himself. Green Jersey Robbie McEwen was beaten by the strong, quick-witted Hushovd who had the distinction of winning both the opening Prologue and the closing sprint.

Final 2006 Tour de France General Classification:
1. Floyd Landis (Phonak): 89 hours 39 minutes 30 seconds.
2. Óscar Pereiro (Caisse d'Epargne) @ 57 seconds
3. Andreas Klöden (T-Mobile) @ 1 minute 29 seconds
4. Carlos Sastre (CSC) @ 3 minutes 13 seconds
5. Cadel Evans (Davitamon-Lotto) @ 5 minutes 8 seconds

Climbers' Competition:
1. Michael Rasmussen: 166 points
2. Floyd Landis: 131
3. David de la Fuente: 113

Points Competition:
1. Robbie McEwen: 288 points
2. Erik Zabel: 199
3. Thor Hushovd: 195

Landis' win made 11 American Tour victories in the past 21 years:

On Monday the Spanish teams engaged in mutual recriminations over who should have taken the responsibility of reining in Landis during stage seventeen. Cyrille Guimard thought that if Dessel's team had ridden with greater intelligence, Dessel could have won the Tour. The newspapers were dominated by stories of the man with the bad hip who had tamed the European peloton.

Then on Wednesday it was leaked that a rider high in the General Classification had tested positive for dope. Moreover, the positive, called an "adverse analytical finding", was from stage seventeen. Speculation was rampant as reporters tried to find out who the rider was. Because rules require the national cycling federations be notified of a doping positive, riders from Germany, France, Spain, Italy and France could be eliminated when their federations said that they had not received any such notice.

Reporters started to home in on Landis when he failed to show up for two lucrative post-Tour criteriums, races where he was to receive $100,000 each in appearance money. On Thursday, with Landis still missing, his team confirmed that indeed he was the rider in question. The test that tripped up Landis measured the ratio between testosterone and epitestosterone, and Landis had shown an elevated level of the testosterone, more than his body would produce naturally.

Landis surfaced Friday and began a series of public appearances, begging for patience while he mounted a defense to show that he had not cheated. The definitive test, called "Carbon Isotope Ratio Analysis" would have to be made to determine if the statistically excessive testosterone in Landis' system was synthetic or naturally secreted.

The test was performed and synthetic testosterone was found to be in Landis' system.

Goaded by others in professional cycling, Landis mounted a million-dollar defense of his Tour title. His understanding was that if he denied doping and fought the charges, he would get help. But, if he were to come clean and explain the doping that he and his teammates had committed, Landis believed he would be the victim of the full force of the Armstrong cycling-industrial complex.

He forced an arbitration hearing that was held in May, 2007. Landis argued that the doping lab's procedural errors were so substantial that his positive for testosterone was invalid.

Just when it seemed as if things could not get worse, they did. Greg LeMond was called to testify in the arbitration hearing. The night before LeMond was to take the stand, Landis' business manager made an anonymous call to LeMond, pretending to be LeMond's uncle. He threatened to reveal the secret of LeMond's childhood sexual abuse. Earlier, trying to convince Landis to admit to doping, LeMond had told Landis about his childhood abuse, telling him that holding secrets like this is very destructive.

The call was traced and the sordid episode came out. Landis had been present when the threatening call was made. Landis claimed that he should be believed when he said he wouldn't cheat to win a race, because his character made him above that sort of thing. That argument now lay in tatters.

On September 21, 2007, the arbitration panel ruled 2-to-1 that Landis had doped. The Tour stripped him of his title and awarded the 2006 Tour to Óscar Pereiro, a decision that has withstood Landis' appeals.

The new 2006 Tour de France General Classification podium:

1. Óscar Pereiro (Caisse d'Epargne) 89 hours 40 minutes 27 seconds
2. Andreas Klöden (T-Mobile) @ 32 seconds
3. Carlos Sastre (CSC) @ 2 minutes 16 seconds

2007 Doping news was all anyone could read about in the winter and spring leading up to the 2007 Tour.

Ivan Basso, who had so effortlessly won the 2006 Giro, seemed to skate past any problems with the Puerto scandal. The Spanish judge examining the Puerto evidence appeared to be looking for a way to ignore as much of the case as possible and to investigate as little of the dossier as would appear seemly. He shelved the case, saying that at the time, while it appeared that doping had occurred, nothing that had happened was against Spanish law.

Next, the Italian Olympic Committee (CONI) tried to investigate Basso. Since they couldn't get their hands on all of the evidence from the Spaniards, in October, 2006 they had to pronounce Basso able to sign for a team and ride. This non-exoneration clearance was all Johan Bruyneel needed to sign Basso to his Discovery team. Making matters worse, alone among the Pro Tour teams, Discovery signed several other Puerto-implicated riders.

The other Pro Tour teams erupted in fury because they had all agreed to avoid signing Puerto riders until the case was closed and the suspected riders truly cleared. Because of this breach, many teams would combine against Discovery during-early season races.

The Puerto inquiry looked like it was going to die, but it didn't. The big break came in early April 2007 when German prosecutors were finally able to match up Jan Ullrich's DNA with blood bags seized from Fuentes. In late April it was revealed that an Italian prosecutor had blood bags from Fuentes that were thought to contain Basso's blood. From then on, Basso's defenses came apart. Knowing what was coming, Basso requested and was granted release from his Discovery contract.

On May 7, 2007, faced with too much evidence, Basso confessed to being involved with Fuentes, but refused to admit he had ever doped. He said he had planned to dope in the 2006 Tour, but that so far, all of his wins were clean. Skeptical observers wondered why he never again raced with the mastery he had shown in 2006 and why he had been paying Fuentes tens of thousands of euros since 2004.

The Giro organizers ruled that the fifty or so riders implicated in the Puerto scandal could not start the Giro. Tyler Hamilton, Michele Scarponi and Jörg Jaksche, all potential contenders, would not be able to ride.

Race organizers had to get a handle on the doping and not just for reasons of common decency. In the wake of the Puerto scandal, the television audience for the Vuelta fell thirty percent. When team sponsors Comunidad Valenciana and Liberty Seguros pulled out of the sport, they took millions of euros out of the sport with them. Sales of racing-related books and DVDs plummeted. It was vital to the economic health of pro racing that the cheating be brought under control.

At the end of April former Telekom *soigneur* Jef D'Hont alleged that during the mid-1990s, Telekom team doctors administered EPO to their riders as part of a team-wide systematic program of doping. The usual denials were made. But the wall of silence started to fall when Telekom riders from that era, Erik Zabel, Rolf Aldag, Brian Holm, and Udo Bölts, among others, came forward and confessed. They said that with the pressure to win and to beat other doped riders, they had to use the needle or risk losing their jobs.

On Friday, May 25, Tour de France winner and CSC team owner Bjarne Riis held a press conference. He finally came clean. The man who had the nickname of "Mr. 60 Percent" for the rumored hematocrit he sported when he won the 1996 Tour admitted he had used EPO, hormones and cortisone in his campaign to win the Tour.

D'Hont said Riis had run his hematocrit up to a frightening 64 percent. That was how Riis had risen from competent domestique to being the dominant rider of the 1996 Tour.

Riis' confession left an important question unanswered. How could Riis, famous for his hands-on, close and careful management of his riders, not know about Basso's relationship with Fuentes and not wonder about Basso's extraordinary performance in the 2006 Giro, especially in light of his own dope-fueled performances?

The series of doping confessions showed that after 1998, teams had continued with their institutionalized doping programs. The wounded denials coming from the accused managers sounded exactly like those that came from Bruno Roussel in 1998.

All this scandal created only the third Tour in the last thirty years (1999, 2006, 2007) in which no former winner was on the starting line. The Tour, wanting to make a symbolic gesture but not having the 2006 winner present, decided not to give any rider the Number 1 back-number (or *dossard*). The riders' numbers would start with numbers 11–19, which were given to Valverde's Caisse d'Epargne team.

Who was left to start the race? Alexandre Vinokourov was the favorite. At thirty-three he knew this was his last, best chance to win. His Astana team was superb, now with Andreas Klöden as part of a one-two punch that could be devastating in the hands of a good strategist. Vinokourov had ridden the Dauphiné for training and displayed good form by winning the time trial and one other stage.

With Basso gone, Discovery fell back on its earlier signing, Levi Leipheimer. Leipheimer was a probable podium finisher, but an unlikely Tour winner, a view Bruyneel seemed to hold.

The two other major contenders were Alejandro Valverde and Cadel Evans. Valverde was riding under a Puerto cloud, but he denied any involvement and no firm evidence at the moment seemed to connect him. While Valverde was a gifted climber, he had wilted under the assault of Vinokourov and his Kazakhs in the 2006 Vuelta. Evans prepared quietly for the Tour, and his condition was looking good when he came in second to Christophe Moreau in the Dauphiné.

Other riders like Alberto Contador, excluded the previous year for alleged involvement in Puerto, were allowed to race in 2007.

Like the 2006 route, the course itself seemed designed for a complete rider. The time trialing, at 117.4 kilometers, was only a kilometer more than in 2006 and there were three hilltop finishes. At 3,570 kilometers, the 2007 Tour's length was in line with recent editions.

For the first time since 1996, the Tour visited Britain. This time, the Prologue was in London, and stage one was to be raced between London and Canterbury. Then the Tour was to cross the British Channel for a clockwise (Alps first) Tour. The riders had to confront the Alps earlier than usual, in stage seven, with an ascent of the Col de la Colombière followed by a day with three first-category climbs.

The Prologue in London was a smashing success, with an estimated crowd of one million lining the streets to watch. World Time Trial Champion Fabian Cancellara won the stage convincingly. Most important, none of the major contenders lost any appreciable time. Andreas Klöden finished second, slightly ahead of the others who had ambitions of Yellow in Paris.

Late in stage one, a crash took down several riders including Robbie McEwen. His team waited for him, and with great effort dragged him back to the fast-moving peloton. As the sprinters started to wind up the final meters, out of nowhere popped the amazing McEwen. He was bruised and battered, but moving far faster than any of the others as he nailed the stage convincingly.

The Tour returned to the continent, and after a detour to Belgium made its way south for the Alps. At the end of stage three Cancellara, still in Yellow, surprised the sprinters, who had a moment of hesitation before the sprint began. The powerful Swiss jumped clear and earned the 20-second time bonus for winning the stage.

Vinokourov, who always seemed to have a bottomless well of bad luck at his disposal, again suffered misfortune, this time in stage five. First, teammate Andreas Klöden crashed and injured a previously fractured tailbone. Then, with about 25 kilometers to go, a slipped chain sent Vinokourov to the ground. His team directed everyone but potential Tour winners Klöden and Andrey Kashechkin to wait for the Kazakh to help him back up to the peloton. On the final climb, Vinokourov left his teammates, chasing the raging pack all by himself. Because there was a break up the road that threatened Cancellara's lead, CSC had been driving the peloton hard. Vinokourov never did make contact and lost 1 minute, 20 seconds.

After spending five hours in the hospital, Vinokourov started the flat sixth stage. Klöden was also able to start. But the effect of their crashes, combined with the ultra-intense racing in stage five, was to further open the Tour to others who had only dreamed of a shot at the podium.

The day's racing allowed the evergreen Erik Zabel to take the Green Jersey for the first time since 2002. The next day Tom Boonen won the last flat stage before the Alps, taking Zabel's Green Jersey.

Worse for Zabel, as a result of having confessed to doping in 1996, the Tour organization announced that it was stripping him of his Green Jersey for that year.

With the Tour scheduled to ascend the tough north face of the Col de la Colombière in stage seven, the General Classification stood thus:

1. Fabian Cancellara
2. Andreas Klöden @ 33 seconds
3. Filippo Pozzato @ 35 seconds
4. David Millar @ 41 seconds
5. Óscar Freire @ 43 seconds

T-Mobile's young Linus Gerdemann rode away from his breakaway companions on the Colombière and came in alone after a skilled descent into Le Grand-Bornand. Gerdemann was now the *maillot jaune* with a lead of 84 seconds over Spanish rider Iñigo Landaluze. While the stage may have removed many non-contenders from the top ranks, the day in the Alps didn't affect the relative positions of the best riders. The real racing would have to wait for Sunday's hilltop finish.

That evening, both Valverde and French champion Moreau said that Vinokourov should be dealt a *coup de grace* while he was still suffering from his crash and before the Kazakh could take advantage of the coming rest day to recover.

Well into stage eight, Michael Rasmussen left the peloton on the Cormet de Roselend. He rode away from a peloton that contained almost all of the big men and did so without the slightest challenge or marking from the other riders. They just let him go, and go he did. He went right through an earlier break and picked up T-Mobile's leader, former world time trial champion Michael Rogers.

The fortunes of T-Mobile now went from the high of Gerdemann's success the day before to the low of having Rogers crash out of the Tour on the descent of the Cormet de Roselend. Doubling the pain of the injuries, when Rogers hit the railing on the descent he was the Tour's virtual Yellow Jersey, "I could see the Yellow, I could taste it, now it's gone," Rogers recalled.

The descent of the Cormet de Roselend took another casualty, but its true effect wouldn't be apparent until the end of the Tour. Leipheimer had problems with his chain, requiring him to freewheel down the mountain and lose contact with the lead riders. After switching bikes he rode next to his team car and got a good, long hard push. This probably would have been allowed in 2006, but in 2007 the judges decided to crack down and assessed Leipheimer a 10-second penalty.

Rasmussen pushed on, riding powerfully and confidently to both the stage victory and the overall lead.

Behind him, Moreau attacked the remnants of the peloton and slightly distanced himself from Vinokourov and Klöden. He tried to get the others in his group, which included Evans and Valverde, to make a coordinated effort to get away from the Astana riders while the getting was good, but each of his accelerations was only matched. The result was some damage to Vinokourov, but not the finality Moreau had sought.

The General Classification after stage eight, going into a rest day before the final alpine stage:

1. Michael Rasmussen
2. Linus Gerdemann @ 43 seconds
3. Iban Mayo @ 2 minutes 39 seconds
4. Alejandro Valverde @ 2 minutes 51 seconds
5. Andrey Kashechkin @ 2 minutes 52 seconds
6. Cadel Evans @ 2 minutes 53 seconds
7. Christophe Moreau @ 3 minutes 6 seconds
22. Alexandre Vinokourov @ 5 minutes 23 seconds

Stage nine had the Iseran and the Galibier. After ascending the Galibier's little brother, the Télégraphe, Mauricio Soler rolled away and was never seen again. But back in the pointy part of the peloton, the speed on the ascent of the Galibier was too much for Vinokourov, who had to concede almost three minutes. This time Astana didn't have Klöden sacrifice his chances by staying with Vinokourov. With the Alps behind them, the standings were thus:

1. Michael Rasmussen
2. Alejandro Valverde @ 2 minutes 35 seconds
3. Iban Mayo @ 2 minutes 39 seconds
4. Cadel Evans @ 2 minutes 41 seconds
5. Alberto Contador @ 3 minutes 8 seconds
6. Christophe Moreau @ 3 minutes 18 seconds
7. Carlos Sastre @ 3 minutes 39 seconds
8. Andreas Klöden @ 3 minutes 50 seconds

Stage ten was on a hot day, and the baking temperatures made Vinokourov miserable enough to consider abandoning. Vinokourov was probably not as unhappy as Bob Stapleton, the American brought in to manage the T-Mobile team under a regime of absolute intolerance to doping. It was announced that T-Mobile's Patrik Sinkewitz, who had quit the Tour a few days earlier after breaking his nose in a collision with a spectator, had tested positive for testosterone in an earlier, out-of-competition test. Tired of the doping, the German public television network, as promised, immediately pulled the plug on their Tour coverage.

The next day there were rumors that some sort of move was afoot. After the feed zone, while Christophe Moreau was at the back of the pack, Astana took advantage of the hot winds blowing across the peloton. They massed at the front and detonated the race with a high-powered attack, breaking the pack apart and catching Moreau, Zabel, and Hushovd napping. Over half the field never saw the lead group again as the Kazakhs furiously hammered at the front. Zabel's chances for Green were about gone and Moreau's loss of over three minutes made a podium place in Paris unlikely. Astana had a newfound morale after showing they were there to race. The 2007 Tour was at least refreshing in its combativeness.

It was the accepted wisdom that the 54-kilometer individual time trial would be Rasmussen's last day in Yellow. Further, it was thought that either Valverde or Evans would take the lead. Nothing was going as planned in this Tour. Rasmussen delivered a superb ride, actually catching Valverde and retaining the Yellow Jersey. Meanwhile, Vinokourov won the stage and took back more than three minutes, saying that he would set off fireworks in the Pyrenees. I am sure no one in the race doubted him.

The standings:

1. Michael Rasmussen
2. Cadel Evans @ 1 minute
3. Alberto Contador @ 2 minutes 31 seconds
4. Andreas Klöden @ 2 minutes 34 seconds
5. Levi Leipheimer @ 3 minutes 37 seconds
9. Alexandre Vinokourov @ 5 minutes 10 seconds

Stage fourteen, the first Pyrenean stage, ended with two *hors catégorie* climbs, the Port de Pailhères and a hilltop finish at Plateau de Beille. Saunier Duval, preparing for an attack by Iban Mayo, set a scorching pace up the Pailhères. There were notable casualties: Mayo, who later finished the day over nine minutes down, and Vinokourov. To make matters worse, near the top of the mountain a zealous fan caused a teammate riding with Vinokourov to crash, forcing Vinokourov to land on his damaged left knee.

The day's final showdown on the ascent to Plateau de Beille was superb, exciting racing. The favorites took turns relentlessly attacking and counter-attacking. An early victim was Klöden, probably still hurting from his earlier time trial crash. Fate seemed to be unforgiving in her treatment of the Kazakh team. From the series of savage blows the racers dealt each other, Contador and Rasmussen emerged and finished together in that order. Contador moved to second and Rasmussen started to look like a man who might wear Yellow in Paris.

But all was not well with Rasmussen. The UCI now revealed that Rasmussen had missed several out-of-competition drug tests over the last two years. Worse, an American ex-racer alleged that in 2002 Rasmussen had tried to trick him into smuggling a box of blood substitute into Europe for him, disguised as shoes. In June, the Danish Cycling Union had kicked Rasmussen off the National Team, making Rasmussen ineligible to contest the World Championship or the coming Olympics. The tardy timing of the news release about his missing the required testing made many suspicious about the UCI, still mired in its ongoing war with the Grand Tour organizers. It was suggested that the UCI timed the release specifically to harm the Tour.

The other teams and the Tour organization became increasingly angry that Rabobank, knowing what it did about Rasmussen, had sent him to ride the Tour anyway. Rabobank played dumb, saying that Rasmussen had not failed any drug tests, so there was no reason to keep him off the team. This explanation satisfied few.

Stage fifteen was still harder than the day before, with the Port, Portet d'Aspet, Menté, Balès and the Peyresourde on the day's menu. Early in the day's racing Vinokourov joined a break that was allowed to go. His nearly half-hour time loss the day before meant that the General Classification men didn't have to worry about him. By the Peyresourde, Vinokourov was clear. He soloed over the crest and rode down the other side into Loudenvielle-Le Louron to win the stage.

Farther back, the Yellow Jersey group was content to let Rabobank domestiques Thomas Dekker and Michael Boogerd set the pace. About two kilometers from the top of the Peyresourde, Contador delivered six brutal attacks that only Rasmussen could answer. With each acceleration, Contador was able to open a gap that Rasmussen struggled to close. Rasmussen was weakening, but Contador had opened the hostilities too late. The two went over the top of the Peyresourde together, making Wednesday (stage sixteen), the final day in the mountains with its hilltop finish on the Aubisque, the 2007 Tour's probable arbiter.

Vinokourov's positive test for a homologous blood transfusion the day of his time trial win was announced during the rest day. The news staggered everyone. Vinokourov was out of the Tour and his Astana team was asked to leave with him, which it did.

There was still a race to be ridden, and what a race stage sixteen was. At the morning sign-in, the announcer had to stop talking for a moment when Rasmussen came forward because the crowd was whistling (the European way of showing contempt) and booing so loudly.

Rabobank's trio of Menchov, Boogerd and Dekker kept the speed high on the climbs. Ten kilometers from the summit of the Aubisque (the Tour's sixty-ninth visit to the big mountain), it was down to the Tour's best four riders: Rasmussen, Contador, Evans and Leipheimer. Contador jumped, but lacked the same punch he had two days before. Rasmussen met each of these attacks and then with about a kilometer to go, soloed away for a 47-second time gain. Again the crowd booed and whistled. Contador revealed that he was coming down with a cold.

The situation looked sewn up. After the mountains were finished, the General Classification stood thus:

1. Michael Rasmussen
2. Alberto Contador @ 3 minutes 10 seconds
3. Cadel Evans @ 5 minutes 3 seconds
4. Levi Leipheimer @ 5 minutes 59 seconds
5. Carlos Sastre @ 9 minutes 12 seconds

That afternoon Cofidis rider Cristian Moreni was revealed to have tested positive for exogenous testosterone and was shown the door.

Cofidis pulled their entire team from the race and withdrew their cars from the publicity caravan.

And then Rabobank sobered up. After Rasmussen's claims to have been in Mexico during his missed tests, Italian TV commentator Davide Cassani remarked that he'd seen the Dane in Italy at that time. This was the final straw, Rabobank finally yanked Rasmussen from the Tour. It was a strange performance. Earlier, team boss Theo De Rooy had been adamant in his defense of his rider. Now, he was angry over Rasmussen's missed tests, claiming that the team had been lied to. It was an inexplicable overnight character transformation, the sort of which one generally sees only in half-hour TV shows.

But, while it was looking like the Tour and cycling were indeed cleaning up, Greg LeMond noted that the mountain ascension times in the 2007 Tour were as fast as or faster than Marco Pantani's. That did not square with a clean Tour.

Two flat stages remained before the final time trial. The General Classification with Rasmussen removed:

1. Alberto Contador
2. Cadel Evans @ 1 minute 50 seconds
3. Levi Leipheimer @ 2 minutes 49 seconds
4. Carlos Sastre @ 6 minutes 2 seconds
5. Haimar Zubeldia @ 6 minutes 29 seconds

It looked like the Tour might still be in play. In the first time trial, Evans had taken about a minute out of Contador. Almost two minutes would be a tall order. He would have to gain an average of two seconds every kilometer. The bigger problem for Evans would be fending off a challenge from Leipheimer, who had won four time trials so far this year.

The time trial made things thrilling and closer, but the top five placings were unchanged. The time trial's results:

1. Levi Leipheimer: 1 hour 2 minutes 44 seconds
2. Cadel Evans @ 51 seconds
3. Vladimir Karpets @ 1 minute 56 seconds
4. Yaroslav Popovych @ 2 minutes 1second
5. Alberto Contador @ 2 minutes 18 seconds

At 53.068 kilometers per hour, Leipheimer had uncorked the fourth-fastest individual time trial in Tour history, which yielded the following General Classification:

1. Alberto Contador
2. Cadel Evans @ 23 seconds
3. Levi Leipheimer @ 31 seconds
4. Carlos Sastre @ 7 minutes 8 seconds

While the top three were now close in time, the Green Jersey competition remained unsettled, making it unlikely Evans could grab bonus seconds to take the lead by outsprinting the specialists in the final stage. Leipheimer said that he would not "pull a Vinokourov", remembering how the Kazakh had taken a placing from him in the final stage of the 2005 Tour.

And remember Leipheimer's 10-second penalty for the help from his team car in the Alps? He was now just 8 seconds behind second-place Evans. Without that penalty he might have been 2 seconds ahead. Leipheimer says that the push was necessary to help him regain contact after his mechanical problem. Without it, he might have suffered a catastrophic time loss.

And that's how the 2007 Tour ended, with the 24-year-old Spaniard taking the victory and the 31-second time spread for the podium being the closest in Tour history. That was the ninth Tour victory for Spain, previous Spanish winners having been Bahamontes, Ocaña, Delgado and Indurain.

The average speed of the 2007 Tour was 38.98 kilometers per hour, the slowest since 1994. The relentless obscene increases in speed that had been going on year after year had been halted, at least for now.

For Discovery, it was an amazing turnaround of fortune after their disastrous 2006 showing. They captured first and third in the General Classification, the Young Rider (Contador) and two stage wins.

Yet, again we had a winner for whom questions remained. There are suspicions that he was involved with Fuentes, suspicions that were not eased by Contador's truculent refusal to give clear answers at press conferences. When asked why he didn't just give the DNA samples that would surely clear him, his response was disheartening, "I don't have to prove everything to everyone." He also gave the meaningless defense that he had passed all of his dope tests.

The Tour organization, furious with the UCI over its continuing attempts to grab power and money from the Grand Tour owners, announced that they would withdraw from the UCI and set up a new cycling organization with the World Anti-Doping Authority. "There can only be one answer for the UCI, either they are incompetent or want to damage the Tour de France", said Tour director Prudhomme after the strange occurrences of July.

UCI president Pat McQuaid countered, "I don't think the Tour de France belongs to the ASO. I think the Tour de France belongs to the cycling family and I am president of the cycling family. I think in that context they should accept that and we should be sitting down together to work out plans for the future." I'm sure ASO could feel McQuaid's hand in its pockets.

Final 2007 Tour de France General Classification:
1. Alberto Contador (Discovery) 91 hours 26 seconds
2. Cadel Evans (Predictor-Lotto) @ 23 seconds
3. Levi Leipheimer (Discovery) @ 31 seconds
4. Carlos Sastre (CSC) @ 7 minutes 8 seconds
5. Haimar Zubeldia (Euskaltel) @ 8 minutes 17 seconds

Climbers' Competition:
1. Mauricio Soler: 206 points
2. Alberto Contador: 128
3. Yaroslav Popovych: 105

Points Competition:
1. Tom Boonen: 256 points
2. Robert Hunter: 234
3. Erik Zabel: 232

2008 Discovery Channel did not renew its title sponsorship. Armstrong and Bruyneel were unsuccessful in finding a replacement and at the end of the 2007 season, the team was disbanded. Bruyneel retired for a few weeks, then accepted an offer from Astana to restructure and run the troubled team. As part of the rebuilding, he brought along several of Discovery's best riders, including Contador, Leipheimer and Rubiera, creating a team so strong *La Gazzetta Dello Sport* labeled it "Fortress Astana".

As powerful as it was, even with the 2007 Tour de France winner, ASO decided it would not allow Astana to compete in any of the races it owned. Tired of the constant doping positives coming from the team dating back to when it was managed by Manolo Saiz, the Tour said that it had just had enough. Every year the team had promised to reform and every year it was a source of scandal, culminating in the troubles Astana had inflicted on the Tour in 2007. Meanwhile, Contador did go on to win both the Giro and the Vuelta in 2008, making him one of only five riders to have won all three Grand Tours.

The Tour announced a counter-clockwise route for 2008, with four mountaintop finishes and only 82.5 kilometers of time trialing. This edition not only did away with time bonuses, it would not have a Prologue. The Tour would just jump right in, with a road stage over some moderately heavy roads in Brittany.

The limited time trialing would favor a superb climber who therefore was less likely to dissipate his lead in a poor time trial. Cadel Evans' careful, race-not-to-lose style might serve him well. Others who looked good were Denis Menchov and Carlos Sastre. Sastre had the particular advantage of being backed by CSC, the strongest and deepest team in the Tour.

Also on nearly everyone's list was Alejandro Valverde, a complete rider whose ambitions seemed to exceed his ability. He had a superb spring, winning Liège–Bastogne–Liège. Three weeks before the Tour's start, he also took the Dauphiné Libéré, finishing off his pre-Tour season by winning the Spanish road championships.

Valverde showed his ambition and ability by winning the first stage. As the sprint was getting wound up, the powerful Spaniard jumped clear. He was now in Yellow, certainly risky behavior with three weeks of racing still ahead.

The third stage with its small winning breakaway forced Valverde to give up the lead to Frenchman Romain Feillu. More importantly, a crash split the field with Menchov and Italian climber Riccardo Riccò losing 38 seconds. Menchov earned a public reprimand from his director, Erik Breukink, who had warned his rider to stay at the front of the peloton on this windy and wet day.

Stage four was the first individual time trial, 29.5 kilometers at Cholet. Stefan Schumacher won the stage and took the Yellow Jersey, but Evans had done himself a wealth of good. He was the best-placed of the contenders, beating Menchov by 7 seconds and most of the others by over a minute.

The General Classification now stood thus:

1. Stefan Schumacher
2. Kim Kirchen @ 12 seconds
3. David Millar @ same time
4. Cadel Evans @ 21 seconds
5. Fabian Cancellara @ 33 seconds

The sixth stage was the year's first hilltop finish. Valverde's Caisse d'Epargne squad roared up the mountain, but in the sprint Riccò showed the same prowess in uphill drag races that he had demonstrated in the Giro, taking the stage just as he had predicted. Meanwhile, Schumacher touched wheels with Christian Vande Velde and crashed. He was back up in a flash, but the lost time meant that he was no longer the leader. A rider who crashes in the final kilometer gets the same time as the group except in hilltop finishes.

That put Kim Kirchen in Yellow and Evans second at 6 seconds. Schumacher was third at 16 seconds while Vande Velde had pulled himself up to fourth place, 44 seconds behind Kirchen.

The next day's furious racing through the Massif Central was so fast that several important riders were unable to stay with a field broken up by crashes and five categorized climbs. Even former Paris–Roubaix winner Magnus Backstedt was eliminated for finishing beyond the time limit, yet there were no changes at the top of the roster. Manuel Beltran's positive for EPO put him out of the Tour, and added him to a long list of former Lance Armstrong teammates who had later been caught cheating.

Sunday's stage nine brought the race to the Pyrenees with the Peyresourde and the Col d'Aspin. With the Aspin's summit 26 kilometers before the finish, it was unlikely to be a stage where the Tour would be won, but it could be a stage where the Tour might be lost.

Early on, just after the feed zone, Evans went down hard. He was up in a flash and his entire team waited for him and dragged their scuffed-up leader back to the peloton.

It was on the Aspin where the shock was delivered. First Riccò tested the field with a probing attack that was brought back. Farther up the slope, as he had promised, Riccò launched a blistering acceleration that left the rest of the best bike riders in the world looking as if they had slammed on their brakes. Riccò soared up the mountain and then pounded his way down the descent for a stunning victory. The man called The Cobra had done it again. Though he had said he was there just for the experience and stage wins, others remembered that in 1998 Pantani had also said that he was not riding the Tour to win.

After stage nine, the top of the General Classification was little changed except for Riccò's improvement:

1. Kim Kirchen
2. Cadel Evans @ 6 seconds
3. Christian Vande Velde @ 44 seconds
4. Stefan Schumacher @ 56 seconds
5. Denis Menchov @ 1 minute 3 seconds
21. Riccardo Riccò @ 2 minutes 35 seconds

Stage ten was 2009's first day with *hors catégorie* climbs and the year's first hilltop finish. Midway through the stage, the riders would ascend the Tourmalet and then finish atop Hautacam.

The action began on the Tourmalet's upper slopes as the tempo started to warm. It was too much for Valverde, who cracked and was never able to rejoin the leaders. On the descent and the run-in to the Hautacam climb, CSC put its strong men at the front and made sure Valverde remained permanently dropped.

It was on the Hautacam that Kirchen's dream went up in smoke. Saunier Duval sent their General Classification hope, Juan José Cobo, up the road. CSC's Frank Schleck tried to close the gap, but blew up. With that, Leonardo Piepoli, who had been on Schleck's wheel, took off and joined Cobo for a 1-2 finish.

Evans, who had started the day still bandaged up after his crash, did a lot of the work to keep the escapees in sight, putting him in Yellow, but just barely.

The General Classification now stood thus:

1. Cadel Evans
2. Frank Schleck @ 1 second
3. Christian Vande Velde @ 38 seconds

4. Bernhard Kohl @ 46 seconds

5. Denis Menchov @ 57 seconds

6. Carlos Sastre @ 1 minute 28 seconds

Again, the performance of the Saunier Duval riders, this time Cobo and Piepoli, had left knowledgeable observers gap-jawed.

While it is an imprecise tool because road conditions and gradients vary, sports physiologists can measure a rider's climbing ability by measuring his VAM, or *Velocità Ascensionale Media* (average rate of ascent). It's an Italian acronym because Michele Ferrari devised it. VAM is usually given in vertical meters gained in an hour.

Through the late 1990s and early 2000s, the best climbers such as Pantani and Armstrong were VAMing (if I may invent a verb) at about 1,800 meters an hour. In the 2006 Giro d'Italia, winner Ivan Basso went up the Colle San Carlo at close to a staggering 2,000 meters an hour.

So far, Riccardo Riccò's Saunier Duval team seemed to be riding on another level. Tour favorites Cadel Evans, Carlos Sastre and Alejandro Valverde and the other angels of the mountains couldn't keep up with the astonishing Saunier riders.

The approximate vertical climbing rates for Evans, Menchov and Sastre were between 1,500 and 1,650 meters an hour. Compare those rates to that of stage ten, won by Piepoli and Cobo who went up the Hautacam at 1,800 meters an hour. Stage winner Leonardo Piepoli was actually climbing faster than 1,800 meters an hour, but at one point in their escape he waited for Cobo.

After a rest day following the Pyrenean stages, it was announced that Moisés Dueñas of the Barloworld team was positive for EPO. The next day a bigger bomb was dropped. Riccò was popped for using a new generation of EPO, called EPO/CERA, for Continuous Erythropoietin Receptor Activator. Riccò and his team of cheaters left the race in disgrace. Riccò later remarked that drug testing had a long way to go because EPO was found in his samples for only two stages while it was in his system during his entire time at the Tour.

Team Columbia's Mark Cavendish showed that when it came down to a drag race at the end of a stage, he had no equal, winning two of the stages between the Pyrenees and the Alps and bringing his stage win total for the 2009 Tour to four. Evans maintained his tenuous hold on the lead with Schleck shadowing him at 1 second.

The chase for the Yellow Jersey resumed in stage fifteen with the Col d'Agnel, an *hors catégorie* climb early in the stage and then a hilltop finish at Italy's Prato Nevoso. The previous day's warm sun deserted the racers and they had to race in cool air under cloudy and rainy skies. Óscar Pereiro crashed on a wet street and was out of the Tour.

During the final ascent, CSC put its cards on the table for all to see. Brothers Frank and Andy Schleck along with Carlos Sastre hammered the group of contenders who were some minutes behind a small break that stayed away. Undaunted by the CSC pressure, Menchov attacked but then crashed after gapping the field.

Evans, left without any teammates on the climb, was dropped. Bernhard Kohl was the first rider in after the four-man break crossed the line. On his wheel was Sastre. Frank Schleck finished 38 seconds later, with Evans another 9 seconds behind. Schleck was in Yellow and the race, after the Pyrenees and after the first Alpine stage, was still tight with the six top riders separated by just 49 seconds.

The General Classification after stage fifteen now stood thus:

1. Frank Schleck
2. Bernhard Kohl @ 7 seconds
3. Cadel Evans @ 8 seconds
4. Denis Menchov @ 38 seconds
5. Christian Vande Velde @ 39 seconds
6. Carlos Sastre @ 49 seconds

A rest day in Cuneo, Italy came before the two remaining Alpine stages. Stage sixteen crested the Cime de la Bonette-Restefond 22 kilometers before the finish. It was the Bonnette-Restefond's tricky descent that made the difference. CSC, as expected, made the pace up the climb hard for everyone. Vande Velde came off and went over the top 35 seconds behind the other contenders. Descending fearlessly, he crashed and lost a little over four minutes. Menchov, not wanting to leave too much of his skin on the road, took the descent carefully, but also lost contact, crossing the line 35 seconds behind the Schleck/Kohl/Sastre group.

The new standings. With Schleck and Sastre, CSC still had two riders in the top four:

1. Frank Schleck
2. Bernhard Kohl @ 7 seconds
3. Cadel Evans @ 8 seconds
4. Carlos Sastre @ 49 seconds
5. Denis Menchov @ 1 minute 13 seconds

The 2008 Tour de France's Queen stage came on Wednesday with stage seventeen. Three legendary climbs were scheduled: the Galibier, Croix de Fer and a hilltop finish on l'Alpe d'Huez.

CSC's ace time trialist Fabian Cancellara buried himself on the Croix de Fer, but at the top, the Yellow Jersey group still contained all of the real hopefuls. This Tour was going to be decided on l'Alpe d'Huez.

By the base of the Alpe, CSC's hot work had reeled in the day's early breakaways. Just as the road started to tilt up, Bam! Carlos Sastre lit his jets. Menchov, with the others on his wheel, clawed their way back up to the flying Spaniard.

Sastre went again. This time no one could answer his attack. He had been riding almost completely under the radar for more than two weeks, carefully saving his energy for this one, grand moment. Up the mountain he rode. Back in the chase group, the Schleck brothers marked anyone who mounted a pursuit. Eventually Evans went to the front, but every time he took a pull, one of the Schleck brothers was quickly on his wheel. For some reason, each time a Schleck found his wheel, Evans would back off, not wanting to drag them up the hill. Since neither rider was in play for the final victory (Andy was too far down in time and Franck couldn't time trial well), Evans' slackening makes no sense. Sastre continued to time trial up the hill and Evans, with his go and slow chase, lost more time.

Sastre crossed the line alone, 2 minutes, 15 seconds ahead of Kohl, Evans and Menchov. It was a brilliant attack.

The General Classification now looked like this:

1. Carlos Sastre
2. Frank Schleck @ 1 minute 24 seconds
3. Bernhard Kohl @ 1 minute 33 seconds

4. Cadel Evans @ 1 minute 34 seconds

5. Denis Menchov @ 2 minutes 39 seconds

There was only one stage left that could affect the final outcome, the 53-kilometer individual time trial. If one were to extrapolate the stage four time trial results, one would have expected Evans to take 2.5 seconds per kilometer back from Sastre, giving Evans a final lead of about a half minute. But Sastre had been racing with the most powerful team in the world working like dogs to protect him, allowing him to ride without burning a single watt needlessly. Evans, on the other hand, had been constantly isolated and forced to fend for himself. Moreover, his crash had also affected his performance. He looked tired.

Evans could take only 29 seconds from Sastre, netting him a second consecutive Tour second place. Sastre, looking fresher than the others, was even able to catch his three-minute man, teammate Frank Schleck. Schumacher won the stage (as well as the stage four time trial), beating the formidable Fabian Cancellara by 21 seconds.

Schumacher's Gerolsteiner teammate Bernhard Kohl sewed up third place, in addition to gaining the Polka-Dot jersey. Gerolsteiner seemed to have ridden an exemplary Tour.

Final 2008 Tour de France General Classification:

1. Carlos Sastre (CSC-Saxo): 87 hours 52 minutes 52 seconds

2. Cadel Evans (Silence-Lotto) @ 58 seconds

3. Bernhard Kohl (Gerolsteiner) @ 1 minute 13 seconds

4. Denis Menchov (Rabobank) @ 2 minutes 10 seconds

5. Christian Vande Velde (Garmin-Chipotle) @ 3 minutes 5 seconds

Climbers' Competition:

1. Bernhard Kohl: 128 points

2. Carlos Sastre: 80

3. Frank Schleck: 80

Points Competition:

1. Óscar Freire: 270 points

2. Thor Hushovd: 220

3. Erik Zabel : 217

Because of the rift between ASO and the UCI, dope testing for the 2008 Tour was handled by the French Anti-Doping Agency (AFLD). AFLD boss Pierre Bodry found several riders' urine samples that exhibited suspicious values, but nothing that could trigger a confirmed positive. But the suspicions were strong enough to examine the suspected riders' blood samples. In September the AFLD announced that Leonardo Piepoli and Stefan Schumacher were positive for EPO/ CERA. A few days later Bernhard Kohl was also found to have been using the new EPO.

Despite its doping problems, this was a superb Tour whose winner came from a team with a well-regarded internal dope testing program. The VAMs for this Tour (at least those of riders not found to be doped) were generally lower than in previous Tours. Pierre Bodry estimated that 80 percent of the peloton was clean. This is a far different picture from 1950 when French team manager Marcel Bidot thought three-quarters of the riders in the Tour were doped.

2009

With rumors swirling everywhere, on September 9, 2008, Lance Armstrong announced that he was returning to professional cycling, on the Astana team, with winning the 2009 Tour de France his ultimate goal.

The reaction to Armstrong's return was mixed. Some welcomed it, knowing that cycle racing's publicity would get a shot in the arm. Tour boss Prudhomme seemed indifferent, but said Armstrong would be welcome if he complied with all of the new anti-doping protocols. Underlying most reactions was the feeling that Armstrong had never dispelled the taint of the doping allegations that had followed him from his first Tour victory in 1999. The German television networks, who were in the midst of negotiating new Tour broadcasting rights, said that they were "not amused" with Armstrong's plans. A network spokesman said he believed that Armstrong belonged to an earlier generation, that he was a piece of the past they did not want to see again.

To counter these feelings, Armstrong said that he would ride the Tour with total transparency. All of his blood values and tests would be posted online for all to see, a promise that was quickly broken. Suspiciously, Astana hired an old hand from Armstrong's past, Pedro Celaya, who according to several members of the US Postal team had helped US Postal riders dope in 1998.

In October, after almost four years of strife, the Grand Tour organizers signed an accord with the UCI. It gave the races much of the independence they had been fighting for, yet also left much of the Pro Tour machinery in place. By 2011, seventeen teams would be automatically qualified to race the Grand Tours, leaving the organizers the chance to include more wild cards.

Simultaneously, Editions Philippe Amaury (EPA)—the owner of ASO and the Tour de France—fired ASO president Patrice Clerc. He was replaced with EPA boss Jean-Etienne Amaury, Philippe Amaury's son. It was with EPA that the deal with the UCI was made, not with Clerc and the ASO.

The settlement of the feud between the Tour and the UCI had a troubling consequence. The French Anti Doping Agency (AFLD) had aggressively and successfully handled the dope testing for the 2008 Tour, culminating with the finding that Schumacher, Riccò and Kohl were cheaters. The Tour was returning dope testing back to the toothless UCI.

Pierre Bodry explained, "Between 2003 and 2007, there were no riders caught for EPO, Well, I got seven in a month! The UCI didn't catch anyone, and we did. Riccò was already known to have doped in the Giro d'Italia. Where were the UCI?" Confirming Bodry's dread assessment of the UCI's handling of doping was the announcement that the UCI would not bother to re-test samples from the 2008 Giro, where it was obvious that many riders where using EPO.

Pat McQuaid, head of the UCI, said that retrospective testing of the Giro samples would be futile and would not advance the anti-doping fight. This was errant nonsense that left the cheaters with their ill-gotten gains and could only encourage future doping.

While the Tour and the UCI were settling their feud, ASO and Armstrong began sniping at each other, with Amaury claiming that Armstrong's performances had embarrassed the Tour. Armstrong hit back, noting that he and his team had never failed a drug test. Seemed like old times.

Meanwhile, Alberto Contador was raising a stink, saying that if he were not given serious, believable assurance that he would be the protected leader of the Astana Tour squad as called for in his contract, he would leave the team.

As that played out, Armstrong complained that the media circus and potential French hostility that would follow him to the Tour was not a good setting for the anti-cancer fight that his re-entry to pro racing was intended publicize. So, answering in the affirmative to Giro boss Angelo Zomegnan's invitation to ride the Giro on its hundredth anniversary, Armstrong simplified Astana's problem for the moment. While confirming that he would ride the Giro, he said a Tour ride had not been not ruled out.

During the Giro, news leaked that Astana's sponsors hadn't been paying the riders for several months, putting the team in danger of losing its racing license. It got to the point the team raced in logo-less uniforms in protest and by June it was still not certain whether Astana would be able to ride the Tour. Wary, Contador came to an agreement with Jonathan Vaughter's Garmin-Slipstream team, which even shipped him new bikes. Just before the Tour started, Astana received sufficient funding to ride the rest of the season, so Contador stayed put.

All still wasn't well within the Astana family. Bruyneel named Contador the team's leader. When Armstrong objected—having decided to ride the Tour after coming in twelfth in the Giro—Bruyneel waffled, saying Contador was the leader, but the team's captain would be determined by who performed best on the road. Furthermore, the Astana Federation and government wanted to change the team's direction after the Tour. They wanted to boot Bruyneel and Armstrong, bring in Vinokourov, whose doping suspension would be over, and give Contador a big wad of cash to stay. The plan was to turn Astana into a team of top Spanish and Kazakh riders.

Astana rider Benjamin Noval, clearly bristling over being left off the Astana Tour team, gave an angry interview to *L'Équipe*. He asserted that since Armstrong had joined the team, Bruyneel gave Contador no respect and the team was riven with factions, presumably riders loyal to Contador versus those for Armstrong. Noval blamed Bruyneel for the team's unity troubles.

The Tour route that was unveiled in October excited race fans. Again, there would be no time bonuses. It would start in Monaco with a 15.5-kilometer individual time trial and climb the Pyrenees first. With only 56 kilometers of individual time trialing, the lightweight climbers looked to be favored. Cementing that impression was a hilltop finish on Mont Ventoux on the penultimate stage rather than a final time trial. Prudhomme said the Tour had never in its history had a mountaintop finish so close to the finale in Paris.

While Contador was clearly the favorite, Armstrong had ridden himself into excellent shape during the Giro. Menchov had fought a brutal, no-holds-barred fight with Danilo Di Luca when he won the Giro in May and would surely be too tired to contend with those who had trained just for the Tour. Andy Schleck, who had so effortlessly toyed with Evans on l'Alpe d'Huez the year before, would be a year older and a year stronger. With the reduced time trialing, this Tour might be made for him. Sastre would also be well served with a Tour that made racing against the clock less important.

The addition of a team time trial with the event's real time being applied to the rider's General Classification standings made Cadel Evans, with his weak Silence-Lotto team, vulnerable to a debilitating time loss.

No one was surprised when chrono specialist Fabian Cancellara won the stage one individual time trial, with Contador the first of the contenders, 18 seconds back, and Evans only 5 seconds slower than the Spaniard. These were superb performances given that Cancellara was the finest living time trialist. Sastre lost 48 seconds and Menchov gave up 73 seconds to Contador in the first stage. Armstrong turned in a solid performance, coming in tenth, 22 seconds behind Contador. Good, but he still was far from his 2005 self.

The third stage headed west over Provence's flat roads and should have been an unimportant sprinters' stage. With about thirty kilometers to go, the peloton turned a corner and was hit by a strong crosswind. The entire nine-man Columbia team hammered the pack with an incendiary acceleration, immediately splitting the peloton in half. Of the Classification contenders, only Armstrong was savvy enough to make the front group. Even though Riis had told the Schleck brothers to be alert and stay at the front, they missed the move, as did Contador, Menchov and Evans. Once the break was established, Armstrong had his two Astana teammates— who were also in the break—work to distance it from the main peloton, which included the supposedly protected Contador.

The result was a 41-second gap, with Armstrong moving up to third in the GC. Contador was stiff-jawed about the incident but downplayed its significance. Armstrong had shown that he knew how to read a race, and where to be in order to stay out of trouble. Being Lance Armstrong, he would give Contador no respect.

It was feeling like 1986 again.

The next day was the long-awaited team time trial, 39 technical kilometers out and back into Montpellier; the first team time trial since Armstrong's last Tour ride in 2005. Astana laid down the law, performing a smooth, machine-like ride that put six Astana riders in the top ten. Several teams suffered crashes or lost several riders early on. Evans lost 1 minute, 55 seconds. Initially it looked like Armstrong was going to be the race's new leader, but he was still behind Cancellara, now by just 0.22 seconds.

A look at the General Classification after the team time trial showed Astana's depth:

1. Fabian Cancellara (Saxo)
2. Lance Armstrong (Astana) same time
3. Alberto Contador (Astana) @ 19 seconds
4. Andreas Klöden (Astana) @ 23 seconds
5. Levi Leipheimer (Astana) @ 31 seconds

On Friday, July 10, came stage seven with its hilltop finish at Arcalis. It seemed as if the Tour had stepped into a time machine and was transported back to the years of US Postal and Discovery. While a break of non-contenders took off, Astana rode hard tempo at the front. The rest of the teams, as in the Postal years, happy to be freed of the obligation to race, simply sat on. In the final kilometers, first Evans and then Andy Schleck tried to get away, but both were unable to counter the stiff breeze blowing in their faces.

With two kilometers to go, Contador bolted. It was a brilliant, irresistible acceleration that grew to a 21-second gap at the finish. The earlier break stayed away. Bruyneel did not want to catch those riders because he didn't want to take the Yellow Jersey this early in the race. One of the break's survivors, Rinaldo Nocentini, was the new leader, the unlikely and happy recipient of Astana's largesse. Contador's bold action moved him up to second place, two seconds ahead of a grim-faced Armstrong.

Both Bruyneel and Armstrong said Contador's action was not according to the team's plan, but no mention was made of how Armstrong's stage three escape, leaving the highest placed rider on the team behind, was according to team plans. It was reported that there was a "frank" talk on the team bus that evening. Armstrong's response to Contador's superb move showed that he was there to win the Tour and Contador was turning into an obstinate obstacle.

The whole drama seemed perverse. On any other team where a Classification rider had successfully put almost a half-minute between himself and the rest of the field, there would be jubilation. In fact, Contador was isolated. Bruyneel, favoring Armstrong, had brought only one rider who could be reliably counted on to ride for Contador, Sergio Paulinho. Almost all the other riders on the Astana squad were loyal to Armstrong. If Contador wanted to win the Tour, he would have to count on his own resources and the help of Spanish riders on other teams, whom it was reported he had been courting.

There were two more Pyrenean stages, but because the crests of the final climbs each day were far from the finish lines, they had little effect upon the standings. This was true even though stage nine included the Aspin and the Tourmalet.

After the Pyrenees, the General Classification stood thus:

1. Rinaldo Nocentini
2. Alberto Contador @ 6 seconds
3. Lance Armstrong @ 8 seconds
4. Levi Leipheimer @ 39 seconds
5. Bradley Wiggins @ 46 seconds

Many critics (including this writer) argue that the use of two-way radios, allowing directors to closely control their teams, lowers the quality of bicycle racing by destroying the racers' spontaneity and initiative. The Tour wanted to experiment by doing away with the radios for two stages. French television had seen a sharp drop-off in bike racing viewership in the key demographic of young men. Without reform, the long-term prospects for cycling's financial health did not look good to the broadcasters. Since a large part of the Tour's income is from television rights, the Tour was highly attentive to this question. As usual, worrying more about their short-term situation, the objections to the test from the team directors and some racers were predictable and furious. At the last minute a compromise was found. Stage ten would be raced without radios but the plan to run stage thirteen without them would be scrapped.

To prove the Tour organizers wrong, the teams made stage ten a miserable, slow truculent day in the saddle. The peloton and team managers have never shown the slightest interest in the sport's long-term health. A break was allowed to get away and then was kept on a short leash. They were eventually caught, and Mark Cavendish won another stage.

The much-anticipated stage fifteen with its hilltop finish at Verbier did not disappoint. The drama was intense, but given the short nine-kilometer length of the ascent, over in a flash. The pack got to the bottom of the climb with all of the big names close at hand. As soon as the road began to bite, Saxo set a pace that immediately reduced the front group to fewer than twenty riders. The casualties were surprising. Among the dropped were 2008 winner Sastre, current King of the Mountains Franco Pellizotti, and Nocentini.

Saxo was preparing things for Frank and Andy Schleck, but Contador was in no mood to let Saxo set the terms of the conflict. With five kilometers left, he bolted with an absolutely irresistible acceleration, a jump reminiscent of Pantani. Contador was soon out of sight, with Andy Schleck in pursuit. Meanwhile, as the riders started to climb the hill in groups, Armstrong, who had made the elite cut, was unable to stay with any of the attackers. His trademark fluid, high-cadence style was gone. Sastre showed up from nowhere and passed many of the group that had dropped him earlier, making common cause with Franck Schleck and a surprising Bradley Wiggins. Armstrong, paced by Andreas Klöden, came in 95 seconds after Contador. An excellent ride by any measure. But the day and the Yellow Jersey were Contador's.

After stage fifteen the General Classification now stood thus:
1. Alberto Contador
2. Lance Armstrong @ 1 minute 37 seconds
3. Bradley Wiggins @ 1 minute 46 seconds
4. Andreas Klöden @ 2 minutes 17 seconds
5. Andy Schleck @ 2 minutes 26 seconds

How remarkable was Contador's ride? Disturbingly good. Until stage fifteen of this Tour, the fastest climb in the Tour (measured by VAM) had been Riis' drug-fueled ascent to Hautacam. Marco Pantani's equally chemically-aided 1995 and 1997 trips up l'Alpe d'Huez came next. All had VAMs of about 1,820 to 1,840. Calculations vary according to how the mountain is measured, but scientists came up with VAMs of between 1,858 to 1,900 for Contador's 21 minutes of climbing, making it the fastest ascent in the history of the Tour de France.

After the second rest day, stage sixteen had two big climbs, the Petit and Grand St. Bernards, with the summit of the second peak coming 30 kilometers before the finish. Andy Schleck tried to smack the Classification riders around on the Petit St. Bernard but at the end, there were no changes to the GC. Armstrong showed flashes of his old brilliance, but Contador looked to be having an easy day of it despite the others going full gas.

Revealing the worst-kept secret in the peloton, Bruyneel said that 2009 would be his last year with Astana.

There were only two mountains stages left, and everyone knew the Schlecks would be throwing bombs.

On the Col de Romme, stage seventeen's second-to-last climb, the warm pace got hot with Saxo and Astana giving it their all. The Schleck brothers broke loose, taking Contador, Wiggins, Armstrong, and Klöden with them.

On the final mountain, the Colombière, everyone went into the red zone. When Contador attacked, only the Schleck brothers could hold his wheel.

Neither the Schlecks nor Contador could drop each other. Frank Schleck was first across the line with Contador second and Andy third. Italian Vincenzo Nibali of Liquigas led Armstrong in 138 seconds later with Klöden a further 9 seconds back.

Later in the day Contador came in for sharp criticism from Bruyneel for his attack that dropped Klöden, which he claimed cost Astana the potential to sweep the podium in Paris. Contador was winning the Tour de France and doing it masterfully, yet in return, all his team manager could do was give him grief and do it publicly. It was a strange Bizarro world where everything was backwards and winning was bad.

That Contador was the finest living stage racer was confirmed in the stage eighteen individual time trial. The slender Spaniard won the 40.5-kilometer stage, beating even the man widely regarded as the best time trialist of the age, Fabian Cancellara. Of the contenders, only Wiggins and Klöden could get within a minute of Contador. Andy

Schleck lost 1 minute, 45 seconds and Armstrong dropped 1 minute, 30 seconds.

Before the race was even over, Armstrong announced he would have a new team in 2010, sponsored by RadioShack.

The penultimate stage with its finish at the top of Mont Ventoux was supposed to be a dramatic conclusion to the 2009 Tour de France.

Before the start of the stage the General Classification stood thus:

1. Alberto Contador
2. Andy Schleck @ 4 minutes 11 seconds
3. Lance Armstrong @ 5 minutes 21 seconds
4. Bradley Wiggins @ 5 minutes 36 seconds
5. Andreas Klöden @ 5 minutes 38 seconds
6. Frank Schleck @ 5 minutes 59 seconds

Only 38 seconds separated Armstrong, Wiggins, Klöden and Schleck. Saxo wanted to put Frank in third place, while Garmin wanted to move Wiggins up to Armstrong's spot. Armstrong had said taking Andy Schleck's second place and moving Klöden to the podium was not out of the question, despite Bruyneels' earlier whining to the contrary.

With two riders off the front, the chasing pack was detonated by Saxo, Astana and Garmin on Mt. Ventoux's lower slopes. Before reaching the tree line, the front chasing group was reduced to Contador, the Schlecks, Armstrong, Wiggins, Nibali and Klöden. Andy Schleck showed no mercy, banging away at the group, trying to break his brother loose. It wasn't to be. Armstrong was having a terrific day and was able to stay with Frank. With each hammer blow from Schleck, Wiggins would get dropped and then claw his way back. Finally it was too much for Wiggins, who came in tenth, but Nibali was able to stay with this elite group. Andy Schleck out-sprinted Contador, but with no time bonuses in play, Contador was uninterested in nailing third place in the stage. He had just won the Tour de France.

In the romp down the Champs Élysées, Cavendish won his sixth stage, but it wasn't enough for the Green Jersey. Thor Hushovd had been industrious in the hillier stages that were beyond the British sprinter's abilities and had racked up plenty of points to put the sprinter's jersey beyond Cavendish's reach.

Contador had won four Grand Tours in only 14 months.

Final 2009 Tour de France General Classification:

1. Alberto Contador (Astana): 85 hours 48 minutes 35 seconds
2. Andy Schleck (Saxo) @ 4 minutes 11 seconds
3. Lance Armstrong (Astana) @ 5 minutes 24 seconds
4. Bradley Wiggins (Garmin-Slipstream) @ 6 minutes 1 seconds
5. Frank Schleck (Saxo) @ 6 minutes 4 seconds

Climbers' Competition:

1. Franco Pellizotti: 210 points
2. Egoi Martínez: 135
3. Alberto Contador: 126

Points Competition:

1. Thor Hushovd: 280 points
2. Mark Cavendish: 270
3. Gerald Ciolek: 172

Alberto Contador on the Champs Élysées, all decked out in Yellow: yellow jersey, yellow helmet, yellow gloves, sunglasses, socks, frame decals...

After the race was over, the depth of the Armstrong/Contador split was revealed. Armstrong did not attend the team's post-race celebratory dinner, preferring to spend the evening with people from his new sponsor, RadioShack. When asked what the most difficult part of the race had been for him, Contador said it was the time in the hotel.

Contador's victory was masterful and done with both a minimum of wasted effort and team support, though his dominance made one wish Bodry and the AFLD had been handling the testing in 2009.

Still burning from the conflict after the race was over, Armstrong sent out several ill-tempered messages on Twitter: "If I were him I'd drop this drivel and start thanking his team" and "What did I say in March? Lots to learn. Restated."

The depth of the dislike boded well for an excellent 2010 Tour.

2010 Like the 2010 Giro d'Italia, the 2010 Tour started in the Netherlands. Beginning with an 8.9-kilometer prologue in Rotterdam, the next three stages were in the Lowlands. The specter of crashes in these streets crowded with road furniture (barriers in streets designed to slow cars) wasn't the only frightening aspect of the northern start. Stage three had 13 kilometers of cobbles, raising the possibility of dramatic time losses by those riders who crashed or got dropped in the pell-mell rush over the pavé. Most Grand Tour racers detest cobbles and the element of chance they bring to a race. Contador went so far as to hire retired classics ace Peter Van Petegem to coach him in dealing with stage three's challenges.

Prudhomme continued his war against individual time trials, scheduling only the prologue and a 52-kilometer penultimate stage as races against the clock. Given the reduced time trialing and the race's hilly profile (23 mountain passes), it looked to favor the climbers, even if there were only three hilltop finishes. After a couple of days in the Alps, the race would spend three days in the Pyrenees, with two trips up the Tourmalet to celebrate the hundredth anniversary of the Tour's first high mountain stages. For only the second time in Tour history (1974 was the other occasion), the Tourmalet would be the scene of a mountaintop stage finish.

Contador was the prohibitive favorite. Armstrong, who announced this would be his final Tour, had suffered a difficult build-up to the Tour, but in June he came in third in the Tour of Luxembourg and was second in the Swiss national tour.

The Schleck brothers remained at the top of the list of contenders, but given their poor time trialing, most writers considered them potential podium placers at best.

Just before the July 3 start, many riders traveled to Belgium to examine the stage three parcours. What they discovered startled them. The cobbles, especially the final sector, were far worse than they had expected. Armstrong summed it up with a twitter message, "Going.To.Be.Carnage." Armstrong said the roads were worse than those used in the 2004 Tour.

Back home, Floyd Landis was miserable. He had done what everyone had told him to do, stay quiet and fight the charges. But as a result, he was now ruined professionally and financially. After a couple of starts and stops to re-launching his racing, he became desperate. In 2009 he'd asked Bruyneel for a spot on his new RadioShack team, but was turned down. Protecting everyone had done him no good. He saw himself as cycling's scapegoat. He had taken the fall, while others who were just as guilty, prospered. If he had confessed and helped the US Anti-Doping Agency (USADA) instead of fighting the charges, he would have likely had a short suspension and then gotten on with his professional racing life, just like dozens of other riders who had been caught. He was tired of lying and tired of protecting others who did nothing for him in return.

In May, Floyd Landis startled the world with a confession that he had indeed doped (denying taking testosterone in 2006, but admitting autologous blood doping and using EPO). But unlike almost every other rider who had 'fessed up, Landis named his former teammates and directors, including Lance Armstrong, George Hincapie and Johan Bruyneel, as having participated in a team-run doping program. Every person Landis accused denied the charges. The U.S. Food and Drug Administration thought the charges merited the appointment of Jeff Novitzky, who had investigated the BALCO athlete doping case, to assess the Landis claims and decide if empaneling a grand jury to charge the US Postal riders and managers with criminal wrongdoing was warranted. The FDA also appointed Doug Millar, who had also worked on the BALCO case, to act as prosecutor, if needed.

If the US Postal team had used Postal Service funds to pay for a doping program, the penalties could be severe. The UCI, which Landis accused of covering up Armstrong's doping, joined nearly everyone in the cycle racing business in condemning Landis as a serial liar. Landis was vilified from all sides, including by cycling sportswriters who should have known better.

Yet, based upon both the government interest and the investigative reporting being done by mainline media outlets like *Sports Illustrated*, the *Wall Street Journal*, the *New York Times* and ESPN, many thoughtful people considered Landis' claims to have a powerful verisimilitude. If he had made up the entire team doping story with all of the believable minute details that fit together perfectly, it would mean Landis had a startlingly brilliant and creative imagination.

Moreover, the reporting of the story by big media meant that the cycling industry had lost its ability to control the narrative. Within the cycling community Landis could be scorned and treated as an angry misfit, which he probably was, but the cycling industry's ability to protect Armstrong seemed to be waning.

And make no mistake, Armstrong was a gold mine to the business of cycling and the cycling media. The Versus television network, which broadcast the Tour de France in the U.S., had an average of 316,000 viewers a day during the 2005 Tour, Armstrong's last before retiring. In 2006 viewership fell by almost half, 165,000. With Armstrong's 2009 return, Tour watching perked up by 35 percent. Tour watchers, like golfers, are valuable to advertisers because their demographics skew toward the affluent and well-educated. Households that earn more than $100,000 are twice as likely to be Tour watchers. Money-wise, Armstrong was well worth protecting.

On July 3rd, the day of the Rotterdam prologue, the *Wall Street Journal* published a summary of an extensive interview with Landis and several former US Postal riders. Landis had added extensive detail to his earlier accusations, saying that US Postal riders were forced to ride old, worn-out bikes so that Bruyneel could sell the new race bikes provided by sponsors in order to pay for drugs. Again all the accused vigorously denied the charges.

Rain during the later hours of the prologue was forecast, so several teams had their top riders take earlier time slots, hoping to avoid the downpour. Mother Nature is rarely cooperative and this day was no exception. Bradley Wiggins, who as the 2009 fourth-place rider and the Team Sky's new captain, was the most prominent of the racers making this choice and got bucketsful of rain for his efforts. The streets were mostly dry at the end of the day. Fabian Cancellara won his fourth Tour prologue and the year's first Yellow Jersey.

Because the Tour continued to score the race in real time, without time bonuses, the Swiss time trial ace looked to be able to keep his lead for a while. Armstrong, at fourth, was the highest placed of any rider thinking of winning the Tour, with Contador losing 5 seconds to his former teammate. The others, riding carefully and desperate to avoid a crash, lost larger but not serious amounts of time. The exception to this being the Schleck brothers. Andy Schleck claimed he had improved his time trialing, but he lost the same amount of time, 42 seconds, that he gave up to Contador the year before at Monaco. He was so distressed by the result he refused to talk to the press after the stage.

Then came the three Dutch and Belgian stages. The first one ended in a series of crashes, including a giant collision with less than a kilometer to go that stopped all of the Classification contenders. No one lost any time, but a day's racing that had at least half the peloton falling did not bode well for the next three weeks. Stage two was more of the same; almost half the peloton fell on wet, slippery streets. The greatest carnage was on the descent of the legendary Stockeu hill, caused when a TV motorcycle following the break crashed, spilling oil on the road. So many fell, the riders decided to neutralize the race to let the fallen contenders catch the main peloton. The leader of the mini-strike was Fabian Cancellara, who sacrificed his Yellow Jersey slowing the field (while also protecting fallen teammate Andy Schleck), allowing breakaway rider Sylvain Chavanel to take the stage and the lead.

Stage three was the feared cobblestone stage and when the peloton hit the third of the seven pavé sectors, Saxo's Frank Schleck crashed hard, breaking his collarbone into several pieces.

But this didn't mean Saxo was out of the fight, not by a long shot. In what was surely a carefully planned set-piece, in the fourth cobbled sector Cancellara, with Andy Schleck on his wheel, took a hard pull and emerged clear of the peloton with Cadel Evans, Thor Hushovd and Geraint Thomas along for the ride. Driving their advantage home, they picked up the sole remaining rider from an earlier break, Canadian Ryder Hesjedal, and raced for the barn.

Behind them, Armstrong was in the first chase group (I can't help wondering if the 2004 Armstrong would have missed the Cancellara move) with Alberto Contador frantically chasing to get back on terms with the leaders. Showing surprising skill at racing on cobbles, the Spaniard made contact just as Armstrong flatted.

The Cancellara/Schleck group stayed away with Hushovd winning the stage and taking the green jersey. For Hushovd it was especially sweet because he was furious at having been deprived of a chance to sprint for points the day before.

The chase group came in 53 seconds later, but without Contador, who broke a spoke and had lost contact and a further 20 seconds.

For Armstrong, the day was a disaster, not so much because he came in 2 minutes, 8 seconds after the Schleck group, but because this day had been pinpointed as a perfect chance for him to take time from the specialist stage race riders who were supposed to be less skilled at racing on pavé. Instead, the frighteningly slender Schleck, with the help of his Paris–Roubaix winning teammate, had scored the triumph. His fifth place meant he took serious time out of his rivals well before the mountains: 53 seconds from Wiggins and Menchov, 1 minute, 13 seconds from Contador, 2 minutes, 8 seconds from Armstrong and 2 minutes, 25 seconds from Basso and Sastre.

The top ranks of the General Classification stood thus:

1. Fabian Cancellara
2. Geraint Thomas @ 23 seconds
3. Cadel Evans @ 39 seconds
4. Ryder Hesjedal @ 46 seconds
5. Sylvain Chavanel @ 1minute 1 second

But let's remove those riders most likely to be eliminated from the top ranks by the climbing. Then the picture would look like this:

1. Cadel Evans
2. Ryder Hesjedal @ 7 seconds
3. Andy Schleck @ 30 seconds
4. Alberto Contador @ 1 minute 1 second
5. Denis Menchov @ 1 minute 10 seconds
6. Bradley Wiggins @ same time
7. Lance Armstrong @ 1 minute 51 seconds

The next three days were flat stages designed for the sprinters and they didn't miss their chance. Alessandro Petacchi snaffled the first of the three while Mark Cavendish took the next two, making a total of twelve career Tour stage wins for the man nicknamed "The Manx Missile".

The Tour had been heading south to the Alps, and in stage seven the appointment was close at hand. The seventh leg traveled through the French Jura, ending in a trio of second-category climbs. Not enough to dislodge a contender, but they did offer the opportunity for an adventurous break to do a little buccaneering. Pirate Sylvain Chavanel did just that, leaving a break in his rear view mirror on the day's penultimate climb, allowing him to retake the lead, which he had lost to Cancellara on the cobbles of stage three. Cancellara, tired from days of hard work, melted on the hot roads and conceded fourteen minutes.

The climbers, miserable after the northern European stages, had been licking their chops for the mountains to start, and in stage eight they got their wish with a hilltop finish at the Avoriaz ski station in Morzine.

For Armstrong, the day was a dismal series of crashes. A mass fall near the start took down a lot of the riders, but Armstrong was able to ride off the road to avoid falling. But shortly before the day's first serious climb, the first-category Col de la Ramaz, Armstrong uncharacteristically clipped a pedal on a traffic circle, sending him flying at 60 kilometers per hour. His team paced their battered captain back up to the field, but the short distance before the start of the climb started forced them to ride à bloc. Armstrong finally made contact with the back of the peloton but he was already tired from the chase, and at the top of the Ramaz, Armstrong was still a minute behind the leaders. Worse, Armstrong got the hunger knock on the Ramaz; a failing for which he had publicly castigated Contador the year before, despite his own near catastrophic bonks in earlier Tours. An attempt to close the gap on the descent was fruitless and on the next climb, Armstrong was stopped by yet another crash. At that point he gave up. He rode the final climb to Morzine grim-faced, making no attempt to regain any of his lost time, which eventually grew to almost twelve minutes.

Up front, Contador's Astana squad had been driving the peloton so hard that only thirteen riders survived to fight out the final kilometers. With about a kilometer to go Schleck jumped. Contador tried to get on his wheel but couldn't, allowing Schleck to win his first-ever Tour stage with a 1 minute, 14 second gap back to the rest of the peloton. Evans, who had been riding a canny, low-key race, now donned the Yellow Jersey. Armstrong said his quest for a Tour victory was over and that he would now work for his team.

Going into the first rest day the General Classification stood thus:

1. Cadel Evans
2. Andy Schleck @ 20 seconds
3. Alberto Contador @ 1 minute 1 second
4. Jurgen Van den Broeck @ 1 minute 3 seconds
5. Denis Menchov @ 1 minute 10 seconds

The stage facing the riders after their day of rest was imposing, though the final climb, the Col de la Madeleine, would come well before the finish.

A break of mostly non-contenders (though Luis-León Sánchez might be considered a real dangerman) rolled away from the peloton. Cadel Evans' BMC squad worked like fiends to keep the escapees' lead from getting out of hand. In fact, they worked so hard that the mountain stage's average speed ended up a leg-breaking 36 kilometers per hour.

When the peloton hit the Madeleine, BMC ceded control to Andy Schleck's Saxo squad, which snapped everyone's neck with a hard increase in tempo and tossed two hopefuls, Wiggins and Michael Rogers, out the back. Then Astana decided to drive the pack harder still. First Vinokourov took a vicious pull and then Daniel Navarro buried himself. Those two efforts ended any hope of winning the Tour for nearly the entire list of challengers. Evans, who it turned out had been hiding a fractured elbow acquired in a stage eight crash, folded under the pressure. Leipheimer, Menchov and Robert Gesink were also unable to handle the savage pace.

When Navarro pulled over there were only two riders left, Andy Schleck and Contador. The two tested each other with some probing attacks and then settled down to leverage their gap into the destruction of any other rider's hopes of winning the Tour.

They were so effective, they caught the remaining riders of the early breakaway who by now had stopped working together. French rider Sandy Casar, of the original escape, won the stage, but Schleck and Contador had done themselves a world of good. Menchov, Leipheimer, Gesink and Joaquim Rodríguez all lost more than two minutes. Basso and Armstrong gave up almost three and Roman Kreuziger just shy of four minutes. Sastre and Wiggins came in nearly five minutes after Casar. Evans broke down in tears after giving up more than eight minutes.

That left the General Classification thus:

1. Andy Schleck
2. Alberto Contador @ 41 seconds
3. Samuel Sánchez @ 2 minutes 45 seconds
4. Denis Menchov @ 2 minutes 58 seconds
5. Jurgen Van den Broeck @ 3 minutes 31 seconds
6. Levi Leipheimer @ 3 minutes 59 seconds

The next three days took the Tour towards the Pyrenees. They were full of spirited riding, but the standings remained unaffected. Stage twelve included an ascent of the Côte de la Croix-Neuve, which the locals had renamed the Montée Laurent Jalabert in honor of Jalabert's 1995 Bastille Day victory at Mende in 1995.

The main peloton was together for the start of the Jalabert climb. Vinokourov jumped away looking for solo victory. Feeling as if his moment had come, Joaquim Rodríguez rocketed out of the peloton in pursuit with an attentive Contador on his wheel. Schleck couldn't make contact and had to watch the Spanish pair go off in search of Vinokourov. They were moving so fast they went right by the Kazakh, with Rodríguez taking the stage. Schleck limited his loss to only 10 seconds, but it was a powerful blow that made Contador's improving form obvious.

Jens Voigt, one of Schleck's teammates, said stage twelve was one of the three hardest days of racing he had ever endured in his entire career.

Stage thirteen brought the race to Revel, at the base of the Pyrenees. Vinokourov again took off, and this time made his escape stick, beating the pack by 13 seconds. This probably worked to Contador's advantage because Vinokourov had now slaked his thirst for a stage win and could be counted on to work exclusively for teammate Contador.

Meanwhile, the Green Jersey had been bouncing between Petacchi and Hushovd and Petacchi's third place in the stage was good enough to give him a two-point lead.

Stage fourteen brought the Tour to the high Pyrenees, with the Port de Pailhères and Ax-3-Domaines climbs at the end of the stage. Astana hammered away, keeping the speed high on the Pailhères, but none of the Classification men dared make a move. On the final ascent, again Astana worked to break the legs of the rest of the peloton with Vinokourov and Navarro putting in especially fearsome pulls. With about five kilometers to go, the Contador/Schleck group had been pared down to only those with wings. Contador slammed the front hard and was immediately matched by Schleck. From there, the two just kept an eye on each other, almost coming to a halt, ignoring the others. It was beginning to look like the 1948 Valkenburg world championships when Coppi and Bartali, so fixed on each other, let the rest of the field ride away from them.

It didn't come to that. Menchov sensed an opening in the chess-playing and took off with Samuel Sánchez hot on his tail. Realizing that the race could well be heading up the road, Schleck and Contador sobered up and chased, coming within 12 seconds of the Russo-Spanish pair. Schleck later said that the gradient wasn't steep enough for either of the two evenly matched riders to get a gap on the other. This played to Contador's advantage, as the chances for Schleck to take time before the time trial were getting fewer.

Before the start of stage fifteen, Schleck was in Yellow, with Contador down 31 seconds. The stage featured the Portet d'Aspet, the Ares and the Port de Balès followed by a technical descent to the finish at Bagnères-de-Luchon. After the Ares, Schleck's Saxo team drilled away at the front until about four kilometers from the summit, where the lead group was down to the top six Classification men. Schleck accelerated a couple of times, and after each hit, the group would slow, allowing a few gapped riders to get back on. Contador seemed especially content to sit on Schleck and finish the stage without any time change.

But with just two kilometers left in the climb, Schleck launched what looked to this writer as the hardest hit yet, instantly gaining him a gap. Vinokourov was quickly on him and Contador jumped as well, with Jurgen Van den Broeck, Menchov and Sánchez in close pursuit. But, just a few seconds after he had jumped, Schleck's chain came off his chainwheel, forcing him to stop. As he was slowing, Contador swerved around him.

Knowing the importance of the moment, Schleck quickly fixed his bike and with Van den Broeck, took off after the escaping trio. At the crest the gap was only 13 seconds. The riders up front, especially with the skilled descender Sánchez, increased their lead down the mountain. At the finish, the Contador group had gained 39 seconds, making Contador the new Yellow Jersey by 8 seconds.

Television commentators, bloggers and forum contributors erupted with fury at Contador's not waiting for Schleck, believing that the unspoken rule was the Yellow Jersey should not be attacked during a mechanical, misunderstanding the rule which merely holds that the Yellow Jersey or his nearest competitor should be able to safely urinate and get food. Schleck was furious, saying he would have waited if the situation had been reversed, an easy statement to make and simply not true—Schleck hadn't waited for Yellow Jersey Chavanel in stage three after Chavanel suffered flat tires.

Contador later posted a video on YouTube apologizing to Schleck.

But to stop racing in the heat of battle, especially when the fight was started by the Yellow Jersey? Several experienced professionals including Bernard Thévenet (who rode right on by Lucien Van Impe after Van Impe was hit by a television car in 1977), Laurent Jalabert and Bernard Hinault thought the complaints against Contador baseless. Armstrong, who had attacked during a competitor's crash several times, also refused to condemn Contador's actions. The careful reader of this history will find only one example of a racer waiting for a disabled competitor in the heat of the moment when the race was truly in play and that was Jan Ullrich in 2003.

Stage sixteen's mountain roster of the Peyresourde, Aspin, Tourmalet and Aubisque mimicked Desgrange's 1910 "Circle of Death". But, as in 1910, no one died. In fact, Schleck and Contador held a cease-fire over all four of the giant peaks.

That doesn't mean the day was without action. Armstrong mounted what was probably his last attempt to win a professional bike race when he got into the day's break and forced the pace on the Soulor portion of the Aubisque ascent. Both he and teammate Christopher Horner were in the eventual nine-man selection, but they were unable to use their numerical advantage against the far speedier Pierrick Fédrigo, who won the stage. Armstrong came in sixth.

Schleck now had all of his Tour de France eggs in one basket, stage seventeen with the Marie-Blanque, Soulor and a hilltop finish at the Tourmalet.

Both Saxo and Menchov's Rabobank felt that the moment to seize time had come, and together they set a fiery pace. Schleck waited until the Tourmalet had been half-climbed, about ten kilometers to go, before making his move. It looked like a mild acceleration, but it wasn't. Only one rider was able to match Schleck's acceleration, and it was Contador. Over and over Schleck attacked; each time Contador matched him. To show Schleck that his efforts were for naught, Contador then mounted an assault of his own, which Schleck was able to handle. As they rocketed up the Tourmalet, they caught and passed all the riders who had been in the day's break. Schleck kept at it, saying later that he accelerated fifteen times trying to drop Contador. At the line, following the normal practice of the rider who further secures his grip on the lead, Contador let Schleck take the stage.

In the mountains, the pair were too evenly matched for either of them to effect a serious Classification change. With the climbing completed the race was interestingly close.

1. Alberto Contador
2. Andy Schleck @ 8 seconds
3. Samuel Sánchez @ 3 minutes 32 seconds
4. Denis Menchov @ 3 minutes 53 seconds
5. Jurgen Van den Broeck @ 5 minutes 27 seconds

That left the penultimate stage's nearly pan-flat 52-kilometer individual time trial in Bordeaux to decide the Tour's outcome. There were really two races in play here. The big one for the Yellow Jersey, of course, but also a second one for that precious last spot on the podium, at that point occupied by Sánchez.

Cancellara won the stage, but Menchov did what everyone expected, blasting the Spanish climber out of third place with the fastest ride of any of the contenders.

Schleck rode with Contador as his three-minute man. Initially Contador struggled to find his rhythm while the Luxembourg rider slowly gained time. At one point Schleck was within one second of the virtual jersey. Perhaps shocked by this reversal of expectations, Contador slowly took back the time loss and then gained 31 seconds. The Tour was Contador's, by 39 seconds, the fourth closest in Tour history and Contador's third Tour win. The final General Classification difference was the same as Contador's time gain in stage fifteen, when Schleck dropped his chain, fueling bar fights for years to come. Schleck's time trial was normal for him, forty-fourth place, more than six minutes slower than Cancellara. But Contador's ride was a surprise. He was thirty-fifth, much slower than riders he regularly beat. Contador later said the entire time trial was a struggle for him. Schleck had missed one of the few chances to catch Contador on an off day. As Contador summed it up, "It's not Andy who was stronger this year, it was I who was weaker."

There was one more episode of drama in this Tour. At the start of the final stage, traditionally a ride into Paris followed by the criterium on the Champs-Élysées, Armstrong's Radio Shack squad showed up in black jerseys with the number "28" on their backs, symbolizing the 28 million cancer sufferers worldwide. The race judges said that the kit change had not been approved in advance and could not be worn. Reluctantly the team threw their regular jerseys over the black ones. Not good enough. The judges said that the riders' race numbers were covered and they could not race that way. Both times the team had to be threatened with disqualification before they would comply. Eventually, with the peloton pedaling slowly, the team complied and the stage could continue. Mark Cavendish won his fifth stage of the year, but second-place Alessandro Petacchi secured the green Points Jersey.

Contador joined Philippe Thys, Louison Bobet and Greg LeMond in the three-time winner's club and became the seventh rider to win the Tour without winning a stage.

Final 2010 Tour de France General Classification
1. Alberto Contador (Astana): 91 hours 58 minutes 48 seconds
2. Andy Schleck (Saxo) @ 39 seconds
3. Denis Menchov (Rabobank) @ 2 minutes 1 second
4. Samuel Sánchez (Euskaltel) @ 3 minutes 40 seconds
5. Jurgen Van den Broeck (Omega Pharma-Lotto) @ 6 minutes 54 seconds

Climbers' Competition:
1. Anthony Charteau: 143 points
2. Christophe Moreau: 128
3. Andy Schleck: 116

Points Competition:
1. Alessandro Petacchi: 243 points
2. Mark Cavendish: 232
3. Thor Hushovd: 222

To this writer, the 2010 Tour seemed to be almost a throwback to racing the way it was before the 1990s, when riders had to be careful to guard their energy stores. Riders tired more easily, unable to throw out massive attack after massive attack. The racers were almost unanimous in saying that this Tour was unbelievably difficult. Yet, at 39.589 kilometers an hour, it was slower than the last two Tours and far slower than the 41.654 of the 2005 Tour. This was evidence that doping was coming under control. Moreover, the VAMs on the giant climbs never hit the obscene 1,800 meters an hour seen in recent years. They were regularly in the 1,600s and low 1,700s.

A common measure of a rider's power is watts per kilogram. The line that causes some observers to reach for their pistols is 6.2 watts per kilogram on long climbs. Earlier, riders had been reaching the high sixes, as high as 6.8. On the Tourmalet, Schleck and Contador didn't even hit 6 watts per kilogram, barely making it to 5.9, and at the end of the climb they were down to the 5.5 range. They were exhausted, the way they should have been.

Michele Ferrari noted that the riders were growing thinner with every passing stage, a sign of physical stress that Desgrange had noticed a hundred years before. Also, no team would drop the hammer early in a stage to force an early selection for fear of running out of gas before the crucial moments late in the stage, just as no rider with Classification hopes dared go too early in a stage.

That fall Landis filed a federal whistleblower lawsuit against Armstrong and several in Armstrong's inner circle, alleging that they had defrauded the government when they took US Postal's $30 million and used some of it to buy dope, which was specifically prohibited in the contract. Given the potential triple damages, Armstrong faced a serious peril. In the face of the Novitzky investigation, he had already lawyered up and was paying huge sums to some of the country's finest and most expensive attorneys to fight the growing threats.

2011

There was plenty of drama during the off-season. The Schleck brothers moved to a Luxembourg-based team, Leopard-Trek, and took four more of Saxo's nine 2010 Tour riders with them. Saxo's boss, Riis, looked around for a Grand Tour rider and signed Alberto Contador, who had long wanted to ride for a team not named Astana.

During the World Championships in September of 2010, it was revealed that Contador had tested positive for Clenbuterol, a marvelous drug that allows a rider to lose weight but still to retain muscle. But wait, there's more! It also improves aerobic capacity and stimulates the central nervous system. Willy Voet described it: "Clenbuterol is one of the most powerful hormones when it comes to developing muscle mass. Beef rearers are well aware of its properties: the more meat they can sell, the more money they make. It can give spectacular muscle growth." Voet says Richard Virenque and Laurent Brochard and others under his care had started taking it back in 1997.

The drug has an inconvenient downside: it's banned, and in many countries ownership can be a serious crime. Contador argued that the amount in his system was minute and was probably caused by eating contaminated beef.

Accepting the explanation, the Spanish cycling federation exonerated Contador and cleared him to race (they would, wouldn't they?). The federation had come under intense political pressure from all corners of Spain to accept Contador's explanation. Even the Spanish Prime Minster called for Contador's exoneration. The UCI filed an appeal of the Spanish federation's decision with the Court for Arbitration of Sport, putting off a final decision until at least the end of the Tour. Meanwhile, Contador had a terrific spring, including a dominating ride in the Giro that earned him his sixth Grand Tour victory. Contador was going for the Giro/Tour double, last done by Pantani in 1998.

Tyler Hamilton, who had lost his fight against his Vuelta doping positive, went on the *60 Minutes* television show and not only admitted his own drug use, but that of his teammates, including Armstrong.

Armstrong's army of lawyers and fanboys crucified Hamilton as they had the others who implicated Armstrong in doping. Former UCI president Verbruggen said, "I repeat again: Lance Armstrong has never used doping. Never, never, never. And I say this not because I am a friend of his, but because it is not true. I say it because I am sure. Even if we would like, it would not be possible to bury a positive test." In 2013, Armstrong would claim Verbruggen encouraged and aided Armstrong's 1999 cortisone positive cover-up, because Verbruggen feared a "knockout punch for our sport" the year after Festina.

The Tour's Prudhomme offered up a route with only 42.5 kilometers of individual riding against the clock along with a 23-kilometer team time trial. With six mountain stages, four of which had summit finishes, this was a climber's heaven.

The race for the green sprinter's jersey was given an overhaul. Historically, the Tour had weighted the points in final sprints to give purer sprinters an advantage: more points on flat stages, fewer in the mountains. This practice continued, but with some adjustments. The Tour differs from the Giro and the Vuelta here, which give the same number of points for all stages. In the past, the Tour would sprinkle intermediate sprints along each stage, with Green Jersey points available to the first three riders. For 2011, each stage was given a single intermediate sprint with points available down to fifteenth place. It was hoped the sprinters' teams would race for the intermediate points, even if a small break were up the road vacuuming up the few placings.

The fear that the 2011 edition would be a boring race settled by a few drag races in the mountains was ill-founded. The opening stages were incredibly difficult and dangerous. The trouble started with the first stage (there was no prologue in 2011) which started at the Passage du Gois in the Vendée, where Alex Zülle lost more than six minutes in 1999. With less than ten kilometers to go, a spectator got in the way of Astana rider Maxim Iglinsky, causing a big crash that seriously delayed Contador. The magic man of the 2011 Classics season, Belgian Philippe Gilbert, stormed up the stage's finishing hill with Cadel Evans just off his wheel for a brilliant stage win. Contador started his Tour down 1 minute, 20 seconds.

The next day, the short team time trial caused Contador still more grief. Garmin-Cervélo won their first-ever stage and put Thor Hushovd in Yellow, while BMC was only 4 seconds behind, cementing

Evans' place as the top contender. Saxo was 28 seconds slower than Garmin, putting Contador in seventy-fifth place, 1 minute, 42 seconds behind Hushovd.

There were no time bonuses in play in 2011, but that didn't keep Contador from trying to win the uphill sprint in stage four. Gilbert tried a repeat of his stage one blitz, but he didn't have the same punch. Contador went after him and was so sure he was the day's winner, he raised his arm in victory. But it was the faultless Evans who had won the stage. Hushovd, however, was not to be dropped, and by just a single second over Evans, he remained the overall leader.

The carnage continued through the next five stages. Northern European winds, narrow wet roads, high speeds and a general nervousness in the peloton made some accidents inevitable, but this first week was probably one for the record books. Classification contenders Janez Brajkovič, Bradley Wiggins, Alexandre Vinokourov, Christopher Horner (who was allowed to finish stage seven despite an obvious head injury, but didn't start stage eight) and Jurgen Van den Broeck, along with Tom Boonen (who apparently rode the stage with a concussion) were part of the list withdrawals that had grown to eighteen by the end of stage nine.

Some riders had suffered horrible injuries. There were scores of other battered riders who were able to soldier on. It wasn't just riders crashing into other riders—a car in the caravan hit Johnny Hoogerland and sent him flying into a barbed-wire fence, while one of the Tour motorcycles knocked over a racer and dragged his bike for some distance. In 2011 there were sixteen accredited photographers on motorcycles, and after the moto-caused crash, it was announced that the Tour would reduce that number to twelve for 2012.

Several teams suffered special misfortune. RadioShack had come to the Tour with four protected Classification riders. Between time losses and withdrawals, they now were down to just Klöden. Sky had built their Tour team around Wiggins and he was gone. Geraint Thomas had been in the white jersey, but after waiting for teammate Wiggins to see if he needed a tow back up to the peloton, Thomas lost his lead in the young rider competition.

Hushovd had confounded the experts by keeping his lead into stage nine. There, a break took advantage of the day's crashes and carved out a four-minute gap. It included the always-canny Frenchman Thomas Voeckler, who became the Yellow Jersey. In 2004 he had worn Yellow for eleven days after getting into the right break. He had no illusions, feeling that the ride to the top of Luz Ardiden in stage twelve would spell the end of his time in the lead.

Contador crashed again, this time in stage nine; a collision with Vladimir Karpets bruised an already tender knee.

Through it all, Cadel Evans maintained his position as the top contender with the Schlecks, Klöden and Basso just a few seconds behind him. Day after day he had put his "big diesels" George Hincapie and Marcus Burghardt to work, protecting him, helping him maintain position and keeping the peloton moving when necessary. Evans came in for a lot of criticism for overworking his team so early in the race. Despite being the best-placed contender, Evans' comment on the first nine stages told volumes about how hard this Tour was: "I've had enough of bike racing this week, thanks very much."

Going into the rest day, with Contador denying rumors that he intended to abandon, here was the General Classification:

1. Thomas Voeckler
2. Luis-Leon Sánchez @ 1 minute 49 seconds
3. Cadel Evans @ 2 minutes 26 seconds
4. Frank Schleck @ 2minutes 29 seconds
5. Andy Schleck @ 2 minutes 37 seconds
16. Alberto Contador @ 4 minutes 7 seconds

After a couple of high-speed sprinters' stages, the first day in the Pyrenees would conclude with an ascent of the Tourmalet and a finish atop Luz Ardiden. While Gilbert teammate Jelle Vanendert had escaped with Samuel Sánchez, the main group had gone over the Tourmalet together and arrived at the base of the final climb, Voeckler thinking he was in his final minutes as the Yellow Jersey.

Voeckler's Europcar team tried to find a speed high enough to keep the others from getting edgy, but not so fast that Voeckler would lose contact. Basso's *gregario* Sylwester Szmyd grew tired of this and inaugurated the festivities with a long, hard brutal turn at the front that quickly made the Yellow Jersey group smaller. There was only one surprise. Not only were the Schlecks, Contador, Evans and Basso there, but so was Voeckler! Meter after meter of the steep mountain was climbed, and no action. With about three kilometers left, Frank Schleck finally gave it a go, marked by Contador.

Contador clearly had trouble staying with Schleck. There had been no rest-day miracles; the Spaniard was still off his feed. Andy Schleck tried to get away, but again he was covered. Frank's third attack was finally too much for the others and he opened up a gap. Up ahead Sánchez easily outsprinted Vanendert.

Evans took on the responsibility of keeping Schleck from running away with the Tour. As Basso led Evans and Andy Schleck across the line, brother Frank had gained 20 seconds. Contador, not looking good, followed in 33 seconds after Frank. But just behind Contador was Voeckler and his domestique Pierre Rolland. Voeckler was still in Yellow, 1 minute, 49 seconds ahead of Frank Schleck. Olympic champion Sánchez's fine ride had made him a dark horse for final victory.

The conventional wisdom was that the Schlecks would use the steep part of the fourteenth stage's final sixteen-kilometer climb to Plateau de Beille to hammer Contador, Evans, Basso and Voeckler into oblivion. Evans predicted "fireworks". Plateau de Beille had been used as a stage finish four times, and all four winners had gone on to final victory in Paris: Pantani (1998), Armstrong (2002, 2004) and Contador (2007).

By the third big climb of the stage, the Col d'Agnes, the Schlecks' team was driving the peloton. At the base of the last ascent, Schleck super-domestique Voigt's leg-breaking pull whittled things down to the favorites. Andy Schleck tried a couple of testing probes that Contador responded to slowly. He looked better than two days before, but he was far from the dominant rider who had cruised through the Giro. One kept waiting for action, but it never happened.

Voeckler and the contenders were still together at the three-kilometers-to-go marker, despite some tentative attacks that had come to nothing. The steepest sections of the climb were long gone and there would be no chance for any attacker to extract serious time.

Near the finish Andy Schleck broke clear, but he couldn't catch stage winner Jelle Vanendert and the ever-resourceful Sánchez, who had again escaped. Andy had gained only two seconds in what was surely his best opportunity to win the Tour de France. The astounding rider was Voeckler, who was closing gaps, keeping things together and riding with incredible tenacity. His reward was retention of his lead of 1 minute, 49 seconds over Frank Schleck.

The recriminations began almost as soon as the riders were unclipped. The Schlecks whined that the others didn't work hard enough to break the lead group apart and that only they had been racing.

Evans answered, "The Schleck brothers are there, they ride all day, they've got the Yellow Jersey to gain and they look at me to pull for them? I feel like saying, 'Hang on a second, I'm not here to tow you to Paris.'"

Talk was starting that Voeckler had a real chance to win the Tour de France. The last thing the Frenchman wanted was to be considered a threat, and he went to great lengths to deny that he had even the slightest chance of wearing yellow in Paris.

With the hard Pyrenean climbing over, the General Classification stood thus:

1. Thomas Voeckler
2. Frank Schleck @ 1 minute 49 seconds
3. Cadel Evans @ 2 minutes 6 seconds
4. Andy Schleck @ 2 minutes 15 seconds
5. Ivan Basso @ 3 minutes 16 seconds
6. Samuel Sánchez @ 3 minutes 44 seconds
7. Alberto Contador @ 4 minutes 0 seconds

A couple of days later Leopard-Trek manager Kim Andersen admitted that a Tour that looked custom-made for the Schlecks was not turning out well and that the coming Alpine stages would probably do them little good. Worse, a couple of technical descents could spell trouble for the Schlecks, forcing the race to be decided by the time trial. There, Evans' adoption of Anquetil-style riding, being careful to avoid losing time, would play to his advantage. And of course, Contador's potential revival hung over everything.

Stage sixteen ended with a climb over the second-category Col de Manse and a difficult descent into Gap. Contador started the fighting with an attack that drew everyone with Classification ambitions. The lead group ascended together until about a kilometer to go, when Contador jumped again, catching most of the group completely by surprise. But not everyone. Sánchez and Evans marked the move while the Schlecks couldn't match the speed. Over the top and on into Gap, the three skilled descenders took advantage of the day's rain and gained time on their chasers. Voeckler, with Frank Schleck and several others, bravely went after the Contador group, but lost 20 seconds. Andy Schleck couldn't bring himself to follow his brother on the dangerous descent and lost a minute.

The next day was almost a carbon copy of stage sixteen. Contador unsuccessfully tried to get away on the final climb, the Pramartino, before a descent more hair-raising than the day before tested everyone's bike handling and courage. Voeckler, always looking to grab time wherever possible, three times overcooked the sharp corners that were often hidden in shadows, costing him 27 seconds, but not the lead.

Up front things were exciting. Contador escaped with his friend Sánchez and the two risked their skins in a daredevil ride that showed what complete riders they were. Once on the flat they performed a two-man time trial to the line. But who was chasing? The Schlecks! The pair had manned-up and come down the Pramartino hot on Contador's tail. Close to the line, with Evans in tow, they made contact. With the exception of Voeckler's time loss, it was *status quo antebellum*.

The standings at this point:

1. Thomas Voeckler
2. Cadel Evans @ 1 minute 18 seconds
3. Frank Schleck @ 1 minute 22 seconds
4. Andy Schleck @ 2 minutes 36 seconds
5. Samuel Sánchez @ 2 minutes 59 seconds

With the race so close, it was the perfect time for the Tour's Queen Stage with three *hors catégorie* climbs, the Agnel, Izoard and for the first time, a finish at the top of the Galibier. Celebrating the one-hundredth anniversary of the Tour's first visit to the Galibier, at 2,645 meters it was the highest finish in the Tour's history. Everyone knew big things would happen. Both Evan's BMC team and the Schlecks' Leopard-Trek squad sent riders up ahead in breaks, making sure their leaders would have help if and when they needed it.

Leopard-Trek set a searing pace up the Agnel. Again, on the lower slopes of the Izoard, the Schlecks had their team go deep, and from that scorching ascent, Andy Schleck erupted off the front and quickly settled into what everyone thought was a foolhardy adventure. There were still 60 kilometers to go and neither of the Schlecks had ever shown they had the stuff for a ride like this.

As he crested the Izoard, Schleck had almost two and a half minutes on his chasers. On the descent, he caught teammate Maxime Monfort. Monfort's job was to now lead Schleck down the mountain, which he did with skill. Constantly, Schleck urged Monfort to go faster, catching him and pushing him ahead. At the start of the Galibier, the gap had ballooned to nearly four minutes. A headwind had been predicted and that's just what Schleck ran into. In 1977, Lucien van Impe had gone on a long adventure in the Alps and had seen his chances crushed by the wind. But Schleck had the legs this day and as he ascended the mountain his lead grew.

Alarmed, Evans personally took up the chase, riding most of the ascent out of the saddle with Contador, Voeckler, Cunego, Basso and Frank Schleck sitting on his wheel. Against all odds and expectations, Andy Schleck crossed the line alone, more than two minutes ahead of the Evans group. It was a day worthy of Merckx or Hinault, a throwback to an era when great racers were willing to do magnificent rides.

Near the top, Contador, who everyone thought was starting to show a little sparkle, slid off the back of the Evans group and lost four minutes. The astonishing rider was Voeckler, who turned himself inside out holding on to the hard-charging Evans. Somehow, he had found the strength to stay in Yellow another day, now by just fifteen seconds. Meanwhile, Evans and Andy Schleck were now separated by less than a single minute.

Over the Galibier again! Knowing the riders would be exhausted by this point, course designer Jean François Pescheux kept stage nineteen short. Short it was, but with the Galibier and an Alpe d'Huez hilltop finish, it was still positively frightening.

The general belief was that Evans always has a bad day in a Grand Tour. It looked like the day had finally come.

The Télégraphe is part of the Galibier's north face, and there Contador gave it another shot, attacking and taking with him the irrepressible Voeckler, Evans and Andy Schleck. As the pace got hotter, Voeckler had to let go while Evans was forced to stop to fix a wheel rubbing against his chainstay. He stopped again and during a third stop, changed bikes. Andy Schleck, of the flexible racing standards, wasn't waiting for a competitor with bike problems.

The men up the road were riding away with the Tour de France, but Evans was undaunted. He chased up and over the Galibier with the Voeckler group behind him. After an impressive pursuit, both Evans and Voeckler caught Schleck and Contador well before the Alpe d'Huez ascent began. Evans later said he should have waited for Voeckler.

The man who had been with Voeckler throughout the high mountains, Pierre Rolland, was now given his freedom to win a stage. He was gone in a flash.

Once the Evans group was on the Alpe proper, the Aussie gave it the gun, but was marked. Contador bolted and Evans led the chase, which was finally too much for Voeckler, who had to watch the others ride away. Contador tried to dispatch Rolland, but the young Frenchman was not to be denied this day. He soloed up to the summit, earning the first French stage win in 2011 and the White Jersey. Farther down, there were a few attacks, but soon the ride to the top settled into a nervous mutual marking and watching.

Cadel Evans led the Schlecks across the line, making Andy the Yellow Jersey, with the 42.5-kilometer time trial the final arbiter of the 2011 Tour de France.

The General Classification now stood thus:

1. Andy Schleck
2. Frank Schleck @ 53 seconds
3. Cadel Evans @ 57 seconds
4. Thomas Voeckler @ 2 minutes 10 seconds
5. Damiano Cunego @ 3 minutes 31 seconds

Andy Schleck hoped the Yellow Jersey would give him the strength to survive the time trial, but Evans needed to gain only 1.4 seconds per kilometer. Given the Schlecks' notoriously poor time trialing and Evans' reputation as was one of the world's premier riders against the clock, things didn't look good for Andy.

Evans came out of the start house fast, and quickly settled into a powerful rhythm, stroking a huge gear with authority. Andy looked nowhere near as good and the first unofficial time check showed Evans was the faster rider. Further time checks showed Evans gaining, and when he had become the virtual Yellow Jersey, Schleck seemed to give up and quickly lost 30 seconds. Evans pounded his bike home. He had at last won the Tour de France after riding a perfect race. The man with caterpillars for eyebrows was the most complete rider of his generation and had ridden a relentless Tour, exploiting every opportunity, riding at the front, staying out of trouble and being willing to shoulder the responsibility of containing threats. None of which could be said about the Schlecks.

The 2011 Tour gave hope that the drug scourge was being contained. Riders and teams were exhausted in a way that hadn't been seen since the 1980s. The days of riders kicking out nearly seven watts per kilogram seemed gone. The best were now in the 5.7 to 5.85 range. VAMs reached into the mid-1,600s, a far cry from the 1,800s of a few years ago. A corner seemed to have been turned.

Final 2011 Tour de France General Classification:
1. Cadel Evans (BMC): 86 hours 12 minutes 22 seconds
2. Andy Schleck (Leopard-Trek) @ 1 minute 34 seconds
3. Frank Schleck (Leopard-Trek) @ 2 minutes 30 seconds
4. Thomas Voeckler (Europcar) @ 3 minutes 20 seconds
5. Alberto Contador (Saxo) @ 3 minutes 57 seconds

Climbers' Competition:
1. Samuel Sánchez: 108 points
2. Andy Schleck: 98
3. Jelle Vanendert: 74

Points competition:
1. Mark Cavendish: 334 points
2. José Joaquin Rojas: 272
3. Philippe Gilbert: 236

seven

2012–2018

The British Invasion: Great Britain goes from one of racing's marginal players to a dominating force

2012 Contador's Clenbuterol doping case was finally resolved in February of 2012 when the Court of Arbitration for Sport ruled he was to be stripped of results since his positive test in the 2010 Tour, including his 2010 Tour and 2011 Giro victories. That made Andy Schleck the 2010 Tour champion and Michele Scarponi the winner of the Giro d'Italia.

Meanwhile, things were not going well for Johan Bruyneel's new RadioShack-Nissan team, created by merging the RadioShack and Leopard-Trek teams of 2011. The Schleck brothers and Fabian Cancellara were under Bruyneel's management, making what should be a stage racing powerhouse. But, the Schlecks are notoriously difficult to manage. The team's problems became public when Bruyneel said that of all his riders, only Cancellara had a sure ride in the Tour.

For Armstrong the news was mixed. The extensive federal investigation into doping in the US Postal and Discovery teams ended without an indictment. Why the two-year investigation was dropped was never explained. Armstrong claimed vindication.

But the head of the U.S. Anti-Doping Agency, Travis Tygart, decided to go ahead with trying to charge Armstrong with doping, and

Bruyneel and a trio of doctors with assisting with Armstrong's teams' drug programs. Tygart interviewed former Armstrong teammates, including Hincapie and Zabriskie, and all the interviewees agreed to testify in return for lenient sentences. Armstrong remained adamant in maintaining his innocence, certain his powerful, highly-paid legal team could steamroller Tygart.

But the USADA and the plaintiff attorneys in the Landis whistleblower suit were working to a different standard than the FDA investigators, who would have had to bring a case that showed Armstrong guilty beyond a reasonable doubt. The USADA merely needed to show that the rules of cycling had been broken, and if it went to arbitration, that Armstrong's misdeeds were proven to the "comfortable satisfaction of the hearing panel." In the whistleblower civil suit, Landis needed only show a preponderance of evidence to prevail.

Amid the clamor, Bruyneel withdrew from leading RadioShack at the Tour.

One of the backers of the team, Flavio Becca, was up to his armpits in financial scandals and problems, and by May he was late in paying team salaries. Andy Schleck crashed in the Dauphiné and had to give up his place on the team's Tour roster. Brother Frank said he was cooked after a long spring season that culminated in a second place in the Tour of Switzerland. He said he would ride the Tour, but was too tired to compete for victory. By late June, the Schlecks were said to be looking for a way out of their team and to have yet another squad formed around them, this one headquartered in Germany.

Prudhomme offered an armistice in his war against time trialing, scheduling 101.4 kilometers of racing against the clock to go against three hill-top finishes (three or four is normal). To compare, 2011 had 42.5 kilometers of individual time trialing, 2010 had 60.9, and 2009 had 56.

At the start, the race looked to be between two riders, Cadel Evans and Bradley Wiggins. Evans seemed to be on track with a careful, measured climb to fitness that aimed to avoid peaking too soon. At the Dauphiné he asserted himself enough to show he had lots of punch, but he wasn't yet at the level Wiggins was displaying.

Wiggins' win at the Dauphiné along with victories in Paris–Nice and the Tour of Romandie made for an historic and stunning spring.

He was the first rider in cycling history to win all three races in a single season. His time-trial skills were unquestionable and he showed he could handle himself in the mountains. The big question mark remained, could a rider who came in third in February's Volta ao Algarve sustain his fitness to the end of July?

All the speculation was put aside as the prologue time trial began in Liège. While Wiggins turned in an outstanding ride, Fabian Cancellara won his fifth Tour de France prologue, beating Wiggins and Sylvain Chavanel by 7 seconds. Evans came in thirteenth, a crucial 10 seconds slower than Wiggins. Vincenzo Nibali showed vastly improved time trial powers when he finished only a second slower than Evans.

Again, during the early stages the peloton was plagued with crashes.

BMC and Sky were so worried about the danger the collisions posed that toward the end of each stage, they would drag their classification men to the front and drill away, keeping the speed high and the peloton strung out until they hit the three kilometers to go sign. From there, if something went wrong, a delayed rider would still get the same time as the peloton. As the riders headed for stage four's finish line in Rouen, another huge pileup left dozens of riders on the ground. And again in stage five. Wiggins and Evans were still safe and Cancellara was still in Yellow.

A battered and wounded peloton came into Metz at the end of stage six with Liquigas' *wunderkind* Peter Sagan winning his third stage. A particularly vicious crash had occurred on a downhill section with about 25 kilometers to go. Rabobank rider Laurens ten Dam tweeted, "Lots of blood and screaming. Carnage." Several riders lost time after waiting what seemed an eternity for new bikes. Frank Schleck, Michele Scarponi, Pierre Rolland, Alejandro Valverde and Janez Brajkovič chased frantically as the peloton raced for its appointment with the sprint, but they were only able to get within two minutes of the peloton. 2012 Giro winner Ryder Hesjedal limped in more than thirteen minutes after Sagan had won.

The wreckage was awful. All but one of Garmin-Sharp's riders had hit the deck, while all of Valverde's Movistar teammates had fallen. Rabobank had similar misfortune. Eleven riders had abandoned the Tour by the next morning. Several more would succumb to their injuries over the next few days.

The General Classification after stage six:

1. Fabian Cancellara
2. Bradley Wiggins @ 7 seconds
3. Sylvain Chavanel @ same time
4. Tejay Van Garderen @ 10 seconds
5. Denis Menchov @ 13 seconds
6. Cadel Evans @ 17 seconds
7. Vincenzo Nibali @ 18 seconds

The top contenders had come through the ordeal with their standings and most of their skin intact.

But why all the crashes? Everyone kept blaming a nervous pack destabilized by race jitters. Sean Kelly asked around the peloton and was told that today's riders are simply taking more chances, going through holes that are too small, moving up when the road was too narrow. But that begs the question. Thomas Voeckler, owner of one of the finest tactical minds actively racing, as well as a rider who was caught in the stage six crash, placed the blame squarely on the race radios. He said all the directors at the same time will tell their riders to move to the front. "Well, if you have 198 riders like that on a road that is only seven meters wide, there's not room for everyone," the Frenchman explained. "With all the pressure that's being put on via the earpieces, I think it's the same on all teams. You then have one point where all the riders try to move up and mathematically that just doesn't add up."

The next day the Tour traveled to the Swiss Jura with a finish atop the challenging La Planche des Belles Filles. The final ascent had places where the gradient approached twenty percent.

Sky's Edvald Boasson Hagen roared up the hill until he was spent and the pack shattered. Next, Christopher Froome (second in the 2011 Vuelta) notched the speed up still more, leaving just eight riders in the lead group. The Tour looked to be over for several riders dropped on 2012's first hard climb. Pierre Rolland (probably suffering from his stage six crash), Frank Schleck, Michele Scarponi, Alejandro Valverde and Christopher Horner suffered significant time losses.

Near the top, Evans jumped, but Wiggins held his wheel while Froome took off to win the stage.

The climb had been too steep for Cancellara; he gave up his lead to Wiggins. Still, for a squad thought to be in trouble, RadioShack's owning the Yellow Jersey for a week and putting two riders in the top ten was trouble almost any other team would like to enjoy.

The next day France got something to cheer about. Thibaut Pinot, the youngest rider on the team with the smallest budget in the race, FDJ-Big Mat, escaped on a day with seven categorized climbs. As he went up the final climb he was alone, with the pack several minutes behind. He pressed his advantage while his director, Marc Madiot (Paris–Roubaix winner in 1985 and 1991), ecstatically screamed at him from the team car (one journalist likened him to a poodle hanging out a car window) that he could win the stage, which he did.

The chasers, reduced to the elite eight best on that same final climb, got a taste of what was to come when the Tour would reach the high mountains. The descent to the finish had technical sections and each time the road got curvy, Vincenzo Nibali would open a gap, only to be chased down when the road straightened. The Italian later said he was probing, trying to see how well the Sky riders could descend and determine whether Evans wanted to work with him. Nibali felt that his best hope was in separating Wiggins from his team.

Come the first long time trial, race leader Wiggins had the privilege of being the last rider off. At all three time checks, he had the best time. Wiggins took a whopping 57 seconds out of Cancellara, who was surely tired from his week-long defense of the *maillot jaune*.

The General Classification after the Besançon 41.5-kilometer time trial:

1. Bradley Wiggins
2. Cadel Evans @ 1 minute 53 seconds
3. Christopher Froome @ 2 minutes 7 seconds
4. Vincenzo Nibali @ 2 minutes 23 seconds
5. Denis Menchov @ 3 minutes 2 seconds

During his rest day press conference, Evans said he would have to attack in the mountains. Not only was he two minutes down, another 53.5 kilometers of time trialing were coming up where he could lose another two minutes, meaning a conservative approach to the remaining stages would not yield victory.

Cadel Evans in the stage nine time trial, with the television motorcycle right at his side.

Stage ten was the 2012 Tour's first day in the high Alps. A large group escaped early in the day and as they went over the huge obstructions, attrition reduced them to just five. The solo winner was Thomas Voeckler, whose dodgy knee had made him a doubtful starter. Farther back in the Yellow Jersey group, Nibali blasted away on the descent of the penultimate climb, the Grand Colombier, and artfully connected with teammate Peter Sagan, who had been part of the early break. The two hammered away in the valley leading to the final ascent, the Col de Richemond, but the relentless Sky tempo machine swallowed the duo before the Richemond began. With a long downhill after the climb, there was a regrouping, with all the contenders finishing together. Wiggins and his team had so far shown no sign of weakness.

304

The next day had more torture for the riders' tired legs, starting with a nearly immediate run up the Madeleine followed by the highest pass in the 2012 Tour, the Croix de Fer with a hilltop finish at La Toussuire.

Again the stage winner was a survivor of an early break, Pierre Rolland, giving his Europcar team its second stage win in a row. But the fight for the Yellow Jersey was where the real drama unfolded.

On the Glandon (a prelude to the Croix de Fer), Evans had attacked. It was good to see real aggression from a contender that far from the finish. Wiggins later said he was surprised Evans attacked so far from the finish while the Sky team was riding such a hard tempo. But Evans' jump was without real punch and the Australian was quickly reeled in. Sky's neutralizing efforts had left most of the peloton gasping, with only eight riders left closing in on Evans.

The contenders were together for the day's final ascent to La Toussuire. Both Nibali and Jurgen Van den Broeck tried to get away, and Nibali's second jump caused Evans to lose contact. White Jersey holder and BMC teammate Tejay Van Garderen dropped back to pace Evans up to the finish.

Wiggins' right hand man, Chris Froome, went with Nibali, easily gaining 100 meters on his captain in a half-kilometer. It was an impressive display of climbing power that some characterized as an attack on Wiggins. As soon as he had carved out this sizable gap, Froome slowed, and with great show, listened with one hand on his earpiece. It was Sky team director Sean Yates giving Froome orders to get back to Wiggins to pace him up to the finish, which he did. Yates says Froome agreed to protect Wiggins all the way to the top.

There was carnage at this, the year's first high hilltop finish. Evans was not the only rider who had shown weakness so early in the Tour: Scarponi, Klöden, Valverde, Leipheimer and Menchov had also been mangled by Sky. Only Nibali and Van den Broeck had finished with Froome and Wiggins. Evan's spring build-up had been troubled by tendinitis and sinusitis, and on this day it looked like his legs were paying the price.

As soon as the stage ended, Froome was peppered with questions about his move and if he had known he had dropped his captain. Froome gave careful diplomatic answers, all to the effect that he was there to help Wiggins. The next day Bjarne Riis threw a little gasoline on the fire by saying Froome was the better rider, speculating that Sky might be considering a change of team leaders. In fact, there was a huge rift between the two riders; and even Wiggins' wife and Froome's girlfriend got into the scrum, waging a short Twitter war over Froome's seeming lack of loyalty to Wiggins' leadership.

After the stage eleven bloodbath, the General Classification was thus:

1. Bradley Wiggins
2. Christopher Froome @ 2 minutes 5 seconds
3. Vincenzo Nibali @ 2 minutes 23 seconds
4. Cadel Evans @ 3 minutes 19 seconds
5. Jurgen Van den Broeck @ 4 minutes 48 seconds

A few days later Froome gave an interview to *L'Équipe*, complaining about the magnitude of his sacrifice. But Froome had earlier been given a chance to be a team leader. After his 13-second second place to Juan José Cobo in the 2011 Vuelta where he beat third-place Wiggins by 1 minute, 26 seconds, his contract with Sky was up. Jonathan Vaughters, owner of the Garmin-Sharp team had offered him a place, but other teams soon priced the talented rider out of Vaughter's budget. By re-signing for Sky, Froome had accepted golden handcuffs and complaining now about the sacrifice was unseemly.

The stages taking the Tour to the Pyrenees were hard-fought. Case in point, stage thirteen to Le Cap d'Agde on the Mediterranean coast. The day's only climb, the third-category Mont St. Clair, turned out to be a leg-breaker, in no small part because it was raced at a red-hot speed. Evans tried to bolt, but Sky was having none of it. However, in the process, several good sprinters were dropped, including Cavendish. Over the crest, the peloton scorched the descent. Once on the flat coastal roads, side winds made the high speed perilous for anyone who couldn't find shelter at the front. Alexandre Vinokourov took off with Michael Albasini in tow. As they pounded away, the peloton broke into pieces. The pair was caught, but still the attacks and counter attacks went off like the final kilometers of a Belgian Classic.

Cavendish may have been dropped, but Sky still had another excellent sprinter, Edvald Boasson Hagen. Now Wiggins, unafraid to stick his nose in the wind, dragged the pack up to the escaping riders, making for a sprint finish, where big German André Greipel won with Sagan second.

Shades of 1904! Saboteurs returned to the Tour in stage fourteen. After the day's breakaway had gone over the crest of the final pass of this first Pyrenean stage, someone scattered tacks on the road. It was chaos. Follow cars, motorcycles and 45 riders suffered punctures. Evans had to stop three times as he frantically chased to get up to the Wiggins group. Once on the flat roads, Wiggins and Nibali slowed the pack to let the sabotaged riders regain contact, the group rolling in more than eighteen minutes after Luis-Leon Sánchez had outsmarted and out-ridden his fellow breakaways to win.

The next day there was little interest in racing as well. With a rest day coming up before two rough days in the Pyrenees, the riders' truculence was understandable. The first two weeks of competition had taken a large toll. There were 156 riders left in the race, many of the 42 abandons the results of injuries from crashes.

On the second rest day, doping again reared its ugly head. Adding to the cloud caused by the USADA action against Armstrong, Bruyneel and US Postal's doctors, Cofidis rider Rémy Di Gregorio had already left the Tour after being arrested on doping charges (the suspicious chemical turning out to be vitamins, and Di Gregorio eventually being cleared).

Then it was announced that Frank Schleck was the subject of an "adverse analytical finding". The UCI said a banned prescription diuretic, Xipamide, was found in his stage thirteen urine sample. Tour management suggested RadioShack-Nissan withdraw their rider rather than battle on while Schleck's "B" sample was tested. Schleck did leave, giving an unreserved denial, saying he had never taken the drug or any other banned substance, suggested that he may have been "poisoned". Poisoning was indeed possible. But there was always the cloud of Schleck's earlier payment of €7,000 to Operation Puerto doctor Eufemiano Fuentes. Schleck claimed it was for coaching advice and that the Luxembourg cycling federation cleared him (again, they would, wouldn't they?). But why consult with such a notorious doctor when there were so many untainted, but competent coaches?

The old "circle of death"—the Aubisque, Tourmalet, Aspin and Peyresourde—greeted the riders after their rest day. Voeckler went over the top of the Tourmalet with Brice Feillu. The two maintained a healthy lead over the pack and on the Peyresourde Voeckler dropped

Feillu and soloed down the mountain for his second high-profile stage win and the polka-dot jersey.

In the Yellow Jersey group, Evans' troubles continued. Stomach problems tormented the BMC rider as he was dropped on the Aspin. He scrambled back on during the descent in time to be the victim of Nibali's Liquigas team acceleration on the Peyresourde. It looked like Liquigas was going to use the same strategy it had used in the Giro: continue winding the speed ever higher before launching the team's classification rider.

That was exactly how it played out. Nibali jumped away near the summit, planning to use the descent to gain time, but Froome calmly closed up to him. Nibali went again, but before the summit Nibali, Wiggins and Froome were together. They raced to the finish to keep Van den Broeck, Van Garderen and Evans from re-catching them. Nibali beat his fellow escapees, but after the perfectly executed Liquigas set-piece, he had been unable to find any gaps in Sky's armor. Evans' hopes for even a podium place were shattered, the Australian was now in seventh place, eight minutes behind Wiggins.

Stage seventeen, with a finish at the top of the first-category Peyragudes, was the last chance for rivals to budge Sky from its place at the top of the standings. Coming before the Peyragudes were four passes—the Col de Menté, Ares, Burs and the *hors catégorie* Balès. Again, Liquigas tried to strip Wiggins of his support by keeping the speed high on the climbs. In the last kilometers of the Peyragudes, it wasn't Nibali who slipped the leash, it was Van den Broeck. When the Belgian jumped, Nibali was shelled.

Near the top, Wiggins asked Froome to up the tempo, and immediately it was just Froome leading Wiggins, the duo chasing Valverde, a survivor of an earlier break. It looked like Froome and Wiggins would easily make up the 38 seconds to Valverde and get a stage win, but when Froome accelerated to close the gap, Wiggins came off his wheel. Rather than catch Valverde, Froome turned and looked back for Wiggins and waited. Froome accelerated a couple of more times, and each time Wiggins came off. Valverde got the stage while the British pair distanced themselves still farther from their competitors. Asked about his trouble staying on Froome's wheel, Wiggins said at that point he realized he had won the Tour and had begun to lose concentration. The whole episode was odd. Did Wiggins pretend to struggle just to deny Froome a stage win?

The General Classification with the climbing finished:

1. Bradley Wiggins
2. Christopher Froome @ 2 minutes 5 seconds
3. Vincenzo Nibali @ 2 minutes 41 seconds
4. Jurgen Van den Broeck @ 5 minutes 53 seconds
5. Tejay Van Garderen @ 8 minutes 30 seconds

No one expected anything but a fabulous ride from Wiggins in the 53.5 kilometer time trial and that was exactly what he delivered. At 50 kilometers per hour he was the fastest at all check points. Froome was second, a little more than a minute slower.

Wiggins had arisen from the catastrophe of his 2010 and 2011 Tours to become the first British Tour winner. In addition to Sky's winning both extended time trials, their Mark Cavendish won three stages, allowing him to surpass by one André Darrigade's twenty-two stage wins. That left André Leducq's twenty-five, Bernard Hinault's twenty-eight and Eddy Merckx's thirty-four ahead of him. At no point was Sky in difficulty. It was a perfectly executed assault on a prize Wiggins had dreamed of winning since boyhood.

To frame Sky's accomplishment differently, €2,020,100 in prize money was up for grabs in the 2012 Tour. Sky took home €824,840. At €204,110, second place Liquigas didn't even earn a quarter of Sky's take.

Tradition holds that the Tour winner gives his prize money to his team (including the mechanics and soigneurs). While everyone else on Sky got his share as expected, Wiggins didn't pay Froome in full until September of 2013.

Final 2012 Tour de France General Classification:

1. Bradley Wiggins (Sky): 87 hours 34 minutes 47 seconds
2. Christopher Froome (Sky) @ 3 minutes 21 seconds
3. Vincenzo Nibali (Liquigas) @ 6 minutes 19 seconds
4. Jurgen Van den Broeck (Lotto-Belisol) @ 10 minutes 15 seconds
5. Tejay Van Garderen (BMC) @ 11 minutes 4 seconds

Climbers' Competition
>   1. Thomas Voeckler: 135 points
>   2. Fredrik Kessiakoff: 123
>   3. Chris Anker Sørensen: 77

Points Competition:
>   1. Peter Sagan: 421 points
>   2. André Greipel: 280
>   3. Matthew Harley Gos: 268

After beating back Armstrong's legal challenges, but still finding him unwilling to confess, USADA sent their "Reasoned Decision" to the UCI on October 10, 2012. This being a seminal document in the fight against doping, the statement from Travis Tygart, CEO of USADA, regarding that document is quoted in full here:

> Today, we are sending the "Reasoned Decision" in the Lance Armstrong case and supporting information to the Union Cycliste International (UCI), the World Anti-Doping Agency (WADA), and the World Triathlon Corporation (WTC). The evidence shows beyond any doubt that the US Postal Service Pro Cycling Team ran the most sophisticated, professionalized and successful doping program that sport has ever seen.

> The evidence of the US Postal Service Pro Cycling Team-run scheme is overwhelming and is in excess of 1000 pages, and includes sworn testimony from 26 people, including 15 riders with knowledge of the US Postal Service Team (USPS Team) and its participants' doping activities. The evidence also includes direct documentary evidence including financial payments, emails, scientific data and laboratory test results that further prove the use, possession and distribution of performance enhancing drugs by Lance Armstrong and confirm the disappointing truth about the deceptive activities of the USPS Team, a team that received tens of millions of American taxpayer dollars in funding.

> Together these different categories of eyewitness, documentary, first-hand, scientific, direct and circumstantial evidence reveal conclusive and undeniable proof that brings to the light of day for the first time this systemic, sustained and highly professionalized team-run doping conspiracy. All of the material will be made available later this afternoon on the USADA website at www.usada.org.

The USPS Team doping conspiracy was professionally designed to groom and pressure athletes to use dangerous drugs, to evade detection, to ensure its secrecy and ultimately gain an unfair competitive advantage through superior doping practices. A program organized by individuals who thought they were above the rules and who still play a major and active role in sport today.

The evidence demonstrates that the "Code of Silence" of performance enhancing drug use in the sport of cycling has been shattered, but there is more to do. From day one, we always hoped this investigation would bring to a close this troubling chapter in cycling's history and we hope the sport will use this tragedy to prevent it from ever happening again.

Of course, no one wants to be chained to the past forever, and I would call on the UCI to act on its own recent suggestion for a meaningful Truth and Reconciliation program. While we appreciate the arguments that weigh in favor of and against such a program, we believe that allowing individuals like the riders mentioned today to come forward and acknowledge the truth about their past doping may be the only way to truly dismantle the remaining system that allowed this "EPO and Blood Doping Era" to flourish. Hopefully, the sport can unshackle itself from the past, and once and for all continue to move forward to a better future.

Our mission is to protect clean athletes by preserving the integrity of competition not only for today's athletes but also the athletes of tomorrow. We have heard from many athletes who have faced an unfair dilemma—dope, or don't compete at the highest levels of the sport. Many of them abandoned their dreams and left sport because they refused to endanger their health and participate in doping. That is a tragic choice no athlete should have to make.

It took tremendous courage for the riders on the USPS Team and others to come forward and speak truthfully. It is not easy to admit your mistakes and accept your punishment. But that is what these riders have done for the good of the sport, and for the young riders who hope to one day reach their dreams without using dangerous drugs or methods.

These eleven (11) teammates of Lance Armstrong, in alphabetical order, are Frankie Andreu, Michael Barry, Tom Danielson,

Tyler Hamilton, George Hincapie, Floyd Landis, Levi Leipheimer, Stephen Swart, Christian Vande Velde, Jonathan Vaughters and David Zabriskie.

The riders who participated in the USPS Team doping conspiracy and truthfully assisted have been courageous in making the choice to stop perpetuating the sporting fraud, and they have suffered greatly. In addition to the public revelations, the active riders have been suspended and disqualified appropriately in line with the rules. In some part, it would have been easier for them if it all would just go away; however, they love the sport, and they want to help young athletes have hope that they are not put in the position they were—to face the reality that in order to climb to the heights of their sport they had to sink to the depths of dangerous cheating.

I have personally talked with and heard these athletes' stories and firmly believe that, collectively, these athletes, if forgiven and embraced, have a chance to leave a legacy far greater for the good of the sport than anything they ever did on a bike.

Lance Armstrong was given the same opportunity to come forward and be part of the solution. He rejected it.

Instead he exercised his legal right not to contest the evidence and knowingly accepted the imposition of a ban from recognized competition for life and disqualification of his competitive results from 1998 forward. The entire factual and legal basis on the outcome in his case and the other six active riders' cases will be provided in the materials made available online later today. Two other members of the USPS Team, Dr. Michele Ferrari and Dr. Garcia del Moral, also received lifetime bans for perpetrating this doping conspiracy.

Three other members of the USPS Team have chosen to contest the charges and take their cases to arbitration: Johan Bruyneel, the team director; Dr. Pedro Celaya, a team doctor; and Jose 'Pepe' Marti, the team trainer. These three individuals will receive a full hearing before independent judges, where they will have the opportunity to present and confront the evidence, cross-examine witnesses and testify under oath in a public proceeding.

From day one in this case, as in every potential case, the USADA Board of Directors and professional staff did the job we are mandated to do for clean athletes and the integrity of sport. We focused solely on finding the truth without being influenced by celebrity or non-celebrity, threats, personal attacks or political pressure because that is what clean athletes deserve and demand.

Two days after the "Reasoned Decision" release, RadioShack sacked Bruyneel. On October 22, 2012, the UCI accepted the USADA's position, stripping Armstrong of all results from August 1, 1998, including his seven Tour victories, and banned him from the sport for life.

Trying to regain control of the situation, Armstrong appeared on Oprah Winfrey's television show and made a partial confession almost devoid of apology. He didn't name others (given his call to Verbruggen to accuse Hamilton of doping, this certainly wasn't because he refused to be a snitch), nor explain how he got his drugs. Armstrong blamed the sport and said he was merely leveling the playing field, and that to a professional cyclist, taking drugs was like airing up bicycle tires, just part of the job.

He was wrong of course. Taking drugs does not level the playing field. It tilts it in the doper's favor. Bjarne Riis was merely a competent domestique before he became a cycling pharmacy that could crush the competition. Marco Pantani went from being a very good climber to the finest living bicycle racer because his body responded so well to dope.

After taking drugs, Armstrong, who previously never shown much talent for stage racing, became the greatest stage racer in the history of the sport. But even worse, he was the sport's greatest and most enthusiastic enforcer of its code of *omertà*. He tried to ruin people's lives, hounding and punishing them for daring to speak the truth.

The 1999–2005 Tours have no winners. Greg LeMond is the only American to have won the Tour de France. As of this writing, several of those whom Armstrong sued are fighting to get their money back. After Nike gave up on him, Armstrong's other sponsors ran from him as if he had the plague. It's calculated that in a single day he lost $75 million in endorsements.

The U.S. Government decided to join Landis' whistleblower lawsuit, seeking $100 million. In April, 2018, shortly before the case was to go to trial, the federal government agreed to settle with Armstrong for $5 million, plus $1.65 million to go to Landis to cover his legal costs.

Mr. Armstrong has been unmasked as a bully, liar, cheater and thug.

2013

Prudhomme unveiled a hillier race than the year before, with six stages in the high mountains and four summit finishes. A 25-kilometer team time trial was included, while the individual time trialing was dialed down from 101.4 kilometers in 2012 to 65 in 2013. As in recent editions, there were no time bonuses. The hundredth edition of the Tour de France would be tallied in real time.

After tiring of the seemingly endless drug scandals tied to its eponymous cycling team, Rabobank had its name scrubbed from the team jerseys. The Dutch banking giant would still honor its sponsorship contract, but so damaging was the connection to cycling, the team raced under the name "Blanco". Just before the Tour's start, the American computer equipment maker Belkin took over as the troubled team's title sponsor.

Cycling couldn't escape its past. The French Senate ordered the results of the 1998 Tour urine sample tests that had been performed in 2004 (the same tests that had shown Armstrong used EPO) be revealed. Just before the Tour's start Laurent Jalabert's positive was leaked with the likelihood that other famous riders would no longer enjoy at least some doubt about their drug use. The riders' union protested vigorously, claiming the 2004 retesting had been unjust and would be of little use during what was now a clean era (they would, wouldn't they?). The Senate gave in to demands that it at least wait until the Tour's end before releasing the damaging report.

Sky had a mess on its hands too, with Chris Froome no longer content to be a *gregario di lusso* for Wiggins. Rumor had it that Froome would only renew with Sky if Wiggins were not on their Tour team. Wiggins would ride the Giro, Froome the Tour and everyone would be happy. But Wiggins didn't quite see it that way and in the days leading up to the Giro, Wiggins said he would try for the Giro/Tour double. That forced Sky director Dave Brailsford to issue a statement confirming Froome as Sky's Tour leader.

Wiggins soon made Brailsford's Tour team management job easier by getting sick and abandoning the Giro. Shortly thereafter it was announced that Wiggins was not recovering, and further, that a stubborn knee injury wasn't healing fast enough to let Wiggins train, meaning he would not be ready for the Tour.

Froome (like Wiggins in 2012) was the dominant rider of 2013 with victories in the Tour of Oman, Critérium International, Tour de Romandie and the Critérium du Dauphiné. Three times in 2013 he had gone head-to-head with his major rival, Alberto Contador (Oman, Tirreno–Adriatico and the Dauphiné) and had beaten him each time. At the Tour's start Contador said he was at ninety percent, the level of fitness he thought optimal to avoid getting overcooked before the Tour ended. But like Ivan Basso, at no time since coming off his doping suspension had he shown much of the spark that had made him the dominant Grand Tour rider of his age.

The first three stages were run in Corsica, the Tour's first visit to France's wild and beautiful island off Italy's Tuscan coast. The first stage turned out to be a near-catastrophe. While the sprinters' teams were dragging the peloton north to the finish in Bastia, the Orica-GreenEdge team bus got stuck under the finish line gantry and couldn't be freed. What to do? The screaming pack was now only fourteen kilometers away. Quickly, an improvised finish line was set up three kilometers before the original, at a point where the road made a dangerous S-curve, chosen because timing equipment was already set up there. As this announcement was made, a big crash at the back of the pack took down a major hopeful, 2012 Giro winner Ryder Hesjedal.

The workmen at the finish line hadn't given up on getting the bus loose and a few minutes later it finally backed away from the banner and the finish was returned to its original place. Another big crash near the front took down most of the good sprinters, including Mark Cavendish, André Greipel and Peter Sagan. Making it through all the chaos, German rider Marcel Kittel was the first of a reduced lead group to cross the finish line. Though the crash had come before the three-kilometer mark, all the delayed riders were given the same time. Many riders said the changes created confusion and instability in the peloton, making the crashes almost inevitable. Kittel said he was oblivious to the whole situation, and rode his normal race.

The next two stages were over hilly terrain made more difficult by the narrow roads and high speeds. Crashes were common and many riders were sporting bandages, hoping they could just survive until the race got to the mainland.

Before the team time trial in Nice, RadioShack's Jan Bakelants was holding onto a slim lead as a result of a narrowly successful escape in stage two.

1. Jan Bakelants
2. Julien Simon @ 1 second
3. Simon Gerrans @ same time
4. Michal Kwiatkowski @ same time
5. Edvald Boasson Hagen @ same time

To save riders on weak teams from crippling time losses, the team trial was kept short, just 25 kilometers, and all the real contenders came through with manageable deficits. Orica-GreenEdge got its second consecutive stage win, putting Simon Gerrans in Yellow and largely erasing the humiliation of the stage one team bus fiasco.

There was another big crash near stage five's end in Marseille. It didn't get better the next day. A big pile-up here separated Mark Cavendish from the field and after a hard chase he didn't have the suds to win the sprint, taken by André Greipel. The Germans were on a roll.

After seven stages Daryl Impey still held the precious seconds Orica-GreenEdge had gained in the team time trial.

The General Classification stood thus:

1. Daryl Impey
2. Edvald Boasson Hagen @ 3 seconds
3. Simon Gerrans @ 5 seconds
4. Michael Albasini @ same time
5. Michal Kwiatkowski @ 6 seconds

For those who had survived the falls and collisions, the real Tour began with stage eight and its two big ascents near the stage's end. First would be the Col de Pailhères (the year's Souvenir Henri Desgrange) followed by a hilltop finish at the Ax-3 Domaines ski station.

The year's first big move happened with five kilometers left to go on the Pailhères, when Movistar sent its young climber Nairo Quintana up the hill. By the mountain's crest, he had a minute on the Sky-led bunch, a lead reduced to 30 seconds during the descent.

With Froome on his wheel, Sky's Richie Porte blasted up the final climb with about thirty riders on his tail. He quickly shelled many of them, including Cadel Evans and Andy Schleck. With five kilometers to go, five riders remained: Porte, Froome, Contador, Valverde and Roman Kreuziger.

Bam! Froome hit the other four with a vicious attack and raced up the hill. He quickly caught and dropped Quintana and by the time he crossed the line he had about a minute in hand. Like Armstrong had done year after year, Froome had used the first hilltop finish to put his competitors to the sword. Sky occupied the first two places in the standings.

1. Christopher Froome
2. Richie Porte @ 51 seconds
3. Alejandro Valverde @ 1 minute 25 seconds
4. Bauke Mollema @ 1 minute 44 seconds
5. Laurens ten Dam @ 1 minute 50 seconds

The peloton was in shock. Some blamed the change from the heat of Corsica and Provence to the Pyrenean cold for their bad day. Contador had looked simply dreadful, needing Roman Kreuziger to guide him up the mountain, while Evans lost more than four minutes.

It wouldn't be easier the next day with four first-category climbs promising a hard day of racing. Garmin-Sharp started firing on the day's first climb, the Portet d'Aspet, revealing Sky's vulnerable condition. Froome's domestiques must have gone very deep the day before, because only Porte was able to stay with Froome over the top, and on the Col de Menté, even Porte was dropped. It was still early in the stage, but Froome had already been stripped of support. He was alone, surrounded by ambitious athletes eager to put the Yellow Jersey *in extremis*.

Or so you would have thought. As had happened countless times before with Armstrong, the Spanish had the numbers but were afraid to confront the leader. Quintana put in a few testing attacks, but never was Froome subjected to the hammering he should have received. Content with dispatching Porte and taking second place, Valverde's Movistar riders, hoping for a stage win, went to the front to chase down non-threatening breakaway riders. Garmin-Sharp rider Daniel Martin won the stage after fleeing near the final summit, an excellent reward for his team's heads-up riding. Froome remained the leader.

Garmin-Sharp had put the ball on the tee, but Movistar wouldn't take a swing.

Froome's Pyrenean riding caused a furor. His ascent of Ax-3 Domaines in stage eight was the third-fastest ever, only 15 seconds slower than Armstrong's drug-fueled 2001 ride. He was 10 seconds faster than Armstrong in 2003, and 26 seconds quicker than Armstrong in 2005. He also beat Ullrich's and Basso's 2003 times up the mountain. Calculations showed Froome had been kicking out 6.5 watts/kilogram of body weight. Sports physiologists found Froome's performance to be of a kind unseen in the last few years. Yet, though both his 6.5 watts/kg and his 1,715 VAM were impressive and disconcerting, neither was so incredible that one could accuse him of doping.

At its start Sky had promised to be a different team, one dedicated to clean sport and transparency. But when asked for physiological data, the team (as Armstrong had before) reneged, saying the data was both a trade secret and too confusing for others to understand. But, Sky assured the world that they were clean and they should be trusted. "At some point in time, clean performances will surpass the doped performances in the past." Sky's boss David Brailsford said, "Bottom line is, it's a rest day. It's 10 o'clock in the morning and I'm trying to defend someone who has done nothing wrong. I'm happy to do it and more than happy to try and convince you guys that we're not doing anything wrong but we need a bit of help." He steadfastly refused to give what was asked for, data such as Froome's VO_2 max. Without the promised transparency, questions would continue. Paralleling American reactions to earlier questions about Armstrong's performance, while the rest of the world expressed doubts born of decades of corruption and lying, British fans and writers rallied to Sky's defense.

During the rest day, the Tour transferred north to bike-mad Brittany where those hoping to find a weak spot in Froome's armor were disappointed. Over the 33 kilometers of the Mont St. Michel individual time trial, Froome schooled the rest of the field in the use of power. Froome went so fast that at one point he was ahead of Tony Martin, the world time trial champion. Martin rode nearly 55 kilometers/hour on average to beat Froome by just 12 seconds, while Valverde and Contador lost more than two minutes. It was an astonishing performance.

The General Classification now stood thus:

1. Christopher Froome
2. Alejandro Valverde @ 3 minutes 25 seconds
3. Bauke Mollema @ 3 minutes 37 seconds
4. Alberto Contador @ 3 minutes 54 seconds
5. Roman Kreuziger @ 3 minutes 57 seconds

By the start of the twelfth stage neither France nor Spain nor Italy had won a stage. One had to go back to 1926 to find a comparable drought. And stage twelve didn't make things any better. Marcel Kittel surprised all by coming around Cavendish in the sprint to score Germany's fifth stage win.

Wind is dangerous. It allows crafty, powerful teams to upset the best-laid plans. The thirteenth leg, run through the heart of France, looked to be an easy stage. But after the day's racing was a bit more than half done, the Belgian Omega Pharma squad suddenly accelerated into a crosswind, catching many riders napping (including their *bête noir* Marcel Kittel). Riders scrambled to form echelons, hoping to regain the front group.

After contact with another rider broke his rear wheel, Valverde waited for a slow arriving wheel change rather than take a teammate's bike, putting him far behind the Kittel group. All Movistar riders but Nairo Quintana were sent back to help Valverde. The Spaniards eventually caught the Kittel group, but this sort of racing was the turf of Belgians and Dutchmen. The Belgians wanted to make sure Kittel stayed dropped, while the Dutch Belkin team saw Bauke Mollema moving up to second place if Valverde couldn't make the catch. The pursuit was on.

With 40 kilometers remaining, the gap was over two minutes. Despite the ferocious chase, the Dutch and Belgian echelon experts were carrying the day. Then things got even worse for Valverde. Contador's Saxo-Tinkoff team had been careful to stay up front but had not been doing any work. They were as fresh as anyone could be this late in a difficult stage.

As the pace in the front group seemed to ease a bit and Froome had drifted to the back, Saxo now went full gas. Instantly a split put Contador, Kreuziger, Mollema and Green Jersey Peter Sagan on the good side of the fracture, while Froome and a couple of teammates were stuck with those who had missed the move. Cavendish said that when a break goes in a crosswind it's like falling through ice. You have just five seconds to close the gap or it's gone.

Cavendish did just that, and there were now fourteen riders motoring away from the Froome group. Contador's Saxo-Tinkoff team might have been the strongest team in the Tour and now he was putting it to excellent use, bludgeoning Froome with power. Sky's ability to dominate the peloton had suddenly evaporated. Yet, Froome displayed extraordinary confidence in his own cause. As the others in his chase group banged away, Froome did not contribute any work, preferring to sit in and save his strength.

Like the Valverde chase that eventually gave up, the Yellow Jersey group couldn't get up to the leaders, and by the end of the stage (won by Cavendish) the gap had grown to a minute. But Froome's losses were trivial compared to Valverde's nearly ten-minute catastrophe. It was time to say a funeral mass for Valverde's podium hopes.

The next day, Italy finally snagged a stage win. Matteo Trentin's canny sprint came from a break the tired peloton seemed happy to let ride into the sunset. Trentin's Tour victory was Italy's first stage win since 2010.

Stage fifteen ended with the Tour's fifteenth visit to Mont Ventoux since it was first ascended in 1951, as well as the ninth time it had been used for a hilltop finish.

Sky wanted this stage. Even before Mont Ventoux had been reached, Froome's men were driving the bunch hard, spitting riders out the back. Nairo Quintana, now Movistar's only GC hope, made his move with more than twelve kilometers of ascent left, and soon had a half-minute. But Sky, led now by Richie Porte, was content to ride its chosen tempo. Porte's steady pacemaking broke the peloton, and soon he had only Froome and Contador for company. He had ridden nearly all of the best cyclists in the world off his wheel.

With seven kilometers remaining, Froome swept around Porte, easily left Contador behind and soon blew by Quintana as well. But Quintana was not to be so easily liquidated and crawled back up to Froome. For a few kilometers the pair worked together, but Froome was itchy. A couple of times he tried to lose Quintana, but the stolid-faced Movistar rider clung to Froome. As they passed under the four-kilometer banner, Froome struck again and this time Quintana couldn't answer. Froome soared up the mountain, speedily spinning his elliptical chainring with his skinny but powerful legs. Froome wasn't a pretty rider. Italian commentator Davide Cassani said Froome's gangly position made him look as if he were pushing a shopping cart while cradling a telephone to his ear. But there is no time-bonus for style and the prestigious stage was Froome's. He had left Quintana a half-minute back and everyone else at least a minute and a half behind.

The General Classification was now:

1. Christopher Froome
2. Bauke Mollema @ 4 minutes 14 seconds
3. Alberto Contador @ 4 minutes 25 seconds
4. Roman Kreuziger @ 4 minutes 28 seconds
5. Laurens ten Dam @ 4 minutes 54 seconds

If Contador couldn't execute Froome on the climbs or in the wind, there remained several challenging descents. Rather than the typical rest before the last time trial, stage sixteen was raced à bloc. Joaquim Rodríguez and his Katusha squad blistered the final climb, with Contador throwing in a couple of whacks of his own for good measure. Despite these efforts, the contenders were still together. When the Yellow Jersey group crested the pass, Froome still had Porte with him. Contador took off on a suicidal descent, attacking out of every corner. Froome marked him and when Contador overcooked a corner, Froome had to go off the road to avoid the fallen Spaniard.

Contador was quickly up, and the race continued with Froome now assisted by Porte. It was a hard day, but with the exception of Nairo Quintana moving up to fifth, no one at the top of the standings had been budged.

With two second-category climbs stuffed into its 32 kilometers, the final stage seventeen time trial was not likely going to be won by a pure rouleur. Froome was slightly behind Contador at the second time check, but like most of the riders that day, Froome chose to switch from a road bike with aero bars to a full time trial bike for the final downhill kilometers. There he pulled ahead slightly to beat Contador by 9 seconds. Froome now led Contador by 4 minutes, 34 seconds.

Brailsford buckled slightly under calls for Froome's data by releasing two years of Froome's power information. It was deemed consistent with itself, but without earlier data before Froome was capable of winning a Grand Tour or his VO_2 max, an effective analysis was impossible. Brailsford was still being coy.

Course designer Pescheux wanted stage eighteen to be a shorter, nervous stage full of attacks, a stage that a bold rider might use to "turn things around". He included two trips up l'Alpe d'Huez. Pescheux's hopes went unfulfilled. Contador tried again to get away on the penultimate descent, but again, the best were together for the second pass up L'Alpe d'Huez and its hilltop finish.

Porte kept the speed high, too high, it seemed, for his team leader. Porte slowed to let his captain close up. Then Froome simply rode away from the others, catching Quintana asleep at the switch. The Colombian struggled up to Froome and then Rodríguez made it up to the duo. Contador and Valverde had no answer as the trio motored up the road.

Rodríguez's announced intention was to make up for his poor first two weeks and attain a place on the podium. He now made good on that plan with a powerful attack that dropped both Froome and Quintana. He was caught just as Porte had found the legs to rejoin the leaders. With four kilometers still to climb, Froome motioned with his hand for Porte to go back to the team car for food, something quite against the rules in the final kilometers of a stage.

Quintana took advantage of Froome's growing hunger knock by jetting away with Rodríguez for temporary company. Further up the road, Christophe Riblon, who had been away for most of the stage, erased France's embarrassment by being the first of his countrymen to win a stage in the 2013 Tour.

Two minutes later Quintana finished, more than a minute ahead of Froome and now in third place. Despite his problems in the final kilometers and a 20-second time penalty for his illegal feed, Froome had extended his lead over Contador to more than five minutes.

Though the next day had a passel of famous passes including the Glandon, Madeleine and the Croix Fry, no one mounted a serious challenge to the GC standings. It was to come down to the penultimate stage, ending with a hilltop finish at Annecy-Semnoz. Though Froome was close to having the race nailed, much was still in play. There were four riders fighting over second and third place, within 47 seconds of each other. While Peter Sagan had only to finish the Tour to be assured of winning the Green Jersey, the contest for the polka-dot jersey was nowhere near settled.

Even before the final climb began, Sky's pace had blown the peloton to pieces, and there were only eight riders left in the Froome group. Once the mountain really reared up, Rodríguez lit up the road with Quintana on his wheel. In an astonishing display of power, Froome whooshed by them both. That was too much even for Froome. He had to relent and let the pair close up to him. But everyone else was gone. Contador lost time with every turn of the cranks and as Rodríguez was dragging the trio, Contador was slipping down to virtual fourth place.

Passing under the kilometer-to-go banner, Froome tried to escape, but Quintana could not be dropped. In fact, he had a lot left in the tank. He zoomed away to take the stage win, second place, best young rider and the polka-dotted jersey. Behind him Rodríguez cruised in second and earned that third sport on the podium. Froome had to be content with third that day, making him the winner of the hundredth edition of the Tour de France. At no point was his leadership in doubt. He consistently rode at a higher level than the rest of his competitors.

This was a good Tour for ASO. Running the Tour costs about €100 million a year. But despite the past fifteen years of scandal, according to French writer Pierre Ballester, the 2013 edition yielded a profit of €30 million (about $40 million USD).

Final 2013 Tour de France General Classification:
1. Christopher Froome (Sky): 83 hours 56 minutes 40 seconds
2. Nairo Alexander Quintana (Movistar) @ 4 minutes 20 seconds
3. Joaquim Rodríguez (Katusha) @ 5 minutes 4 seconds
4. Alberto Contador (Saxo-Tinkoff) @ 6 minutes 27seconds
5. Roman Kreuziger (Saxo-Tinkoff) @ 7 minutes 27 seconds

Climbers' Competition:
1. Nairo Alexander Quintana: 147 points
2. Christopher Froome: 136
3. Pierre Rolland: 117

Points Competition:
1. Peter Sagan: 409 points
2. Mark Cavendish: 312
3. André Greipel: 267

On the Wednesday after the Tour's end, the French Senate finally released the names of riders found to have had EPO in their samples during the 1998 Tour, or whose tests had at least triggered suspicions. Because only some of the samples were actually tested, it was no exoneration for those not named. The list of positives contained no surprises to anyone paying close attention to the sport, among them: Mario Cipollini, Jacky Durand, Bo Hamburger, Laurent Jalabert, Abraham Olano, Marco Pantani, Andrea Tafi, Jan Ullrich, and Erik Zabel.

Meanwhile, riders called for a ceasefire from scientists and journalists who continued to insist that close scrutiny of riders' past performances was necessary. Riders insisted that mass doping was a thing of the past and they shouldn't be tainted with the sins of previous generations. We've all been told this before. Without rigorous scrutiny fueled by a skepticism born of decades of lies put forth by an unbelievably corrupt sport, racing could again easily descend to the dark depths from which it seemed to be arising.

"This is one Yellow Jersey that will stand the test of time", Froome promised. We all hope this is true.

2014

For just the fourth time, the United Kingdom hosted the Tour de France. Previous British visits were in 1974, 1994 and 2007. This time the riders began the Tour on July 5 from the city of Leeds and finished the year's first stage in Harrogate, in Yorkshire.

On the start line were several favorites, notably Chris Froome, Alberto Contador and Vincenzo Nibali. Coming off his 2013 season and a clear Tour win, Froome's spring seemed an inevitable continuation of the talented racer's career. He came to the Tour with victories in the early-season Tour of Oman as well as the Tour de Romandie and the Critérium du Dauphiné. As he stood ready to start the Tour, Froome already had a successful season under his belt.

Coming off his poor 2013 with its single victory, Contador was clearly back to his old self in 2014. After a second place in the Portuguese Volta ao Algarve, he won the prestigious Tirreno-Adriatico and the Tour of the Basque Country, coming second only to Froome in the Dauphiné.

Vincenzo Nibali, 2013 Giro d'Italia victor, said the Tour was his main objective for 2014. He had a very quiet spring with no race wins until he claimed the *tricolore* jersey of the Italian road champion the week before the Tour began. Without fanfare, the man nicknamed *Lo Squalo* ("The Shark") had brought himself to peak form.

The first day's racing in the modest Yorkshire hills yielded the expected sprint finish, won by German rocket Marcel Kittel. Swiss escape artist Fabian Cancellara had tried his disappearing act, but within sight of the finish, the speeding peloton (despite being slowed a bit by a crash involving Mark Cavendish and Simon Gerrans) hoovered him up, setting things up for the big romp to the line.

Yorkshire wasn't going to let the riders leave without feeling the sting of the lash, as stage two had nine categorized climbs, all levels three and four, plus rolling terrain that made this a challenging stage. By the final climbs, the lead group was down to just twenty, with all of the contenders watching each other. Then Bam! Nibali blasted away while the others looked at each other, hoping someone would spend some energy chasing him. They hesitated for a few fatal seconds. The Italian was gone.

The chase did get organized, but The Shark crossed the line alone, two seconds ahead of the others. That was good enough to make him the new Yellow Jersey. Clearly, not only was Nibali not a man afraid to take a chance, but he also had the horsepower to make an escape stick.

After another Marcel Kittel sprint win, the Tour transferred to France for the fourth stage, again won by Kittel. That made three of the first four stages won by the German. But without the time bonuses of past years in play, Nibali remained the overall leader.

That brought the Tour to its first truly important day, the fifth stage with its trip over nine sectors of Belgian and French cobblestones. Rain was already falling on the riders when they headed south from Ypres, though Roubaix, on their way to the finish at Arenberg-Porte du Hainaut. The *pavé* would be dangerously slippery with water and oil. The bad weather forced the organizers to remove two of the cobbled sectors, but that still left thirteen kilometers of dangerous, worn and slippery stones to navigate. Dutchman Koen de Kort tweeted what everyone was feeling, "I have to somehow feel like I'm about to be witness to an epic and historic stage. This is a day to never forget."

Contador voiced the GC contenders' anxiety, "I will cross my fingers for tomorrow—it will be a really difficult day. The weather forecast is very bad. Already without bad weather it will be a complicated stage, but with rain it will be like ice-skating with bikes."

After only thirty kilometers Froome was on the ground. He was quickly up and paced back up to the peloton. As the stage progressed, riders kept falling, yet the peloton's relentless, take-no-prisoners speed yielded a 47.6 kilometers/hour pace after 100 kilometers. Contador was having trouble with the terrain and was unable to maintain his usual position near the front. Froome was in even worse condition. After a second crash, he refused a new bike from the team and instead, climbed into the team car. His Tour de France was over, making him the first defending Tour champion to abandon since Bernard Hinault's bad knee forced him to quit in 1980.

With all the carnage, Nibali seemed at home on the difficult terrain. He was with two other riders, former world cyclocross champ Lars Boom and Jakob Fuglsang. Near the finish, a mud-splattered Boom went clear to take a solo win with Nibali and Fuglsang a short distance behind. Contador crossed the line almost three minutes later.

The day had transformed the 2014 Tour. Froome was out of the race, Contador was more than two minutes down and Nibali was in Yellow, displaying superb form, tactics and courage.

GC after stage five:
1. Vincenzo Nibali
2. Jakob Fuglsang @ 2 seconds
3. Peter Sagan @ 44 seconds
4. Michal Kwiatkowski @ 50 seconds
5. Fabian Cancellara @ 1 minute 17 seconds
19. Alberto Contador @ 2 minutes 37 seconds

The Tour returned to racing on paved roads in stage six, but that didn't mean things were going to be any easier. It was a windy day with rain falling on the start line. As the peloton closed in on the finish town of Reims, Omega Pharma riders began taking hard, ferocious pulls at the front, upping the speed to 55 kilometers/hour. The high speeds combined with strong crosswinds shattered the peloton. Several sprinters, including Marcel Kittel, never saw the front again. Then, obviously following a pre-determined script, Omega Pharma rider Michal Kwiatkowski took a flyer, but was caught. As the stage ended, André Greipel unleashed an irresistible sprint to keep the Tour's fast finishes German property. Nibali stayed up front and out of trouble, keeping his lead.

A couple of days later the Tour had its first real climbing with two second-category ascents. Blel Kadri was the last survivor of a five-man break, and late in the stage, on the Col de la Croix Moinats, he motored away and rode alone for twenty kilometers to give the French their first stage win of the year.

Back in the peloton, Contador's Tinkoff-Saxo team decided this would be a good day to see if they could put a little daylight between Contador and Nibali. They pounded away and momentarily dropped the Italian, but Nibali closed back up. On the final climb to the finish Contador was able to get clear of The Shark, but only by 3 seconds.

Meanwhile, Sky's backup GC rider Richie Porte moved up to third place, two minutes behind Nibali.

Now the real climbing started. Stage nine was the first day in the Vosges with six categorized climbs, but the day was only a prelude to stage ten's relentless profile. Not wanting to waste energy, the pack allowed Tony Martin and Alessandro de Marchi to roll off the front. A good-sized chase group then formed, but they didn't put too much effort into the pursuit. Martin was able to make a solo break of it to win the stage. But in the first chase group of eighteen riders was Tony Gallopin. His savvy riding put him in the lead, allowing him to be a Frenchman in Yellow on Bastille Day.

Playtime was over. Stage ten had those six tough climbs with a hilltop finish at the top of the first-category, six-kilometer-long Le Planche des Belles Filles.

After just 60 kilometers, the race's character was completely changed. While Alberto Contador was reaching into his back pocket, he went down hard. Perhaps his front wheel hit a rock or he hit a hole in the road. No one knows for sure. As the race went up the road, his bloody knee was bandaged, he was given a new bike and his team set about pacing him back up to the pack. But it was no use. After 18 kilometers Contador gave up, climbed into the team car and abandoned the race. Later, x-rays showed the Spaniard had been chasing with a broken right tibia. The determination of the men who race at this level is nothing short of incredible.

Now both Froome and Contador were out.

As the final climb began to bite, Michal Kwiatkowski and Joaquim Rodríguez were off the front with Nibali's Astanas giving serious chase. Nibali went clear, passed Rodríguez and crossed the line alone, a quarter-minute ahead of his nearest chaser. Porte did himself a world of good when he came in seventh, a half-minute behind Nibali. Porte was now in second place.

Nibali said, "This was the hardest stage I've ever done in a Grand Tour, with seven climbs and so many crashes."

After a rest day and several stages with rolling terrain that didn't affect the standings, it was time for the big stuff in the Alps. Stage thirteen had it. There were just three rated ascents. While they were small in number, they were crucial in character. It was the final slope that mattered, the *hors categorie* Montée de Chamrousse, eighteen kilometers averaging 7.3 percent.

The stage was ridden with gusto. The cold, wet days of the Tour's start were history as the riders unzipped their jerseys looking for some relief from the heat. Two-thirds through the stage, just before the real climbing began, the pack had been averaging almost 45 kilometers/hour, putting the riders twenty minutes ahead of the organizers' most optimistic schedule.

At the start of the Chamrousse, the Spanish Movistar team went to the front to keep the pace high for Alejandro Valverde. Porte was soon left behind. The speeds stayed high, finally leaving just a few riders in the front group. Ten kilometers from the summit, Valverde rolled the dice and off he went in search of a pair of riders a little farther up the hill. But he couldn't drop Nibali. Then with seven kilometers remaining, Nibali showed why he was the man wearing the yellow jersey. He was soon alone and off the front.

Nibali had left everyone well and truly behind. He had time to zip up his jersey and cross the line in style. Ten seconds later, Rafal Majka finished, while Valverde ended the stage almost a minute behind Nibali. At one point in the climbing, Richie Porte had gut troubles so bad he had to call for medical assistance. The Sky rider finished the stage but his Yellow Jersey hunt was over.

The GC after the first day in the Alps:
1. Vincenzo Nibali
2. Alejandro Valverde @ 3 minutes 37 seconds
3. Romain Bardet @ 4 minutes 24 seconds

The Story of the Tour de France

4. Thibaut Pinot @ 4 minutes 40 seconds
5. Tejay Van Garderen @ 5 minutes 19 seconds
16. Richie Porte @ 11 minutes 11 seconds

One might reasonably expect the next day with its menu of the Lautaret, Izoard and a hilltop finish at the top of the first-category Montée de Risoul to continue the turmoil in the standings. Nibali predicted a fearsomely difficult stage. He was right.

Though riders had been trying to get away all day, there was a general regroupment at the base of the Risoul ascent with eleven riders in a front group. Rafal Majka wasn't done trying to win a Tour stage and from this small group he took off. And that was the stage, the peloton never saw him again.

Meanwhile, a half-minute back, Nibali shook off the rest of his group and finished just 24 seconds behind Majka. Valverde, however, cracked and came in eleventh. He didn't lose enough time to fall out of second place, but third-place Bardet was only 13 seconds behind him.

The race rolled across southern France for its appointment with the Pyrenees. The steep stuff began with stage seventeen, which was the year's shortest, at 124.5 kilometers. But as Merle Travis sang, it was so round, so firm, so fully packed. Those few kilometers had some of the Tour's most renowned climbs: the Portillon, Peyresourde, Val Louron-Azet and a hilltop finish at Saint-Lary-Soulan/Pla d'Adet.

Just two kilometers into the stage, Blel Kadri escaped the pack with seven other riders. As they climbed the Col du Portillon, Joaquim Rodríguez bridged up to them, while the Astana team pulled the peloton. Rodríguez and Majka were locked in a fight for the KOM classification and when Rodríguez was first over the Portillon, he became the new King of the Mountains, taking the classification lead from Majka.

There was some re-ordering on the Peyresourde and when it was time for Val Louron-Azet, Vasil Kiryienka was a minute and a half in front of his nearest chasers. But near the crest, Rodríguez was again at the front…along with Majka.

After just a couple of kilometers into the final ascent, Majka, with Giovanni Visconti hanging on to his wheel, was away. Well back down the mountain Nibali, with Jean-Christophe Péraud on his wheel, revved things up and started steaming by everyone.

329

Majka dropped Visconti and gave a wink to the camera at the Red Kite on his way to winning the stage and re-taking the mountains classification. Visconti came in 29 seconds later, followed another 17 seconds later by Nibali. Nibali now had a 5 minute, 26 second lead over second-place Valverde.

The 2014 Tour didn't get any easier. Stage eighteen had the seventeen-kilometer Tourmalet ascent about two-thirds into the day's racing, followed by a hill-top finish at Hautacam.

Almost from the gun riders scrambled off the front, eventually coalescing into a break of about twenty riders. At this point Astana wasn't going to let anyone do anything silly like get a big gap. The team stayed at the front, and at the start of the Tourmalet, the break—with some quality riders such as Lars Boom and Thomas Voeckler—was three and a half minutes up the road.

Once over the top, Valverde, a gifted descender, left the peloton behind, hoping to build a time gap between himself and the riders who threatened his second place. His Movistar team played this perfectly. Jesus Herrada and Jon Izaguirre had been in the break and now waited for Valverde. Together, they set about building a gap on the Yellow Jersey group.

No dice. Astana had no intention of letting the GC second-place rider ride off into the wild blue yonder. After fourteen kilometers of hard work, Valverde was caught. But the effort had taken its toll. Very early in the Hautacam ascent, Nibali was down to a single teammate.

Bam! Chris Horner attacked and only Nibali could go with him. So much for worrying about teammates. After just a couple of kilometers, Nibali dropped Horner, went by the final uncaught break rider, Mikel Nieve, and was alone off the front.

In Yellow, alone, off the front. That's how to win the Tour de France.

Further back, the spent Valverde couldn't maintain his place as riders went right on by him.

Nibali spun his smallish gear across the line to win his fourth stage this Tour, 70 seconds ahead of his nearest chaser, Thibaut Pinot.

GC after stage eighteen:

1. Vincenzo Nibali
2. Thibaut Pinot @ 7 minutes 10 seconds
3. Jean-Christophe Péraud @ 7 minutes 23 seconds

4. Alejandro Valverde @ 7 minutes 25 seconds

5. Romain Bardet @ 9 minutes 27 seconds

Since only 15 seconds separated second from fourth place, stage twenty's 54-kilometer individual time trial would matter, and matter a lot.

Time trial specialist Tony Martin won the stage, but Nibali was fourth behind the big, fast chrono men. The feeling that Valverde had run out of gas in stage eighteen was reinforced by his coming in twenty-eighth in the time trial, four and a half minutes slower than Martin and now well back, solidly in fourth place.

Marcel Kittel won the final stage, the now-traditional blast up and down the Champs Élysées, allowing him to bookend this Tour with wins in the first and last stages, as he had done in 2013. That gave Germany seven stage wins this Tour.

Nibali finished safely in the field, giving him a solid lead and making him the sixth winner of all three Grand Tours. Nibali again showed that he was a complete rider, being able time-trial, climb, descend and handle himself in a tight, large peloton. It's hard to beat a man with that sort of capability when everything is working, as it did in July of 2014.

Final 2014 Tour de France General Classification

1. Vincenzo Nibali (Astana): 89 hours 59 minutes 6 seconds

2. Jean-Christophe Péraud (Ag2r La Mondiale) @ 7 minutes 37 seconds

3. Thibaut Pinot (FDJ) @ 8 minutes 15 seconds

4. Alejandro Valverde (Movistar) @ 9 minutes 40 seconds

5. Tejay Van Garderen (BMC Racing Team) @ 11 minutes 24 seconds

Climbers' competition:

1. Rafal Majka: 181 points

2. Vincenzo Nibali: 168

3. Joaquim Rodríguez: 112

Points competition:

1. Peter Sagan: 431 points

2. Alexander Kristoff: 282

3. Bryan Coquard: 271

2015 Rematch. Contador and Froome had both crashed out of the 2014 Tour and were hungry for another trip down the Champs Élysées in Yellow. Contador had won the Giro in May, beating Fabio Aru by about two minutes. And just before the Tour start, Contador won the Route du Sud. Would he be able to sustain such sparkling form through July? If he could, he would be the first rider to perform the Giro-Tour double since Pantani in 1998.

Froome also had brought his condition to a high level. He won the early-season Ruta del Sol, both GC and Points, beating Contador by a mere 2 seconds in the GC and 1 point in the Points Competition. He went on to wins in the Tour of Valencia and the Dauphiné, taking the latter in both the GC and points. But, Froome had a cloud hanging over him. In 2014 he got sick during the Tour de Romandie and had acquired a Therapeutic Use Exemption (TUE), allowing him to take a steroid to alleviate his symptoms. All perfectly legal. But some saw the move as cheating and Froome would pay the price in the weeks to come.

The defending Tour champion, Vincenzo Nibali, repeated his careful conditioning. He had no notable results until, as in 2014, he won the Italian road championship. There were issues about his Astana team's doping positives in the off season.

And there was another rider who would bear watching, Nairo Quintana, second in 2013 Tour. Young Quintana had won the 2014 Giro, beating second-place (and fellow Colombian) Rigoberto Uran by three minutes. With a win in the Tirreno-Adriatico in early 2015, Quintana was clearly a rider who had arrived.

The race opened in Netherlands with 2015's only individual time trial, a pan-flat 13.8 kilometers around the city of Utrecht. Australian Rohan Dennis blasted around the course at more than 55 kilometers an hour, allowing him to start stage two in Yellow. The four contenders finished within 18 seconds of each other, Nibali being the fastest.

That this Tour would be a brutal, hard fight every meter of the way was made clear part way into the windy, rainy second stage. With about a hundred kilometers to go, Tinkoff-Saxo and Etixx-Quick Step went to the front, hammering with a hard acceleration and splitting the peloton. About fifty kilometers later a crash further fractured the pack. The results were profound. Contador and Froome were attentive and made the front group. Quintana and Nibali did not and conceded a minute and half. Already some were singing a requiem for the pair of delayed contenders.

Though German sprinter André Greipel won the stage, the time bonus Fabian Cancellara earned for coming in third was enough to give him the overall lead.

If Holland had been tough, the racers now had to face what *L'Équipe* called "a taste of Flèche Wallone at the Tour de France" in stage three. The day was to finish atop the Mur de Huy, which averages 9.6 percent, but has a section of 19 percent gradient.

By the time the final climb began, the front group had been reduced to 40 riders. Immediately Froome and Contador began to duel up the steep hill. But it was Spanish rider Joaquim Rodríguez who soared up the Mur, taking the stage. Froome, though, took second with the same time. Contador couldn't match Froome's speed and finished twelfth, 18 seconds back. Froome was now in Yellow.

It had been a day of crashes and Cancellara was one of the victims. The carnage was so bad stage three had been neutralized for eighteen minutes. Cancellara remounted and with help from his teammates, finished the stage. A trip to the hospital revealed Cancellara had finished the stage with two broken vertebrae. Of course, he abandoned.

The organizers kept the race tough. Stage four, 2015's longest stage at 223.5 kilometers, was a mini Paris–Roubaix with seven sectors of pavé, finishing in the northeastern French city of Cambrai. At the first cobbled sector, Contador, Quintana and Uran suffered mechanical problems. Since many riders needed to answer the call of nature, the peloton slowed to let everyone get his business done. That allowed the riders with bike troubles to regain the pack.

Then things got worse. As the stage left Belgium and entered France, rain began to fall, making the cobbles even more treacherous. Wanting to protect Nibali by keeping the pack stretched out over the difficult roads, his Astana team went to the front and upped the speed. As the race covered the stage's final twenty kilometers, all four contenders were in the front group, now down to 50 riders. Quintana looked the most uncomfortable, but he bore down and hung in with the other leaders.

Nibali was clearly at home on the stones and several times went to the front and put in murderous accelerations. Over and over again Nibali took hard, vicious turns at the front. His efforts didn't go to waste. As the leaders exited the final cobbled sector, the front group was down to just eight, with Contador not among them. With a huge effort the Spaniard and about twenty other riders bridged up to the leaders.

Bam! With three kilometers to go, time trial specialist Tony Martin took flight. It worked. Martin crossed the line well in front the peloton to win the stage and take the *maillot jaune*.

The next several stages were flattish days that yielded sprint victories. But stage six mattered. First, race leader Tony Martin crashed and broke his collarbone. He was able to finish the stage and keep the Yellow Jersey, but his 2015 Tour de France were over. When Martin couldn't start stage seven, Chris Froome resumed his ownership of the Yellow Jersey. Out of respect for Martin he did not wear it as he rode stage seven, though he did accept it at the post-race awards.

More importantly, the African MTN-Qhubeka team had received a wild-card invitation, making them the first African team to ride the Tour. That made it possible for team member Daniel Teklehaimanot, from Eritrea, to become the first black African to wear the polka-dot jersey, which he did after stage six. Times were changing, for the better.

Stage nine was a 28-kilometer team time trial finishing in the Brittany town of Plumelec. This was not going to be a monster-gear, straight, flat time trial. The course was hilly, finishing on a hill often used in French racing, the 6.2 percent Côte de Cadoual. Though BMC won the stage by riding 52 kilometers/hour, Froome's Sky team was only a second slower.

That yielded the following GC:
1. Christopher Froome
2. Tejay Van Garderen @ 12 seconds
3. Greg Van Avermaet @ 27 seconds
4. Peter Sagan @ 38 seconds
5. Alberto Contador @ 1minute 3 seconds
6. Rigoberto Uran @ 1 minute 18 seconds
7. Alejandro Valverde @ 1 minute 50 seconds
9. Nairo Quintana @ 1 minute 59 seconds
13. Vicenzo Nibali @ 2 minutes 22 seconds

During the rest day that followed stage nine, the Tour transferred to the Pyrenees. Some argued that with stage ten, the real 2015 Tour de France began. Certainly the roads started pointing to the sky more often. The 167-kilometer tenth stage had three category-four ascents before an *hors catégorie* hilltop finish at La Pierre-Saint-Martin. That final challenge involved fifteen kilometers of more than a seven-percent gradient. *L'Équipe* called the day a chance for the dark horse contenders such as Rigoberto Uran, Bauke Mollema and Robert Gesink to emerge.

Near the start of the last climb, Froome moved up to the front as both Europcar and FDJ teams put riders at the front to round up the early escapees and keep the pace high. As the climb began to bite, Sagan and Teklehaimanot were quickly dropped.

While Sky riders were pegging their watt-meters leading the very-reduced front group, Robert Gesink was a short distance ahead, off the front. Further back, Nibali was the first big casualty. Then Contador came off, soon to be joined by Van Garderen. Gesink was caught.

Having put the other contenders to the sword, Froome knew this was the moment, and attacked. Hard. He simply rode away from the others, all gifted climbers who were already maxed out.

Froome was on song as he spun away, gaining time with every stroke. With three kilometers to go, he was a minute ahead of his nearest chaser, Nairo Quintana. Chasing Froome was his teammate, Richie Porte, who was able to pass Quintana.

Stage ten results:

1. Christopher Froome
2. Richie Porte @ 59 seconds
3. Nairo Quintana @ 1 minute 4 seconds
11. Alberto Contador @ 2 minutes 51 seconds
21. Vincenzo Nibali @ 4 minutes 25 seconds

Yielding the following GC:

1. Christopher Froome
2. Tejay Van Garderen @ 2 minutes 52 seconds
3. Nairo Quintana @ 3 minutes 9 seconds
4. Alejandro Valverde @ 4 minutes 1 second
6. Alberto Contador @ 4 minutes 4 seconds
10. Vincenzo Nibali @ 6 minutes 57 seconds

People who are paid to know about these things had predicted that Froome would get into trouble in the early Lowlands stages, surely losing time in the crosswinds and cobbles. He handled them like a Belgian, exiting them in the lead. As we have seen, he then proceeded to savage his competition in the first day in the mountains as well.

The next day was no easier, with six rated climbs including the Aspin and Tourmalet before a hilltop finish on the third-category Cauterets. This eleventh stage started in Pau, the sixty-sixth time the town had hosted a Tour stage.

Astana had an interesting change in its hierarchy. Though Jakob Fuglsang was behind Nibali in the GC, he was nevertheless made the team leader. Team management must have felt Nibali was out of gas from the Giro and with the mountain stages just beginning, he would lose still more ground.

When the race reached the Tourmalet, Tinkoff-Saxo rider Rafal Majka took off and went by the day's early escapees. As he crested the legendary climb, he was alone, riding with authority, five minutes ahead of the now 14-man Yellow Jersey group.

Majka flew down the mountain with Daniel Martin chasing like a fiend. Majka was having a terrific day and soloed in alone exactly one minute ahead of Martin and more than five minutes in front of the Froome group. Nibali couldn't stay with Froome and lost another half-minute. But Astana team leader Fuglsang? He came in nearly sixteen minutes after Majka.

Stage twelve, finishing atop the *hors catégorie* Plateau de Beille was 200 kilometers of exhausting effort with nothing but second, first and *hors catégorie* ascents.

Here's how the organizers saw the day: "It gets harder and harder every day in the Pyrenees. With just one big climb to start with after the rest day in Pau, a light uphill finish in Cauterets after climbing the legendary Tourmalet, stage twelve is the queen stage of the first block of mountains. The first difficulty is the col de Portet d'Aspet where a tribute will be paid to Fabio Casartelli twenty years after his tragic death. The Col de Core and Port de Lers will take their toll before the expected big fight between the top guns."

As is normal in stages like this, a big break went clear early, but the mountains took their toll as some riders joined the leaders while others were dropped. As the final climb began, rain wasn't enough. It started to hail. Joaquim Rodríguez pulled away from the other escapees and no one was going to catch him this day. With three kilometers to go he was more than a minute ahead of his nearest chaser, a now-revived Fuglsang.

In the Froome group, both Contador and Nibali tried to escape, but both were soon rounded up.

While Rodríguez took the stage, his second stage win in this Tour, Froome and the other contenders finished safely, about seven minutes behind the Spaniard.

That was it for the Pyrenees. Across southern France, the riders faced a couple of transition stages. The fourteenth, with two second-category climbs, cost Van Garderen his second place, with Quintana slotting himself just behind Froome, 3 minutes, 10 seconds back.

But also during this fourteenth stage, the crowd's hostility to Froome boiled over. Many believed he bent the system to take drugs (remember that TUE?). Some spectators held up accusatory signs and in one disgusting incident, early in the stage a miscreant threw urine on Froome. Froome soldiered on, but after the stage, he blamed the press for creating an atmosphere of suspicion.

This Tour had so far given the sprinters very few chances, but the fifteenth stage, finishing in Valence, finally gave the men with giant legs a chance to show their stuff. André Greipel, one of the sport's fastest men, took the stage in front of John Degenkolb, Alexander Kristoff and Peter Sagan. Sagan now had a firm ownership of the green jersey.

Regarding those jerseys that are presented at the end of each stage. No one races in them. They are strictly ceremonial with a full-length zipper up the back, allowing for an easy-on and an uninterrupted front-of-the-jersey sponsor's logo. A van with a printer travels with the Tour and the operator prints eight to twelve of each color. Many of them are autographed post-race and given to the sponsors or auctioned for charity fund-raising while the front-zip versions are for the riders to use the next day.

Stage sixteen was the last day of racing before a rest day and the Alps. It had two second-category ascents, and with the contenders wanting to conserve their energy, it was a perfect day for a break.

A big group went clear, and indeed, the contenders were uninterested in chasing them. On the second of the day's climbs, the Col de Manse, Ruben Plaza left the other breakaways and crested a minute ahead of the others. He flew down the mountain, hoping to stay away for the day's final twelve kilometers.

Peter Sagan was having none of that. He went after Plaza, descending like a madman. But being crazy wasn't enough as Plaza still had 30 seconds on Sagan when he crossed the line alone. The Froome group came in eighteen minutes later.

At the second rest day and before the Alps, the GC stood thus

1. Christopher Froome
2. Nairo Quintana @ 3 minutes 10 seconds
3. Tejay Van Garderen @ 3 minutes 32 seconds
4. Alejandro Valverde @ 4 minutes 2 seconds
5. Alberto Contador @ 4 minutes 23 seconds

Stage seventeen's 161 kilometers were designed to become increasingly vicious as the day wore on. Starting with a pair of third-category climbs, next came the second category Colle-Saint-Michel. Forty kilometers later was the first-category Allos followed by a hard (*L'Equipe* called it "tricky") descent before the hill-top finish at Pra Loup. Because of the descent's challenging character and Pra Loup's difficulty, at racing speed it's very difficult to eat on the way down as well as on the way up to the finish. If a rider bonks, his race is lost. The stage would have to be ridden both with strength and intelligence.

It was on the Pra Loup climb in 1975 that Bernard Thévenet left Eddy Merckx behind to keep the Cannibal from winning his sixth Tour. Could history repeat itself? Might a challenger topple Froome?

Tejay Van Garderen would not be leading the *coup d'etat*. The BMC rider, who had dropped Froome on a like stage earlier in the Dauphiné, had been quietly enduring an infection since stage thirteen. He had hoped to be over the illness by the Alpine stages, but during the rest day had had been feverish and suffering chills.

Van Garderen was dropped on the day's first climb, the Col des Lèques. Aided by the pack's slowing so that the riders could take a "natural break" in the middle of the stage, Van Garderen fought his way back to the pack. Then, as the third-to-the-last climb, the Col de la Colle St Michel began to bite, Contador accelerated hard and Van Garderen was well and truly dropped.

Van Garderen spent ten agonizing minutes trying to rally his sick body and re-catch the field. But it was impossible. He slowed, got off his bike and collapsed in tears. His director Yvon Ledanois held him, knowing Van Garderen's Tour was over. It was a stunning breakdown for a man who had been in third place.

As the race started the Allos, dangerous-looking black clouds loomed ahead. Though there was a good-sized contingent well up the road, in the Yellow Jersey group Nibali attacked and quickly drew Froome, Quintana, Valverde and Contador. Contador crashed twice on the descent and never saw the others again.

On the Pra Loup ascent Quintana hammered away, but each time Froome would close up. Just before the finish Quintana tried one last time and crossed the line in front of Froome, but the judges gave them the same time. Besides Van Garderen's sad withdrawal, the only other major change to the top of the GC rankings was Contador's losing another two minutes, allowing Geraint Thomas to slip into fourth position.

Challengers to Froome's Yellow Jersey had made it clear in stage seventeen that they were willing to attack all day. Froome expected no less the next day with its roughly fifty-kilometer ascent from the small town of Séchilienne to the crest of the monstrous Glandon. But it wasn't to be. Froome rode the day unchallenged as riders well down in the GC standings broke away and fought for the stage win. Romain Bardet was the day's victor, crossing the line three minutes ahead of Froome's group.

What the other contenders didn't know was that Froome was sick. And after the huge ruckus that had been raised over his 2014 TUE, he decided not to take strong medicines beside antibiotics. Froome explained his decision: "After everything we had been through in this year's Tour, especially the hostility from different people along the way, it just felt that if we go down this route, we are opening the door for a whole new wave of criticism and aggression. It would have been within the rules, but I didn't want it to be the Tour de France that was won because he took this medication in the last week."

Stage nineteen wasn't for sissies. The first-category Col du Chaussy began just as the riders were snapping into their pedals. It was followed by the Croix de Fer, the Col du Mollard and then another hilltop finish after a first-category ascent, this time at La Toussuire. Sixty-one of the stage's 138 kilometers were uphill. The La Toussuire ascent is where

Froome was held back by his director in 2012 at the request of Sky team leader Bradley Wiggins.

That this Tour was not over in the minds of Froome's competitors was made clear the morning of the stage with some remarks by Quintana's director José Luis Arrieta, "Second and third, it looks good on paper. But it's not enough for us. We came for winning and the whole team has been working for three weeks to make Nairo a winner. Unfortunately, there was this special stage in Zealand where Nairo lost one and half minutes. Three minutes deficit is a lot, but in the two coming stages, failures can happen. We've seen it in the past. Those two hard stages are made to create differences. We have no choice but attack. However we have to do it smartly. Nairo is motivated. We keep hoping."

The racing started almost with the gun. Joaquim Rodríguez blasted up the hill along with others who didn't want to miss out. After eight kilometers there were twenty-one riders off the front. Near the top of that first big climb, the Chaussy, Contador attacked. That drew Valverde and Thomas and then Nibali. All bridged up to the front attacking group.

But all was not well with Sky. First Richie Porte couldn't stay with the group around Froome, then Geraint Thomas couldn't stay with Contador's group.

And then Froome simply rode up to the lead group with little trouble.

On the way down, the leaders descended with caution, allowing the peloton to be reunited. But the day was too important, and before the Croix de Fer, more than twenty riders escaped, gaining two minutes before the giant mountain began to bite.

In the Froome group, Nibali's teammates started applying pressure, trying to put Froome's clearly tired team out the back door. It worked. Soon Froome was down to one teammate, Wouter Poels.

Valverde attacked five kilometers from the crest. Poels slowly dragged Froome up to the Spaniard, but Froome had to stop to fix a mechanical problem. That was a signal to Nibali to try his luck. Froome was soon back up to his group, but Nibali was gone.

Nibali was on song. Pierre Rolland had been sporting about off the front and went over the next climb, the Mollard, a few seconds ahead of Nibali. Quickly they were together, Nibali having a few friendly words with the Frenchman. The pair went to work, they had one more climb to negotiate, the hill-top finish at La Toussuire. The duo began the climb two minutes ahead of the Froome group.

Midway up the mountain Nibali dropped Rolland. Surprisingly, with his fifth place in serious danger from Nibali's move, Alberto Contador made no move to bring Nibali back, content to sit in. Valverde, who might lose his third place, also failed to counter the move. Tinkoff-Saxo put Rafal Majka at the front of the Yellow Jersey group to work control Nibali's gap. With nine kilometers to go, Nibali's lead was 2 minutes 20 seconds.

With five kilometers to go Nibali's gap was down to 2 minutes 12 seconds.

Quintana attacked. Froome quickly went around the riders between them and started trying to close the gap. None of the others could go with Froome, whose face clearly showed the depth of the effort he was making. Froome was going deep as he worked to contain the Quintana move.

Nibali never slowed as he drove for the finish line to win the stage. Quintana, finally able to crack Froome, followed in 44 seconds later, finishing 30 seconds ahead of Froome.

The GC after stage nineteen:

1. Christopher Froome
2. Nairo Quintana @ 2 minutes 28 seconds
3. Alejandro Valverde @ 5 minutes 25 seconds
4. Vincenzo Nibali @ 6 minutes 44 seconds
5. Alberto Contador @ 7 minutes 56 seconds

There was one more day in the high mountains before riders could blast up and down the Champs Élysées, and it was a bear. First there was the 29-kilometer ascent of the Croix de Fer followed by a hilltop-finish on the leg-breaking Alpe d'Huez.

Movistar said second-place Nairo Quintana would attack on the Croix de Fer. They knew that if Quintana were to win the 2015 Tour, he couldn't wait until the final climb to gain the needed two and a half minutes.

Attacks went off, but the first one that mattered was Valverde's acceleration partway up the Croix de Fer. Froome's team went to the front to contain the menace. Doing what looked to be a well-planned set-piece, as Froome's tired Sky team dropped back, Quintana exploded from the Froome group and quickly joined teammate Valverde. At this point Froome only had Richie Porte to help him.

Needing Valverde's superb descending skills to help him get down the mountain, Quintana slowed a bit to keep Valverde with him. Farther back, Contador was dropped and it was only Froome and Nibali chasing Quintana and Valverde. The race was in play. Quintana went over the Croix de Fer 15 seconds ahead of Froome.

On the valley floor the riders re-grouped. As the Alpe began to bite, Quintana began attacking over and over again. Each time he was brought back. Then Valverde went and he was allowed to escape.

With about nine kilometers remaining, Quintana put in another huge effort and this time he was rewarded with his freedom. Quintana quickly motored up to Valverde. The teammates made common cause as they proceeded in their attempt to wrest the Tour from Froome and win the year's most prestigious stage.

Quintana used up Valverde and then climbed up to another teammate off the front, Winner Anacona. At that point he was a half-minute ahead of Froome. He still needed another two minutes.

With 4.4 kilometers to go, Quintana dropped Anacona and was now a full minute ahead of Froome. With two kilometers to go he had 1 minute, 15 seconds, plus the 10-second time bonus he might gain for winning the stage.

Thibaut Pinot won the stage with Quintana following in 18 seconds later. Valverde and Froome finished 1 minute, 38 seconds after Quintana.

"I was on my absolute limits. I was dying a thousand deaths", Froome told reporters after the stage. Froome said he had been waking up congested. He had worked hard to hide his troubles, not wanting other racers to hear his breathing troubles. "I was trying to hold it in, so my rivals wouldn't hear me coughing and wheezing. The most difficult times were on the start line where I had Quintana on one side, Contador on the other."

"I would be standing there with a burning sensation to cough or needing to get some phlegm up, but I would hold my breath to stop myself. I didn't want them to see I was battling with this. Just don't let them see anything. I couldn't wait for the neutral zone so I could get to the side of the road, blow my nose and get it all up."

Froome had handled his burden well. Barring some other terrible misfortune, Christopher Froome had won the 2015 Tour de France. And after the final stage in Paris, that was just how it turned out. Froome had won his second Tour as well as the King of the Mountains classification.

Final 2015 Tour de France General Classification:
1. Christopher Froome (Sky): 84 hours 46 minutes 14 seconds
2. Nairo Quintana (Movistar) @ 1 minute 12 seconds
3. Alejandro Valverde (Movistar) @ 5 minutes 25 seconds
4. Vincenzo Nibali (Astana) @ 8 minutes 36 seconds
5. Alberto Contador (Tinkoff-Saxo) @ 9 minutes 48 seconds

Climbers' competition:
1. Christopher Froome: 119 points
2. Nairo Quintana: 108
3. Romain Bardet: 90

Points competition:
1. Peter Sagan: 432 points
2. André Greipel: 366
3. John Degenkolb: 298

2016

The 2016 route Tour boss Christian Prudhomme presented in late October was surely one of the most challenging in recent history. With seventeen stages having at least some climbing (starting with the fifth stage, containing six rated climbs, two of them second-category), the race might very well come down to being a test of brute endurance. Who will have the legs to survive the twenty-one stages?

The real mountains started with stage seven where the Col d'Aspin crested seven kilometers from the finish. And then they kept coming. Normally there is a bit of respite between the Alps and Pyrenees. Not this year. After the Alps the riders would face Mont Ventoux on their way to the Pyrenees.

And in what might end up being a trademark for this Tour, the finish at stage seven's Lac de Payolle came after a hair-raising descent.

This feature was repeated in stages eight, fifteen, and twenty, the Tour's penultimate stage. The 2016 winner would need endurance, climber's legs and superb descending skills. And courage.

While there were 54.5 kilometers of time trialing in this Tour, stage thirteen's 37.5 kilometers was the only normal time trial course as stage eighteen was a timed-hill-climb. More fodder for the pure climbers.

And who would be contending to win this special edition? Cycling journalists agreed on three. Of course, Chris Froome was the favorite. He won February's Herald Sun Tour and showed he still had superb mid-season form by triumphing in June's Critérium du Dauphiné.

Alberto Contador was the second rider considered a potential victor. The seven-time Grand Tour winner started the season firing on all cylinders, winning the Tour of the Basque Country and coming in second in Paris–Nice and the Tour of Catalonia.

After four stages in the Dauphiné, Contador had a slim four-second lead over Froome. But near the end of the fifth stage, Froome attacked with stunning force on the final climb, and only BMC's Richie Porte could go with him. Contador could not handle Froome's display of power and followed in twenty-one seconds later. The next day Contador lost still more time. He eventually finished the Dauphiné in fifth place, a half-minute behind Froome.

Colombian climber Nairo Quintana was the third rider expected to do well, especially given the 2016 Tour's steep profile. Quintana won the Tour de Romandie, the Tour of Catalonia and the Route du Sud. Though illness partway through the season slowed his preparation, no one thought Quintana, the 2014 Giro d'Italia winner, and second-place finisher in both the 2013 and 2015 Tours de France, was going to be a pushover this year.

These were three superb athletes who promised to deliver a ferociously fought Tour.

What a stunning start! The first stage started at Mont St. Michel, an island just 600 meters off the Norman coast with a road to the mainland navigable only during low tide. That road had been used for an individual time trial in the Tour's 2013 edition. The peloton then headed north to Utah Beach, one of the beaches used for the D-Day invasion in 1944.

With a flat profile and only a couple of fourth-category climbs early in the stage, sprinter Mark Cavendish's win was no surprise. This was his twenty-seventh Tour stage win, but only the first time for him to wear the race leader's Yellow Jersey. There was still bigger news. With about 80 kilometers to go, Alberto Contador crashed. He finished with the other contenders, but he crossed the line beat-up, bandaged and with torn clothing. A bad way to start the hardest race in the world.

The next day was a trip north up the Cotentin Peninsula. Ominously for Mark Cavendish, the stage ended with a third category climb with a patch of fourteen-percent gradient. And indeed, it was a stage for punchers. Just 500 meters from the line, solo escapee Jasper Stuyven was caught. World Champion Peter Sagan won his fifth Tour stage, though he thought he was sprinting for third place, not realizing an early break had been caught. Like Cavendish the day before, he put on his first Yellow Jersey. And again, Contador hit the deck. He finished, but almost a minute behind the front group containing GC contenders.

Sprinters took the next two stages. It was stage five, with its six categorized climbs—two of them second category—that would show who was ready to race. A break of non-contenders led in by Belgian Greg Van Avermaet was allowed to finish five minutes ahead of the field, making Van Avermaet the leader.

But showing the wear and tear of his mishaps in the early stages, Contador was unable to finish with the contenders, losing a valuable half-minute to Froome and the others.

GC after stage six:

1. Greg Van Avermaet
2. Julian Alaphilippe @ 5 minutes 11 seconds
3. Alejandro Valverde @ 5 minutes 13 seconds
4. Joaquim Rodríguez @ 5 minutes 14 seconds
5. Christopher Froome @ 5 minutes 17 seconds
25. Alberto Contador @ 6 minutes 38 seconds

Stage seven featured the seventy-second ascent of the Col d'Aspin, followed by that hair-raising seven-kilometer descent to Lac de Payolle. Stephen Cummings crossed the line alone, but the GC men held their fire and finished together.

Well, it wasn't quite that simple. The Tour's inflatable arch at the one-kilometer to go point collapsed, causing Adam Yates, who had been off the front of the main group, to crash. A careless spectator had accidently unplugged the air compressor that inflated the arch.

That also held up the main chasing group. The Tour said it would give the delayed riders their times at the 3-kilometers to go point. And, after a protest from his Orica-BikeExchange team, Adam Yates (officially seventy-third in the stage) was given a finishing time of 3 minutes, 30 seconds after winner Stephen Cummings, 7 seconds ahead of the Froome group. That made Yates second in GC and first in the Young Rider classification.

Stage eight was a big day in the high mountains, featuring the Tour's eightieth ascent of the Tourmalet, followed by three more serious ascents, the last one being the Peyresourde. The organizers had a trick up their sleeves. The finish line was at the bottom of the Peyresourde. After cresting the first-category mountain, a wild, sixteen-kilometer descent to the line would determine the day's winner.

There were the usual attacks and escapes, but Froome's Team Sky had been working like dogs to keep the race under control. Froome tried to escape two kilometers from the top, but he was quickly reeled in. At the crest of the Peyresourde Froome led fourteen riders over the top. And then Bam! Froome escaped as the road began fall away and quickly built a lead as he descended the treacherous road with skill. Froome not only won the stage alone, he was the new Yellow Jersey. It was an impressive display of skill, power and tactical savvy.

GC after stage eight:

1. Christopher Froome
2. Adam Yates @ 16 seconds
3. Joaquim Rodríguez @ same time
4. Daniel Martin @ 17 seconds
5. Alejandro Valverde @ 19 seconds
20. Alberto Contador @ 3 minutes 12 seconds

The next day was no easier. Stage nine was this Tour's queen stage and included five major ascents with a hilltop finish at Arcalis. Early on, a break of non-contenders went clear while the GC men kept a wary watch on each other.

One hundred kilometers into the stage, beat up from his early race crashes and now suffering from a fever, Alberto Contador climbed off his bike and abandoned the 2016 Tour de France.

As the stage approached the day's final climb, the contenders still showed no interest in anything besides making sure none of them did anything silly like try to gain time. Up front, Tom Dumoulin broke away from the escapees to win the stage alone under torrential rain and hail while the GC remained basically unchanged.

After the first rest day, again, the contenders showed little interest in being at the front, despite the 22-kilometer Envalira climb in the day's opening kilometers. This time, the main group with Froome finished almost ten minutes after stage winner Michael Matthews. The Tour was finished with the Pyrenees and headed towards the Alps.

Stage eleven ended in Montpellier. There Froome proved he had not shown everything stowed in his toolbox. After the day's break had been rounded up, with about twelve kilometers to go, Green Jersey Peter Sagan put in a massive acceleration. Froome and a couple of other riders were quickly on his wheel. That was the stage. Sagan's speed nearly guaranteed him the stage win, but Froome was strong enough to be second. The net effect was to give Froome another twelve seconds in what was turning out to be a tight race.

With a Mont Ventoux finish in a stage held on Bastille Day, stage twelve looked to be a fan's delight. It turned out to be so much more than that. Race leader Froome donned his thirty-fourth yellow jersey, putting him in the race's top ten list of Yellow Jersey owners, tying Louison Bobet and Ottavio Bottecchia.

With a forecast of dangerously high winds at the top of the usually windy mountain, the finish was moved down six kilometers to Chalet Reynard. This late decision did not give the organizers enough time to move the fencing used to protect the riders from fans in the closing kilometers.

Again, a break was allowed to gain a lot of time while the GC men rode at their own pace. As the peloton approached Mont Ventoux, Simon Gerrans crashed, taking down three Sky teammates behind him. Froome, not involved with the crash, asked the group to slow and allow him to wait for his teammates, a request the other riders inexplicably granted. Froome and the rest of the Sky team were soon back with the peloton.

With 3.5 kilometers to go, Richie Porte hit a TV motorbike, taking down Froome and Bauke Mollema. Froome's bike was ruined by a following motorbike. Knowing the value of every second, Froome went running up the steep mountain, calling via radio for a new bike as riders passed him. He finally got a new machine and finished the stage in twenty-fifth place. Initially Adam Yates was made the new race leader with Froome now in sixth place. Then, the officials gave Froome his time gap when he crashed, putting Froome back in Yellow.

Adam Yates was generous about the incident, saying, "Nobody would have wanted to take the Yellow Jersey like this, so it's a good decision the jury has taken." Not every rider agreed with the decision, but Froome did start the stage thirteen 37.5-kilometer individual time trial in Yellow.

Froome turned in a smashing ride, finishing second to Dutch strongman Tom Dumoulin to increase his lead to 1 minute, 47 seconds over new second-place Bauke Mollema.

After Mark Cavendish won stage fourteen, for the first time in Tour history, there had been no stage winner from any of the European Latin countries (France, Italy, Spain & Portugal) in the first fourteen stages.

It took a beast of a stage to shake things up. Stage seventeen closed with the Forclaz and a hilltop finish at Finhaut-Emosson. As usual, riders with no GC hopes were allowed to ride away. On the final ascent, Vincenzo Nibali tapped out a hard pace, but Alejandro Valverde was feeling ambitious. He went to the front of the group of GC contenders and put in a series of hard accelerations. Each time Froome needed time to close back up while Nairo Quintana stayed glued to Froome's rear wheel.

Near the top there were nine riders well up the road. Richie Porte attacked hard, dropping even Mollema. Froome and Porte were together, with most of the peloton behind them. Porte finished just ahead of Froome, who increased his lead in this tight race.

The GC after stage seventeen:
1. Christopher Froome
2. Bauke Mollema @ 2 minutes 27 seconds
3. Adam Yates @ 2 minutes 53 seconds
4. Nairo Quintana @ 3 minutes 27 seconds
5. Romain Bardet @ 4 minutes 15 seconds
6. Richie Porte @ 4 minutes 27 seconds

Might Froome be tiring? Stage eighteen's 17-kilometer timed hill-climb would tell the tale. There Froome showed his complete superiority, winning the stage by beating Tom Dumoulin by 21 seconds. He increased his lead on Mollema to nearly four minutes.

Rain and a hilltop finish at Saint-Gervais-Mont Blanc: a perfect recipe for trouble. And trouble is what several riders got with the peloton slipping and crashing as the racing continued in the Alps. Among the day's casualties were Tom Dumoulin and Daniel Navarro, who had to abandon, and Bauke Mollema, who lost fistsful of time. Even Froome and Nibali crashed, but Froome was back up and on Geraint Thomas' bike in time to maintain his place.

On the Mont Blanc ascent, Romain Bardet darted out of the main group and bridged up to escapee Rui Costa of Lampre-Merida. Feeling on-form, Bardet dropped the former world champion to come in alone, a half-minute ahead of his closest chasers, including Alejandro Valverde. That brilliantly executed exploit pulled Bardet up to second place in the GC, 4 minutes, 11 seconds behind Froome. And at last France had a stage win.

There was one last day in the mountains, and it was the real thing. Stage twenty had the riders ascend the Aravis, Colombière, the Ramaz and the Joux-Plane, all legendary Tour climbs. Mother Nature tossed in rain to make the day a true test. Jon Izaguirre bridged up to the day's break, dropped them all and then masterfully sped down the Joux-Plane to win alone. Froome, who said he was feeling tired after the previous day's crash, finished with the other GC men.

On the eve of the final stage, Tour director Prudhomme reiterated his desire to reduce Tour teams by one man, from nine to eight. His intent was to reduce team dominance. He said Team Sky, "overpowered and locked the others out of the race in the mountain passes". One could not argue his point after Froome still had four teammates with him on the Joux-Plane. It was an extraordinary display of power by Sky.

German speedster André Greipel won the final stage on the Champs Élysées while Team Sky surrounded their precious teammate Froome over the final kilometers. Froome had won his third Tour and done it with skill, intelligence and power.

Final 2016 Tour de France General Classification:

1. Christopher Froome (Sky): 89 hours 4 minutes 48 seconds
2. Romain Bardet (Ag2r La Mondiale) @ 4 minutes 5 seconds
3. Nairo Quintana (Movistar) @ 4 minutes 21 seconds
4. Adam Yates (Orica-BikeExchange) @ 4 minutes 42 seconds
5. Richie Porte (BMC Racing Team) @ 5 minutes 17 seconds

Climbers' classification:

1. Rafal Majka: 209 points
2. Thomas de Gendt: 130
3. Jarlinson Pantano: 121

Points classification:

1. Peter Sagan: 470 points
2. Marcel Kittel: 228
3. Michael Matthews: 199

The recent Tours de France were not without a resurgence of worry about drugs. Scottish racer David Millar, who won a total of ten Grand Tour stages and also served a two-year racing suspension for doping, explained the problem: "Therapeutic Use Exemption (TUE) is the official name for an athlete's right to use a banned substance—under medical supervision and with a doctor's approval. The TUE rightfully exists in order to enable an athlete who has a legitimate medical condition to continue to compete. In baseball, there has long been widespread use of TUEs to enable players to take the attention deficit disorder drug Adderall. And as the Fancy Bears hack shows, the practice of obtaining TUEs—ostensibly to treat disorders like asthma and allergies—is common among world-class athletes, not just in running and cycling, but in rowing, hockey, tennis and even golf."

Bradley Wiggins' World Anti Doping Agency files were released by Russian hackers, the Fancy Bears hack Millar referred to above. They showed that Wiggins had been given a TUE for triamcinolone acetonide (Kenecort), a powerful anti-inflammatory corticosteroid for what Wiggins' said was terrible hay fever and asthma. The drug does help mitigate those problems, but it also reduces body weight while preserving muscle mass, allowing a rider to become a leaner and more efficient racer. Moreover, Wiggins had taken the drug before his wins in both the Dauphiné and the Tour de France. While it was all perfectly within the rules, Wiggins surely gained some competitive advantage from taking the drug. Fancy Bears revealed that Wiggins was not the only rider with a TUE for what can be performance-enhancing drugs. Froome had been given one before the 2014 Tour. In fact, TUEs were given to a surprisingly significant part of the peloton, though there's no knowing what the percentage is.

Cycling was still mired in the same drug mess that has soiled the sport since its earliest days. The rational solution to the TUE performance-gain problem is to allow the rider to take the drug, but be suspended from competition for several months so that the rider enjoys no performance gain from the drug.

It remains to be seen if the sport will finally get truly serious about drugs.

2017

How do you keep something fresh and new that has been done 103 times before? That's always the challenge facing the Tour organizers and the in the hundred-fourth edition they largely succeeded.

The two components of the race that most affect the outcome are the climbs and the time trials. The mountains for 2017 could be summed up in two words: fewer, harder. Though the riders would hit all five of France's mountain ranges: the Vosges, Jura, Pyrenees, Massif Central and Alps for the first time since 1992, there would be just three hilltop finishes. The hard mountain stages would only come in pairs, not stacked up one after another. A few of the climbs selected were leg-breakingly steep, such as the 20-percent section of the Planche des Belles Filles in stage five. Though the Tour had climbed the Col d'Izoard 34 times before since its first inclusion in 1922, it had never been the scene of a stage finish. In 2017 it would.

Christian Prudhomme continued to minimize individual time–trialing. In 2017 there would be just 36.5 kilometers against the clock, with no team time trial.

Time bonuses were brought back. After a seven-year absence 10, 6, and 4 seconds would be awarded to the top three finishers respectively, of each stage.

And who would be contending to win this interesting race? None of the top picks were strangers to the Tour. Romain Bardet, 2016's second-place, longed to be the first French winner since Bernard

Hinault's 1985 victory. France has been waiting a long time to see a Frenchman wear Yellow in Paris.

Romain Bardet had been racing all spring—with sixth places in Liège–Bastogne–Liège and the Dauphiné—and it looked like he was making a careful, tempered approach to the Tour.

Richie Porte, 2016's fifth place, had been flying since the season's beginnings in Australia with overall victories in the Tour Down Under and the Tour de Romandie. Could he hold that form through July?

The same question had to be asked about Colombia's ace climber, Nairo Quintana. He had won both the Tour of Valencia and Tirreno–Adriatico. He was in the Giro race-leader's pink jersey going into its final stage, a 29.3-kilometer individual time trial. That last day he lost enough time to end up second overall. This Tour, with its hard climbs and reduced time trialing, looked to be a good fit for the Colombian.

But all eyes were on three-time winner Chris Froome, who hungered to join Anquetil, Merckx, Hinault, Indurain in the five-time club. Froome had spent a quiet spring on the bike with no wins, not even a stage victory to his credit when he started the 2017 Tour's opening individual time trial in Düsseldorf. His conditioning seemed to be the product of very careful planning, resulting in a fourth place overall in the Dauphiné. Clearly, he was not in bad shape. "I've had a slow build-up, but that was always part of the plan. I haven't done as many race days as I have in previous seasons. That will hopefully mean I'm going to be a lot fresher coming into this period, when I'll be racing a lot."

He thought the 2017 Tour's design a poor fit for his skills. "It means that it's going to be a lot closer race and a lot more exciting for the fans. I'm going to have to make sure I'm absolutely at my best and to take advantage of any situations out on the road."

The Tour's start in Düsseldorf answered a lot of questions. The twisty, but nearly dead-flat 14-kilometer time-trial course was dominated by Team Sky who put four riders in the top eight. Sky's super-domestique Geraint Thomas won the stage with Froome coming in sixth, just 12 seconds slower. This performance was amazing given that the stage was run under heavy rain and because it hadn't rained in a while, Düsseldorf's roads had accumulated a lot of oil. Every corner was a slippery invitation to crash.

Movistar's Alejandro Valverde slid, slamming into a corner barrier so hard he was taken away in an ambulance wearing a neck brace. Before the first stage was over Nairo Quintana had lost his most powerful teammate. Others decided to ride cautiously, willing to lose time rather than risk a race-ending fall. Richie Porte rode 35 seconds slower than Froome, while Quintana, Bardet and Contador chose to take significant time losses in the name of safety. Froome and Team Sky had started on the right foot.

The next two stages were fodder for the sprinters as the race headed south to France. Stage four changed the race. As Frenchman Arnaud Démare was streaking for the finish line, the riders behind him fought for his wheel. Mark Cavendish was coming up next to the barrier as Peter Sagan also moved left. The inevitable crash from two speeding riders trying to occupy the same space at the same time sent riders flying and Cavendish to the hospital with a broken shoulder blade. Initially, Sagan was penalized 30 seconds for his move, and docked 80 points in the Green Jersey competition. But after reviewing the films the race jury kicked Sagan out of the race. The reigning world road champion thought the decision unjust, saying later "This I don't accept, because I didn't do something wrong."

Geraint Thomas had been delayed by a slightly earlier crash and crossed the line more than two minutes after stage winner Démare. But since he was delayed within three kilometers of the finish, he was given Démare's time and kept his Yellow Jersey.

Stage five's hilltop finish at La Planche des Belles Filles provided some distraction from the fury that erupted from Sagan's fans after his expulsion. More than a few had stopped watching the race after Sagan's exit. At our BikeRaceInfo.com website we saw a notable decrease in viewership after Sagan's disqualification.

There was still a race to ride, and what a day in the Vosges it was. Though there were the usual early attempts to break away, at the foot of the final ascent Team Sky massed at the front. Italian road champion Fabio Aru took off with a couple of kilometers left to climb and that was the last they saw of 2015 Vuelta winner. It looked to this writer like Sky had decided to let Aru fly away. Daniel Martin was just 16 seconds behind Aru and just off his wheel were Froome and Porte. Thomas finished 20 seconds after Froome, making Froome the new *maillot jaune*.

Froome had laid down the law. The form he brought to the Tour gave him the power to time-trial and climb with the best. Beating him would be no easy thing. But Aru was now third, at just 14 seconds.

The next two stages were again the territory of the men with fast-twitch muscles. Stage seven's escape of the day was rounded up with perfect timing at six kilometers to go. That allowed the sprinter's teams to get organized and unleash their speedsters. Marcel Kittel won his third stage of this Tour and earned his twelfth career Tour-stage win. He was now in green while Froome remained in his bright yellow top.

With those two sprinters' stages done, it was time for the next set of mountains, the Jura in eastern France. Stage eight finished at Station des Rousses, near Lake Geneva (or Lac Léman in French), twelve kilometers after cresting the first-category, twelve-kilometer long Côte de la Combe de Laisia-Les Molunes. The day's bumpy profile made winning the stage a matter of survival. After a few unsuccessful escape attempts, a big group of 46 riders went away after 75 kilometers. Twenty kilometers later all but 16 had been shed. There were still 9 riders sweating away off the front in the 91-degree sun with 25 kilometers to go.

Bam! Direct Energie rider Lilian Calmejane took off. Nicolas Roche and Robert Gesink tried to catch the fleeing Frenchman, but he was not to be caught that day. Horrible cramps hit Calmejane with five kilometers left, but the worst climbing was done and he crossed the line alone with Gesink following in a half-minute later. Calmejane had won his first Tour stage in his first Tour de France. Froome and the other GC leaders followed in about a minute behind Calmejane. None of the contenders had used the difficult stage to try to take time from Froome.

Before allowing the riders a day off, the organizers gave the peloton another lick of the Jura's lash. This time there were seven rated ascents including the *hors categorie* Col de la Biche, the Grand Colombier and the Mont du Chat. Worse, rain was forecast.

The day began taking its terrible toll when Both Geraint Thomas and Rafal Majka crashed descending the wet road of the Col de la Biche. Thomas was ambulanced off with a broken collarbone. Majka finished the stage, but abandoned early in stage ten.

As the Mont du Chat began to bite, the various escapees were quickly losing ground to the Sky-led Yellow Jersey group, a mere three minutes back. Then, things got strange. Tony Gallopin took off from the front in search of solo glory while Froome put his hand up, signaling that he had a mechanical problem. Fabio Aru attacked (he later said he did not know Froome was having trouble with his bike, but it looked to this writer as if the mechanical triggered the acceleration) with Nairo Quintana and Richie Porte on his wheel. Quick-Step Floors GC man Dan Martin protested and the Aru group waited for Froome, who quickly caught Aru and the others.

With Alberto Contador withering under the pressure, Aru again attacked and then Porte came through even harder. Then Aru went again. Each time Froome was able to withstand the accelerations.

Near the top of the Mont du Chat Froome attacked with Porte on his wheel. Aru and Quintana came off and clearly had to go very deep to close back up.

On the fast and technical descent Porte crashed, taking Martin down with him. Martin was back up and chasing, but Porte had broken his clavicle and pelvis. He finished the stage in an ambulance.

Romain Bardet made a bid for solo glory, but Froome rode at the front of his group as if he were trying to simply ride them off his wheel. He couldn't do that, but it was a select group that was first across the finish line. Despite having an ailing bike from his involvement in the Porte crash, Rigoberto Uran won the stage in a photo-finish from Warren Barguil. Froome was third, followed by Bardet, Aru and Jakob Fuglsang.

Stage four winner Arnaud Démare of the FDJ squad was among the riders who couldn't handle the day's high-speed crossing of the difficult terrain. He had two teammates with him who were trying to get him to the finish before the time cutoff, but they failed. At one swoop, FDJ lost three riders.

The GC after nine stages and two mountain ranges:
1. Chris Froome
2. Fabio Aru @ 18 seconds
3. Romain Bardet @ 51 seconds
4. Rigoberto Uran @ 55 seconds
5. Jakob Fuglsang @ 1 minute 37 seconds

The Tour moved west for a day of rest in Dordogne. Then there would be a couple of days for the big, fast men before a few days to enjoy the gentle slopes of the Pyrenees. Riders generally go for an easy spin on a rest day. After crashing a couple times in stage nine, Contador chose to simply rest and let his body heal. There was lot more Tour left to race.

Marcel Kittel had certainly found his legs. When he won stage ten that made four wins out of the five bunch sprints he had contested so far. And then Kittel-the-Flash did it again, winning stage eleven and making it five wins. He had now won nearly half the 2017 Tour's stages.

That wasn't going to happen in stage twelve with its six rated climbs, some of them Tour legends: the Ares, Menté, Peyresourde and a hilltop finish at Peyragudes.

To make things even tougher, bad weather hit the Tour. For the first couple of hours the riders rode in the rain, though this Tour's case of the falls didn't hit the pack this stage. As usual, a large group escaped early in the stage. Even Marcel Kittel joined the break, surely hoping to minimize his time loss on roads poorly suited to his 195 pounds of muscle. Sky led the peloton and on the Peyresourde all the escapees had been caught. There were now just eleven of the best in the front group. Quintana showed that he hadn't completely recovered from his Giro ride when he was the first of the favorites to lose contact. Contador, who had been having a terrible Tour with four crashes so far, starting in stage one, was dropped near the top of the Peyresourde.

Then, as Sky tried to keep control of the race on a patch of 20-percent gradient leading to Peyragudes, Aru went deep and looked like he might win the stage. No, he wouldn't. Bardet went right on by with Uran on his wheel.

The surprise: Froome couldn't handle the final rush on the ultra-steep road to the finish. He cracked slightly as others went by. He finished seventh, 22 seconds behind Bardet. Aru was now in yellow.

The new GC after stage twelve:
1. Fabio Aru
2. Chris Froome @ 6 seconds
3. Romain Bardet @ 25 seconds
4. Rigoberto Uran @ 35 seconds
5. Daniel Martin @ 1 minute 41 seconds

This was a race.

At 101 kilometers and with three first-category ascents, stage thirteen was a beast. But the crest of the last climb, the eight percent Mur de Péguère came 26 kilometers before the finish. It would require a brave, fast downhill scramble to win the stage.

Showing signs of recovery, Contador was first over the second of the three big mountains, the Col d'Agnes. Again Froome had one of those rare moments of weakness, but seemed to quickly recover and maintain his place in the Sky-led group of chasing contenders.

On the Mur de Péguère, Warren Barguil led Contador, Landa and Quintana over the top. With Sky rider Mikel Landa in the Contador Group, Sky had two GC cards to play. Two minutes back down the road Froome, showing absolutely no sign of weakness, attacked his small group. Aru was instantly on his wheel.

Froome wasn't done. On the descent he tried again to get away and again Aru closed up to him. Then Uran slipped away, but he wasn't allowed any rope. Martin, however wasn't seen as a dangerman and was allowed to scoot away from the Froome group.

Up the road, Contador made the first move to win the stage, but Barguil went by, becoming the first Frenchman to win a Tour stage on Bastille Day since David Moncoutié in 2005. Froome, along with Aru, Uran, Bardet and Louis Meintjes finished 1 minute, 48 seconds later. Sky now had two riders in the top five.

To keep his lead Aru, who had no teammates with him for much of this stage, would need eyes in the back of his head.

The GC after stage thirteen:

1. Fabio Aru
2. Chris Froome @ 6 seconds
3. Romain Bardet @ 25 seconds
4. Rigoberto Uran @ 35 seconds
5. Mikel Landa @ 1 minute 9 seconds

Stage fourteen should have been a day of little drama. The two third-category ascents along the way might provide launching pads for an opportunistic breakaway, but nothing looked dangerous for the GC men as the Tour traveled to the foot of the Massif Central.

After ace opportunist Thomas Voeckler and his escape group were rounded up with five kilometers to go, it looked like a big bunch finish.

The uphill finale broke the peloton into pieces. Fastman Michael Matthews won the stage from Greg Van Avermaet. There was just a single second's gap back to a seven-man group with Froome, Martin and Uran. Bardet was a further four seconds back. And where was Aru?

Alone and isolated without teammates, he finished thirtieth, 24 seconds behind Froome. Froome was back in yellow with Aru now second, at eighteen seconds.

When questioned about the critical lapse, Astana team director Dmitri Fofonov said, "He was on his own, isolated. We had crosswinds the whole day. We needed to be up front all the time to avoid the splits. Then the finish was explosive with sprinters climbing very fast, not Fabio's favorite ground, Today we lost a battle, but not the war."

It was later revealed that in the hectic, high-speed run-in to the finish, Aru had failed to eat and was weakened by hunger-knock. When the hammer fell, Aru simply did not have the strength to respond. This was the sort of failure the nearly faultless Sky team almost never committed. Froome's teammate Luke Rowe said the team had been very disappointed when Aru took over the lead. "It won't happen again," Rowe promised.

Time for the fourth mountain range, the Massif Central, a huge area of mountains and volcanos that covers fifteen percent of France. Stage fifteen had two first-category ascents with a downhill finish at Le Puy-en-Velay. The day's escape was allowed to stay away to the finish where race veteran Bauke Mollema crossed the line alone. Though Mollema was riding his seventh Tour, this was his first stage win.

Several minutes back, again there was high drama. On the penultimate climb, the first-category Col de Peyra Taillade, Froome had another mechanical. Teammate Michal Kwiatkowski was right there and gave Froome his own back wheel. This allowed Froome, following a very demanding chase, to be back with the Aru/Bardet group that was being led by Bardet's hard-charging Ag2r team. That moment showed the depth of the Sky team. Froome had Michal Kwiatkowski, the 2014 world road champion, for a selfless domestique. More importantly, serious GC contender Mikel Landa also dropped back to help Froome. Team Sky wasn't holding Landa in reserve. All its money was on Froome.

Bardet kept banging away, and despite having gone deep in his chase after his mechanical, Froome answered each attack. Froome finished with Simon Yates, Uran, Aru, Contador and Bardet. The day's big loser was Nairo Quintana. Looking exhausted, he crossed the line about four minutes after Froome. The Giro-Tour double was looking like too much to ask of the small Colombian climber.

After the second rest day, the peloton rode off the Massif Central in a stage with strong crosswinds that meant every rider had to be alert for splits in the peloton. Froome said he would be careful about this dangerous day.

Sky had more horsepower than any other team and during the day's final twenty kilometers, the squad decided to use that power and the crosswinds to deliver a shock to the peloton. What followed was an incredible display of strength. Despite the flattish terrain, Sky was able to bust up the pack so that only twenty riders were in the front group that crossed the line. Bardet had been caught out, but after a hard scramble, regained contact with the leaders. Dan Martin was dropped and never saw the Froome group until after the finish.

So, after stage sixteen and the pack headed to the Alps, this standings were thus:

1. Chris Froome
2. Fabio Aru @ 18 seconds
3. Romain Bardet @ 23 seconds
4. Rigoberto Uran @ 29 seconds
5. Mikel Landa @ 1 minute 17 seconds

Stage seventeen visited mountains deeply embedded in Tour culture: the Croix de Fer, the Col du Télégraphe and the Col du Galibier, the year's highest point. Because the Galibier's crest came 28 kilometers before the finish, there would be another hell-bent-for-leather descent to the finish line.

Attacks went off from the gun, as did the crashes. One involved Marcel Kittel, but the German sprinter was quickly back up on his bike and chasing. Early on, Thibaut Pinot, who had crashed in stage eleven and was an hour and a half down, abandoned. That left FDJ with just three riders in the Tour.

After ascending the Croix de Fer, his points leader Green Jersey bloodied from his crash, Kittel abandoned the Tour. Later his team revealed that Kittel had been suffering from stomach troubles during the rest day. Adding a crash and some of the Tour's most challenging climbs was too much. "I couldn't do anything to avoid that crash and lost some skin on my shoulder, back, elbow and hip, which are a bit swollen. I tried to carry on, but pedaling was just painful, especially as in the last couple of days I had to fight with stomach problems and a cold." Michael Matthews took over the points classification lead.

At that point, with two more big mountains to climb, there was a large group with Contador off the front and the Sky-led pack three minutes back. Contador's 2017 Tour luck held. Approaching the Galibier, he had a problem with his chain and needed a new bike. After getting a new mount he wasted no time chasing back up to the break.

This was the Tour's fifty-ninth trip up the Galibier. As soon as the road tilted up, Quintana was spit out of the Froome group. Up front, Primoz Roglic attacked the break, taking Contador and Serge Pauwels with him. A few kilometers later Pauwels tried to get away, but was caught and passed by Roglic. Contador was unable to respond.

Roglic was first over the Galibier's crest. Bardet had tried several times to get away from Froome, but Froome had no intention of letting the Frenchman get out of sight. As the attacks kept coming, Aru yo-yo'd off the back of the Froome group as it caught Contador.

Roglic performed what can only be called an insane, but highly skilled, super-fast descent of the Galibier. Near the finish he faced a headwind, but the former ski-jumper had plenty of time in hand, finishing alone, 73 seconds ahead of Uran, Froome, Bardet and Barguil. Contador and Aru finished another half-minute later. Uran was now in second place with the same time as Bardet.

The new GC:

1. Chris Froome
2. Rigoberto Uran @ 27 seconds
3. Romain Bardet @ same time
4. Fabio Aru @ 53 seconds
5. Mikel Landa @ 1 minute 24 seconds

One more day in the high mountains. Though the Tour had used the Col d'Izoard 34 times since its first inclusion in 1922, this would be the first-ever finish at the top of the giant Alp.

A huge group of more than fifty riders went clear early on and it wasn't until the Col de Vars, almost 120 kilometers into the stage that the break really fractured. At the start of the Izoard there were still nearly forty riders scattered behind Astana's Alexey Lutsenko, but ahead of the Sky-led group of leaders.

Froome expected to get hit hard on the Izoard. Both Uran and Bardet knew they would wrest no time from Froome in the second time trial. If the Tour was to be won it would be on these final, steep fourteen kilometers.

Not carrying an extra ounce, Chris Froome stays in Yellow after stage eighteen.

Polka-dot jersey owner Warren Barguil jetted away from the Froome group. Being well down in the GC (a not uncommon tactic of men chasing polka-dots), he was given the freedom to escape and soon passed an already off-the-front Darwin Atapuma.

With just three kilometers to go Bardet jumped, surprising no one. Froome quickly closed up to him with Uran on his wheel. Then it was Froome's turn, and now Uran closed the gap with Bardet on his wheel.

Barguil held his slim lead to win the stage and cement his ownership of the climbers' competition. Just 20 seconds later Darwin Atapuma led Bardet and Froome across the line with Uran just two seconds behind the trio. The time gap and bonus moved Bardet to second and Uran third in the GC.

Froome had survived the mountains and all the attacks the best climbers in the world could dish out. If Uran and Bardet were to take the lead, there was just the final race against the clock and this would be against the man who had earned Olympic time trial bronze medals in 2012 and 2016.

Froome didn't win the winding 22.5-kilometer seafront stage, but a third place, just 6 seconds slower than winner Maciej Bodnar, was good enough to cement his first place. Rigoberto Uran was eighth, just 25 seconds slower than Froome, despite Uran's taking a corner too fast and bouncing off the barriers. It was Romain Bardet's meltdown that shocked. He finished fifty-second, nearly two minutes slower than Froome. Uran moved up to second while Bardet had a desperate hold on third, just 1 second ahead of Mikel Landa.

The final stage, with its traditional finish on the Champs-Élysées had a few moments of worry for two important riders. Before arriving on the Champs, Froome had yet another mechanical problem, but he was able to wait leisurely for a new bike and rejoined with teammate Mikel Landa's help. But King of the Mountains Barguil had a flat at the worst possible time, as the peloton was screaming up and down the Champs.

The big question hanging over the race was Landa. Would he try to make up that simple 1-second deficit? No. He played at attacking, but seemed to have accepted his fourth place.

As rain fell, Barguil's wheel was changed and he was soon back on the road and chasing, desperate to close up the nearly one-minute gap. He put his head down and was soon slipstreaming in the caravan of the team cars following the peloton. From there he was able to leapfrog past each car and with about 30 kilometers to go, was safely back in the pack.

Dylan Groenewegen led the final sprint out from way back. As he closed in on the line, André Greipel, the man who had won in Paris in both 2015 and 2016 came screaming past everyone. Everyone, that is, but Groenewegen.

Greipel had started his sprint just a little too late and passed stage winner Groenewegen just after the line. For the first time, Greipel had raced a Tour without winning a stage. Froome finished safely to win his fourth Tour de France. At 54 seconds over Uran, this was his closest Tour win and his first victory of the 2017 season.

Final 2017 Tour de France General Classification:
1. Christopher Froome (Sky): 86 hours 20 minutes 55 seconds
2. Rigoberto Uran (Cannondale-Drapac) @ 54 seconds
3. Romain Bardet (Ag2r La Mondiale) @ 2 minutes 20 seconds
4. Mikel Landa (Sky) @ 2 minutes 21 seconds
5. Fabio Aru (Astana) @ 3 minutes 5 seconds

Climbers' Competition:
1. Warren Barguil: 169 points
2. Primoz Roglic: 80
3. Thomas de Gendt: 64

Points competition:
1. Michael Matthews: 370 points
2. André Greipel: 234
3. Edvald Boasson Hagen: 220

That September Froome won the Vuelta a España (Tour of Spain), both GC and Points, confirming his status as the finest Grand Tour rider of his generation.

2018

Following his 2017 Tour de France victory, Chris Froome won not only the 2017 Vuelta a España, he was victorious in the 2018 Giro d'Italia. That put Froome in rare company. Eddy Merckx had won four consecutive Grand Tours in 1972-73 and Bernard Hinault won three in a row in 1982–83. A 2018 Tour win would allow Froome to join Merckx in the 4-time club and would make him the first rider to win the Giro and the Tour in the same year since Pantani in 1998.

There was a cloud hanging over Froome. After the Vuelta's eighteenth stage, Froome triggered what is known as an "adverse analytical finding" [AAF] for the asthma drug Salbutamol. An AAF is not a drug test positive. It is a potential violation of anti-doping rules that requires further investigation. In December, 2017, news of Froome's AAF was leaked to both the British *Guardian* newspaper and France's *Le Monde*.

Froome and his Team Sky fought back with vigor, insisting that the stage eighteen AAF was an outlier and that there were many reasons for the high reading of the drug that opens up airways, making it easier to breathe. Froome was an asthmatic and had a Therapeutic Use Exemption (TUE) to use Salbutamol. There are strict limits to how much of the drug a rider can use. Even after Sky's careful re-working of the numbers that accounted for dehydration, kidney problems and maybe coriolis forces and God-knows-what-else, Froome was still found to have an illegal amount of the drug in his system.

The case dragged on, and after winning the Giro, there was still no resolution. Bernard Hinault spoke contemptuously of Froome and the doping scandal, saying Froome should not be allowed to ride.

Surely tired of asterisks in its list of winners, on Sunday, June 30, just days before the Tour start, ASO moved to prevent Froome from starting. Tour boss Christian Prudhomme cited the Tour's own rules that allow it to block a rider who could damage the image or reputation of ASO or one of its events.

ASO's attempted ban woke up the UCI. After months of foot-dragging, on Monday, July 1, the UCI miraculously found Froome innocent of wrongdoing. He could ride the Tour.

That brought up the question of why a rich, powerful team like Sky could save its rider from the penalties of a clearly broken rule when other riders such as Alessandro Petacchi and Diego Ulissi had been harshly punished for the same infraction. More than a few writers and race fans felt that an unjust decision had been made.

There was more drama. Tour of Switzerland winner Richie Porte's BMC team had so far been unable to find a 2019 sponsor, despite being one of the most successful teams in recent history. In the week before the Tour start, BMC began to bleed important technical staff including Porte's main coach, David Bailey. During the Tour's second day, word leaked out that Porte would move to the Trek-Segafredo squad for the 2019 season. BMC looked to be the walking dead.

The French were desperately hoping that Ag2r's Romain Bardet could move up from his third and second placings in the Tour's GC to a Yellow Jersey in Paris at the end of July. He would be the first French winner since Hinault in 1985. *La Belle France* was still waiting.

At 3,349 kilometers, this Tour was the shortest edition since 2002's 3,276 kilometers. There was some brutal climbing in the later stages, and stage nine had 15 sectors of cobbles totaling almost 22 kilometers. Combined with the penultimate stage's 31-kilometer individual time trial, light, pure climbers would need to enjoy both good fortune and big time gains in the mountains to win. This looked to be a Tour for an all-rounder. That group might also include 2017 Giro winner Tom Dumoulin.

The teams were presented on Thursday, July 5. French fans made their feelings clear when Froome was booed by many spectators. ASO knew it had a problem on its hands. One of the glories and beauties of bicycle road racing is that the riders and spectators are so close. Yet one of the problems with bicycle road racing is that the riders and spectators are so close. Knowing the volatility of the situation, ASO let it be known that extra security was being ordered up to protect the riders (I assume that meant Froome) from angry spectators.

The 2018 Tour rolled out from Noirmoutier-en-l'Île, an island town just off the west coast of France. The first stage sported a flat profile with just a single fourth-category ascent to trouble the sprinters. The Tour's early flat stages are usually nervous affairs and this stage was no exception. Several GC contenders went down late in the stage. Richie Porte, Adam Yates, Nairo Quintana, Egan Bernal and Chris Froome were among the riders who either fell, were delayed by crashes or suffered mechanical problems. All five lost around a minute. Notably, neither Tom Dumoulin nor Froome's teammate Geraint Thomas (winner of the Critérium du Dauphiné in June) lost time.

Up front, the Quick-Step Floors team delivered their fastman Fernando Gaviria to the front. He won the stage and became the first Colombian to win a Tour bunch sprint.

The next day it was Gaviria's turn to be among the fallen as world road champion Peter Sagan took the stage and exchanged his rainbow jersey for one of Yellow.

Sagan couldn't get too comfortable in his Yellow Jersey with stage three's team time trial. Over and over again, BMC had shown itself to be the master of the event, having won six of the last ten major team trials the team had entered. Froome's Sky team were not pushovers, finishing just 4 seconds slower. That put BMC's Greg Van Avermaet in Yellow with Tejay Van Garderen in second, at the same time. Thomas was close by, down just 3 seconds.

Stage four. Another flat stage. Gaviria was again the speediest of the fast-twitch set. The next day had the first serious bumps in the road, with four third and fourth-category climbs. That was perfect for Sagan, who thrives on rolling stages. He let Philippe Gilbert go early, bided his time and sped by everyone.

The Tour amped up the difficulty another notch with stage six's hilltop finish on the third-category Mûr de Bretagne Guerlédan. Close to the finish Richie Porte took off. For a moment nobody chased. Then Dan Martin went after Porte, blew by him and won the stage. Van Avermaet was in a group just 3 seconds back, preserving his GC lead.

Highlighting the fact that every rider in a massed-start road race is millimeters from trouble as he speeds down the road, Tom Dumoulin bumped into Romain Bardet on the second of the day's two trips up the Mûr. The resulting broken spokes forced the 2017 Giro champion Dumoulin to get a new bike and lose nearly a minute. Bardet gave up 31 seconds.

A couple of flat transfer stages took the race up to northern France. LottoNL-Jumbo's Dylan Groenewegen won both. That brought the race to the highly anticipated ninth stage with its fifteen sectors of cobbles. Those 21.7 kilometers of rough stones would certainly re-order the standings of the GC contenders.

Before the first cobblestone saw rubber the race was turned side down. After about seven kilometers of racing Richie Porte, Jens Keukeleire and José Joaquin Rojas were among the fallen riders so badly injured they had to withdraw from the race. Porte, later diagnosed with a broken collarbone, had quit the Tour during stage nine of the

2017 Tour as well. Riders kept falling on the bumpy road to Roubaix, including Chris Froome, Mikel Landa and Rigoberto Uran. Tejay van Garderen crashed early in the race and never regained contact with the peloton.

By the penultimate pavé sector, it was down to a lead trio of Yves Lampaert, John Degenkolb and Greg Van Avermaet. Degenkolb won the sprint and Van Avermaet extended his lead.

Two contenders who made it to the finish were probably now out of contention: Rigoberto Uran lost 1 minute, 55 seconds, and Tejay Van Garderen dropped 5 minutes, 47 seconds.

Going into the first rest day after stage nine's bumpy ride, here was the GC:

1. Greg Van Avermaet
2. Geraint Thomas @ 43 seconds
3. Philippe Gilbert @ 44 seconds
4. Bob Jungels @ 50 seconds
5. Alejandro Valverde @ 1 minute 31 seconds
6. Rafal Majka @ 1 minute 32 seconds
8. Chris Froome@ 1 minute 42 seconds
10. Mikel Landa @ same time
12. Vincenzo Nibali @ 1 minute 48 seconds
13. Primoz Roglic @ 1 minute 57 seconds
15. Tom Dumoulin @ 2 minutes 3 seconds

Things really went right for BMC's general manager Jim Ochowicz that same day. Polish firm CCC announced that it would become the title sponsor of the team starting in 2019.

After the rest day, the peloton hit the Alps. Despite stage ten's three first-category climbs and the HC-rated Montée du Plateau des Glières, the GC contenders were content to let their legs recover after a rest day and let others do the racing. Against all predictions, Van Avermaet was able to slightly increase his GC lead, though he knew he was in for a caning. "I give myself zero chance for tomorrow," he said.

The next day's racing was a whole 'nother thing. The day's ride was very short, just 108 kilometers, but it sported four tough climbs with a first-category hilltop finish. It was finally too much for Van Avermaet, who succumbed to the day's second climb, the Col du Pré. This would be his last day in Yellow. Sky showed it intentions by spending the day riding at the front of the peloton.

On the ascent to the finish at La Rosière, Tom Dumoulin was up the road when Mikel Nieve made a bold move for the stage win. He went by Dumoulin, but behind him Geraint Thomas had jumped. In the final kilometer Thomas passed Nieve (as did several other riders) to take a dramatic solo win. Dumoulin and Froome crossed the line 20 seconds later.

The result was a Sky one-two. Geraint Thomas was in Yellow with Froome 85 seconds back in second place. Dumoulin was third and Nibali fourth. The 2018 Tour de France had begun in earnest and Team Sky looked to be in control.

2017's runner-up Rigoberto Uran finally succumbed to his Roubaix-stage injuries and did not start stage twelve with its highly anticipated finish atop l'Alpe d'Huez.

First, the riders had to get over the giant Col de la Madeleine. Thirty riders separated themselves on the 23.5-kilometer ascent. On the penultimate climb, the 29-kilometer Col de la Croix de Fer, a member of the 30-man break, Steven Kruijswijk, was off the front alone with the Sky-led bunch four minutes back.

Kruijswijk began the 21 switchbacks of the Alpe d'Huez 4 minutes, 20 seconds ahead of a thirty-man group that had all the top fifteen GC riders. Attacks went off from the chase group as Kruijswijk's lead shrank. Froome caught Kruijswijk just 3.5 kilometers from the finish and soon thereafter Bardet counter-attacked. Meanwhile a spectator caused Nibali to crash into a police motorbike (or perhaps he caught a spectator's camera strap; there are no films of the accident) with Thomas riding over the Italian's rear wheel. Nibali was back on his bike, but the race had gone up the road. Two kilometers from the summit there were five riders in front: Bardet, Froome, Thomas, Dumoulin and Landa.

Close to the finish Landa tried to get the drop on the others, but again Thomas had the horsepower to blast by and take the stage. Dumoulin crossed the line second, 2 seconds later, followed by Bardet and Froome.

Nibali was seventh, making him fourth in the GC. But after the stage Nibali was found to have broken a vertebra and of course, had to withdraw.

Both Froome and Thomas were jeered at by the roadside spectators, clearly skeptical of Froome's clearance by the UCI. Thomas said, "I would rather be on the podium and be booed than be on the bus and have everyone cheering me."

After the Alps, the GC stood thus:

1. Geraint Thomas
2. Chris Froome @ 1 minute 39 seconds
3. Tom Dumoulin @ 1 minute 50 seconds
4. Vincenzo Nibali @ 2 minutes 37 seconds
5. Primoz Roglic @ 2 minutes 46 seconds

The big sprints would be quite different after stage twelve. Mark Cavendish and Marcel Kittel had been eliminated in stage eleven for missing the time cut. Fernando Gaviria, André Greipel and Dylan Groenewegen were not on the start line for stage thirteen, having abandoned the race during stage twelve. That made Peter Sagan's task of winning the flat stage thirteen a bit easier. The Slovak said that with the marquee sprinters missing the big rushes were chaotic. "Everyone wants to do a sprint now. It's pretty messy."

After the day's break was caught near the finish, Sagan went by twenty riders in the final kilometers to earn a close win over Alexander Kristoff and Arnaud Démare.

The weekend stages, numbers fourteen and fifteen, would be spent in the Massif Central, southern France's highland region with no shortage of mountains, plateaus and gorges.

Stage fourteen was a brutal day with lots of hard climbing in the second half of the 188-kilometer stage. A big group went away while the GC contenders watched each other and waited for the steep stuff. The mountains whittled down the break until it was mostly lone riders crossing the line at Mende, with Astana's Omar Fraile getting his first Tour de France stage win.

Back in the Yellow Jersey group Sky kept everything under control. Dumoulin tried to get away with two kilometers to go, but Thomas was having none of that. He towed Froome up to Dumoulin. Froome beat Dumoulin across the line, but Froome, Dumoulin and Thomas were given the same time. *Status quo antebellum.*

Before the second rest day, stage fifteen had, in order, category three-, category two- and category one-rated ascents, but the final peak came forty kilometers from the finish. As on the day before, a big group escaped early, but it was down to just three riders in front at the end. Astana got its second consecutive victory when Magnus Cort Nielsen was first across the line.

Sky led in the GC contenders thirteen minutes later. That day Sky lost an important mountain *gregario*, Gianni Moscon. Moscon had a short, but intense history of bullying behavior. In 2017 Team Sky suspended him for racially abusing black racer Kevin Reza at the Tour de Romandie. Shortly thereafter he was accused (but because there was no tape, it could not be proved) of causing Sebastien Reichenbach to crash because Moscon thought Reichenbach was responsible for making the Reza incident known. Early in stage fifteen Moscon punched Fortuneo-Samsic's Elie Gesbert. After the judges reviewed the video tape, Moscon was tossed from the Tour.

Team Sky seemed to be living in a world of its own. The British newspaper *The Telegraph* reported rest day complaints from Team Sky's boss:

> Team Sky principal Sir Dave Brailsford believes the spitting, booing and physical intimidation to which his riders have been subjected at this Tour de France is a phenomenon particular to "French culture", adding that unless French fans start to "respect top international teams" they may find they do not come any more.

> Speaking on the Tour's final rest day on Monday ahead of the first of five Pyrenean stages which will decide the race, Brailsford said the treatment being meted out to his team was unacceptable.

> "I don't think it's going to stop," he said. "I'm not too optimistic on that front. We're trying to remain dignified, we're trying not to react and we're trying not to get distracted by it. But I don't think spitting and throwing things has a place in professional sport.

> "I'm not sure it's got a place in everyday life but it seems to be the thing that's done here. It's a shame but we're not going to let it distract us."

Brailsford was quite correct that a few spectators had acted reprehensibly. In 2015 Froome had been splashed with urine. As Brailsford had rightfully complained, other spectators had also crossed the line.

It was not quite as simple as the Sky boss has made things look. French team Groupama-FDJ's manager Marc Madiot felt that cycling's credibility had been harmed by the way Chris Froome's case had been handled and that the fans had every right to express their unhappiness at how the sport had been run. He thought little of Sky's playing the victim and wondered why the team had never joined the "Movement for Credible Cycling", an organization of teams, organizers, sponsors and federations dedicated to promoting clean cycling. "I'm convinced that cycling is paying a price now for not being properly regulated over the years. We have a problem of credibility, quite simply."

There was still a race to be ridden and the first day in the Pyrenees had three legendary climbs. After a couple of fourth-category ascents, the riders would cross the Col de Portet d'Aspet, the Col de Menté and then face a hilltop finish on the Col du Portillon.

The race would have to wait just a bit. Shortly after the riders rolled off, French farmers angry with government agricultural policies blocked the road with hay bales. It took police armed with pepper spray and tear gas to break up the protest. A few riders, including Froome, Thomas and Sagan, were hit with the pepper spray causing some riders to seek medical help.

After a quarter hour the riders again hit the road. It took nearly a hundred kilometers before a break formed. It was a big one, 47 riders. One of the riders in the break, Christophe Laporte, won the day's intermediate sprint. That was important because now there were not enough points in play to take the Green Jersey from Peter Sagan. If he finished the 2018 Tour, he would win the points competition for the sixth time.

Philippe Gilbert went clear on the Portet d'Aspet, going over the top a minute ahead of the break. He pointed his bike down the mountain and while making a difficult left-hand turn, went over a wall and down a ravine. He climbed out and after a quick medical check, resumed the stage, eventually being reabsorbed by the peloton. This was the same descent where Fabio Casartelli had died in the 1995 Tour.

Riders kept going off the front from the break while a peloton suffocated by Team Sky was uninterested in chasing. On the day's final climb, the Col du Portillon, Adam Yates took off just three kilometers from the summit. He went over the top alone followed by polka-dot jersey owner Julian Alaphilippe. Yates crashed on the descent allowing a supercharged Alaphilippe to pound his way to the finish to take his second stage of the Tour. Almost nine minutes later the Yellow Jersey group crossed the line, Thomas and Froome easily maintaining their positions at the head of the GC.

But for Philippe Gilbert, the story turned out to be very grim. Taken to the hospital after the stage, he found he had broken his left kneecap. Gilbert's Tour was finished.

The next day's stage was Hobbesian: nasty, brutish and short. Just 65 kilometers long, it crammed in three giant climbs, the Montée de Peyragudes, Col de Val Louron-Azet and the Col de Portet. That final ascent, sixteen kilometers averaging 8.7 percent, was the Souvenir Henri Desgrange, the 2018 Tour's highest peak. While there have been short half-stages, a short mountain stage like this was unprecedented. Another innovation, the riders were lined up at the start in GC order, ready to race from the start. There was no pre-race neutral zone.

With the climbing starting with the first pedal stroke, the peloton broke up immediately. Though riders were allowed to dangle off the front a bit and try to seek glory, Team Sky stayed close to any escapees.

Polka-dotted Julian Alaphilippe was first over the Col de Val Louron-Azet with Thomas' group just 130 seconds back. On the mountain's descent Peter Sagan crashed badly. Later he told reporters, "I crashed in a turn, in the corner I made a mistake. It looked like a fast corner, but after I just went a little more right, I was braking, but it wasn't enough. After I flew through the forest, I hit a big rock with my ass."

He remounted and several teammates escorted him to the finish. X-Rays showed no broken bones and the speedster fully planned on starting stage eighteen.

On the Col de Portet, Movistar's Nairo Quintana raced up the mountain with Rafal Majka for company. With six kilometers to go he dropped Majka and wasn't seen until the stage was over. Dan Martin gave a mighty chase and closed to within 28 seconds of the Colombian. Thomas finished third with Roglic and Dumoulin 5 seconds behind him.

The surprise was Froome, who needed another half-minute to reach the summit. That changed the GC order in a big way.

1. Geraint Thomas
2. Tom Dumoulin @ 1 minute 59 seconds

3. Chris Froome @ 2 minutes 31 seconds
4. Primoz Roglic @ 2 minutes 47 seconds
5. Nairo Quintana @ 3 minutes 30 seconds

Dumoulin wasn't showing any tiredness from his Giro ride, but he thought Thomas' form made beating the Welshman quite unlikely.

Though Tour officials had pleaded with fans to leave the riders alone and just let them race, even making repeated posts on social media platforms, Team Sky riders continued to be harassed by angry spectators. Near the finish a fan (wearing an Ag2r shirt) grabbed Thomas by the arm. The Yellow Jersey managed to stay upright, and as we know, continue to close in on Quintana.

In a more innocent incident, Froome put on a grey windbreaker after the stage and as he was descending to the team bus, a policeman stopped him, thinking he was just a race fan. In the ensuing confrontation Froome fell. Froome was fine and uninjured.

The climbers got a chance to rest a bit during stage eighteen, a largely flat stage finishing in Pau. Before the stage, André Greipel tweeted the accusation that French sprinter Arnaud Démare had held on to a team car during stage seventeen's ascent of the Col de Portet. A furious Démare denied that he had cheated and then won the stage with enough speed that he could sit up as he crossed the line. Greipel quickly apologized for passing on what he said was "incorrect" information. Incredibly, beat-up Peter Sagan finished eighth. This was the 2018 Tour's first win by a French team, Démare being a Groupama-FDJ rider.

Friday's stage nineteen was the last day in the tall stuff and the riders were not allowed to go gentle into that good mountain. There were six rated ascents including the Col d'Aspin, Col du Tourmalet, Col des Bordères and the Col d'Aubisque before a 28-kilometer descent to Laruns.

While Sagan may have been doing well on the flat eighteenth stage, he was already off the back on the day's first climb, the fourth-category Côte de Loucrup. A brutal, long stage like this has a long cut-off time and Sagan hunkered down and worked on getting to the finish in time.

The real action began on the final climb, the Col d'Aubisque. Rafal Majka attacked a couple of times, bringing Thomas and Dumoulin with him. Froome couldn't stay with them. He was dropped! With help from Dan Martin and Egan Bernal he regained contact. Majka went over the top a few seconds ahead of the Yellow Jersey group. He was soon caught.

On the descent Primoz Roglic made a daring attack, showing extraordinary courage on the twisting descent made more dangerous with the fog and clouds that hung over the Aubisque. Fearlessly, he crouched low in a "supertuck" position with his butt in front of the saddle. Roglic crossed the line 19 seconds ahead of the chasers who were led in by Thomas.

After the stage Tom Dumoulin accused Roglic of drafting a motorbike. The judges didn't see it that way and Roglic's victory stood. Roglic took Froome's third place on the podium, bumping the Sky rider to fourth. With the time bonus for second place, Thomas had extended his lead over Dumoulin to 2 minutes, 5 seconds.

As the organizers planned, it would all come down to the Tour's penultimate stage, a hilly, winding 31-kilometer individual time trial. After stage nineteen's mountains Thomas had said, "It's going to be a tough day tomorrow. I'm really knackered." Would the Welshman be able to keep his two-minute lead against world time-trial champion Dumoulin?

Thomas turned out to be a complete rider, capable of turning in a first-rate ride against the clock after a three-week race. He was the fastest through the first two checkpoints and was only surpassed by Froome and Dumoulin in the final section. Dumoulin won the stage, beating Froome by just a single second. Thomas successfully defended his lead with a third place, just 14 seconds slower than Dumoulin. Roglic's time trial skills weren't in that league. His eighth place, 72 seconds slower than Dumoulin, let Froome reclaim his third spot on the podium.

The final stage followed the usual script. The remaining 145 riders rode to Paris at just 32.3 kilometers an hour. When the Tour reached the Avenue Montaigne, Sylvain Chavanel, finishing his last and eighteenth Tour, was allowed to do a solo lap of honor on the Champs Elysées. Then the day's real racing started. It came down to a 70-man sprint, won by Alexander Kristoff. Thomas sat up as he crossed the line. He had just won the Tour de France.

Final 2018 Tour de France General Classification:

1. Geraint Thomas (Team Sky): 83 hours 17 minutes 13 seconds
2. Tom Dumoulin (Team Sunweb) @ 1 minute 51 seconds
3. Chris Froome (Team Sky) @ 2 minutes 24 seconds
4. Primoz Roglic (LottoNL-Jumbo) @ 3 minutes 22 seconds
5. Steven Kruijswijk (LottoNL-Jumbo) @ 6 minutes 8 seconds

Climbers' competition:

1. Julian Alaphilippe: 170 points
2. Warren Barguil: 91
3. Rafal Majka: 76

Points competition:

1. Peter Sagan: 477 points
2. Alexander Kristoff: 246
3. Arnaud Démare: 203

eight

The Greatest Tour Winner

Who is the greatest Tour de France rider? If the definition is limited to merely who is the most successful, the question is easily answered. Though drugged (as were many of his predecessors) and stripped of his victories, Lance Armstrong's seven consecutive Tour wins would make him the greatest Tour rider. Cross Armstrong off the list and then we have the five-time quartet of Jacques Anquetil, Eddy Merckx, Bernard Hinault and Miguel Indurain.

But I am looking for a more sublime and meaningful definition that accounts for the changes to the sport and the event that have occurred over the last 100 years. By great, I am asking who is the giant, the man whose victories were larger than life? The greatest Tour rider of all time must display an imposing superiority to all others of his age and those of all other ages. His Tour wins must be characterized by duration, quantity, quality and above all, eminence.

Cross-generational comparisons are very dangerous. We must be alert to the trends and changes in cycling in order to make this judgment.

There is a core fact of Tour history: The basic tendency over the last 100 years in stage racing has been to increase the chances for the superior rider to be the winner and for him to win ever more consistently. Here are a few of the reasons for this evolution.

1. The bicycle has become a more reliable machine. Metallurgical advances make the broken forks that crushed Christophe's chances almost unheard of.

2. Roads are better. The first racers competed on dirt roads and climbed ascents that were little more than goat paths. Broken wheels such as the one that kept Philippe Thys from winning the 1922 Tour are a thing of the past.

3. The rules that magnified the consequences of mechanical difficulties have been relaxed. Christophe had to walk to a blacksmith shop

and repair his own fork. Even Koblet had to wait mid-race while his mechanic glued on a new tire to the spare wheel before it could be mounted on his bike. Today a flat tire is fixed in seconds. Thys' broken wheel that cost him three and a half hours would have been replaced on the spot today.

4. Teams are unified and dedicated to bringing a chosen athlete to Paris in Yellow. Bobet and Anquetil had to contend with intra-team feuds that sapped their strength and morale, and hurt their chances. Gaul never really had a team. Coppi rode in fear that his team and director would betray him.

5. Early Tour riders were forbidden to ride in pacelines. Today a team captain might see the front of the race for only a few minutes (individual time trials excepted) during the entire three weeks of the Tour. The rest of the time team captains are surrounded, coddled and protected by a dedicated team. Earlier racers had a much more rugged time of it.

6. Time trials, which improve the superior rider's chances by isolating each rider's efforts and allowing him to gain time without fighting the unified efforts of the peloton, were not introduced until 1934.

7. Tour contenders now have the privilege of being more specialized. Gone are the days when Eddy Merckx would win Milan–San Remo in March, race Belgian Classics in April, contest the Giro and the Tour of Switzerland, and then race the Tour de France. In 1974, after riding the spring Classics, Merckx raced almost nonstop from the start of the Giro on May 16 until the end of the Tour on July 21, winning the Giro, the Swiss Tour and the Tour de France, and having surgery performed in between. A modern stage race contender can start an important race fresh, at an optimal level of fitness.

8. Modern training techniques as well as advances in sports medicine can allow a contender to start a Tour Prologue with only about 25 days of racing in his legs. His chances of a race-induced injury in the run-up to the Tour are reduced. Thys' broken collarbone from a crash in the 1920 Milan–San Remo and Coppi's 1950 broken pelvis come to mind here.

9. A modern team captain can have his entire season and his team built around him and the Tour. Lance Armstrong wasn't the first; he was only the culminating result of a two-decade long tendency. This is

in no small way a consequence of big-time sponsors who need the major-event win to get the mass media coverage they covet. In years past a bike manufacturer wanted his riders racing as often as possible, showing the bike and the equipment in every city and village. The crushing expense of team sponsorship has the unexpected effect of helping the better rider consistently win the Tour.

The trajectory of these tendencies can be seen in the Tour results. After Philippe Thys won three Tours in 1913, 1914 and 1920, no one won three Tours again until Louison Bobet did it in 1953, 1954, and 1955.

Then, Anquetil began his five wins in 1957. Merckx then won five, starting in 1969. Hinault began his streak soon thereafter in 1978. Indurain won five in a row starting in 1991. Armstrong began his seven wins in 1999. Barring his hunting accident LeMond would surely have slotted himself between Hinault and Indurain.

The trend is clear. Consistency became possible with the evolution and improvement of the bike, rules, teams, sponsor's goals and roads.

Therefore, the threshold by which a racer is judged changes over the passing years. Indurain's 5 consecutive wins are remarkable, but they do not stand out from the age.

So who is the Giant of the Road? To me it is very clear. One man stands heads and shoulders above the rest: Philippe Thys with his three victories spanning the First World War.

He showed his mastery of the nature of stage racing in his 1913 win.

In 1914 he won the first stage and was one of the rare riders to hold the lead from the beginning all the way to the end. All Tour winners from 1905 (Trousselier) to 1923 (Pélissier)—except René Pottier, who was dead—started the 1914 Tour. In addition, Lucien Buysse, the 1926 winner, also started. That made eleven men at the line who were either past or future Tour winners. Thys emerged supreme. I know of no other racer who has mastered competition with that much depth.

Thys didn't take the lead in 1920 on the first stage, he took it on the second and held it all the way to the end.

This start-to-finish stranglehold on a Tour doesn't happen often because it is considered suicide to expend so much energy keeping the lead for weeks on end. Often a rider who fancies himself in Yellow in Paris will purposefully relinquish the lead if he finds himself in Yellow too early in the Tour. Roger Walkowiak did this in 1956. Thys showed no such fear.

The writers at *L'Auto* (and presumably Desgrange) thought it likely that Thys would have won seven Tours if the war hadn't intervened. Given his consistent performance in the Tour over such a long period of time this seems a very likely possibility.

Thys' three victories stand out from those of his age. All the post-World War Two multiple Tour winners, while all wonderful and magnificent athletes, were fulfilling the predictable expectation of the trends of the Tour. Thys did not. His three-Tour achievement would not be equaled again until 1955.

Maurice Garin won both the 1903 and 1904 Tours, holding the lead in both from start to finish. His second victory was taken from him in the aftermath of the 1904 cheating scandal. Might he have been the greatest? He had the physical ability but he didn't ride and win enough Tours to enter our elite club.

Coppi, like many great Italian riders, seems to have been intimidated or at least reluctant to ride the Tour. Given his prodigious talent he could have made a much larger mark on the Tour even with the war taking away so many of his best years. Like Garin, his Tour footprint is too small to be considered. That said, Coppi remains perhaps the most extraordinarily talented rider in the history of the sport.

If Merckx had won all five of his Tours the way he won 1969, the judgment would be much harder. His 1969 Tour was won with startling ease. He rode it with complete tyrannical control over the race. But in the context of the era, he was, if one may be so bold, just another of the five-time winners. If Merckx had slowed only a little to allow his body to recover between seasons, he would not have been worn out prematurely. He would surely have won more Tours with even greater authority and would probably be the greatest Tour rider of all time. But that pushes us into the realm of hypotheticals, not the facts.

Armstrong's seven wins were extraordinary. But they in no way contradict the expectations of the era. With each passing decade one expects greater consistency from the best riders and Armstrong was far and away the best of his time. While no one had won seven before, no one had won five before Anquetil.

So here's to you Philippe, The Tour's true Giant of the Road.

Why the Tour de France is the greatest sporting event in the world

The Tour de France is the greatest sporting event in the world. No annual sports event has the television viewership that the Tour has. The Olympics and soccer's World Cup come along every four years and don't have the same impact on our consciousness. Only the most extraordinary Olympic accomplishment stays with us. Franz Klammer's insane skiing at Innsbruck, Mark Spitz's total domination of the swimming events at Munich or Abebe Bikila's marathon at Rome are remembered, but most of the rest of the myriad Olympic events are forgotten. The World Cup mesmerizes the planet for a while and then we move on for another four years.

But every July the world knows that a struggle of epic proportions will occur, and the man who emerges victorious will have achieved truly lasting fame and glory. The Tour's consistent yearly intrusion into our lives gives the race an iron grip on us. And being three weeks long, it is a marvelous event that has time to develop like a giant novel. While we can become captivated or repulsed by its players, we don't ignore them.

But why the Tour? Spain and Italy have their national tours and there are other important races. Why have we devoted years of our lives chronicling this race? The reasons are several and most go back to the vision, methods and authoritarianism of its founder, Henri Desgrange.

1. Desgrange was originally looking for a cheap sales tool to promote his newspaper's circulation. As he grew into his task of running the Tour he wanted more from his race. He wanted it to be a

true test of the mind and body of the competitor. The Tour had to be so difficult that just finishing it was a monumental accomplishment. But he wanted more than that from his Tour. After her defeat in the Franco-Prussian war, France went through a long period of self-doubt and self-examination. Like all educated Frenchmen, Desgrange was aware of this. He wanted the Tour to be a tool to promote French industry and sport, to lift his countrymen to a higher economic and physical plane and wipe away the miasma of the war loss. He implemented this vision with an iron fist that infuriated many riders. Yet it was his race that they wanted to win.

2. The Tour has always been adaptable. From the very start, the Tour has shifted nimbly when the occasion demanded. This gave a life and vitality to the Tour and made sure it never grew old.

3. The Tour has been reasonably fair. It hasn't been perfect in its judging—the 1937 victory of Lapébie must be considered tainted, and in the 1970s it seemed that drug penalties were not enforced as stringently against French riders—but overall, it has treated its riders justly. For that reason, the Tour has always been an international affair. Early in the Tour's history there were foreign winners and they were acclaimed. In contrast, for a host of reasons, the Giro didn't have a non-Italian winner until 1950.

4. Both Desgrange and Goddet could write. They could get their readers excited about the riders and the race. Also, they skillfully exploited the attention of the growing media—including films, radio and eventually television—to their event and the resulting exploding commercialization of the Tour.

5. The Tour was the first major stage race and being the senior Tour matters. Marketers know that being the first into a niche creates a lasting advantage that late-comers must struggle to overcome.

6. The Tour has been run consistently since 1903, interrupted only by the two wars. Spain's Vuelta had a late start and wasn't run consistently until 1955.

It's a combination of all the above that make the Tour a well-run, fair race of unbelievable difficulty with a gloriously rich history. For those reasons, we race fans already have those three weeks in July marked on our calendars.

Afterword

The Tour keeps going, a new edition every year. It is our intention from here on to publish a Kindle book every year, to be available in August or September, covering that summer's Tour. This will enable you to keep up with our story as time goes by.

@: In English language race results an asperand (or "at" sign) is used to denote the amount of time or number of points behind the winner. In the example below Luis Ocaña won the race, taking 6 hours, 51 minutes, 15 seconds to complete the course. Joop Zoetemelk was behind him and crossed the finish line 15 seconds later. Pollentier was still further behind and crossed the line 3 minutes and 34 seconds after Ocana. Van Impe and Thévenet were with Pollentier but slightly behind him. The "s.t." means that they were given the same time as Pollentier. If a rider finishes close enough to a rider who is in front of him so that there is no real gap, he will be given the same time as the first rider of that group. French or Spanish results will use often use "m.t." to denote same time. If no time is given, same time is assumed.

1. Luis Ocaña: 6 hours 51 minutes 50 seconds

2. Joop Zoetemelk @ 15 seconds

3. Michel Pollentier @ 3 minutes 34 seconds

4. Lucien van Impe s.t.

5. Bernard Thévenet s.t.

à : French for @ in race results

Abandon: To quit a race. See also Broom Wagon

Arc-en-ciel: French for rainbow. See Rainbow Jersey

Arrivée: French for the finish line

Arrivée en altitude: French for hilltop finish.

Attack: Generally a sudden acceleration in an attempt to break free of the peloton. On flat roads it is usually done by riding up along the side of the pack so that by the time the attacker passes the peloton's front rider he is traveling too fast for the pack to easily react. In the mountains it is usually enough to accelerate from the front.

Autobus: French. In the mountains the riders with poor climbing skills ride together hoping to finish in time to beat the time limit cutoff. By staying together in a group they hope that if they don't finish in time they can persuade the officials to let them stay in the race because so many riders would otherwise be eliminated. It doesn't always work. Often the group lets a particular experienced racer who knows how to pace the Autobus lead them in order to just get in under the wire.

This risky strategy minimizes the energy the riders have to expend. Synonyms include Grupetto (Italian) and Laughing Group. See Time Limit.

Azzurri: Italian for the Men in Blue. The Italian National team wears blue jerseys, hence the name.

Bell Lap: If the riders are racing the final meters of a race on a velodrome or on a circuit in a town, a bell is rung at the start of the final lap.

Bidon: Water bottle. Now made of plastic, early ones were metal with cork stoppers. Until 1950 they were carried on the handlebars, sometimes in pairs. Around 1950 riders started mounting bottle cages on the downtube. The trend to dispensing with the bar-mount cages started in the early 1960s and by 1970 they were a thing of the past. In the early 1980s, as a result of the sport of Triathlon, builders started brazing bosses on the seat tube allowing mechanics to attach a second cage so that riders could again carry 2 bottles.

Bonification: Time bonus (actually time subtracted) awarded to a rider. Stage races vary and the Tour is always tinkering with its rules. Bonifications can be earned several ways: winning or placing in a stage, winning or placing in an intermediate sprint, being among the first riders over a rated climb. The rules have changed over the years. At one time in the early 1930s the Tour awarded a 4-minute time bonus for winning a stage. In 2005 the bonification was 20 seconds.

Bonk: To completely run out of energy. Sometimes a rider will forget to eat or think he has enough food to make it to the finish without stopping to get food. The result can be catastrophic as the rider's body runs out of glycogen, the stored chemical the muscles burn for energy. Famously José-Manuel Fuente didn't eat during the long stage 14 in the 1974 Giro. He slowed to a near halt as his body's ability to produce energy came to a crashing halt. Merckx sped on and took the Pink Jersey from the Spaniard who had shown such terrible judgment. It's happened to many great riders including Indurain and Armstrong but not always with such catastrophic results. The French term is défaillance but that term can also mean exhaustion or mental failure, such as when Gaul attacked in the Cévennes in the 1958 Tour. Bobet was unable to respond, mostly because he suffered a loss of confidence. This also would be a défaillance.

Break: Short for breakaway.

Breakaway: One or more riders escaping from the front of peloton, usually as the result of a sudden acceleration called an "attack". Riders will work together sharing the effort of breaking the wind hoping to improve their chances of winning by arriving at the finish in a smaller group. This can also be called a "break". Some riders do not possess the necessary speed to contest mass sprints and therefore try very hard to escape the clutches of the peloton well before the end of the race. Franco Bitossi was a master of the lone break even though he possessed a fearsome sprint. Hennie Kuiper won many famous victories this way as well. Sometimes a break will escape during a Tour stage and no team will take responsibility to chase it down. Sometimes the gap results in an unexpected winner as in the case of Roger Walkowiak in 1956. See Chapatte's Law.

Bridge: Short for bridge a gap. To go from one group of cyclists to a break up the road.

Broom Wagon: When Desgrange added high Pyrenean climbs to his 1910 Tour he thought it would be necessary to have a rescue wagon follow the riders in case the mountain roads were beyond their ability to ascend, hence the Broom Wagon to sweep up the exhausted racers. It is still in use, following the last rider in a stage. Today when a rider abandons he usually prefers to get into one of his team cars. Years ago the Broom Wagon had an actual broom bolted to it but today this wonderful bit of symbolism is gone. In the 1910 Tour if a rider could not finish a mountain stage he could restart the next day and compete for stage wins but he was out of the General Classification competition. Today an abandonment sticks. The rider is out of the Tour for that year. Before a rider enters the broom wagon an official removes the dossard or back number on the rider's jersey. In French the Broom Wagon is called the Voiture Balai.

Bunch: When preceded by "the", usually the peloton. Far less often a group of riders can be "a bunch"

Cadence: The speed at which the rider turns the pedals.

Caravan: The long line of vehicles that precede and follow the racers.

Caravan publicitaire: The line of cars and trucks that precedes the race, promoting various companies' goods and services. When Henri Desgrange switched the Tour to using National instead of trade teams, he became responsible for the racers' transport, food and lodging. By charging companies money for the privilege of advertising their goods to the millions of Tour spectators along the route he was able to help pay the new expenses. When the Tour reverted to trade teams the publicity caravan remained.

Category: In European stage racing it is a designation of the difficulty of a mountain climb. This is a subjective judgment of the difficulty of the ascent, based upon its length, gradient and how late in the stage the climb is to be ridden. A medium difficulty climb that comes after several hard ascents will get a higher rating because the riders will already be tired. The numbering system starts with "4" for the easiest that still rate being called a climb and then with increasing severity they are 3, 2, 1. The most challenging are above categorization, or in the Tour nomenclature, "Hors catégorie", HC. In the Giro the hardest climbs are rated a Category 1.

Chairman Bill McGann: A man mad about bikes. A harmless drudge.

Chapatte's Law: Formulated by former racer and Tour commentator Robert Chapatte, it states that in the closing stages of a race a determined peloton will chase down a break and close in at the rate of 1 minute per 10 kilometers traveled. If a break is 3 minutes up the road the peloton will need to work hard for 30 kilometers to catch it. It is now calculated by computer on French television. TV race commentator Paul Sherwen regularly uses Chapatte's Law to come up with his often surprisingly accurate predictions of when a break will be caught.

Chrono: Short for time-trial. See also Cronometro, Time Trial.

The Story of the Tour de France

Circle of Death: In 1910 Desgrange introduced high mountains into the Tour. The big stage with the Peyresourde, Aspin, Tourmalet and Aubisque was called the "Circle of Death" by the press who doubted that the riders could perform the inhuman task that was asked of them. Now the hardest mountain Tour stage is still occasionally called the Circle of Death.

Classic: One of 7 one-day races whose history and prestige will make the career of its winner. They are: Milan–San Remo, Tour of Flanders, Gent–Wevelgem, Paris–Roubaix, Flèche Wallonne, Liège–Bastogne–Liège and the Tour of Lombardy. Gent–Wevelgem is traditionally held mid-week between Flanders and Paris–Roubaix. Only Rik Van Looy has won them all. Some writers include a few other races in their list of Classics: Omloop Het Volk, Amstel Gold Race, Rund um den Hernniger Turm, San Sebastian Classic, Paris–Brussels and Paris–Tours.

Col: French for mountain pass.

Combine: The Tour has had a competition that uses an aggregate of General Classification, Mountains and Points competitions to arrive at the winner of the Combine category.

Commissaire: A race official with the authority to impose penalties on the riders for infractions of the rules. A common problem is dangerous or irregular sprinting. The commissaire will usually relegate the offending rider to a lower placing.

Contre-la-montre: French for time trial

C.L.M.: French abbreviation for contre-la-montre or time trial.

CLM par équipes: French for team time trial.

Criterium: A bike race around and around a short road course, often a city block. Good criterium riders have excellent bike handling skills and usually possess lots of power to enable them to constantly accelerate out of the corners. The Dutch and the Belgians are the masters of the event.

Cronometro: Italian for time trial. Cronometro individuale is individual time trial and Cronometro a squadre is team time trial.

Départ: French for the start line of a race.

Défaillance: French for a total mental or body collapse. See Bonk for more.

Directeur Sportif: The on-the-road manager of a bike team. Although French, it is the term used in English as well.

DNF: Did not finish. Used in results to denote that the racer started but did not complete the race.

DNS: Did not start. Used in results to denote a racer who was entered in a race but failed to start. Often seen in results in stage races where the rider abandons after the completion of a stage.

Domestique: French but used in English as well. Because bicycle racing is a sport contested by teams and won by individuals, a man designated to be the team leader has his teammates work for him. These men have been called domestiques since Tour founder Henri Desgrange used it as a term of contempt for Maurice Brocco whom he believed was selling his services to aid other riders in the 1911 Tour. Today the term has lost its bad connotation and serves as an acknowledgement of the true nature of racing tactics. Domestiques will chase down competitors and try to neutralize their efforts, they will protect their team leader from the wind by surrounding him. When a leader has to get a repair or stop to answer nature his domestiques will stay with him and pace him back up to the peloton. They are sometimes called "water carriers" because they are the ones designated to go back to the team car and pick up water bottles and bring them back up to the leader. In Italian the term is "gregario".

Dossard: French for the rider's race number on the back of his jersey.

Drafting: At racing speed a rider who is only a few inches behind another bike does about 30% less work. Riding behind another rider in his aerodynamic slipstream is called drafting. This is the basic fact of bike racing tactics and why a rider will not just leave the peloton and ride away from the others, no matter how strong he is. Only in the rarest of cases can a racer escape a determined chasing peloton. To make an escape work he needs the pack to be disinterested in chasing for some length of time so that he can gain a large enough time gap. Then, when the sleeping pack is aroused they do not have enough time to catch him no matter how fast they chase. Hugo Koblet's wonderful solo escape in the 1951 Tour is one of the rare instances when a solo rider outdid a determined group of elite chasers. A rider who drafts others and refuses to go to the front and do his share of the work is said to be "sitting on." There are a number of pejorative terms for a rider who does this, the best known is "wheelsucker".

Drop: When a rider cannot keep up with his fellow riders and comes out of their aerodynamic slipstream, whether in a break or in the peloton, he is said to be dropped.

Échappée: French for breakaway

Echelon: When the riders are hit with a side wind they must ride slightly to the right or left of the rider in front in order to remain in that rider's slipstream, instead of riding nose to tail in a straight line. This staggered line puts those riders further back in the pace line in the gutter. Because they can't edge further to the side, they have to take more of the brunt of both the wind and the wind drag of their forward motion. Good riders then form a series of echelons so that all the racers can contribute and receive shelter. Although this is a French word, it is unknown in that sense in French, where it is known as an éventail or bordure.

Équipe: French for team

Escape: When used as a noun it is a breakaway. When used as a verb it is the act of breaking away.

Étape: French for stage.

Feed zone: The specific point along a race route where the riders pick up food and drink. Racing etiquette generally keeps racers from attacking at this point, but there have been some famous initiatives that have started while the riders were having musettes (bags) of food handed up. In 1987 a carefully crafted plot to attack Jean-François Bernard who was then in Yellow was executed by Charly Mottet and his Système U team. They informed Stephen Roche and Pedro Delgado of their plans so that there would be enough horsepower to carry it through, which they did.

Field: See Peloton

Field Sprint: The race at the finish for the best placing among those in the peloton. The term is usually used when a breakaway has successfully escaped and won the stage and the peloton is reduced to fighting for the remaining lesser places.

Fixed gear: A direct drive between the rear wheel and the cranks. The rear cog is locked onto the rear hub so that the rider cannot coast. When the rear wheel turns, the crank turns. Because this is the most efficient of all possible drive trains riders in the early days of cycle racing preferred fixed gears to freewheels. When the Tour added mountains in 1905 the riders had to mount freewheels so that they could coast down the descents; otherwise their velocity was limited by their leg speed. Track bikes use fixed gears.

Flamme Rouge: French. A red triangular flag hung at the beginning of the final kilometer of a race.

Flyer: Usually a solo breakaway near the end of a race.

Fugue: Romantic French for breakaway

GC: General Classification

General Classification: The ranking of the accumulated time or placings, whichever basis the race uses to determine its winner. The Tour (since 1913) and the Giro use time. Lance Armstrong was the winner in the General Classification for all Tours between 1999 and 2005. See Stage Race.

Giro d'Italia: A 3-week stage race, like the Tour de France. It is held in Italy, traditionally in May. It was first run in 1909.

Grand Tour: There are three Grand Tours, all lasting 3 weeks: the Tour de France, the Giro d'Italia and the Vuelta a España.

Green Jersey: In the Tour, awarded to the leader of the Points Competition (except 1968 when the Points Jersey was red). In the Giro, the leading climber wears a green jersey.

Gregario: Italian, see Domestique.

Grimpeur: French for a rider who climbs well. Italian is scalatore.

Gruppo: Italian, literally, "group". In road racing it is the peloton. When they are all together without any active breakaways, it is "gruppo compatto". When referring to the bicycle, "gruppo" means the core set of components made by a single manufacturer, such as a Campagnolo Gruppo.

HD: 1. The initials of Henri Desgrange, the father of the Tour de France. For years the Yellow Jersey had a stylized "HD" to commemorate Desgrange's memory. Sadly, to make room for commercial sponsors for several years Desgrange's initials were removed from the Yellow Jersey. For the Tour's centenary and since, the initials have been replaced. 2. Hors délais or finishing outside the time limit. See time limit.

Hilltop finish: When a race ends at the top of a mountain, the rider with the greater climbing skills has the advantage. It used to be that the finish line was far from the last climb, allowing the bigger, more powerful riders to use their weight and strength to close the gap to the climbers on the descents and flats. The Tour introduced hilltop finishes in 1952 and did it with a vengeance ending stages at the top of L'Alpe d'Huez, Sestriere and Puy de Dôme. In order to reduce Anquetil's advantage in the time trials and flatter stages the 1963 Tour moved the finish lines closer to the last climbs of the day, further helping the purer climbers.

Hook: To extend an elbow or thigh in the way of another rider, usually during a sprint, to impede his progress while he is attempting to pass. Often it is said that a rider "threw a hook". Means the same thing.

Hors-délais: French. See time limit

Hot Spot: See intermediate sprint

Individuel: French. Independent rider in the Tour. See Touriste-Routier

Intermediate sprint: To keep the race active there may be points along the race course where the riders will sprint for time bonuses or other prizes (premiums, or "preems"). Sometimes called "Hot Spots".

Isolés: A class of independent rider in the Tour. See Touriste-Routier

ITT: Individual time trial

Jump: A rider with the ability to quickly accelerate his bike is said to have a good "jump".

Kermesse: A lap road race much like a criterium and associated with a city fair. Bill Kund, one of the first modern-era Americans to race in Europe, says that the course can be longer in a kermesse, as long as 10 kilometers.

King of the Mountains: Winner of the Grand Prix de la Montagne. In 1933 the Tour de France started awarding points for the first riders over certain hard climbs, the winner of the competition being the King of the Mountains. In 1975 the Tour started awarding the distinctive polka-dot jersey or maillot à pois to the leader of the classification. The first rider to wear the dots was the Dutch racer Joop Zoetemelk. The classification has lost some of its magic in recent years because of the tactics riders use to win it. Today a rider wishing to win the KOM intentionally loses a large amount of time in the General Classification. Then when the high mountains are climbed the aspiring King can take off on long breakaways to be first over the mountains without triggering a panicked chase by the Tour GC contenders.

KOM: King of the Mountains

Lanterne Rouge: French for the last man in the General Classification. In earlier years riders competed to be the Lanterne Rouge because of the fame it brought and therefore better appearance fees at races.

Laughing Group: See Autobus

Loi Chapatte: See Chapatte's Law.

Maglia Rosa: Italian, see Pink Jersey.

Maillot à Pois: French for Polka Dot jersey awarded to the King of the Mountains.

Maillot Blanc: White Jersey. Currently worn by the best rider under 25. In the 1970s white was worn by the Combine leader.

Maillot Jaune: See Yellow Jersey.

Maillot Jaune Virtuel: French for Virtual Yellow Jersey

Maillot Vert: French for Green Jersey. In the Tour de France it is worn by the leader of the points competition.

Massed Start Road Race: All the riders start at the same time. This is different from a time trial where the riders are set off individually at specific time intervals. Known in French as course en ligne

Mechanical: A problem with the function of a racer's bicycle, usually not a flat tire. Because rules have sometimes been in place that prevents rider's changing bikes unless a mechanical problem is present mechanics have manufactured mechanicals. In the 1963 Tour de France Anquetil's manager Géminiani cut one of Anquetil's gear cables so that he could give him a lighter bike to ascend the Forclaz.

Minute Man: In a time trial the rider who starts a minute ahead. It's always a goal in a time trial to try to catch one's minute-man. See Time Trial

Musette: A cloth bag containing food and drinks handed up to the rider in the feed zone. It has a long strap so the rider can slip his arm through it easily on the fly, then put the strap over his shoulder to carry it while he transfers the food to his jersey pockets.

M.T.: French for même temps or same time; Spanish for mismo tiempo. See "@"

National Team: From 1930 to 1961, and 1967 and 1968 the Tour was organized under a National Team format. The riders rode for their country or region. See Trade Teams.

Natural or nature break: Because races can take over 7 hours the riders must occasionally dismount to urinate. If the riders are flagrant and take no care to be discreet while they answer the call of nature they can be penalized. Charly Gaul lost the 1957 Giro when he was attacked while taking such a break so he later learned to urinate on the fly.

Off the back: To be dropped.

Paceline: Riders riding nose to tail saving energy by riding in each others slipstream. Usually the front rider does the hard work for a short while, breaking the wind for the others, and then peels off to go to the back so that another rider can take a short stint at the front. The faster the riders go the greater the energy saving gained by riding in the slipstream of the rider in front. When the action is hot and the group wants to move fast the front man will take a short, high-speed "pull" at the front before dropping off. At lower speeds the time at the front is usually longer. See echelon

Palmarès: French for an athlete's list of accomplishments.

Parcours: The race course.

Pavé: French for a cobblestone road. Riding the pavé requires skill and power. Some riders such as the legendary Roger De Vlaeminck can seem to almost glide over the stones knowing exactly what line to take to avoid trouble. De Vlaeminck, who won the Paris–Roubaix 4 times, rarely flatted in this race famous for its terrible cobbles because of his extraordinary ability to pick his way over the tough course while riding at high speed.

Peloton: The main group of riders traveling together in a race. Breaks leave the front of it, dropped riders exit its rear. Synonyms: bunch, group, field, pack.

Piano: Italian for soft. It can mean slow or easy when riding. The Giro often has "piano" stages where the riders intentionally take it easy until the final kilometers leading up to the sprint.

Pink Jersey: Worn by the rider who is currently leading in the General Classification in the Giro d'Italia. It was chosen because the sponsoring newspaper *La Gazzetta dello Sport* is printed on pink paper.

Podium: The top three places, first, second and third. Many racers know that they cannot win a race and thus their ambition is limited to getting on the podium. In major races such as the Tour and the Giro, attaining the podium is such a high accomplishment that it almost makes a racer's career.

Poinçonnées: Riders in early Tours who had their bikes hallmarked or stamped so that the officials could know that the competitors started and finished with the same bike.

Point Chaud: French for Hot Spot. See intermediate sprint.

Points: The usual meaning is the accumulation of placings in each stage. Today the Tour gives more points to the flatter stages so the winner of the points competition is a more likely to be sprinter. See General Classification. In the Tour the Points leader wears a green jersey, in the Giro he dons a purple jersey.

Polka-Dot Jersey: Awarded to the King of the Mountains

Prologue: French. An introductory stage in a stage race that is usually a short individual time trial, normally under 10 kilometers. The Tour has also used a team time trial format in the Prologue.

Pull: A stint at the front of a paceline.

Rainbow Jersey: The reigning world champion in a particular cycling event gets to wear a white jersey with rainbow stripes. The championships for most important events are held in the fall. A former World Champion gets to wear a jersey with rainbow trim on his sleeves and collar. If a World Champion becomes the leader of the Tour, Giro or Vuelta he will trade his Rainbow Jersey for the Leader's Jersey. In the 1975 Tour after Thévenet defeated Merckx on the climb to Pra Loup, Merckx gave up his Yellow Jersey to Thévenet and wore his Rainbow Jersey the rest of the Tour.

Ravitaillement: French for taking on food and drink, usually in the feed zone. Zone de ravitaillement is French for the Feed Zone. Often shortened to ravito.

Rouleur: French for a rider who can turn a big gear with ease over flat roads. Rouleurs are usually bigger riders who suffer in the mountains.

Routier: French for road racer.

Same time: See "@"

Scattista: Italian for a climber who can explode in the mountains with a devastating acceleration. The most famous and extraordinary of these pure climbers were Charly Gaul and Marco Pantani.

Soigneur: Today a job with many duties involving the care of the riders: massage, preparing food, handing up musettes in the feed zone and sadly, doping. Usually when a doping scandal erupts the soigneurs are deeply involved.

Souvenir Henri Desgrange: A prize to the first rider of the highest summit of the Tour. In 2005 the Tour awarded Alexandre Vinokourov a 5,000 euro purse when he was first over that year's highest point, the 2,645-meter high Galibier. In 1974 it was also the Galibier and the prize of 2,000 francs was won by Spanish climbing ace Vicente Lopez-Carril.

Sprint: At the end of a race the speeds get ever higher until in the last couple of hundred meters the fastest riders jump out from the peloton in an all-out scramble for the finish line. Teams with very fine sprinting specialists will employ a "lead-out train". With about 5 kilometers to go these teams will try to take control of the race by going to the front and stepping up the speed of the race in order to discourage last-minute flyers. Sometimes 2 or 3 competing teams will set up parallel pace lines. Usually the team's train will be a pace line organized in ascending speed of the riders. As the team's riders take a pull and peel off the next remaining rider will be a quicker rider who can keep increasing the speed. Usually the last man before the team's designated sprinter is a fine sprinter who will end up with a good placing by virtue of being at the front of the race in the final meters and having a good turn of speed himself.

Squadra: Italian for team

S.T.: Same time. See "@"

Stage race: A cycling competition involving 2 or more separate races involving the same riders with the results added up to determine the winner. Today the victor is usually determined by adding up the accumulated time each rider took to complete each race, called a "stage". The one with the lowest aggregate time is the winner. Alternatively the winner can be selected by adding up the rider's placings, giving 1 point for first, 2 points for second, etc. The rider with the lowest total is the winner. The Tour de France used a points system between 1905 and 1912 because the judging was simpler and cheating could be reduced. Because points systems tend to cause dull racing during most of the stage with a furious sprint at the end, they are rarely used in determining the overall winner. Because points systems favor sprinters most important stage races have a points competition along with the elapsed time category. In the Tour de France the leader in time wears the Yellow Jersey and the Points leader wears green. In the Giro the time leader wears pink and the man ahead in points wear purple or more accurately "cyclamen". The race's ranking of its leaders for the overall prize is called the General Classification, or GC. It is possible, though rare, for a rider to win the overall race without ever winning an individual stage.

Stayer: A rouleur

Switchback: In order to reduce the gradient of a mountain ascent the road engineer has the road go back and forth up the hill. The Stelvio climb is famous for its 48 switchbacks as is L'Alpe d'Huez for its 21. In Italian the term is Tornante.

Tappa: Italian for stage

Team time trial: See time trial. Instead of an individual rider, whole teams set off along a specific distance at intervals. It is a spectacular event because the teams go all out on the most advanced aerodynamic equipment and clothing available. To maximize the slipstream advantage the riders ride nose to tail as close to each other as possible. Sometimes a smaller front wheel is used on the bikes to get the riders a few valuable centimeters closer together. With the riders so close together, going so fast and at their physical limits, crashes are common. Some teams targeting an overall win practice this event with rigor and the result is a beautifully precise fast-moving team that operates almost as if they were 1 rider. Sometimes a team with a very powerful leader who is overly ambitious will shatter his team by making his turns at the front too fast for the others. Skilled experienced leaders take longer rather than faster pulls so that their teammates can rest.

Technical: Usually refers to a difficult mountain descent or time trial course on winding city streets, meaning that the road will challenge the rider's bike handling skills.

Tempo: Usually means riding at a fast but not all-out pace. Teams defending a leader in a stage race will often go to the front of the peloton and ride tempo for days on end in order to discourage breakaways. It is very tiring work and usually leaves the domestiques of a winning team exhausted at the end of a Grand Tour.

Tifosi: Italian sports fans, sometimes fanatical in their devotion to an athlete or team. The term is said to be derived from the delirium of Typhus patients.

Time Bonus: see Bonification

Time Limit: To encourage vigorous riding the Tour imposes a cutoff time limit. If a racer does not finish a stage by that time limit, he is eliminated from the race. This prevents a racer's resting by riding leisurely one day and winning the next. The time limit is a percentage of the stage winner's time. Because it is the intention of the Tour to be fair, the rules are complex. On flat stages where the riders have less trouble staying with the peloton and the time gaps are smaller, the percentage added to the winner's time to arrive at the cutoff is smaller. On a flat stage it can be as little as 5% of the winner's time if the speed is less than 34 kilometers an hour. In the mountain stages it can be as high as 17% of the winner's time. The faster the race is run, the higher the percentage of the winner's time allowed the slower riders. The Tour has 6 sets of percentage time limits, each a sliding scale according to the type of stage (flat, rolling, mountain, time trial, etc.) and the stage's speed. If 20% of the peloton fails to finish within the time limit the rule can be suspended. Also riders who have unusual trouble can appeal to the commissaires for clemency. More than once Paul Sherwen, now a television racing commentator, was given special dispensation for riding courageously when he had suffered misfortune but bravely continued and yet finished outside the time limit.

Time trial: A race in which either an individual or team rides over a specific distance against the clock. It is intended to be an unpaced ride in which either the individual or team is not allowed to draft a competitor. The riders are started at specific intervals, usually 2 minutes. In the Tour the riders are started in reverse order of their standing in the General Classification, the leader going last. Usually the last 20 riders are set off at 3-minute intervals. If a rider catches a racer who started ahead of him the rules say that he must not get into his slipstream but must instead pass well to the slower rider's side. This is one of the more often ignored rules in cycling. The Tour's first time trial was in 1934.

Touriste-Routier: A class of riders in early Tours who did not ride on a team and were entirely responsible for their own lodging, food and equipment. Various classes of independent or "individuel" and "isolé" riders persisted through 1937. As with all aspects of the Tour, the rules and designations regarding the riders constantly changed. Generally the best riders rode on teams. The best independent performance was Mario Vicini's second place in the 1937 Tour.

Track: See Velodrome

Trade team: A team sponsored by a commercial entity. Until the mid-1950's, cycle team sponsorship was limited to companies within the bicycle industry. That changed in 1954 when Fiorenzo Magni's bicycle manufacturer fell into financial difficulty. Magni was able to supplement the shortfall by getting the Nivea cosmetics company to sponsor his team. The move was initially resisted but it is now the standard. Bicycle companies do not have the monetary resources to finance big-time racing teams. Because the Tour organization suspected collusion between the various trade teams the Tour banished them from 1930 to 1961, and 1967 and 1968. During those years the teams were organized under a national and regional team format. Riders rode for their country, such as France or Italy, or if need be to fill out the race's roster, regions such as Ile de France.

TTT: Team time trial

Transfer: Usually a Tour stage will end in a city one afternoon and start the next morning from the same city. When a stage ends in one city and the next stage starts in another, the riders must be transferred by bus, plane or train to the next day's starting city. This schedule is normally done so that both the finish and start city can pay the Tour organization for the privilege of hosting the Tour. The racers loathe transfers because this delays their massages, eating and resting.

UCI: The governing world body of cycling, the Union Cycliste Internationale.

Velodrome: An oval bicycle racing track with banked curves. It can be sited either indoors or outdoors. Olympic tracks are usually 333 1/3 meters around but indoor ones are smaller and have correspondingly steeper banking. Some road races like Paris–Roubaix have the riders ride into the velodrome and finish after a couple of laps on the track. In the past the Tour would regularly do this, often with the rider's time being clocked as he entered the velodrome. With a 200-man field in modern Tours this is impractical.

Virtual Yellow Jersey: Not the leader of the Tour in fact. When a rider has a large enough lead on the Tour leader, so that if the race were to be ended at that very moment he would assume the leadership, he then is called the Virtual Yellow Jersey.

Voiture Balai: French. See Broom Wagon.

Washboard: A rough riding surface with small bumps or irregularities. Like the pavé, riding on washboard requires a lot of power and puts the smaller riders with less absolute power at their disposal at a disadvantage.

White Jersey: See Maillot Blanc

Yellow Jersey: Worn by the rider who is leading in the General Classification in the Tour de France. Traditional history says that Eugène Christophe was awarded the first Yellow Jersey on the rest day between stages 10 and 11 during the 1919 Tour. It is further believed that yellow was chosen because the pages of the sponsoring newspaper L'Auto were printed on yellow paper. Both may not be true. Philippe Thys says that he was given a Yellow Jersey by Tour founder Desgrange during the 1913 Tour and yellow may have been chosen because jerseys of that color were unpopular and therefore cheap and easy to get.

Bibliography

Books

Those marked * are highly recommended.

Lance Armstrong: *It's Not About the Bike: My Journey Back to Life*. New York, Berkley Books, 2000

Lance Armstrong: *Every Second Counts*. New York, Broadway Books, 2003

Samuel Abt: *Breakaway, On the Road with the Tour de France*. New York, Random House, 1985

Samuel Abt: Up the Road: Cycling's Modern Era from LeMond to Armstrong. Boulder, Colorado, Velopress. 2005

David Armstrong: *Merckx: Man and Myth*. Silsden, England, Kennedy Brothers Publishing, undated

Don Alexander and Jim Ochowicz: *Tour de France '86 The American Invasion*. South Pasadena, Alexander and Alexander Publishers. 1985

Philippe Brunel: *An Intimate Portrait of the Tour de France, Masters and Slaves of the Road*. Denver, Colorado, Buonpane Publications. 1995

Daniel Coyle: *Lance Armstrong's War*. New York, Harper Collins, 2004

Eric Delanzy: *Inside the Tour de France: the pictures, the legends, and the untold stories of the world's most beloved bicycle race*. USA, Rodale, Inc. 2006

Martin Dugard: *Chasing Lance*. New York, Little, Brown and Company, 2005

Jacques Duniecq: *1972 Tour de France*. Silsden, England, Kennedy Brothers Publishing, Ltd.1972

Peter Duker: *Tour de France 1978*. Silsden, England, Kennedy Brothers Publishing, Ltd. 1978

Graeme Fife: *Tour de France. The History, the Legend, the Riders*. Edinburgh, Mainstream Publishing Company. 1999.

William Fotheringham: *A Century of Cycling*. St. Paul, MN. MBI Publishing. 2003

Godaert, Janssens, Cammaert: *Tour Encyclopedie* (7 volumes) Gent, Belgium, Uitgeverij Worldstrips. 1997

*L'Équipe: *The Official Tour de France Centennial 1903–2003*. London, UK. Weidenfeld & Nicolson. 2004

N.G. Henderson: *Continental Cycle Racing*. London, England. Pelham Books. 1970

N.G. Henderson: *Fabulous Fifties*. Silsden, England. Kennedy Brothers Publishing, Ltd. Undated

N.G. Henderson: *Yellow Jersey*. Silsden, England. Kennedy Brothers Publishing, Ltd. Undated

*Marguerite Lazell: *The Tour de France, An Illustrated History*. Buffalo, NY. Firefly Books. 2003

Eddy Merckx: *The Fabulous World of Cycling*. Belgium, Editions André Grisard. 1982

Pierre Martin: *The Bernard Hinault Story*. Keighley, UK, Kennedy Brothers Publishing, Ltd. 1982

*Owen Mulholland: *Uphill Battle*. Boulder, Colorado, Velopress. 2003

Owen Mulholland: Various essays published over the years

Svend Novrup: *A Moustache, Poison and Blue Glasses!* London, UK. Bromley Books. 1999

*Peter Nye: *Hearts of Lions*. New York. W.W. Norton Company. 1988

*Jean-Paul Ollivier: *Maillot Jaune*. Boulder, Colorado, Velopress. 2001

Bob Roll: *The Tour de France Companion*. New York, Workman Publishing. 2004

Jacques Seray: *1904, the Tour de France Which Was to Be the Last*. Boulder, Colorado, Buonpane Publications. 1994

James Staart: *Tour de France—Tour de Force*. San Francisco, Chronicle Books. 2003.

David Saunders: *1973 Tour de France*. Silsden, England, Kennedy Brothers Publishing, Ltd. 1973

David Saunders: *Tour de France 1974*. Silsden, England, Kennedy Brothers Publishing, Ltd. 1974

Pascal Sergent: *100 Anni di Storia del Tour de France*. Milan, Italy, SEP Editrice, 2003

Pascal Sergent: *Paris–Roubaix*. London, UK. Bromley Books. 1997

J.B. Wadley: *Eddy Merckx and the 1970 Tour de France*. Silsden, England, Kennedy Brothers Publishing. Undated

*Christopher S. Thompson: *The Tour de France: A Cultural History*. Berkeley and Los Angeles, University of California Press. 2006

*David Walsh: *From Lance to Landis*. New York, Ballantine Books, 2007

Geoffrey Wheatcroft: *Le Tour. A History of the Tour de France*. London, UK. Simon & Schuster. 2003

John Wilcockson: *23 Days in July*. Cambridge, MA, Da Capo Press, 2004

*Les Woodland: *The Crooked Path to Victory*. San Francisco, Cycle Publishing, 2003

*Les Woodland: *The Unknown Tour de France*. San Francisco, Van der Plas Publications, 2000

*Les Woodland: *The Yellow Jersey Companion to the Tour de France*. London, UK, Yellow Jersey Press, 2003

Les Woodland: *This Island Race*. Norwich, UK, Mousehold Press, 2005

Magazines: Various issues of *Velonews, Procycling, Cycle Sport, Bicisport, Bicyclist*

Websites

http://www.memoire-du-cyclisme.eu/
www.letour.fr
www.bikeraceinfo.com
www.cyclingnews.com
www.procyclingstats.com

www.velonews.com
www.radsport-news.com
www.gazzetta.it (the website of La Gazzetta dello Sport)

Conversations, letters and e-mails over the years with the following generous people, not in any particular order: Owen Mulholland, Les Woodland, James Witherell, Fiorenzo Magni, Giorgio Albani, Greg LeMond, Brian Robinson, Marcel Tinazzi, Felice Gimondi, Frankie Andreu, Joe Lindsey, Steve Lubanski, Celestino Vercelli, Paolo Guerciotti, Valeria Paoletti, Antonio and Mauro Mondonico, Faliero Masi, Rene Moser, Derek Roberts, Franco Bitossi, Ferdy Kübler. Thank you all so much.

Memories of stories told to me over the years of my career by the many people in the bike industry whom I have had the good fortune to meet.

Index

About the Authors

Bill and Carol McGann have had their lives inextricably tied up with bicycles about as long as they can remember. Their first date was a bike ride. Bill, formerly a Category One racer, has been a contributor to several cycling magazines and is widely acknowledged as an expert on road bikes and cycling history. Since his father gave him a small one-speed English lightweight bicycle when he was five years old, Bill has been in love with everything about bikes. Carol, a former college biology instructor is also an accomplished rider, having cycle-toured extensively. Together they started Torelli Imports in 1981, a firm specializing in high-performance cycle equipment.

OCT 2 9 2020

CPSIA information can be obtained
at www.ICGtesting.com
Printed in the USA
LVHW051953260220
648294LV00001BA/24